Islamic Revivalism in Syria

Contemporary studies on Syria assume that the country's Ba'thist regime has been effective in subduing its Islamic opposition, placing Syria at odds with the Middle East's larger trends of rising Islamic activism and the eclipse of secular ideologies as the primary source of political activism. Yet this assumption founders when confronted with the clear resurgence in Islamic militantism in the country since 2004.

This book examines Syria's current political reality as regards its Islamic movement, describing the country's present day Islamic groups – particularly their social profile and ideology – and offering an explanation of their resurgence. The analysis focuses on:

- Who are today's Syrian Islamic groups?
- Why and how are they re-emerging after 22 years of relative silence as an important socio-economic and political force?
- How is the Syrian state dealing with their re-emergence in light of Syria's secularism and ideologically diverse society?

Bridging area studies, Islamic studies, and political science, this book will be an important reference for those working within the fields of Comparative Politics, Political Economy, and Middle Eastern Studies.

Line Khatib is a senior research fellow at the ICAMES (Inter-University Consortium of Arab and Middle Eastern Studies), McGill University, and a visiting scholar at the Dubai School of Government. Her research interests lie within the fields of Comparative Politics, Political Economy, Political Islam, and Secularism, with a particular focus on Islamic groups as both social and political movements.

Routledge studies in political Islam

1 **The Flourishing of Islamic Reformism in Iran**
   Political Islamic groups in Iran (1941–61)
   Seyed Mohammad Ali Taghavi

2 **The Political Thought of Sayyid Qutb**
   The theory of Jahiliyyah
   Sayed Khatab

3 **The Power of Sovereignty**
   The political and ideological philosophy of Sayyid Qutb
   Sayed Khatab

4 **Islam and Political Reform in Saudi Arabia**
   The quest for political change and reform
   Mansoor Jassem Alshamsi

5 **Democracy in Islam**
   Sayed Khatab and Gary D. Bouma

6 **The Muslim Brotherhood**
   Hasan al-Hudaybi and ideology
   Barbara Zollner

7 **Islamic Revivalism in Syria**
   The rise and fall of Ba'thist secularism
   Line Khatib

Islamic Revivalism in Syria
The rise and fall of Baʿthist secularism

Line Khatib

LONDON AND NEW YORK

First published 2011
by Routledge
2 Park Square, Milton Park, Abingdon, Oxfordshire OX14 4RN

Simultaneously published in the USA and Canada
by Routledge
711 Third Avenue, New York, NY 10017
First issued in paperback 2014

Routledge is an imprint of the Taylor & Francis Group, an informa company

© 2011 Line Khatib

The right of Line Khatib to be identified as author of this work has been asserted by her in accordance with sections 77 and 78 of the Copyright, Designs and Patents Act 1988.

All rights reserved. No part of this book may be reprinted or reproduced or utilized in any form or by any electronic, mechanical, or other means, now known or hereafter invented, including photocopying and recording, or in any information storage or retrieval system, without permission in writing from the publishers.

Trademark notice: Product or corporate names may be trademarks or registered trademarks, and are used only for identification and explanation without intent to infringe.

British Library Cataloguing in Publication Data
A catalogue record for this book is available from the British Library

Library of Congress Cataloging in Publication Data
Khatib, Line.
 Islamic revivalism in Syria: the rise and fall of Baʿthist secularism/Line Khatib.
 p. cm. – (Routledge studies in political Islam; 7)
 Includes bibliographical references and index.
 1. Syria–Politics and government–2000– 2. Islamic renewal–Syria. 3. Islam and politics–Syria. 4. Islam and state–Syria. 5. Secularism–Syria. I. Title.
 JQ1826.A58K43 2011
 320.5′57095691–dc22
                                                                2011003875

ISBN 13:978-0-415-78203-6 (hbk)
ISBN 13:978-1-138-78934-0 (pbk)

Typeset in Times
By Wearset Ltd, Boldon, Tyne and Wear

Contents

Acknowledgements   viii

1 **Introduction to the subject of secularism and Islamic revivalism in Syria**   1

   1 Scope of the study 1
   2 Key research questions and key variables 4
   3 "Islamic," "Islamist" and "fundamentalist" defined 5
   4 Why study Syria's relationship with its Islamic movement? 6
   5 Theoretical contribution to scholarship 7
   6 Map of the work 10

PART I
The origins of the conflict   13

2 **The rise of a secular party to power**   15

   1 Introduction 15
   2 The Syrian model of secularism 15
   3 Baʿth Party doctrine and ascent to power 21
   4 Conclusion 34

3 **The rise and fall of political Islam in Syria**   35

   1 Introduction 35
   2 The Muslims Brothers: a different kind of social base and agenda 35
   3 Political Islam vs. the secular Baʿth 43
   4 Conclusion of Part I 50

PART II
Hafez al-Asad's era and the conflict with the Muslim Brotherhood: muting of Baʿthist secularism in Syria 51

4 Conflict with the Muslim Brotherhood 53

1 Introduction 53
2 Hafez al-Asad's rise to power 54
3 Explanations of the violent contention: political and economic grievances, anomie and social alienation 56
4 An open challenge, with emphasis on the secular element 67
5 Conclusion 81

5 Resurgence of neo-fundamentalism and decline of political Islam as a model for change (1982–2000) 82

1 Introduction 82
2 Control and the blurring of borders between the state and society 83
3 Co-optation, compromise and the muting of secularism 85
4 Conclusion 106

PART III
Bashar al-Asad's era: fundamentalist and Islamist revivalism 109

6 Bashar al-Asad following in his father's footsteps: the promotion of moderate Islam from above in the name of de-radicalization 111

1 Introduction 111
2 Islamization from above: how is today's Baʿthist regime further empowering Syria's Islamic sector? 113
3 The resulting above-board and underground activity 137
4 Conclusion 142

7 Islamization from below: Islamic revivalism as a model for social change and the erosion of Baʿthist secularism 145

1 Introduction 145
2 The dawn of an Islamic renaissance: general discourse 146
3 Outreach methods and Islamization from below 153
4 Syria's fundamentalist groups 162
5 Conclusion 171

8 Re-emergence of political Islam: Syria's Islamist groups   174

1 *Introduction: opposition pacifism and opposition activism in the search for systemic change* 174
2 *Ideology: Islamists vs. fundamentalists* 175
3 *Syria's pacifist Islamists:* al-Tayar al-Islami al-Dimuqrati *and the Syrian Islamic Front* 176
4 *Islamist militant groups and the call to Islamic resistance* 189
5 *Conclusion* 199

9 Islamic activism and secularism in Syria   200

1 *Introduction* 200
2 *The state's betrayal of the populist myth could come back to haunt it* 201
3 *Future trends in Syria: Islamizing or secularizing?* 209
4 *Syrian secularism today: containment measures and current attitudes towards the Islamization of the state* 216
5 *Conclusion* 224

10 Conclusion   227

1 *Scope of study* 227
2 *Questions explored and findings* 228
3 *Theoretical analysis* 229
4 *Contribution* 230
5 *The work's main arguments* 231

Bibliography   236
Index   250

Acknowledgements

I am indebted in the writing of this work to my father, whose vast knowledge, passion for politics and consistent and wholehearted support have enlightened my way. Without him, none of this would have been possible. I am also indebted to my mother, whose intelligence and learning go far beyond politics. During my fieldwork, she took time away from her own work to join me, and was both an amazing companion and an extremely talented researcher and communicator. My husband took the time to read the entirety of this work, despite his own lack of free time and the demands of his work. His insightful intellect and penetrating remarks showed me that I was never rigorous enough, and his love and backing carried me through the most difficult moments. The cheerfulness and support of my cousin, my brother and my sister-in-law allowed me to take refuge away from my academic pursuits whenever I needed to do so. My family's unconditional support has carried me through the many impasses that academics encounter on their journey: the loneliness of writing, the self-doubt and the uncertainty about the purpose behind all of the seemingly endless work.

Many scholars shape our minds and ultimately affect our lives. I will never forget my first class with Professor Rex Brynen, who makes academic work appear a great deal easier and, dare I say, cooler than it actually is. I am deeply grateful for his succinct comments and critical guidance of my work, and for his continuous support. I am also indebted to Professor Khalid Medani, whose exemplary scholarship and enriching interlocutions have allowed me to continue writing and reach the end of this project. Beyond scholarship, Rex Brynen and Khalid Medani's encouraging emails always arrived when I needed them the most. Laila Parsons' scholarship, patient advice and invaluable support have truly touched me and lifted my spirit. Raymond Hinnebusch's penetrating questions and remarks guided this work, and I thank him deeply for reading and commenting on my PhD dissertation. I also owe a debt of gratitude to the anonymous Routledge reviewers and for Francesco Cavatorta for their invaluable comments, and for editors Joe Whiting and Suzanne Richardson whose patience and guidance made the whole process an enjoyable and smooth quest. I also thank Georgina Boyle and Phillippa Nichol for their invaluable editorial assistance.

My research and writing was funded by the Institute of Islamic Studies Fellowships, the Alma Mater Travel Grant award, the Arts Graduate Student Travel award and the Social Sciences and Humanities Research grant, which have allowed me to do the needed research and intensive fieldwork. My affiliation with ICAMES at McGill University, where many of the discussions that informed this work took place and where many nights of hard work were spent, has been vital and helped to shape my research. The welcoming environment at the Dubai School of Government where I finished writing this work has provided me with both the much-needed space and the serenity to see this project through to its conclusion.

I also owe a debt of gratitude to the personal and scholarly friends who stuck with me throughout the toughest time, encouraged me to keep on writing and kept me sane along the way: Manon Lavoie, Jean-Marie Seznec, Bok Young Hoon, Elodie Lacroix, Laila Sahyoun and Sobhi Sweidan, Nadia Wardeh, Dia Traore, Dima Ayoub, David Mason, Noora Lori and Tabitha Decker – in times of doubt, their cheerfulness, encouraging phone calls and passionate words meant the world to me. I also benefited greatly from years of intellectual exchanges with various other scholars at McGill, as well as with Syrian observers and academics, all too numerous to mention.

Last but not least, I owe thanks to Steve Millier for proofreading the first chapters of my dissertation. And I owe a special thanks to my editor and friend Robert Stewart for the effort and hours spent reading and commenting on this lengthy research. Robert's intellectual exchanges, valuable comments and patient interlocutions kept me grounded from the beginning and through the many, many stages of writing. He has influenced this work in many ways.

I dedicate this book to my parents and my husband with love and gratitude.

1 Introduction to the subject of secularism and Islamic revivalism in Syria[1]

1 Scope of the study

Syria is a secular state with no official religion. It is facing many of the same issues and witnessing many of the same debates as other secular states currently wrestling with religious revivalism.[2] Yet despite the rise in religious fervour in the Middle East and the eclipse of secular ideologies as primary sources of social and political activism, present-day studies on religious revivalism and secularism have ignored the Syrian case. Indeed, studies on Syria have tended to assume that since the Hama battle of 1982, the country's Ba'thist command has been effective at subduing religious activism and at muting and suppressing the country's Islamic political opposition. But this assumption founders when confronted with the clear resurgence in Islamic *militantism* in the country since 2004.

This study posits that the resurgence since 2004 of Islamist militantism in the country represents a key analytical puzzle, one that warrants a closer examination of Syria's political environment. It argues that the death of Hafez al-Asad in May 2000 marked the beginning of an era of more complex, often shifting and sometimes opaque relations between the secular Syrian regime and the country's Islamic movement, relations that have been characterized by a mixture of co-optation, dialogue and confrontation.[3]

The new dynamics were evident from the outset. In spite of the fact that the new president of Syria, Bashar al-Asad, made it clear that he would be following in his father's secular footsteps when he decided to forsake the traditional "*Bism*

---

1 Syria is witnessing a general increase in religiosity among its two major religions communities. That is, the country is not just seeing increased Islamization, but also increased religiosity among Christians. For instance, in 2009, many Syrians celebrated the year of Paul the Syrian Apostle, and the government declared Syria to be the "cradle of the Christian message." During the festivities, Syria's Grand Mufti, Badr al-Din Hassoun, said: "our faith is our way of life ... we [Syrians] do not monopolize the light of Apostle Paul." Moreover, the last few years have seen Christmas parades in Damascus for the first time. But this Christian element in the de-secularization of Syrian society is beyond the scope of this work.
2 Syria's secular model will be discussed in Chapter 2 of this work.
3 See Eyal Zisser's article "Syria, the Ba'th Regime and the Islamic Movement: Stepping on a New Path?" *Muslim World* 95, January 2005: 43–65.

2 *Introduction*

Allah al-Rahman al-Rahim" (in the name of all-merciful God) at the opening of his inaugural presidential address to the Syrian People's Assembly, he nonetheless made as one of his first executive decisions the repeal of his father's 1982 decree prohibiting the wearing of Islamic headscarves by girls and women in any part of the country's educational system.[4] The repeal of the ban was a symbolic move, since it signalled the Syrian regime's explicit willingness to open up the previously secular public sphere to an Islamic vision of society. Then in September 2001, the Bashar al-Asad command promulgated a bill allowing those in forced political exile to return safely to Syria, including opposition figures who were prominent members of the banned Syrian Muslim Brotherhood. Between 2001 and 2004, the government also released around 800 Muslim Brotherhood political prisoners.

Even the Syrian military, which is known for its strictly anti-religious atmosphere, was affected by this trend, with the lifting of a long-standing ban on prayer in the military barracks.[5] Early in 2006, the military academy also invited Muslim and Christian religious authorities to lecture cadets for the first time.[6]

In February 2004, Syria hosted for the first time in 40 years an Islamic conference entitled "*Tajdid al-Khitab al-Dini*" (Renewal of the Religious Discourse). The government asserted that the conference would help to promote the "right" sort of Islam, both modern and moderate. In the same vein, the Ba'th Party Conference of June 2005 saw Bashar al-Asad declare that Syrians should support the revival of a moderate Islam instead of shying away from the subject, insisting that it would be a grave mistake not to give Islamic groups a platform to express their views given that frustration only leads to fanaticism.[7] The president has since promoted the ideas of "*Takrees al-Akhlaq wa Nashr Thaqafat al-Tasamuh, wa Isal al-Risala al-Haqiqiya lil-Islam*" (diffusing morality, spreading the culture of tolerance and communicating the true message of Islam) in many of his addresses and interviews.[8] That same year, Syria established a Financial Intelligence Unit to counter money laundering and to combat the financing of terrorism, thereby taking a definitive step in trying to separate extreme Islamists from their more moderate counterparts.[9]

---

4 Ibid., p. 54.
5 Ibid. pp. 43 and 54–5.
6 These events will be discussed further in Part III of this work.
7 Ba'th Party Conference in June 2005. See also Sami Moubayed, "The Islamic Revival in Syria," *Mideast Monitor* 1(3), September–October 2006. Online: www.mideastmonitor.org/issues/0609/0609_4.htm.
8 See, for instance, the Syrian President's meeting with the Turkish minister of religious affairs on 23 April 2010.
9 See article 7 of the Legislative Decree No. 33 of 2005, which states that

> An independent judicial Commission called CMLTFC with legal personality shall be created at the Central Bank of Syria, with the following mission: Perform financial investigations in operations which are suspected to include illicit money laundering or terrorist financing, and comply with the rules and procedures provided for in this LD; Provide judicial authorities and other bodies in charge of the implementation of this LD, with information required by these authorities regarding the LD.

These various initiatives took place within the context of the reappearance of a religious bourgeoisie as an important client to the authoritarian regime, a severe economic recession in the country, the US-led invasion of Iraq and the re-emergence of militant Islamist activity in the region, all of which have influenced the Syrian command to further compromise with domestic Islamic groups in order to consolidate its power. The compromises have involved promises of social acceptance, but more significantly, have included acquiescence to the idea of the creation of an Islamic political party within the Syrian Progressive National Front,[10] something that would have been unthinkable less than ten years ago.[11]

When taken together, all of these developments demonstrate a clear willingness on the part of the Syrian state to open a new chapter in its relations with the country's Islamic groups. They also signal an official shift in the country's long-time secular stance, away from the previous understanding that religion was to remain outside the realm of politics and of the public sphere in general. Indeed, visitors to Syria today cannot but notice the increasing Islamization of public spaces, this in a society where public spaces have long been religiously neutral. It can be clearly seen in daily public conduct, styles of dress and speech, the charity work that is being done, the school system, summer camps, entertainment activities, financial institutions and even in architecture. And while secular governance still remains the guiding principle of the Syrian state, this movement of Islamic Renewal is also beginning to infiltrate the political sphere, challenging – although still indirectly – the secular state apparatus.

The re-Islamization of the public sphere and the accommodating measures adopted by the state have not prevented the resurgence of militant Islamist activity in the country, as was made clear by the bloody attack of September 2008.[12] The compromises have also recently given rise to a heated debate among Syria's secular intellectual and political leaders regarding what the next move should be to halt the spread of what some are calling "de-secularizing interpretations and requests" within the country's Islamic discourse.

While these issues and events will be more closely examined in this work, one conclusion can already be drawn: that nearly 30 years after the Ba'thist regime's harsh victory over the Muslim Brotherhood at the city of Hama, not

---

10 The National Progressive Front (*al-Jabha al-Wataniya at-Taqaddumiya*, NPF), established by Hafez al-Asad in 1972, is a coalition of left-wing political parties in Syria that support the socialist and Arab nationalist orientation of the government and accept the leading role in society of the Arab Socialist Ba'th Party.
11 Sami Moubayed, "The Islamic Revival in Syria."
12 See Chapter 6. A number of "Islamist" militant attacks have since 2004 occurred in the capital. For example: in April 2004, Syrians witnessed what was later labelled the Mezzeh Attack, launched by an "al-Qaeda linked group" that was made up of Islamists returning from Iraq. In September 2008, a car packed with 200 kg of explosives exploded on the Damascus Airport road near the area's central intelligence headquarters, killing 17 people. The regime later described it as an Islamist terrorist attack. See Syrian TV, 29 March 2008; *SANA*, 30 March 2008.

only is Baʿthist secularism[13] receding in Syria's political and social domains, but a new battle is underway between religious interests, secular interests, and the authoritarian state.[14] Effectively, Islamic groups in the Syria of Bashar al-Asad are no longer under the control of the state,[15] to the point that 2010 saw the Syrian Command directly announce the need to protect "Syrian secularism."[16]

2 Key research questions and key variables

This work examines the relationship between three main variables: Syrian secularism, Syrian authoritarianism and Islamic revivalism. It does so by focusing upon one main question, namely, why and how are Syrian Islamic and Islamist groups re-emerging as an important socio-economic and political force in the country after 22 years of relative quietism? Several subsidiary empirical questions are also addressed: Who are today's Syrian Islamic and Islamist groups? How has the state contributed to their re-emergence? Does Syria use Islamist groups to wield influence in the region, particularly in Iraq and Lebanon? If yes, how is this affecting the Syrian domestic scene? Beyond the state apparatus, how have Syria's Islamic groups organized and evolved as micro-powers within the authoritarian and secular context of Syrian politics? How successful are they at recruiting followers? And how is the Syrian state dealing with their re-emergence in light of the country's multi-sectarian society on the one hand, and its secular – yet authoritarian – political culture on the other? How has this helped consolidate the regime's power?

In answering these questions, the present study begins by examining the ways in which the secular Baʿthist state dealt with the Islamic militant opposition from its rise in 1963 to the seeming demise of the Islamist movement in Syria at the beginning of the 1980s. It also illustrates how the current political command is re-deploying in the face of recent existential threats that are similar to those faced by the previous command – that is, economic crisis, domestic unrest, and a new regional reality – and highlights its similar economic and socio-political survival strategies in the face of systemic strain. These strategies are aimed at

---

13 It is a Baʿthist view of secularism to which I am referring. Thus the decline of secularism is in this case measured against the high point of militant secularism in the mid-1960s in Syria, and not relative to other Arab states in the region. The intellectual secular history of Syria and more specifically its Baʿthist secularism are addressed hereinafter.
14 See Zisser's article "Syria, the Baʿth Regime and the Islamic Movement."
15 To cite a few of the articles that anticipate an Islamic revival in Syria and debate the secular question in the country, see Baʿthist website All4Syria, which routinely criticizes the new Islamic trends "restricting" the daily lives of Syrians; *Dar Al-Hayat* has writers such as Husam Jazmati, George Katan, Wael al-Sawah, Louay Hussein and Ibrahim Hamid who often discuss the secularizing/religious implication of events in Syria. See also "Syria, Long Ruthlessly Secular, Sees Fervent Islamic Resurgence," *New York Times*, 24 October 2003; "In Secular Syria, an Islamic Revival," *Christian Science Monitor*, 3 October 2003; "Religious Surge Alarms Secular Syrians," *Washington Post*, 23 January 2005; "Outside Iraq but Deep in the Fight: A Smuggler of Insurgents Reveals Syria's Influential, Changing Role," *Washington Post*, 8 June 2005.
16 See, for example, *Al-Hayat* (27 July 2010 and 26 August 2010) at: www.daralhayat.com.

keeping religious discontent – the focus of this study – from spilling over into militancy, eradicating the militant religious opposition, and limiting popular unrest while still maintaining the unity of the ruling coalition. More formally, this study explores the above-mentioned questions through a comparative analysis of the shifts in the state's responses to, and relationship with, the Islamic movement (independent variable), and its impact on Islamic revivalism (dependent variable) in the Syria of Hafez al-Asad and Bashar al-Asad.

In so doing, it offers an explanation for the state's shift from promoting secularism, to muting secularism and co-opting the religious class under Hafez al-Asad, and then to promoting Islamic revivalism under Bashar al-Asad. In effecting this shift, the Baʻth has employed an admixture of incentives and disincentives to consolidate its power and ensure its survival, in a manner typical of Populist Authoritarian (PA) regimes.[17] Along the way, it has also concocted a new state–Islamic relationship in an attempt to retain a considerable degree of control over one of the most active sectors in society, that is, the Islamic groups. Ironically, this has resulted in: (1) the transformation of Syrian secularism; and (2) an opportunity for Syria's Islamic groups to mobilize and recruit.[18] In other words, the regime's re-organization of state–society relations and socio-political manipulation of the Syrian Islamic element has played a crucial role in promoting both Islamic and Islamist revivalism in secular Syria.

The essence of this book is focused upon the evolving nature of the ruling regime's attempts to create a balance between its own interests, domestic concerns about terrorism and the rising influence of various Islamic groups within Syria. Before discussing my methodology and outlining the manner in which this research will unfold, two issues need to be addressed: the first is a brief discussion of the meaning and use of terms such as Islamic, Islamist and neo-fundamentalist, and the second is to offer some comments on the significance of Syria's often conflictual relationship with its fundamentalist and Islamist movements.

3 "Islamic," "Islamist" and "fundamentalist" defined

The term "Islamic" is used to denote groups that are made up of Muslims and that define themselves as such, while the term "Islamist" is used to indicate that

---

17 PA regimes are modern artefacts and products of the de-colonization period. They seek to modernize as a defensive mechanism and a way to control their fate as new states within a global economic and political order. Thus they are propelled to power through the support of the plebeian masses, who are promised the end of the feudal and capitalistic order and a redistribution of power and resources. But as modernization is undertaken, PA regimes encounter an inherent limitation: the once constrained capitalistic class is increasingly needed in order to continue the process of modernization. As a result, étatist reforms are countered and a new capitalistic era is re-activated (see David Apter, *The Politics of Modernization*, Chicago: University of Chicago Press; Raymond A. Hinnebusch, *Syria: Revolution from Above*, New York and London: Routledge, 2001).

18 At the expense of the initially more active and influential secular groups.

6 *Introduction*

the designated group has a particular reading and understanding of Islam that has become political and at times militant in nature.

There is a slight difference between "Islamist party" and "fundamentalist party" or "neo-fundamentalist party" in this work. An Islamist party tends towards political action through the state. More particularly, it focuses upon struggling to change the political regime and to impose Islamic values on society after a revolution from above. A fundamentalist party can also have political aims in the longer run, but it is first and foremost concerned with the restoration of an Islamic ethical model through the "re-establishment" of a Muslim ethos and the "re-Islamization" of each individual. This is with the goal of creating a perfect Muslim society from below. The rationale behind prioritizing ethics over political activism is that it is believed that this passive Islamization from below will create pious Muslim citizens, which will ultimately lead to the creation of an Islamic state.[19]

The terms "Islamic Revivalism" and "Islamic Renewal" do not necessarily refer to an increase in religiosity, but more to an increase in overt, public religiosity. As such, *Islamic* revival is the permeation of society with activities, organizations, speech and attire that are considered to be "Islamic," and that palpably impact upon the way of life of the public masses on a daily basis.[20] In Syria, this means the adoption of the veil, the reinvention of an attire tradition, the flourishing of neighbourhood mosques and Islamic institutes and the proliferation of Islamic organizations in poor neighbourhoods, who often end up partly supplanting the state in providing social welfare and medical assistance.[21] "Islamic Activism" is defined as "[t]he mobilization of contention to support Muslim causes."[22]

4 Why study Syria's relationship with its Islamic movement?

The present work argues that developing an understanding of the major elements underlying Islamic revivalism and the resurgence of Islamism in Syria demands a comparative political examination of the Ba'th regime's responses to the Syrian Islamic movement, particularly under the administrations of Hafez al-Asad and of Bashar al-Asad. This is particularly true because while there has been significant attention devoted to the Syrian regime's struggle with the Muslim Brethren in the 1970s and early 1980s, no published works have yet dealt extensively with the impact of that struggle on Syrian society today.

---

19 It is important to note that parties often oscillate between Islamism and fundamentalism. See Olivier Roy, *The Failure of Political Islam*, Cambridge, MA: Harvard University Press, 1996, ch. 3.
20 Saba Mahmood, *Politics of Piety*, Princeton, NJ and Oxford: Princeton University Press, 2005, p. 3.
21 This is not to say that there is not also a Christian revival in Syria, but this is beyond the scope of this work.
22 Quintan Wiktorowicz, ed., *Islamic Activism: A Social Movement Approach*, Bloomington and Indianapolis: Indiana University Press, 2004, p. 2.

Moreover, there have been no works dealing with the considerable social and political influence that the new Syrian Islamic movement has attained under the Bashar al-Asad government, a development that is especially significant in light of the country's mosaic of ethnic, religious, regional, ideological and class contrasts.[23] Indeed, the movement has already begun to make a direct impact upon Syrian society, with some Syrian Secularists, Muslims and non-Muslim minorities expressing their apprehension about its effects upon their daily lives. Yet some of these have also stated, however, that they do not want to stop pious Syrians from carrying out their religious duties and acts of worship, but simply that they do not want to see their own freedoms impacted upon. Their concerns are related to the closing of pubs in the vicinity of mosques, and to a number of incidents of women being physically harassed for wearing short skirts and of restaurants owners being hassled for serving alcohol or playing loud music during the call to prayer.

The changes occurring in the Syrian environment were seen as inconceivable less than ten years ago. Some observers have even warned about possible broader, regional implications, in that a failure to safeguard the country's secular environment risks not just de-stabilizing Syria but also bolstering the forces that are causing turmoil and factionalism in the region. According to Patrick Seale, Syria's centrality "derives from the fact that it lies at the heart of the Arab Asian power system where, for good or ill, it affects every political relationship in the region. All must take it into account."[24] In other words, Syria is a pivotal country in the Middle East where outcomes of domestic politics often have wide regional implications. At the same time, Syria's ideological and political centrality as a bastion of secular Arabism means that examining the resurgence of its Islamic movement can shed light on future ideological trends within the regional political context.

5 Theoretical contribution to scholarship

This book uses a historical institutional comparative approach. It employs theories and concepts from comparative politics and the socio-economy approach as a unifying framework of analysis. However, its interdisciplinary sensibilities and focus on intervening variables such as the roles of ideological framing, women and informal institutions allow it to also contribute to theory building in the domain of Social Movement Theory.

---

23 In terms of ethnicities, Syria is 90.3 per cent Arab, 9.7 per cent Kurds, Armenians and others. In terms of religions, 74 per cent of Syrians are Sunni Muslim, 16 per cent are other Muslim (includes Alawite and Druze) and 10 per cent are Christian (of various denominations). It also includes small Jewish communities in Damascus, Al Qamishli and Aleppo. See the Syrian Central Bureau of Statistics, 2009 Syrian Statistical Abstract, online: www.cbssyr.org; the CIA World Factbook at www.cia.gov/cia/publications/factbook/goes/sy.html.
24 Patrick Seale, *The Struggle for Syria*, London: I.B. Tauris, 1986, p. xxii.

8 Introduction

Furthermore, this work diverges from the literature on authoritarian regime models which routinely assumes a static notion of state and state–society relations, particularly within the context of Middle Eastern politics. In contrast, this work suggests that there has been an important change in state–society relations and of secular political culture in Syria. It does so by tracing the evolving and shifting nature of the Syrian state's relationship with Islamic groups, and shows that these shifts have been determined by domestic and regional imperatives and security interests.

This study also contributes to the literature on Islamic movements. It complements the work by previous scholars that focused upon the earlier phase of Syria's Islamic movement, by addressing the root causes and motivations and social profile of the new Syrian Islamic groups. It offers a typology of Syria's current Islamic movement, dividing it into two analytical streams: one that is fundamentalist and has formed a patron–client relationship with the state, and another that is Islamist and anti-regime. Within this typology, fundamentalists are divided into modernizers and textualists, while Islamists are divided into pacifists and militants. Importantly, the four streams are not hermetically sealed off from each other – if anything, it will be argued that each empowers the other, at the same time as the leftist, socially liberal and secular elements within the Syrian state and Syrian society continue to grow weaker. Indeed, they have now grown so weak that the Islamic groups could conceivably draw upon the same centres of support that once propelled the statist Ba'th to power, by focusing on the marginalized elements in society who are today in particularly dire need because of the country's ongoing process of economic liberalization without political democratization. In so doing, Syria's Islamic movement could potentially move beyond its present control of the country's social milieu and finally achieve the political power that it has sought since the early 1930s.

A number of works have tackled aspects of the issues addressed in this study, and can be broadly collected under the theme of the resurgence of Islamic movements in the Arab world and internationally. More specifically, they can be grouped under the headings of authoritarianism in the Middle East (and especially in Syria), and Islamic activism or Islamism in its modern forms. The various authors adopt different theoretical approaches: the political culture approach, the political economy approach, the Social Movement Theory approach and geo-political approaches.[25] Part of my contribution to the literature lies in a broadened consideration of the questions and insights arising from each alternative approach, with the goal of testing and verifying the different theories against the Syrian case. These questions include: How did sudden shifts in ideational culture promote Islamist militant activity? And, how do class issues, poverty and the economy trigger the seeming re-emergence of Islamist activity within Syria, and allow the Islamists to successfully expand their platform?

---

25 This taxonomy of the key theoretical issues involved in this analysis builds upon the introductory chapter in Rex Brynen *et al.*'s *Political Liberalization and Democratization in the Arab World: Theoretical Perspectives*, Boulder, CO and London: Lynne Rienner Publishers, 1995.

The Social Movement approach is utilized in this book to explain the mechanisms of Islamic resurgence. It also highlights other important questions, such as: Are more actors willing to join the Islamic movement in Syria today compared to 20 years ago? If yes, why, given that the same authoritarian Baʿth regime is still in power and the same kind of economic and political grievances are still largely present? What kind of informal institutions have evolved in the last 25 years that have enabled Islamic groups to mobilize more actors? And finally, how has the authoritarian Baʿthist state played a role in supporting this mobilization?

The focus of the geo-political school on the regional and international dimensions suggests different but equally important questions: What are the regional and international changes that have caused Syria's Islamists to re-emerge and mobilize? Has the "Islamic International" played a role in their recent successes? And, what role has been played by the cultural polarization and inter-cultural tensions that prevail in today's global environment? This book uses insights from the geo-political approach to explicate the regional dimension of Islamic revivalism in Syria's secular environment.

While the present work considers questions arising from the various theoretical approaches and draws upon insights made by them, it primarily explains Islamic revivalism in Syria through the lens of the political economy approach. In so doing, it provides a new case for testing the limits of the PA model, since it illustrates how the process of selective economic liberalization meant to maintain the political power of the Syrian regime has been closely linked to the opening of an important space for Syria's Islamic organizations to mobilize and recruit a growing pool of members.

The study also shows that understanding this connection requires recognizing how it has been shaped by other intervening variables at the domestic and regional levels. These include: (1) the Syrian Islamic movement's successful use of the organizational space provided by the state; (2) its internal methods of outreach developed in the last 20 years (such as the use of ideological framing and of informal institutions, which have provided an important space for Islamic groups to expand their membership and activities, as well as the role played by women); and (3) the need for the Syrian state to control its regional environment in view of its desire to maintain Syria's central role in the Middle East.

Given the many political barriers to fieldwork in Syria, as well as the relative absence of reliable previous research focusing on this study's subject, my methodology was designed in such a way as to combine several data-collection techniques. These include in-depth, focused interviews, more open-ended interviews, research based on a variety of primary sources (from Islamic sermons and published materials to government archives and Baʿth Party documents), and research based on many secondary sources from both the West and from the Arab world. One of my aims was to understand whether Syrian observers and experts anticipate an outbreak of violence inside Syria, and what influence they believe the Islamic and Islamist groups, as well as regional and international forces, have on Syrian society and Syria's secularism.

Regarding my interviews, I focused upon talking with members of small and large Islamic institutions, mostly using the open-ended interview format. These interviews helped me to define the boundaries of the "legal" and "official" mainstream Islamic message in Syria, as well as what kind of future its members foresee for Syrian society and political life. Most of my interviewees agreed to talk to me "off the record," though with full knowledge of how I would be using the information provided. They almost all expressed reservations about being identified or quoted given the sensitive issues dealt with in this work, as well as the Syrian regime's history of conflict with the country's Islamic movement. Hence in nearly all cases, only the date and the location of the interview are mentioned, though occasionally the title of the interviewee is also provided, as per their wishes.

I also did content analysis on a large sample of Islamic materials, including recorded sermons, religious lessons, pamphlets and books, which I gathered directly in Syria or took from Syrian websites, in order to understand the legal and not-so-legal Islamic message in the country.

In addition to this fieldwork, my research incorporated a variety of secondary material: Arab and Syrian print media, historical records, memoirs, Islamic programmes and pamphlets and Arabic and Western qualitative sources including works from both official and opposition presses available mainly on the Internet. I also consulted primary sources such as government archives, Ba'th Party documents and government agencies' data – for instance, electoral records, parliamentary memberships and electoral programmes – in order to trace the rise of Islamic individuals to government positions and to assess the shift of a supposedly secular Syrian regime towards tolerance of overt religiosity, in such spheres as education, television programmes and the news media.

6 Map of the work

Part I of this work (Chapters 2 and 3) provides an account of the roots of Syria's secular heritage and model. It also provides historical context, by examining the rise to power of the secular Ba'th Party and the formation of the Syrian Muslim Brotherhood, first as an Islamic political democratic party and then as it shifted towards militant Islamism. While much of this information will be familiar to some readers, Part I provides an essential background to those who are less familiar with the Syrian case, and informs the rest of the study.

Part II of this work examines the conflict between Hafez al-Asad's regime and the Muslim Brotherhood between 1970 and 1982 (Chapter 4), and the resulting decline in the 1980s of political Islam as a model for change in Syria (Chapter 5). It does so by tracing the domestic socio-economic and political roots of the conflict, and by unravelling the bloody contours of the clash between the regime and the Muslim Brothers, paying particular attention to those aspects of the conflict that have impacted upon the dynamics of secularism and religiosity in the country. Part II's main contribution is an examination of Syria's secular culture and of the survival strategy of confrontation and compromise deployed by the PA regime. It is argued that in an attempt to subdue and institutionally co-opt Syria's Islamic sector, the authoritarian command put a halt to its secular programmes, intensified patronage and bureaucratic clientelist relations, reinforced corporatist institutions, manipulated religious symbols and abandoned women's emancipation programmes.

Ultimately, Parts I and II of this work demonstrate both how and why Hafez al-Asad's regime paved the way for today's Islamic and Islamist revivalism after 22 years of relative calm on the Syrian social and political scenes. While Part II draws mainly upon secondary sources (some of which have been ignored by the literature up until now), it re-examines fundamental aspects of the various events thereby shedding new light on questions and issues essential to the rest of the study.

In Part III, the focus is on the Syrian domestic and regional contexts between Bashar al-Asad's rise to power in June 2000 and the writing of this work. It answers such questions as who are the Islamists in Syria today, and how is the state under Bashar al-Asad dealing with their re-appearance? In answering such questions, Part III will elucidate the implications and complications underlying today's relations between Syria's various Islamic groups and the Syrian regime under a new president. It will become clear that the regime's balancing act between the different social forces, while successful in the 1980s, became more tenuous in the 1990s, and still more tenuous again under Bashar al-Asad's government (Chapter 6), resulting in a significant change in the nature of both state and society in Syria (Chapters 7 and 8).

Chapter 9 of this work uses interviews to generate a number of arguments about the regime's current policies (especially regarding the enabling and constraining impacts of these policies), and pays particular consideration to the question of whether the new Islamic/Islamist pressures are detrimental to the survival of the secular political culture in the country. The last chapter of this study recapitulates the book's general themes and advances a number of concluding arguments.

Part I
The origins of the conflict

2 The rise of a secular party to power

1 Introduction

An understanding of the rise of Islamic and Islamist activity in contemporary Syria must be grounded in an appreciation of the factors contributing to the origins and evolution of Ba'thism in the country. This is particularly the case because of secularism's important role in the formation and subsequent trajectory of Syrian Ba'thism. As a result, this chapter has two main focuses: the Syrian secular heritage at its inception and later under the Ba'th, and the rise to power of *Hizb al-Ba'th al-'Arabi al-Ishtiraki* (Arab Ba'th Socialist Party, hereafter called ABSP or Ba'th Party) shaped as it was by domestic constraints and the regional context.

The chapter opens with a brief examination of the Syrian model of secularism. It then presents a survey of the Ba'th doctrine and organizing paradigm, as articulated by its different ideational sources and dominant theorists. The Ba'th Party's path to power, and the implications of the particular path taken, are subsequently explored. The chapter then examines the Ba'th regime's actions and first salient policies from 1963 to 1970, that is, up until Hafez al-Asad took power as president.

2 The Syrian model of secularism

A *Overview and historical roots*

A national version of secularism has existed since the early twentieth century in Syria,[1] and the Syrian nation-state has never had an official religion. In general, the Syrian secular model is different from most others in the Arab world, being closer to the "separatist" pole[2] and to the "French *laïcité*"[3] than to the

---

1 See, for instance, the 1920 Constitution.
2 The strict separation of church and state.
3 This will be further examined hereinafter. Briefly, French *laïcité* is different from Anglo-Saxon secularism in that it would like religion to be limited to the private sphere. The Anglo-Saxon model does not deny religion a place within the public sphere.

16 The origins of the conflict

"established official religion" pole[4] and the "Anglo-Saxon" model. As a result, Syrian secularism was not born with Ba'thism, although Ba'thist ideology is aggressively secular. Its ideological roots can arguably be traced back to late-nineteenth-century Ottoman policies that sought to "modernize" the Caliphate's provinces and thus maintain the Empire in the face of challenges from Western Europe.[5] These policies did prove successful at secularizing the political, judicial and educational systems in what would later become the Syrian nation-state.

After the fall of the Ottoman Empire, the 1920 Constitution's secularizing agenda[6] – and indeed the overall discourse that prevailed during the early to mid twentieth century – were widely welcomed as an opportunity for change and improvement in Syria, especially given that many Syrians were tired of the old Ottoman Caliphate and its claim to possess ultimate Islamic authority. The following expresses the overall mood at the time:

> the question of a state religion ... has ultimately, to do not merely with the status of non-Muslim minorities in an "Islamic" state, but rather with the status of the Muslims themselves and the fate of the entire nation. It is a question of the source of authority and power in the state. Is the government in Syria to be one of the people and on behalf of the people? Or is it to be one on behalf of the unimpeachable Deity through His unalterable laws? Are ecclesiastical interests and authorities to continue to maintain, by such a concept of government, their reactionary hold over men's minds and actions in matters that are not of the essence of the faith and the supernatural? Or are reason and the national interest to be finally recognized as the guiding factors in those matters? It is this double phased question of choice between

---

4 The state has an official religion but follows a secular system of rule.
5 See, for instance, the 1876 Constitution. For a history of the early twentieth century in English that touches upon questions of secularism, liberalism and nationalism, see James Gelvin, *Divided Loyalties: Nationalism and Mass Politics in Syria at the Close of Empire*, Berkeley, CA: University of California Press, 1998; Elizabeth Thompson, *Colonial Citizens: Republican Rights, Paternal Privilege, and Gender in French Syria and Lebanon*, New York: Columbia University Press, 2000; Philip S. Khoury, *Syria and the French Mandate: The Politics of Arab Nationalism 1920–1945*, Princeton, NJ: Princeton University Press, 1987.
6 Edward Webb explains:

> In 1920 Article 14 forbade absolutely any bar to freedom of beliefs or religion (diyanaat) nor to the ceremonies of "all sects" (Tawaa'if), so long as these did not damage public security nor the rites of the other faiths or schools (madhaahib). This is notable in contrast to the 1876 Constitution in its emphasis on the multiple sects and traditions within religions rather than simply referring to "religions".

See: Edward W.F. Webb, "Turkey's France, Syria's France: La Laïcité in Two Ottoman Successor States," Conference on Migration, Religion and Secularism: A Comparative Approach (Europe and North America), Paris, 17–18 June 2005. Online: http://histoire-sociale.univ-paris1.fr/Collo/Migrations/Webb.pdf.

a static and a progressive society, between a democratic and a theocratic form of government, which ultimately presents itself in an issue of state religion.[7]

The logic advanced in this extract is that confronting established traditions by keeping religion strictly out of the state apparatus is a requirement for the Syrian nation to modernize and develop.[8]

B Underlying reasons behind the secular agenda

The secularizing agenda was perceived to be an organic transformation by the leading elite and intelligentsia. This was mainly due to the fact that the transformation came from within rather than being imposed by foreign powers. Furthermore, Syria has seen myriad historical shifts, cultural changes and ideologies over its long history, all of which have mixed and interacted with, as well as tangibly impacted upon, Syrians' lives, culture and collective memories, ultimately making it very difficult to assign one religious identity to the overall Syrian culture and to the nation's constitutions. This is argued explicitly in the following passage:

> "Let the advocates of nationalism distinguish between Europe and the East, between the Christianity of the West and the Islam of the Arabs," warns Shaikh Mustapha [leader of the Syrian Muslim Brothers who was arguing against the secularizing trends in Syria during the mid twentieth century].
> But in what sense is the West Christian? Was not Syria an important cradle of this Western civilization? Such questions seem to be of no concern to the protagonists of an Islamic theocracy in Syria. To them the history of the country is arbitrarily circumscribed and made to begin only from the coming of Islam. All that came before may arouse their curiosity, but never their pride. This dichotomy between pre- and post-Islamic Syria, coupled with a rejection of the former, which nevertheless is an integral part of the cultural heritage of the Syrian people, is not a question of only academic historical importance. It is a question of the utmost significance to the rising generations of Syrians.[9]

The result is that while Syrian secularism is certainly informed by European, Turkish and Russian iterations of secularism, the Syrian model was not perceived as being a "Western" or "foreign" model by the majority of Syrians. Rather, it was considered to be an organic product of the country's rich and varied experience, its history and cultural identities.

---

7 George N. Sfeir, "Islam as the State Religion: A Secularist Point of View in Syria," Muslim World 45(3), July 1955: 246.
8 See al-Bina' newspaper, the mouthpiece of the SSNP and a main source on secularism and secular debates during the mid twentieth century in Syria.
9 Sfeir, "Islam as the State Religion," pp. 248–9.

18 The origins of the conflict

In addition to representing a strong ideological inclination among the broader Syrian public, secularism served another important purpose: it helped to create a sense of national unity, at a time when there was a nascent desire to become an independent nation within the new international order of nation-states. Moreover, secularism's ability to transcend ethnic and religious particularity and so-called traditions by asserting an inclusive political identity was perceived by many intellectuals as the only way to unite the Syrian nation.

As was stated earlier, the Syrian secular heritage is closer to the French system of *laïcité* than to the "established official religion" pole and the Anglo-Saxon secular model, which could be because many Syrians studied in Paris during the early part of the century. As a result, it does not see religion in general as being a necessary part of the nation's identity, and posits that the creation of a modern Syrian nation is not possible while faith is imposed from above or remains the overarching ideology of the majority. This fact caused a number of prominent intellectuals and politicians, such as Zaki al-Arsuzi, Antoon Sa'adeh, Michel 'Aflaq and Salah al-Bitar (among many others),[10] to press for a state and a public space free of religious discourse and practices, something that the Ba'thist state actively pursued in the 1960s.[11]

The all-encompassing nature of the Syrian secular model became more significant, at least on a practical level, as a result of the existential threat that Zionist Israel is believed to pose. Indeed, the formation of the state of Israel has often prompted Syrian intellectuals to proudly extol the virtues of the Syrian secular model of common living as the antithesis of the Israeli exclusionary and "reactionary" religious vision.[12]

Asserting a separation of religion from the state was also seen as important in light of the traditional (mis-)conception that religion in general is an all-encompassing system whose fundamental precepts apply to every aspect of life, and thus that Islam (and all religious discourse for that matter) is not compatible with secularism:[13]

> Religious institutions regard themselves as the bearers of a total complete ideology which encompasses all the needs and requirements of human life and deals with all the necessities of man – spiritual and material. From this point of view, these institutions regard themselves as the ultimate authority over

---

10 One of the main inspirers of the Ba'th ideology, Zaki al-Arsuzi, was pro an atheist sort of secularism. He often asserted in his writings that the *Jahiliya* (the pre-Islamic era) was the golden age of the Arab nation.

11 More particularly reflected in the Constitution of 1 May 1969, which gave birth to the current 1973 Constitution.

12 Indeed, Zionism and reactionary movements are often equated in Syrian contemporary discourse. See Ahmad Qurna, *Hafez al-Asad: Sane' Tarikh al-Umma wa Bani Majd al-Watan: Mawsu'a Kamila, 1970–1985*, Aleppo: Dar al-Sharq al-'Arabi, 1986; Patrick Seale, *Asad of Syria: The Struggle for the Middle East*, London: I.B. Tauris, 1988, p. 337; *Der Spiegel*, 28 August 1979.

13 See R. Bayly Winder, "Islam as State Religion: A Muslim Brotherhood View in Syria," *Muslim World* 44(2–3), July–October 1954: 215–26; and Sfeir, "Islam as the State Religion."

human societies and their conditions. And since they are the keepers of the message of the faith, the revelation of God and his laws to men, they are bound to believe that they are in fact the ideal instrumentality to direct human life in its entirety. From here arises their tendency to become the last and absolute authority in all that relates to the spiritual and functional (al-ruhiyat wal-ʿAmaliyat) in life.[14]

The last point in the above extract is reminiscent of the Papacy's powerful resistance to French secularization, resistance that was at once theological and political. It underlines the challenge that Syrian religious leaders posed to the country's politicians and intellectuals. Driven as they were by a fear of being marginalized and a conviction that Islam does in fact apply to all aspects of living and dying, religious leaders resisted the sweeping secular transformations.[15] Yet their resistance did not really hinder the political secularizing process between the time of Syrian independence from the French Mandate in 1946 to the 1970 rise to power of Hafez al-Asad. As will be explained in Chapter 3 and the following chapters of this work, in the late 1940s and early 1950s, the Syrian parliament had a number of debates – which included the leader of the Syrian Muslim Brothers, Mustafa al-Siba'i – about making Islam the official state religion in the Constitution. Al-Siba'i's pleas in favour of the proposition were ultimately rejected by Parliament. The decision was a political one to make, not a religious one.

C God, Islam and the evolution of Syria's secular culture

The Syrian Constitution of 1950 and the Constitution of 1953 were secular constitutions in the sense that Article 3 of both constitutions prescribed strict separation of church and state: "Freedom of belief is guaranteed. The State respects all the heavenly religions and guarantees the free exercise of all forms of worship as long as they do not disturb the public order." The general ease with which successive parliaments pressured Islamic shaykhs to accept the secularizing trend during the first decades of the new Syrian nation-state's existence underlines the strength of the developing secular political culture among most Syrians. Having said this, while Syria's consecutive constitutions were secular, had no official religion and were not meant to encourage religiosity, they still made Muslim law *the* main source of jurisprudence and conceded Islam to be the religion of the president.

The Baʿthist Revolution of 1963 promised to continue Syria's secular heritage, though more aggressively. Thus, the president no longer had to be Muslim, Islam was no longer the leading source of legislation, and morality was no longer religiously driven. The Baʿth encouraged Syrians to shed "reactionary ideologies"; it called for a "scientific culture" rather than a "moral" one and for the

---

14 Quoted and translated from *al-Bina'* newspaper by Sfeir in "Islam as State Religion in Syria," p. 246.
15 See Thompson, *Colonial Citizens*.

family to be seen as a "basic" unit rather than as a "genuine" one; marriage was to be conducted in a civil court, with religious marriage not considered "official"; and women's secular emancipation was to be constitutionally supported by the state.[16] Clauses within the provisional 1969 Constitution (which gave birth to the 1973 Constitution) referring to God were modified and "God" was replaced by "Humanity."[17] For instance, while in the previous secular constitutions, education was meant to create a generation "strong in body and thought, and believing in God," the 1969 constitution article on education reads:

> The educational and cultural system aims at creating an Arab, nationalist, socialist generation, scientific in its thought, tied to its history, seized of its heritage, imbued with the spirit of the struggle to achieve the goals of its nation in unity and freedom and socialism, and in the service of humanity and its progress.[18]

The Ba'th also sought to ensure a secular public sphere by *promising* to abolish religion courses in schools.

Generally speaking, while previous governments were secular in the sense that they guaranteed freedom of faith, refused to declare an "official religion," and separated religious practice from state institutions, the Ba'th's more aggressive secularization was aimed at weakening faith and weakening the position of religion in society. Indeed, the party's model does not assign any role to religion in the public sphere. Instead, the Ba'th – and especially the neo-Ba'th of the mid-1960s – has aimed to define, shape and control the religious discourse even within the private sphere.[19] This effort has included making religious teachers and leaders, whether imams or priests, state officials who are hand-picked and trained by the state. And while religion continued to be taught in schools as a compromise deal with the pious, it is only a very truncated version of it,[20] not to

---

16 For more on Ba'thist feminist agenda, see Annika Rabo, "Gender, State and Civil Society," in Chris Hann and Elizabeth Dunn, eds, *Civil Society: Challenging Western Models*, London and New York: Routledge, 1996.
17 If one compares the 1950 Constitution to the 1969 Constitution. See Webb, "Turkey's France, Syria's France."
18 Ibid., p. 22.
19 More on this in Chapter 3. On the subject of secularism and Islam in France, see Olivier Roy, *Secularism Confronts Islam*, New York: Columbia University Press, 2007.
20 I partly disagree with Joshua Landis's paper "Islamic Education in Syria," which argues that the Sunni Islam that is being taught in Syria is an "undoing of secularism" (see Joshua Landis, "Islamic Education in Syria: Undoing Secularism?" in Eleanor Doumato and Gregory Starrett, eds, *Teaching Islam: Textbooks and Religion in the Middle East*, Boulder, CO: Lynne Rienner Publishers, 2007). I argue that the version being taught is disguised as orthodox Sunnism, but is essentially a secularized version of Islam; a basic, almost caricatural sort of dogma – given its brevity and lack of sophistication compared to the rest of the courses – that few students pay attention to, especially given that the class grade does not count as part of the student's overall grade point average. Specifying the different schools, trends and divisions would mean recognizing that religion, with all its history and complexity, matters.

mention that the student's grade in their religion course does not count as part of their overall grade.[21]

Other aspects of Syrian Ba'thist secularism will be examined in more detail in the following section and later in this book. But for now, it is important to realize that the last 20 years have seen the Ba'thist state oscillate away from a secular rhetoric that is essentially against religiously driven morals and an outward manifestation of faith, and towards one that sees secularism co-existing with religion. In other words, away from a nominally strict Ba'thist *laïcité* and towards a more Anglo-Saxon secular model.[22] As is argued later in this work, this is due to the populist regime's survival needs.

3 Ba'th Party doctrine and ascent to power

A Formation and secular doctrine

Formation

The Ba'th (Resurrection) Arab Party was founded in 1942, four years before Syria's independence from French control,[23] by two upper-middle-class men from Damascus: Michel 'Aflaq (1910–1989), a Christian Arab raised in the old Damascene Maydan Quarter, and Salah al-Din al-Bitar (1912–1980), a Sunni Muslim who also hailed from the Maydan Quarter, and who was the son of a well-off grain merchant.[24] In 1940, inspired by Syria's unstable yet promising domestic and regional environment,[25] the two men founded *Harakat al-Ihya' al-'Arabi* (Arab Revival Movement), which would a few years later give birth to the Ba'th Party. In 1942, they abandoned their teaching careers and dedicated

---

21 In one conversation, a Syrian woman explained that her parents told the school that they did not want her to follow the religion class. As a result, she had no classes during religion class.
22 For more on the difference between *laïcité* and secularism, see Roy, *Secularism Confronts Islam*. See also Alfred Stepan, "Multiple Secularisms of Modern Democratic and Non-Democratic Regimes," in Craig Calhoun and Mark Juergensmeyer, eds, *Rethinking Secularism*, New York: SSRC Press, forthcoming 2010.
23 Syria had been under the control of the French since July 1920. For works relating to Syria's formative years after its independence, see Zeine N. Zeine, *The Struggle for Arab Independence*, Beirut: Khayats, 1960; A.L. Tibawi, *A Modern History of Syria*, London: Macmillan, 1969. On the Syrian state that emerged in the aftermath of independence, see Tabitha Petran, *Syria*, New York: Praeger, 1972, and Moshe Ma'oz, "Attempts at Creating a Political Economy in Modern Syria," *Middle East Journal* 26(4), 1972: 389–404.
24 See Sami al-Jundi, *Al-Ba'th*, Beirut: Dar al-Nahar, 1969. See also Muta' Safadi, *Hizb al-Ba'th: Ma'sat al-Mawlid, Ma'sat al-Nihaya* [The Ba'th Party: The Tragedy of Birth, the Tragedy of the End], Beirut: Dar al-Adab, 1964; George Jabbour, *Al-Fikr al-Siyasi al-Mu'aser fi Suriya* [Contemporary Political Thought in Syria], London: Riad al-Rayyes lil Kutub wa al-Nashr, 1987.
25 At that time, the French and the British colonial powers were engaged in the Second World War and were willing to give the colonies more autonomy. Moreover, the region was boiling with independence movements, and was particularly excited by socialist and communist ideas. In Syria itself, there did not exist any governing strata that could stifle possible future change.

themselves to political activism against the French and British colonial powers, who they felt were manipulating the region's religious, socio-economic and political divisions to their advantage, thereby impeding the growth of national unity.[26] The Ba'th officially achieved the status of a political party in 1946, a milestone that was soon followed by the adoption of its constitution during the first party conference between 5 and 7 April 1947. The year 1946 was later seen to mark the beginning of the end of Syria's so-called "politics of the notables" era.[27]

In 1952–1953, a reconfigured political landscape saw the Arab Ba'th Party merge with *al-Hizb al-'Arabi al-Ishtiraki* (Arab Socialist Party, hereafter called ASP) of Akram al-Hawrani. 'Aflaq and Bitar had previously met Hawrani in prison in 1941 after having organized strikes against the French and the British. The ASP, whose constituency mainly came from the rural, lower middle classes of the Hama region – an area known for its quasi-feudal culture and its military cadres – was to form the pro-Soviet left wing of the party. The merger producing the ABSP "was an impressive coalition of complementary class allies bound together by grievances against common class enemies: the agrarian oligarchy and commercial and industrial bourgeoisie."[28] Indeed, the party's earliest supporters largely belonged to the urban middle classes, mainly white-collar urban workers who believed that the old oligarchic system was incapable of meeting their modern needs, but also included the rural intelligentsia, rural migrants who had come to the cities for further education and the peasantry. The party soon became an instrument of empowerment for a rising middle-class and peasant coalition, while also successfully linking the urban middle class to the village.[29]

That a large number of the ABSP's members came from minority and rural backgrounds can be linked to the appeal of the party's emancipatory and secular ideas among people from these backgrounds, an appeal that was burnished by

---

26 At the time, Arab Sunni Muslims amounted to about 57.4 per cent of the population in Syria, 'Alawis about 12 per cent, Christians around 14 per cent, Druze about 3 per cent and Isma'ilis made up about 1.5 per cent of the population. A small Jewish community of about 30,000 individuals also existed. The majority of these religious minorities considered themselves to be Arabs, and spoke Arabic. Ethnic minorities included the Armenians, most of whom arrived after the First World War and who amounted to 4 per cent of the Syrian population, the Kurds, who represented 8.5 per cent of the population, and the Circassians and Turkomans, who amounted to around 3.5 per cent. The Kurds, Circassians and Turkomans are predominantly Sunni Muslim. If divided along religious lines, Sunni Muslims constituted 68.7 per cent of Syria's then five-million-strong populace.
27 Albert Hourani, "Ottoman Reform and the Politics of the Notables," (1969) in Albert Hourani, *The Emergence of the Modern Middle East*, Berkley, CA: University of California Press, 1981, pp. 36–66.
28 Bassel Salloukh, "Organizing Politics in the Arab World: State–Society Relations and Foreign Policy Choices in Jordan and Syria," McGill University: PhD thesis, 2000, p. 192.
29 Raymond A. Hinnebusch, "Class and State in Ba'thist Syria," in Richard T. Antun and Donald Quataert, eds, *Syria: Society, Culture, and Polity*, Albany, NY: State University of New York Press, 1991, p. 32. See also Nikolaos Van Dam, *The Struggle for Power in Syria*, London: I.B. Tauris, 1996, pp. 15–16.

the fact that these ideas were usually promoted by local supporters rather than simply emanating from Damascus. Indeed, the Ba'th doctrine would soon become the villages' vehicle of revolt against the city, which had historically been dominant in terms of power and wealth, and continued to be the long-established birthplace of the ruler.[30]

Secular doctrine

Ideologically speaking, the roots of the Ba'th doctrine can be traced directly to the League of National Action of Zaki al-Arsuzi (1899–1968), which had challenged the traditional land-owning urban elite after the First World War. The League of National Action paved the way to a more radically secular Arab nationalism in Syria, one that did not shy away from contesting the docile, elite-advanced Arabism of the inter-war period.[31] Inspired by Arsuzi's revolutionary ideology, the Ba'th aimed to take on the traditional patrimonial political and social structure that was prevalent in Syria in the 1940s. In the interest of insulating the domestic arena from external manipulation by the Western bourgeoisie, Syrians were to abandon divisive sectarian, religious and tribal group affiliations and unite with the larger Arab World. To do so, Ba'th Party ideologues posited a direct relationship between the "justice" of economic socialism and an understanding of Arab nationalism that includes all citizens.[32]

30 R.A. Hinnebusch, "The Islamic Movement in Syria: Sectarian Conflict and Urban Rebellion in an Authoritarian-Populist Regime," in Ali E. Hillal Dessouki, ed., *Islamic Resurgence in the Arab World*, New York: Praeger, 1982, pp. 138–9.
31 Zaki al-Arsuzi was a 'Alawi intellectual and philosopher born in Latakia. He studied philosophy in Paris from 1927 to 1930, and founded the Arab Nationalist Party (*al-Hizb al-'Arabi al-Qawmi*) in 1939, and then the Arab Resurrection (*al-Ba'th al-'Arabi*). Most of his followers joined 'Aflaq and Bitar's party when Arsuzi grew increasingly suspicious of political involvement. For more on Zaki al-Arsuzi and his role within the Ba'th, see Hanna Batatu, *Syria's Peasantry, the Descendants of Its Lesser Rural Notables, and Their Politics*, Princeton, NJ: Princeton University Press, 1999, p. 135. See al-Jundi, *Al-Ba'th*, pp. 19–36. See also Safadi, *Hizb al-Ba'th*, pp. 55–66. See also Zaki al-Arsuzi, *al-Mu'alafat al-Kamila* [The Complete Writings], Damascus: Matabe'al-Idara al-Siyasiya lil Jaysh wal Quwat al-Musalaha, 1972.
32 Article 10 of the Ba'th Constitution explains that "The Arab person is the one who speaks Arabic and lives on the Arab territory, or aspires to do so, and believes in his affiliation to the Arab Nation." Article 20 adds: "All rights of citizens shall be given to any citizen who lives in the Arab land and paid sincerity to the Arab Homeland and separates himself from any racist blocking." See Kamel S. Abu Jaber, *The Arab Ba'th Socialist Party: History, Ideology and Organization*, New York: Syracuse University Press, 1966; John F. Devlin, *The Ba'th Party: A History from its Origins to 1966*, Stanford, CA: Hoover Institute Press, 1976; and George Jabbour, *al-fikr al-siyasi al-mu'aser fi suriya*. See also Michel 'Aflaq, *Fi Sabil al-Ba'th*, Damascus: 1963, pp. 177–85. On the rise of Arab nationalism in Syria, see Ernest Dawn, "The Rise of Arabism in Syria," *Middle East Journal* 16(2), 1962: 145–68; James Gelvin, *Divided Loyalties: Nationalism and Mass Politics in Syria at the Close of Empire*, Berkeley, CA: University of California Press, 1998; Muhammad Muslih, "The Rise of Local Nationalism in the Arab East," in Rashid Khalidi, ed., *The Origins of Arab Nationalism*, New York: Columbia University Press, 1991.

Like most other Syrian political parties, the Ba'th Party was disillusioned with absolute monarchies such as the Ottoman Caliphate. It was also avowedly secular (some may even say atheist), and was more outspoken about its secularism than the rest of the traditional notables' parties (although not as outspoken about it as the Syrian Social National Party and the Communists). Thus the Ba'th Party doctrine avoided calling Islam an expression of Arab identity – which would have made it possible to use Islam as a valuable vehicle for the promotion of Arab unity – choosing instead to follow in the footsteps of Arsuzi's atheist ideas by defining Arab nationalism away from religion in general, and Sunni Islam in particular, through an emphasis on secular values that stripped religion of its normative social role.[33]

The position being articulated by Ba'thists was one that recognized Islam as an important cultural and revolutionary heritage for all Arabs, including Muslims, Christians, Kurds, Berbers and Armenians, but that simultaneously rejected the use of Islam as a divisive force or as a tool to politically empower one group at the expense of others: "The Ba'th wanted a united secular Arab society ... a society in which all Arabs would be equal, irrespective of their religion."[34]

Islam as an "Arab" ideology was understood to refer to the desire of the Arabs to contribute to humanity in a positive way. According to 'Aflaq, "Islam is Arab in its reality and universal in its ideals and goals." Arabism in this sense was to replace Islam as a "humanist" ideology.[35] Said Aflaq: "If certain nationalisms have followed the way of bigotry and oppression, is it necessary that we follow their tracks? Our nationalism has a guarantee from the past because it is accompanied by a humane message."[36] He added,

> Humanity is a whole solidified in its interest and commonly linked by its values and civilization. Therefore, the Arabs give the world civilization and take from it. They extend a brotherly hand to all other nations and cooperate with them for establishing just systems, which safeguard, for all peoples, peace, prosperity and sublimation in spirit and temper.[37]

---

33 Michel 'Aflaq, *Fi Sabil al-Ba'th*, pp. 105–29. See also Salem Babikian, "A Partial Reconstruction of Michel Aflaq's Thought: The Role of Islam in the Formulation of Arab Nationalism," *Muslim World* 67(4), October 1977: 280–94.
34 Ibid. See also 'Aflaq, *Fi Sabil al-Ba'th*, ch. 1, parts 4 and 5.
35 See 'Aflaq, *A la Memoire du Prophete Arabe*, April 1943. Online: www.albaath.online.fr.
36 See Aflaq, *The Abstract Thinking*, January 1943. Online: http://albaath.online.fr/English/Aflaq-04-on%20heritage.htm.
37 Third Principle of Bathist Constitution. Online: www.baath-party.org/eng/constitution.htm. Later on, we will see how Islam, interpreted to exclude socialism, will serve as a medium for the traditional merchant community – historically linked to the religious community in Syria – to contest Ba'thist rule. For the interpretation of those slogans and the ideology of the Ba'th, see Michel 'Aflaq, *Fi Sabil al-Ba'th*; idem, *Ma'rakat al-Masir al-Wahid*, Beirut: Dar al-Adab, 1958; idem, *Nuqtat al-Bidaya: Ahadith Ba'da al-Khames min Huzayran*, Damascus, 1971. See also Devlin, *The Ba'th Party*, pp. 23–45.

This statement clearly implies that sublimation in spirit requires secularism, which the Baʻth advanced as a necessary condition for transforming and reforming the Arab self. Indeed, articles 3, 5, 15, 17, 18, 20 and 44 of the Baʻth Party Constitution stressed the need for a "new Arab generation" that adopts "scientific thought" free from "superstitions and reactionary tradition."[38] Article 5 of the Baʻth Constitution[39] reads:

> The [ABSP] is a people's Party which believes that sovereignty is the people's, and they alone are the source of every authority or leadership, and that the value of the state comes from its stemming from the will of the masses. The sacredness of the state is dependent on the masses' will in choosing it. Therefore, the Party, in performing its mission, depends on the people and seeks to contract with them closely and works for lifting their rational, moral, economic and upright standards in order to allow them to sense their character and exercise their rights in individual and national life.

Article 15 explains that,

> The Pan-Arab National link is the only link that exists in the Arab State and assures harmony among the citizens and their fusion in one crucible of one Nation and combats all kinds of denominational, sectarian, tribal, ethnic and regional fanaticism.

Article 17 adds:

> The Party works on the dissemination of the people's spirit (the Rule of the People) and rendering it a living fact in the individual's life. It seeks to put in place a State Constitution that ensures to the Arab citizens absolute equality before the law and the voluntary expression of their freedom and the choice of their representatives honestly and thus prepares them for a free life within the law.[40]

---

38 The words "scientific thought" are posited within the text to replace "reactionary traditions." Although this is not directly stated, "scientific thought" is understood to stand against belief in the supernatural (*ghaybi*), while reactionary traditions are assumed to refer to religious practice in general.
39 For the Constitution of the *Baʻth* Party, see www.baath-party.org/eng/constitution.htm.
40 Webb tells us,

> This compares to Article 28, part 2 of 1950, which says education must aim to produce a generation "strong in body and thought, believing in God..." as well as "seized of the Arab heritage..." and "...imbued with the spirit of solidarity and brotherhood among all citizens.
> Webb, "Turkey's France, Syria's France."

These reforms were in keeping with the overall spirit prevalent in Syria at the time:

> It is suggested that if the Syrian people suffer today from the stings and trials of a deep moral crisis, this moral crisis, if indicative of anything, is indicative of the bankruptcy of the justification for the dominant traditional social order. The justifications for that order are predominantly religious – they are the lingering political interpretations of Islam and the continued entanglement of "Church" and state in the national and individual lives of the people.[41]

Once in power, the Ba'th's social strategy pledged the creation of a nexus of modern social institutions, unions and collective organizations under a strong party apparatus, to discourage "reactionary" ideologies and to promote the establishment of a "progressive" culture that had "human aims" rather than belief in God (see Chapter 3).[42]

Unity, freedom and socialism

The party advanced a trinity of cardinal and organically linked slogans: *Wihda* (unity), *Huriya* (freedom) and *Ishtirakiya* (socialism).[43] In Ba'thi parlance, the term "Unity" symbolized the oneness of the Arab nation and of the Arab Land. The Arab nation[44] was seen as constituting a cultural and historical unit that would form the foundational, ontological basis of Arab nationalism. In the words of 'Aflaq:

> Arab unity is an ideal and a standard, not the outcome or a consequence of the fight of the Arab people for liberty and socialism. It is a new ideal that should accompany and direct that fight. The potentialities of the Arab nation are not the numerical sum of the potentialities of its parts when they are in the state of separation; they are greater in quantity and different in kind.[45]

---

41 Sfeir, "Islam as State Religion in Syria," p. 246.
42 See also section on "Syria's Secular Culture" above; the *Ba'th* Party website at www.baath-party.org, the social policies of the party, articles 38 to 43; Robert W. Olson, *The Ba'th and Syria, 1947 to 1982: The Evolution of Ideology, Party, and State*, Princeton, NJ: Kingston Press, 1982, p. 55. Education was to become a right of every citizen and thus was to be free for all. See articles 44 to 48 in the declaration of principles of the *Ba'th* Party.
43 See *Ba'th* Party website, www.baath-party.org. These axioms will establish Syria as the bastion of secular Arabism and the heart of the Arabs for years to come.
44 According to the *Ba'th* Constitution, the Arab Homeland is the land inhabited by the Arab Nation, extending from the Torus Mountains and those of Bishtekwih to the Gulf of Basra, the Arab Sea, the mountains of Ethiopia, the Greater Sahara, the Atlantic Ocean and the Mediterranean Sea (article 7 of the General Principles). The Arab person is one who speaks Arabic and lives on the Arab territory, or aspires to do so, and believes in his/her affiliation to the Arab Nation (article 10 of the General Principles).
45 'Aflaq, *Fi Sabil al-Ba'th*, pp. 206–7. Translation online: www.albaath.online.fr.

The Ba'th Party was expected to be the vanguard in the spiritual resurrection of the Arab nation. It was felt that the spirit of that nation needed to be transformed and awakened so as to ultimately create a viable non-reactionary, non-religious, non-sectarian identity for a majority of the people who share the Arab language and history, of which a key aspect has often involved being controlled by others.

"Freedom" for the Ba'th meant an emphasis on personal freedom, but also freedom of the people from the corrupt status quo of political tyranny and exploitation at the hands of the oligarchy, as well as freedom from factionalism and the intrusion of foreign powers.[46]

Ba'thi "Socialism" meant social equality, and was seen as the instrument for morally improving the Arabs and awakening their consciousness so that all enjoy a prosperous and just life, thus replacing religiously driven morality. Only with socialism could unity and freedom be achieved.[47] The Ba'th economic programme was populist, promising the redistribution of resources and the regulation of ownership of land and of small industries. It also pledged to achieve social and economic transformation (*Inqilab*) by nationalizing public utilities, major industries and medium-sized companies: "The establishment of public interest, huge natural resources, and means of transportation shall be directly administered by the State. All companies and foreign concessions shall be cancelled" (article 29 of the Ba'th constitution). The party's rural plans called for the forging of a link between the rural masses and the urban political centre through agricultural reform, by partially co-operatizing land under state control, as well as by funding infrastructure projects and the agro-industrial economy.[48]

We will see in Part II of this work that as a result of its social populist thrust and its implications for the Syrian subalterns, the Ba'th doctrine appealed to the rural masses, to minorities and to the lower and middle classes who were naturally drawn to the reformist ideology of the party. Having said this, it was access to education and the military that finally broke the political monopoly enjoyed by Syria's oligarchy rather than the Ba'thist and other leftist groups' revolutionary ideology.

B *The Ba'th Party's ascent to power*

The socio-political and ideological challenges that the Ba'th regime faces today under Bashar al-Asad are not new, and are in fact often intimately connected to old tensions and battles. Hence, before examining the current rise of Islamist activity in Syria, it is important to at least briefly consider the nature of Syrian politics before the 1963 coup that brought the secular Ba'th regime to power.

The Arab Socialist Ba'th Party emerged as a reaction to a number of challenges that faced post-independence Syria. At the time, Syria was a diverse and

---

46 See www.albaath.online.fr.
47 See www.baath-party.org; www.albaath.online.fr.
48 See articles 26 to 37 in the declaration of principles of the Ba'th Party; Olson, *The Ba'th and Syria, 1947 to 1982*, p. 55.

fragmented society clearly lacking an overarching national identity. The state that emerged in the last year of the French Mandate was a truncated one, in that it represented only a small part of the Syrian population, namely the old urban mercantile class and landowners who had gained much power as intermediaries between the foreign rulers and the local population.

In the pre-First World War period, the increasingly precarious state of the Ottoman Empire prompted the Syrian mercantile and political elite to slowly abandon their imperial allegiances in favour of the rising tide of Arab nationalism. Joining with the latter was seen as a means for them to maintain their social status and political power in the face of the resolute French desire to be the sole rulers of Syria. At the same time, the Syrian notables successfully portrayed themselves to the French as intermediaries between the European power and the locals in the patronage system.

The post-Second World War era brought an end to this delicate balancing act. As France vacated Syria on 17 April 1946, a newly emerging generation of intellectuals felt that the politics of the notables were self-serving at best, and lacking in legitimacy. At the time, the Syrian political environment was one of successive and unstable short-lived coups. Moreover, the country's economy was weak, and it faced the new phenomenon of a rural exodus and low rates of social mobility. Stability was also in short supply at the regional level, particularly due to ongoing interference by Western powers.

The new context meant that the ABSP now stood a chance against the traditional (secular) parties such as the Damascene National Bloc and the Aleppo-based People's Party, whose in-fighting during a last-ditch effort to hold on to power opened the door wide to the new progressive parties.[49]

At the time of the September 1954 parliamentary elections, which took place just before the overthrow of President Shishakli, the Ba'th Party had a core of 6,000 members, of whom the majority came from Damascus, Homs, Hama and Jabal al-Druze. The election saw 64 of the 142 seats go to independents, 30 to the People's Party and 22 to the Ba'th Party.[50] Akram al-Hawrani's election in Hama, coupled with the electoral success of four other Ba'th candidates and of Bitar in Damascus, represented a clean sweep of the agrarian oligarchy. These results marked the decline of the traditional notables' parties in favour of alternative ideological currents such as the Ba'th, the Communists and the Syrian Social National Party. More specifically, the People's Party (considered to be one of the important notables' parties) took 43 out of the 119 seats in the 1949 parliamentary elections, but won only 30 seats out of a total of 142 in the 1954 contest. By contrast, the Ba'th won only one seat in 1949, but took 22 seats in the 1954 election.[51]

---

49 Raymond A. Hinnebusch, "Syria under the Ba'th: State Formation in a Fragmented Society," *Arab Studies Quarterly* 4(3), 1982: 178.
50 Olson, *The Ba'th and Syria, 1947 to 1982*, pp. 24–5.
51 Olson, *The Ba'th and Syria, 1947 to 1982*, p. 25. See also Khalid al-'Azm, *Mudhakarat Khaled al-'Azm*, vol. II, Beirut: al-Dar al-Muttahidah lil-Nashr, 1973, pp. 285–324.

From 1955 to 1963, Islamists, Communists, secular nationalists and independents all battled against each other as much as they did against the traditional ruling elite. The de-stabilizing effect that this had on what was already a fragile situation in Syria was further compounded by the penetration of Syrian politics by Iraq, Saudi Arabia and Egypt, each of whom backed competing factions and military conspirators. A further factor was the fragmenting of the country's military apparatus. It is fair to say that it was partly the political instability of post-independence Syria that made the Ba'th revolution possible.[52]

It is perhaps ironic given the political instability that facilitated the Ba'th revolution that the party itself was riven by in-fighting at precisely this moment of opportunity. Yet the Ba'th was able to overcome these internal divisions and out-manoeuvre its political rivals, aided by such blunders as the assassination of Ba'thist Colonel 'Adnan al-Malki, which helped to discredit the Syrian Social National Party (hereafter referred to as the SSNP). SSNP officers were subsequently systematically purged from the army, in favour of Ba'thist officers. The Ba'th was also aided by the fact that the 1956 Suez War that pitted Britain, France and Israel against Egypt, coupled with the earlier triumph of Nasser, helped to indirectly remove another of its formidable enemies, the pro-Iraqi People's Party. By late 1957, the Ba'thists were growing apprehensive about the increasing popularity of the Communists, as well as of their strong and well-organized presence in the army. They thus opted to play the unity card with Egypt, reasoning that a union was the only way to eliminate their rivals. They also believed that they would play a major role in the delivery and rearing of the United Arab Republic because of their having initiated the unity process.[53]

On 1 February 1958, after much deliberation on the part of Nasser, the United Arab Republic was proclaimed. By then the Ba'th, which had successfully rid itself of most of its political enemies – including the redoubtable Communists under Khaled Baqdash – was hoping that Nasser would reward them for their efforts to promote the union.[54]

From the outset, the unity plan sought to end all intertwined and competing civilian and military coalitions. Michel 'Aflaq stated that "we will be officially dissolved, but we will be present in the new unified party, the national union. Born of the union of two countries, this movement cannot be inspired by principles other than those of the Ba'th."[55] Yet the hope of the Ba'thist leaders that Nasser would share power with them once the union was in place proved misplaced. In fact, Nasser agreed to an immediate merger with Syria based on three

---

52 On the de-stabilizing effect of Syria's regional environment, see Patrick Seale, *The Struggle for Syria*, London: I.B. Tauris, 1986.
53 See Nabil M. Kaylani, "The Rise of the Syrian Ba'th, 1940–1958: Political Success, Party Failure," *International Journal of Middle East Studies* 3(1), January 1972: 3–23.
54 Khaled Baqdash was the first Communist to be elected in the Arab world. He won a seat in Damascus in the 1954 parliamentary elections. See Kaylani, "The Rise of the Syrian Ba'th, 1940–1958."
55 Salloukh, "Organizing Politics in the Arab World," pp. 200–1. *L'Orient*, 25 February 1958.

30 The origins of the conflict

conditions that ended up shaping Syrian politics for years to come: first, that the merger be a union rather than a federation, with a presidential political system rather than a parliamentary one like that in Syria prior to the union. Second, that the Syrian army be de-politicized and Nasser given the right to appoint and dismiss officers to civilian posts. Finally, "that all Syrian political parties dissolve themselves into a single corporatist political organization called the National Union (*al-Ittihad al-Qawmi*)."[56]

During the union's short life span, anyone within the Syrian branch of the army who was suspected of posing a threat was purged and transferred to Egypt. Those purged included the Communists, what was left of Hawrani's followers and Baʿthist officers and supporters of ʿAflaq and Bitar. In fact, anyone who was suspected of opposing the union was either expelled from the Syrian army or transferred abroad.[57] Yet this divisive strategy produced a backlash, since a number of exiled Baʿthist officers became fed up with the "Egyptianization" of Syria and thus set up a secret military committee (*al-lajna al-ʾaskariya*) in Cairo. The committee's members, who would later go on to launch Syria's bumpy ride towards Baʿthist rule, blamed the party's founding fathers for the disintegration of the Baʿth. They considered themselves to be the only hope for rebuilding the dismantled party, and awaited an opportune moment to take Syria out of the union.[58]

The Military Committee, which was formed in 1959 by Lieutenant-Colonels Mazyad Hunaydi, Muhammad ʿUmran and Bashir Sadeq and Captain ʿAbdul Ghani ʿAyyash, was by 1960 made up of the following officers: Majors Muhammad ʿUmran, Salah al-Jadid and Ahmad al-Mir, and Captains Hafez al-Asad, ʿAbdul Karim al-Jundi, Hamad ʿUbayd, ʿUthman Kanʾan and Munir el-Jerudi. A majority of these officers came from rural, religious minority backgrounds in the Latakia district of Syria, a fact that was not surprising given that a majority of the officers exiled by Nasser belonged to minority groups.

At the Fourth Baʿth National Congress of August 1960, disillusioned Baʿthists fought over how to re-build their party and to stop the "Egyptianization" of Syria. Hawrani's faction called for immediate secession from the union with Egypt, while others were much more committed to the union and chose to split from the Baʿth.[59]

With Nasser busy fending off the Syrian left, right-wing Syrian officers launched a coup against the union on 28 September 1961. Syria's business leaders and their representatives sought to use the coup to immediately organize a new socio-economic coalition in the cabinet. But that initial coup set off multiple competing business-dominated coups. The resulting confusion was compounded by the Iraqi branch of the Baʿth seizing power in Baghdad on 8

---

56 Salloukh, "Organizing Politics in the Arab World," p. 201. See also al-Jundi, *Al-Baʿth*, p. 85.
57 Olson, *The Baʿth and Syria, 1947 to 1982*, pp. 32–3.
58 Ibid., p. 34. See also al-Jundi, *Al-Baʿth*, pp. 85–6; Seale, *Asad of Syria*, pp. 60–4; Batatu, *Syria's Peasantry*, pp. 144–56.
59 Devlin, *The Baʿth Party*, pp. 169–86.

February 1963, thereby imparting a certain momentum to the Ba'thist officers in Syria. The arrival to power of the Syrian Ba'th Party would follow swiftly.[60]

C The Ba'th in power

The dissolution of the union with Egypt laid bare myriad rival power blocs within the Ba'th Party's ranks. Among these were Bitar and 'Aflaq's group, which controlled the so-called National Command; the Social Unionists' Movement led by Sami al-Jundi and Sami Sufan; Hawrani and his supporters; and the so-called *Qutriyun* or Regional Command formed in December 1961, which advocated a Syria-first policy. These emerging blocs first became visible during the Fifth Congress of the Ba'th Party held on 8 May 1962 in the city of Homs. 'Aflaq, who was then the Secretary General of the National Command, expelled Hawrani and his supporters from the Ba'th because they condemned Aflaq's aim of reviving the union with Egypt.[61]

At the same time, the right-wing, secessionist regime was growing increasingly unpopular. On 8 March 1963, a revolution from above was set in motion by a coalition of non-Hawrani Ba'thists, Nasserists and other anti-secessionist independent officers led by Major Ziyad al-Hariri.[62] Salah al-Din Bitar was tasked with forming a new government, while Amin al-Hafez, a non-Ba'thist Sunni army colonel, was promoted to the rank of major general and was appointed minister of the interior.[63] The events of 8 March 1963 would set the stage for subsequent events in Syria.

The Ba'th had an advantage within this coalition. Unlike the rest of the officers, Ba'thist commanders had both military power and a Ba'thist civilian wing to help with the task of state formation. State formation was thus dominated by Ba'th members, and took place under the watchful eye of Ba'thist army officers. Yet at the same time, sectarian blocs, tribal blocs and personal blocs began to trigger urban–rural splits among the Ba'th Party's members. Emphasizing personal alliances became a major tactic to gain and maintain power in this environment, which concretely resulted in the National Command or old guard being separated from the younger and more radical populist Regional Command, composed of rural petit-bourgeois army officers rather than peasant leaders.[64]

The Military Committee was the real repository of power after the 8 March 1963 coup, and its members felt it imperative to purge the army of anyone threatening their revolution.[65] This resulted in a clear "Ba'thization" and

---

60 On 8 March 1963.
61 See Kaylani, "The Rise of the Syrian Ba'th, 1940–1958."
62 Al-Hariri, who was a relative of Hawrani and the commander of the Syrian forces on the Israeli border, staged a military coup against the traditionalist coalition that had ended Syria's very brief union with Egypt in 1961.
63 See Hinnebusch, "The Islamic Movement in Syria," p. 143; Olson, *The Ba'th and Syria, 1947 to 1982*, p. 92.
64 See Van Dam, *The Struggle for Power in Syria*, pp. 98–103.
65 These purges did not go unnoticed; the Nasserites, with full Egyptian co-ordination, attempted on 18 July 1962 to overthrow the Ba'th. The plotters were executed.

32 *The origins of the conflict*

"ruralization" of the army. It also resulted in its 'Alawization,[66] because the purged independents and Nasserite officers happened to be Sunni in the majority. The bureaucracy was also indoctrinated and reshaped, with between 30 and 300 civilians ousted from the civil administration in favour of Baʻth loyalists.[67] This favouring of the minority 'Alawis would later be viewed as the practising of confessional politics by the Muslim Brotherhood, as will be seen later in this work.

On 25 September 1965, the Regional Command voted "no confidence" in Bitar's government, and Amin al-Hafez became head of the presidential council. By that time, the civilian faction (that is, the National Command) under 'Aflaq and Bitar had lost a large portion of its power, and was no longer capable of ousting the Military Committee and its civilian partner, the Regional Command.[68]

With the Military Committee – composed of Baʻthist officers – now firmly in power, the populist corporatist revolution intensified. "Liberal parliamentarism" was judged a bourgeois aberration and was replaced by "popular democracy," which was ensured by a single, Leninist-style party. In fact, in order to retain power and compensate for the lack of party discipline of past years, the Baʻth in its new radical populist form felt it necessary to expand its social base of support. Organizational networks and popular councils were created to indoctrinate and empower the efforts aimed at ensuring the revolutionary and popular practice of democracy.

> By the late 1960s, they had created an amazing array of social and political institutions, ostensibly to incorporate peasants, workers, students, youth, women, and professionals into the Bath's populist ruling coalition, but also to control them along rigid corporatist patterns.[69]

Furthermore, between 1964 and 1966, legislative decrees (mainly decrees 46, 35, 36, 76, 24, 57, 77, 84 and 88) nationalized all Syrian banks and about three-quarters of Syrian businesses. These decrees set in place strict trade barriers and placed nationalized companies – of which there were 114 – under

---

66 The 'Alawis, or Nusayris, were considered an extreme sect of the Shi'a; they were considered infidels by Sunnis in general and, under the Ottomans, were heavily taxed. For a brief history of Ottoman Syria and Syria's heterogeneous population, see Moshe Ma'oz, "Society and State in Modern Syria," in Menahem Milson, ed., *Society and Political Structure in the Arab World*, New York: Humanities Press, 1973, pp. 29–92.
67 Salloukh, "Organizing Politics in the Arab World," p. 222. The terms "Baʻthization" and "Ruralization" are Batatu's, and are found in *Syria's Peasantry*, ch. 12. They are also Hinnebusch's, found in his "Class and State in Baʻthist Syria," p. 35. See also Yaacov Bar-Siman-Tov, *Linkage Politics in the Middle East*, Boulder, CO: Westview Press, 1983, p. 127.
68 For 'Aflaq's comments on this period of time, see 'Aflaq, "al-Mu'amara al-Tarikhiya 'ala Hizb al-Baʻth", also available in *Niqtat al-Bidaya*, under the title "Tariq al-Wihda Tamur Bi-Filastine," p. 281 (delivered in July 1970).
69 Salloukh, "Organizing Politics in the Arab World," p. 220.

the administration of "state capitalism."[70] Meanwhile, agrarian reforms were sped up.[71] This populist-étatist thrust and social engineering from above did not go unnoticed. It is estimated that up to one billion Syrian liras were smuggled out of the country by the business class, while the religious leaders preached civil disobedience and organized a number of strikes, which were dealt with swiftly and firmly by the authorities. Through such measures, Syria's traditional Sunni elite was essentially silenced.[72]

By 1966, the Military Committee itself was fragmenting. Two interlocking conflicts defined the party's inner workings: The first was largely ideological, generational and urban–rural, pitting the party's older, more moderate urban leaders against the younger, rural radicals. The second was a personal competition between the three ranking party officers, Amin al-Hafiz, Salah Jadid and Muhammad 'Umran, each of whom ultimately joined either the moderate or the radical camp.[73]

The radicals under Salah Jadid finally staged a coup against Amin al-Hafez on 23 February 1966. Al-Hafez had made a number of mistakes, one of which was to accuse Salah Jadid of engaging in sectarian politics. His use of the sectarian and minority card backfired, and more officers defected towards Jadid's radical satellite.[74]

Under Jadid, prominent Sunni party politician Nur al-Din Atasi became Head of State; Ahmad Suwaydani, a prominent Sunni officer, became Chief of Staff; and Hafez al-Asad, an 'Alawi officer who had contributed enormously to the coup, was appointed Defence Minister. Al-Asad subsequently resigned from the Regional Command and focused exclusively on the armed forces.[75]

Salah Jadid's takeover of the party clearly put an end to 'Aflaq's and Bitar's domination of it, and moreover marked the rise of what was to become informally known as the neo-Ba'th Party.[76] This version of the Ba'th Party was more hard-line, seeing itself as part of the World Communist Revolution and subscribing to radical secularist (sometimes even atheist, as will be shown in the

---

70 Ibid., pp. 224–5. See also Hizb al-Ba'th al-'Arabi al-Ishtiraki, *Hawla Mafhum al-Hizb al-Thawri wa al-'Ilaqa Bi-al Bunyatayn al-Fikriya wa al-Tanzimiya* [On the Concept of the Revolutionary Party and the Relation with the Ideological and Organizational Foundations], Damascus: Maktab al-Thaqafa wa al-Dirassat wa al-I'dad al-Hizbi, n.d., pp. 17–19.
71 Olson, *The Ba'th and Syria, 1947 to 1982*, p. 92.
72 Ibid., pp. 92–3.
73 Hinnebusch, "The Islamic Movement in Syria," p. 143.
74 Olson, *The Ba'th and Syria, 1947 to 1982*, pp. 98–9. The subsequent coup was led by Salim Hatum and 'Izzat Jadid, and resulted in the defeat of a number of prominent factions who were perceived as being loyal to Amin al-Hafezi. Members of Umran's faction were also purged. See Van Dam, *The Struggle for Power in Syria*, p. 47.
75 Hinnebusch, "The Islamic Movement in Syria," p. 144.
76 The neo-Ba'th Party was made up of three main groups: the Atasi-Jadid group supported by Chief of Staff Ahmad Suweydani, by Head of Military Intelligence 'Abd al-Karim al-Jundi, and by the Commander of the 70th Regiment, 'Izzat Jadid, as well as by a number of neutral officers; the al-Asad group, supported mainly by the Air Force; and the Hatum group, supported by the Druze of Hamad 'Ubayd.

34 *The origins of the conflict*

following chapter) and scientific socialist positions, which would become a major problem for religious leaders and for the religious class of Syria and the rest of the Arab world. On the international front, Syria strengthened its ties with the Soviet Union and took a strong stance against Zionism and Israel.

Following the Syrian and Arab defeat in the 1967 war with Israel, Chief of Staff Ahmad Suwaydani was replaced by another Sunni, Mustafa Tlas. Meanwhile, Hafez Al-Asad managed to hold on to his post of Defence Minister. Despite attempts by the ruling coalition to ensure sectarian balance among the political elite, the top of the political pyramid exhibited strong rural 'Alawi predominance.[77]

The 1967 Syrian defeat had the additional effect of undermining the leaders' confidence in charting a radical course for the country, and ended up further splitting the Ba'thist elite (mainly Jadid and al-Asad) over what steps to take next. This disagreement between Jadid, who by now controlled the civilian party apparatus, and Hafez al-Asad, who controlled the armed forces, dominated Syrian politics from 1969 to 13 November 1970:

> Once again both coalitions in the intra-elite conflict cut across sectarian lines and were largely cemented by personal and ideological loyalties, but the fact that both sides were led by Alawite officers indicated for many Syrians the ascendancy of this sectarian community.[78]

The November 1970 "Corrective Movement" of Hafez al-Asad finally managed to break the see-sawing power struggle, concentrating power in the hands of his faction's officers, which dismayed competing elites such as the Arab Socialists of Hawrani, the Nasserites and the Muslim Brethren. In February 1971, al-Asad became Syria's first non-Sunni ('Alawi) President, much to the alarm of the traditional Sunni elite.

4 Conclusion

The rise of Ba'thism was a result of the forging of a secular ideology based on a rising social base of the plebeian masses, as well as a new economic orientation towards state socialism. Ideology, secularism and economic forces were key in its advance. But the development of the Ba'th Party and the eventual ascent of Hafez al-Asad to power was not the only significant political development in Syria. In the following chapter, we turn our attention to the rise of the Muslim Brotherhood both as an ideological movement and a political party in the country, as well as to its later shift towards Islamic militantism.

---

77 Hinnebusch, "The Islamic Movement in Syria," p. 144. After an abortive plot prepared by Ahmad Suwaydani in August 1968, Suwaydani was caught in July 1969 and imprisoned until 1994. All his Hawrani followers were also arrested or purged from the military.
78 Ibid., p. 144.

3 The rise and fall of political Islam in Syria

1 Introduction

This chapter explores the Syrian Islamic movement, with a particular focus upon the formation and history of the Muslim Brotherhood in the country (*al-Ikhwan al-Muslimin fi Suriya*). Before explaining the rise of the Syrian Muslim Brothers as a democratic political party and as an Islamic opposition in Syria, it is important to say a few words about the movement's social base and the kind of socioeconomic and political programmes that were advanced by its creators. Doing so will unpack the Brotherhood's positions on issues relevant to its subsequent quest to re-capture an elusive Syrian *imaginaire*. More importantly, it will provide the background necessary for understanding the arguments in later chapters regarding the current rise of Islamic groups in the country. Thus this chapter will explain the reasons behind the failure of the Muslim Brothers to recruit the masses in the mid twentieth century, which will in turn make it easier to understand the successes of the current Islamic movement in Syria. It will also shed a significant degree of light on the secular debate taking place in the country today.

2 The Muslims Brothers: a different kind of social base and agenda

In its early years, the Muslim Brotherhood was far from being one of Syria's largest political organizations. Indeed, the Islamic movement never achieved the degree of ideological influence and social importance of comparable movements in the Arab World, such as those in Egypt and Jordan. One main reason for this is Syria's blend of some 17 different ethnic and religious groups, with over 30 per cent of the population not Sunni Muslim. This heterogeneity is in stark contrast to Egypt and Jordan's overwhelming Sunni majorities, and means that there is relatively less support for a rising regional Sunni movement.[1]

---

1 In Syria, there is no Shi'i Islamic movement, and Syrian 'Alawi culture was and remains for the most part a secular culture, despite present-day attempts at Islamizing this minority (which will be discussed in later chapters).

Another factor is that secular ideologies eclipsed Islam as a primary source of socio-political activism in Syria very early on in the twentieth century (see Chapter 2). As explained earlier, this was partly due to late-nineteenth-century Ottoman policies that "modernized" the Syrian political system and secularized the leading urban elite. Islam at the time was still perceived as the culture of the leaders and as a religion rather than as one particular socio-political movement among the many such movements competing for ideological hegemony. By the time Syria's Islamic leaders were inclined to compete in parliamentary elections, the country's political scene was already dominated by secular tendencies. Moreover, the Islamic leaders and pious Muslims had not fought against the French occupation of Syria as a unified, Islamic entity, instead doing so as part of the overall resistance. This cost them in terms of establishing their resistance credentials, since they were superseded in the popular imagination by myriad secular nationalist groups that had resisted in a more identifiable manner, such as the People's Party, the Nationalist Party, the Communist Party and the Syrian Social National Party.

The weakness of Syria's Islamic movement in the early to mid twentieth century can also be linked to socio-economic factors. That is, unlike in Egypt, Syria's Muslim Brothers tended to embody the defensive ideological protest of the declining traditional bourgeois class, and indeed were often associated, at least in the popular imagination, with that societal class. This meant that the group's socio-economic programme was often seen as serving a feudalistic status quo, and hence did not appeal to the increasingly educated middle to lower urban and rural strata of society, whose political awareness was by then permeated with socialism and with secular Arabism.

A final factor in the group's weakness is best summed up by Hinnebusch, who points out that given

> the diversity of elements and ideological shadings embraced by the Islamic movement [in Syria] ... it is unclear whether it should be considered one movement or many and to what extent it has been able to act in a unified way.[2]

(See Section 3.C in this chapter.) This complex reality resonated in the words of the movement's first superintendent, Mustafa al-Siba'i: "Our movement is neither a society nor a political party but a spirit that permeates the very being of the *Umma*: it is a new revolution."[3]

---

2 Raymond A. Hinnebusch, "The Islamic Movement in Syria: Sectarian Conflict and Urban Rebellion in an Authoritarian-Populist Regime," in Ali E. Hillal Dessouki, ed., *Islamic Resurgence in the Arab World*, New York: Praeger, 1982, p. 153. That being said, whenever discussing Syria's Islamic political movement in this chapter, the main focus will be on the ideology and actions of the Muslim Brothers, for the simple reason that they represented the majority of the Sunni political Islamic movement in Syria, notwithstanding their leaders' quarrels, different visions and their sponsors' ideological diversity, as we will see hereafter. Therefore, throughout the following chapters and until the end of Part II, "the Syrian Muslim Brotherhood" and "Syria's Islamic Movement" are interchangeably used to denote the same political movement.

3 Quoted in Umar Abd-Allah, *The Islamic Struggle in Syria*, Berkeley, CA: Mizan Press, 1983, p. 21.

A Formation and initial social base

Syria's Islamic Movement did not initially emerge as a reaction to the Ba'th or to al-Asad's rule, or indeed to the secularization and modernization attempts by the Ba'th regime in Damascus, though it did become more visible and partly radicalized – or one might say, politicized – during al-Asad's first term. In fact, Syria's religious scholars (*'ulama' al-din*),[4] recruited as they were from notable urban and merchant families, had long been influential actors on the Syrian political stage. And although they were significantly weaker than the Ba'th, the Muslim Brothers had to ward off the same political challengers as the latter.[5] These included Syria's domestic and regional environment, dominated as it was by Western powers; Syria's diverse religious communities, which were believed to be responsible for an increasingly fragmented society and the resultant lack of an overarching national identity; and more importantly, an unstable economy troubled by high rates of social mobilization.[6] However, it is important to reiterate that unlike the Ba'th Party, the Muslim Brothers defended and endorsed the socio-economic status quo in which they flourished, and were wary of the secularizing trends that permeated the country.

It was in this context that a number of political associations, in particular social-welfare societies at first, gained considerable ground in the 1930s. These associations were primarily concerned with providing Islamic education and health care, though later switched their attention to broader cultural and political objectives. In their initial iterations, they believed that a sound Islamic education and a strong social-welfare net would re-establish Islamic culture in its true essence and thus remove the West's unwelcome authority over Syria and the rest of the Arab world.[7] These urban social-welfare organizations met regularly to discuss social reform, and were collectively known as *Shabab Muhammad* (Youth of Muhammad). Then in 1944, the *Shabab Muhammad* joined together in a unified group under the name of the Muslim Brotherhood of Syria and Lebanon,[8] at which point the movement began to shift from being a social-welfare organization towards being an established political party.[9]

---

4 Used alone (without *al-din*), the word *'alem/'ulama'* means scientist/scientists. It is thus important to add (*al-din*, meaning "of religion") in order to specify that one means "the religious scholars." Yet for the sake of brevity, 'ulama' al-din and 'ulama' are interchangeably used hereinafter.

5 These were the secular traditional notable parties such as the Aleppine People's Party, the Damascene National Front, the Syrian nationalists, the Socialists and the Communists, in which originally rural middle class and minority groups played an important role.

6 Raymond A. Hinnebusch, "Syria under the Ba'th: State Formation in a Fragmented Society," *Arab Studies Quarterly* 4(3), 1982: 178.

7 Among these social-welfare associations were *Dar al-Arqam* (the Arqam House) in Aleppo, *Jam'iyat al-Rabita al-Diniya* (the Religious Accord Organization) in Homs, *Ansar al-Haqq* (the Supporters of Righteousness) in Dayr al-Zor and the association of the Muslim Brothers in Hama.

8 Faysal Daraj and Jamal Barut, *Al-ahzab wa al-harakat wa al-jama'at al-islamiya* [The Islamic Parties, Movements and Groups], Damascus: The Arab Center for Strategic Studies, 2006, p. 255.

9 See Abd-Allah, *The Islamic Struggle in Syria*.

The majority of the leaders of Syria's Muslim Brothers were young men who came from a small but powerful group of urban merchants and notable families that combined great wealth with religious office. These men, whom Hanna Batatu calls the "religious class,"[10] soon pressed political Islam into joining the fight against the West, as well as into defending religion and private property. For the most part, the men were attending shari'a schools in Syria or al-Azhar Islamic University in Cairo when they became acquainted with the ideas of Hasan al-Banna, the founder of the Egyptian Muslim Brotherhood and the ideological inspiration for the Syrian Islamic movement. The group of young men included: Mustafa al-Siba'i, who later became a professor of Islamic law at the Syrian University in Damascus and the first superintendent general of the Muslim Brothers society from 1945 to 1961; 'Umar Baha' al-Amiri, who was one of the first founders of Dar al-Arqam; Muhammad al-Hamed, one of the founders of the Muslim Brothers of Hama; 'Isam al-'Attar, who succeeded Mustafa al-Siba'i as superintendent general of the Muslim Brothers and who was also the imam at Damascus University's mosque; and 'Abdul Fatah Abu Ghuda, who as a shari'a teacher set up the Aleppo branch of the Muslim Brothers in 1935, and who in 1972 led the group that seceded from the Muslim Brothers.[11] Unlike the Muslim Brotherhood movements in Syria's neighbouring countries, there were no muftis and only a few judges who were members of the organization.[12]

B Dogma

Although they were ideologically committed to Islamic orthodoxy in their outlook, Syria's Muslim Brothers were also in general loyal to their Sufi roots and to Hasan al-Banna's inclusion of Sufi elements in the Muslim Brothers' belief set. This balancing act was made much easier by the fact that in Syria, the Salafiyya movement – arriving from Egypt and the Arabian Peninsula – had been mostly allied with orthodox Sufism since the late nineteenth century. Indeed, Sufism was Syria's overarching Sunni dogma, for the simple reason that the early representatives of Salafism in Syrian cities tended to come from an orthodox Sufi background, and thus believed that Sufism provided Islam with an important spiritual-ethical component. As a result, the Syrian Muslim Brothers believed that the Sufi *Tariqas* (orders, paths) were an efficient tool for attracting the masses to their new, populist Islamic association.[13]

---

10 Hanna Batatu, "Syria's Muslim Brethren," *MERIP Reports* 110, November–December 1982, p. 14. The "religious class" accounted for around one man out of every 2,500 Syrians in the 1960s and 1970s.
11 Faysal Daraj and Jamal Barut, *Al-ahzab wa al-harakat wa al-jama'at al-islamiya*, pp. 255–8.
12 Batatu, "Syria's Muslim Brethren," p. 14.
13 See Itzchak Weismann, "The Politics of Popular Religion: Sufis, Salafis, and Muslim Brothers in 20th Century Hamah," *International Journal of Middle East Studies* 37, 2005: 39–58; idem, *Taste of Modernity: Sufism, Salafiyya and Arabism in late Ottoman Damascus*, Leiden: Brill, 2000.

At least initially, the Muslim Brotherhood "did not contribute greatly to the Syrian discourse on the definition of nationhood and the nation" as it did not have a specific programme or charter, instead concentrating almost exclusively on emphasizing the importance of Islamic history and its interpretation of Islamic heritage.[14] Accordingly, it was left to the individual religious leaders to call for an Islamic resistance (resistance made up of Muslims) to the French occupation in particular and to the imperialist agendas of the Western powers in general.

Once Syria became independent, the Muslim Brothers were forcefully confronted with the aggressive secularizing tendencies in the country that had effectively replaced its once-overarching Islamic culture. As mentioned in the last chapter, the 1940s and 1950s saw Shaykh Mustafa al-Siba'i initiate major debates and lead a few demonstrations against secularizing trends, especially during the drafting of the 1950 Syrian Constitution.[15] Al-Siba'i argued that Islam is the religion of 90 per cent of Syrians, and that "the opinion of the majority is to be followed and acted upon," which he interpreted as dictating that Islam must be the religion of the state. He added that the establishment of Islam as the religion of the state has a functional or *realpolitik* justification, as it "will stimulate the people" (1) into executing the regulations and decrees of the government, and (2) "to be attached to the State and to be defenders of the fatherland." Al-Siba'i also argued that the establishment of Islam as the state religion "will be a strong factor for unity between us ('the Syrians') and our Arab brethren."[16] Yet ultimately, as was mentioned in the last chapter, al-Siba'i had to yield to the parliament's decision to enforce a secular constitution that included some Islamic colourings. Talhami explains:

> Siba'i led the fight over declaring Islam the sole religion of the state. But he lost in favor of those who insisted only on delineating Islam as the religion of the president of the republic. This statement was then buttressed by declaring Islamic jurisprudence to be the main source of legislation and the state to be the sustainer of all divine faiths. The debate over secularizing the state was also joined by some of Syria's Christian religious leadership. The Greek Orthodox Bishop of Hama, Ignatius Harika, protested in the pages of the national press that the new constitution threatened to relegate Christians to the status of a permanent minority.[17]

C Political and economic agenda

Syria's secular tendencies impacted upon the politics of the Muslim Brothers to a significant extent from the very beginning. Indeed, by the time of its official

---

14 Ghada Hashem Talhami, "Syria: Islam, Arab Nationalism and the Military in Syria," *Middle East Policy* 8(4), December 2001: 113.
15 See *al-Samir* newspaper, 9 and 13 March 1950; *al-Ayyam*, 9 March 1950.
16 Quoted by George Sfeir, "Islam as State Religion: A Secularist Point of View in Syria," *Muslim World* 45(3), July 1955: 242.
17 Talhami, "Syria," p. 120.

40 *The origins of the conflict*

formation as a political party in 1946, Syria's Muslim Brotherhood had already broken ranks with its Egyptian counterpart over the issue of whether or not to be part of a secular political system, by agreeing to actively participate in Syria's burgeoning parliamentary life. The Syrian Muslim Brotherhood also departed from the more "orthodox" interpretations of Islam by including elements of social reform and socialist solidarity in its programme, in an attempt to reconcile traditional Islam with the new concepts of modernism and progress.[18] Hinnebusch explains that

> Siba'i held that the Quran supported state ownership of key industries and a more equitable distribution of wealth than obtained in traditional Syria ... Siba'i went so far as to favour closer relations with the USSR as a means of neutralizing Western influence.[19]

It bears underlining that notables who supported the Muslim Brothers in a behind-the-scenes capacity often themselves shifted from the left to the right on the ideological political spectrum, thus adding to the already difficult task of defining the social position of the Syrian Brothers.[20]

What emerges therefore is that the Brothers' initial lack of a clear and consistent political ideology within an Islamic rubric could be attributed to the following reasons: (1) the pyramid-like structure of the group, (2) the ideological diversity of both its members and its supporters,[21] (3) and most importantly for this work, its *political* ambitions within a *secular* environment. Indeed, an explanation put forward by Michel Seurat among a number of other observers is that the priority for the leading Muslim Brothers simply lay elsewhere than theology.[22] According to these observers, once Syria had achieved independence, it became more important to reclaim the country's 14-century-long Islamic legacy, with an eye to emphasizing the "inalienable" right of its Sunni traditional elite to lead and manage Syrian affairs. This political focus would end up alienating the movement from the masses. Yet as will be shown later, today's movement has latterly gained a great deal of influence by turning away from politics and focusing on socio-ethical change.

It was not until January 1981, even as it was losing its battles on the Syrian domestic front, that the Muslim Brotherhood finally published a comprehensive and detailed manifesto. The document, entitled "Declaration and Program of

---

18 Talhami, "Syria," pp. 113–15. See also R. Bayly Winder, "Islam as State Religion: A Muslim Brotherhood View in Syria," *Muslim World* 44(2–3), July–October 1954: 215–26; Hanna Batatu, "Syria's Muslim Brethren," in F. Halliday and H. Alavi, eds, *State and Ideology in the Middle East and Pakistan*, Basingstoke: Macmillan, 1988, pp. 115–22.
19 Hinnebusch, "The Islamic Movement in Syria," p. 151.
20 Ibid., p. 153.
21 This ideological uncertainty is particularly clear in the scattered views published in its clandestine journal issued in Syria throughout the 1970s and early 1980s, *al-Nadhir*.
22 Michel Seurat, *L'Etat de barbarie*, Paris: Collection Esprit/Seuil, 1989, p. 60.

the Islamic Revolution in Syria," was aimed at attracting the support of a larger section of the Syrian public,[23] and was the first working guide ever published by an Islamic movement in the Arab world that discussed in detail the ideal life of an Islamic polity. The 65-page document consists of a strategy and an ideological platform according to which so-called Islamic laws are to organize constitutional, legal, economic, cultural, military, intellectual and educational affairs in Syria.[24] Of particular note is that freedom of expression and the rights of minorities are to be guaranteed, and political parties are to be allowed to compete freely as long as they do not oppose the main precepts of the monotheistic religions and are not bound by loyalty to a foreign state. Moreover, Arab unity under the wider umbrella of the Islamic Nation (*Umma*) is to be pursued. At the societal level, gambling, alcohol and nightclubs are to be eradicated and the citizenry is to be morally regenerated through a return to *Sunna*. Economically, the document promises a return to free enterprise, privatization and *zakat*, although natural resources and "special economic interests" are to be kept nationalized.[25]

D Political base of support

The economic aspect of the Brotherhood's political programme is particularly significant, since it shows that the party of the Muslim Brothers of Syria did not come from the same background as Islamists in the rest of the Arab world. In Egypt, for instance, the Muslim Brothers arose initially from out of the middle to lower-middle classes, and more often than not came from rural backgrounds. They shared feelings of estrangement from the existing system, having experienced in Cairo the "moral decadence" of urban "Westernized" life for the first time. Often enough they were young men who were pursuing professional, technical and scientific education as a way of moving up the social ladder, but who longed for the strong communal attachments that they had once had. Studies explaining the rise of Islamic movements in the Arab world tend to identify the economic crisis, especially following the defeat in the 1967 war by Israel, as partly responsible for the successful mobilization of this rural youth under the aegis of the Muslim Brotherhood.[26]

In contrast, as was mentioned above, Syria's Islamic Movement was initially drawn from an entirely different class and background. Moreover, its membership gravitated towards the movement for slightly different reasons than their counterparts in Egypt, as is made clear by the fact that Syria's movement advocated a return to free enterprise and an independent

---

23 Thomas Mayer, "The Islamic Opposition in Syria, 1961–1982," *Orient* 24, 1983: 599–600.
24 Ibid., p. 603.
25 Raymond A. Hinnebusch, *Syria: Revolution from Above*, London: Routledge, 2001, p. 95. See also Abd-Allah, *The Islamic Struggle in Syria*.
26 See Laura Guazzone, ed., *The Islamist Dilemma*, Reading: Ithaca, 1995.

economy.[27] Later on, in the late 1970s, the Syrian Islamic movement's support base did expand to include a number of young students from the lower classes.[28] Nonetheless, the Syrian branch of the Brothers was not claiming to be an ally of the workers and the rural constituencies. Indeed there is some question as to whether such an alliance could even be forged, given that the poor and the rural minorities were more interested in challenging the long-standing hold on power enjoyed by the Brothers' core support groups – the urban traditional middle class and traditional labour – than in joining the organization that they controlled.[29]

Similarly, Islamic revivalism did not enjoy widespread support at Syrian universities, and in fact religion in general did not rank high on the students' priorities according to a number of surveys conducted in the 1960s.[30] Despite the disintegration of notable parties and the decline of Nasserism in the 1970s in Syria, the traditionally secular and liberal salaried middle class and professional upper middle class remained deeply opposed to the rise of a non-secular movement to power, though some did applaud the Brothers' economic challenge to the socialist Ba'th.[31] Only the traditional small merchants and artisans could be said to be truly receptive to the Muslim Brothers' calling.

This overview of the Brothers' base of support underlines that the spread of Islamic ideology was overwhelmingly reliant on Syria's traditional urban Sunni heritage, and that the spread was contained by leftist parties' mobilization of students and workers. It is important to note that both high school students and organized workers who were supportive of the Muslim Brothers came chiefly from the older city quarters of Damascus rather than from the newer urban neighbourhoods and rural districts, as was the case in Egypt. One main reason for the success of the Muslim Brothers in recruiting these elements in Syria was the historical influence of the 'ulama', coupled with the latter's permeation of religious institutions in traditional quarters such as al-Midan and al-Shaghur in old Damascus. The corollary of the 'ulama's influence in the traditional quarters was that these areas were less receptive to the secularizing programme of the state.[32] But the 'ulama' did not enjoy the same level of influence in modern parts of the Syrian cities or in the villages, and thus were not similarly successful at recruiting there. Moreover, attempts on the part of the Islamic movement

---

27 In the Syrian Islamic Front's programme, "[t]he liberation of the economy from internal domination and external bondage ... [and] individual ownership should be protected and private capital encouraged." See Abd-Allah, *The Islamic Struggle in Syria*, pp. 220–1.
28 Due to government patronage, favouritism of minorities and corruption. Hinnebusch, *Syria: Revolution from Above*, p. 97.
29 See ibid., pp. 97–8. The Syrian Islamic movement's support base will be further discussed in Chapter 4.
30 Ibid., p. 98.
31 Hinnebusch, "The Islamic Movement in Syria," p. 154; *idem*, *Syria: Revolution from Above*, p. 98.
32 Hinnebusch, "The Islamic Movement in Syria," pp. 154–5. We will discuss further reasons for the successful recruitment of those within the Muslim Brothers in Chapter 4 of this volume.

following the Ba'th's rise to power to convince inhabitants of the newer urban quarters that the new regime was unrepresentative, sectarian and corrupt, and thus deserving of being brought down by political Islam, were to no avail.

These patterns of support can be explained with reference to two main factors, which are also relevant to the success of Islamic groups in recruiting followers today: (1) economically speaking, the Islamic movement supported the traditional capitalistic and feudal class; and (2) the modern parts of the city did not enjoy the long history of apolitical relations built on personal trust with the religious leaders as did the traditional parts. Having said this, however, the 1970s saw the seeds of Islamic popularity successfully planted in the fertile soil of disillusionment with the Ba'th and its increasingly authoritarian rule. As we will see, Syria's Islamic groups were able over time to turn themselves into politically quietist groups more interested in creating large and influential social networks than engendering a political base of support.

3 Political Islam vs. the secular Ba'th

As noted earlier, a majority of the Muslim Brotherhood's members were drawn from the urban traditional classes – that is, notables, the middle class and traditional labour – and especially from bazaar merchants and professionals who inhabited the traditional popular quarters of Damascus and Aleppo, as well as the older sections of smaller towns. The group's members aimed to challenge the Ba'th and other leftist parties for influence over the Syrian public.[33] Yet despite al-Siba'i's serious flirtation with Islamic socialism in the political programme, the Muslim Brotherhood's attempts to become an activist mass movement by galvanizing the urban masses and by penetrating the ranks of the armed forces met with no success. This is in contrast to the Brotherhood in Egypt, which made considerable headway among these segments of society.

A *The Syrian Muslim Brothers as a democratic party*

Mustafa al-Siba'i led the Syrian Muslim Brothers into the 1947 national parliamentary election, in which it won only four seats out of 119 available.[34] From that year until President al-Shishakli's imposition of a dictatorship and suppression of all political parties in 1952, the Muslim Brotherhood competed in parliamentary elections and openly organized and rallied the public, and, although it was not a dominant actor within Syrian political life, it did play an important role in several important political developments such as helping to determine the Syrian response to the Palestine question as well as pushing forward amendments to agricultural policy and certain Syrian constitutional matters.[35]

---

33 See Abd-Allah, *The Islamic Struggle in Syria*, pp. 90, 92–3. See also Batatu, "Syria's Muslim Brethren," p. 16. Batatu argues that the 1948 Arab defeat "gave a considerable impetus to the movement."
34 Seale, *Asad of Syria: The Struggle for the Middle East* London: I.B. Tauris, 1988, p. 322.
35 Daraj and Barut, *Al-ahzab wa al-harakat wa al-jama'at al-islamiya*, p. 258.

44 The origins of the conflict

From 1954 to 1961, the Syrian Muslim Brotherhood had to avert strong challenges and face some remarkable rivals. This was partly due to President al-Shishakli's direct repression of the Muslim Brothers, but also to Egyptian President Jamal Nasser's attempts to crush the Muslim Brothers in Egypt through the use of secular Arabism and the promotion of his own programme among the same urban masses that the Brothers were appealing to. Yet despite these challenges, the Syrian Muslim Brothers enjoyed some limited success in the 1957 elections, winning one seat in a contest that pitted them against a pro-Nasser Ba'thist candidate in Damascus.[36] The 1958 union of Syria and Egypt in the United Arab Republic led to Syrian political parties being dissolved. This included the Muslim Brothers, who in spite of the fact that they supported President Nasser, felt that their best strategy was to agree to being dissolved rather than to challenge the edict (though they did covertly continue some of their political work). At this time, the Muslim Brotherhood lost many of its members to the Nasserist Unionists.

Yet as soon as Lieutenant-Colonel al-Nihlawi's 1961 coup took Syria out of the United Arab Republic, the Muslim Brotherhood under their new leader 'Isam al-'Attar entered into a close alliance with Nihlawi's conservative government, and as a result won an unprecedented 6 per cent of the seats (electing ten deputies) in the Syrian Parliament.[37] 'Isam al-'Attar ranked third in Damascus with 28,404 votes, just behind Khaled al-'Azm (an independent who was close to the National Bloc coalition, and who received 33,278 votes) and Ma'mun al-Kizbari (another independent, who received 31,935 votes). The Muslim Brothers did not, however, win a single seat in Hama, a city whose political inclinations were split between the Socialists under Hawrani and the Muslim Brotherhood, while their candidate in Aleppo, 'Abdul Fatah Abu Ghudda, came only fifth.[38] The new Islamic bloc in the national parliament was thus positioned closer to the conservative, traditional urban right, and moreover reflected the dominance enjoyed at the time by the Damascene traditional right in parliament.[39]

The Syrian Islamic movement's relative political success was very short-lived, coming to an end when the leftist Ba'th-led coup against the Nihlawi government toppled their allies on 8 March 1963. This unexpected setback set the stage for a new kind of Islamic activism, one that would take shape outside the now closed political realm. Indeed, as a result of the coup, a number of significant events directly linked to the arrival of the Ba'th Party in power would ultimately promote militancy outside the political arena for a new generation of Muslim Brothers.[40]

36 Hinnebusch, "The Islamic Movement in Syria," p. 154. The role of repression might have given an important push to the Muslim Brothers. For more on this, see Chapter 4, the Social Movement Theory school.
37 It is important to note that the Ba'th Party had won around 18 per cent of the seats during that year. Batatu, "Syria's Muslim Brethren," p. 18.
38 Daraj and Barut, *Al-ahzab wa al-harakat wa al-jama'at al-islamiya*, p. 264.
39 Ibid.
40 Hinnebusch, "The Islamic Movement in Syria," p. 140.

B Reactions to Baʿthist secularization measures

The arrival of the Baʿth Party to power in March 1963 drastically changed the political and socio-economic environment in Syria's urban centres. The Baʿth regime was radically secular and populist, with a minoritarian, rural membership that threatened to marginalize the urban, mainly Sunni merchant class in two main ways. One was subtle, consisting in the loss of prestige that resulted from the erosion of their position as cultural shapers and leaders of the Syrian environment, while the other was more tangible, that is, political and economic.

This erosion was evident right from the beginning. During its Sixth National Congress in 1963, the Baʿth put forward a text called *Baʾd al-Muntalaqat al-Nadhariya* (Some of the Theoretical Starting Points) in which it advanced its hard-core secular ideology, proposing a revolutionary social and educational transformation of Syria along rigorously "scientific" and "socialist" lines.[41] This pointed the way away from the status quo of Syrian secularism being limited to freedom of the state from religion and freedom of religion from the state, and towards a much more radical secularism that would involve completely excising religious discourse from both state and society. Thus the *Muntalaqat* text could be said to have initiated an overall transformation. Furthermore, the ideal of Arab unity was replaced by Arab revolution. Liberal parliamentarianism was judged unfit for Syria's socio-political realities, and was replaced by a *Dimuqratiya Shaʾbiya* (popular-democracy) supervised by the Baʿth Party through corporatist channels and a democratic-centralizing system that linked all public organizations to the Baʿthi National Committee. More importantly, given this work's focus, the Baʿth's Sixth National Congress called for the radical social transformation of Syrian society through the removal of religion as a classroom subject in the nation's schools, as well as the secularization of the shariʾa-based Syrian Personal Status Law, all moves that betrayed the Baʿth's aim of secularizing society as well as the state.

The mere articulation of these measures infuriated certain religious figures attending the Congress.[42] To add insult to injury, the purges of the army and of the state bureaucracy launched by the Baʿth were accompanied by large-scale dismissals of certain religious figures who had previously been seen as untouchable. Thus Grand Mufti Abu al-Yusr ʿAbidin was dismissed from his post, while Baʿth-backed Shaykh Ahmad Kuftaro was elected in place of the popular Shaykh Hasan Habanaka in 1964. Böttcher explains that, "The Sunni clerical establishment never forgave Shaykh Kuftaru for his willingness to run against Shaykh Habanaka and has remained at distance from him, isolating him from an

---

41 See *Baʾd al-Muntalaqat a-Nadhariya li-Hizb al-Baʿth al-ʾArabi al-Ishtiraki: Aqaraha al-Muʾtamar al-Qawmi al-Sades* [Some of the Theoretical Starting Points of the Arab Baʿth Socialist Party: Adopted by the Sixth National Congress], Damascus: Ministry of Information, n.d..

42 Ibid. To indoctrinate the army, Zaki al-Arsuzi, known for his totalizing secular views, was recalled from retirement.

46 *The origins of the conflict*

important power base."[43] On 28 January 1965, the Baʿthist government gave itself the right to dismiss and appoint religious leaders, in an attempt to marginalize and neutralize such leaders by reducing their sway over the traditional segments of society.[44] It also aimed to control the religious message rather than just render religion a private matter, arguing that there is a basic incompatibility between religion and change, a message that the Syrian people did not in general object to at the time.

In February 1966, as part of the Baʿth's own internal transformation, relatively moderate party members were purged. This meant an increased emphasis on the regime's rural and secular minority character (since the secular rural elements were the ones left over), a development that further alienated traditional Sunni urbanites and conservatives. Hinnebusch notes that "[c]o-optation into government, the forging of a close alliance with the Soviet Union, more overt secularism and antagonism toward the urban establishment, tightened control over commerce ... further alienated conservative and pious Islamic opinion."[45]

On 25 April 1967, an article entitled "The Means of Creating a New Arab Man" appeared in the Syrian People's Army (*Jaysh al-Shaʿb*) newspaper. The article, which was written by a junior ʿAlawi officer named Ibrahim Khalas, called on the people to deliver themselves from "God, religion, feudalism, capitalism, colonialism, and all the values that prevailed under the old society," which were described as "mummies in the museums of history." It added, "There is only one value ... the new man who relies on himself and on his own contribution to humanity." The article caused widespread religious right-wing protest strikes and clashes.[46] It was one thing to marginalize religion, but quite another to equate religion with colonialism and capitalism and to propagate atheism. Bar-Siman-Tov summarizes the ensuing response as follows:

> On 4 May, Muslim religious leaders (the 'Ulama') met in Damascus to discuss steps to be taken against the regime. The following day (Friday), Shaykh Habanka, head of the 'Ulama' in Damascus, gave a sermon attacking the regime in the Manjak mosque. A large state demonstration followed the sermon; more than 30,000 people (including Christian religious leaders) attended, shouting anti-Baʿth slogans. Other religious demonstrations were

---

43 Annabelle Böttcher, *Official Sunni and Shiʿi Islam in Syria*, Florence: European University Institute, 2002, p. 8.
44 For a better understanding of this process, see www.syrianawkaf.org; see also Batatu, "Syria's Muslim Brethren," p. 14; Robert W. Olson, *The Baʿth and Syria, 1947 to 1982: The Evolution of Ideology, Party, and State*, Princeton, NJ: Kingston Press, 1982, p. 93; Tabitha Petran, *Syria*, New York: Praeger, 1972, p. 178; see also Steven Heydemann, *Authoritarianism in Syria: Institutions and Social Conflict*, Ithaca, NY: Cornell University Press, 1999. pp. 172–5.
45 Hinnebusch, "The Islamic Movement in Syria," p. 159.
46 Olson, *The Baʿth and Syria, 1947 to 1982*, p. 113; Bar-Siman-Tov, *Linkage Politics in the Middle East*, Boulder, CO: Westview Press, 1983, p. 158.

The rise and fall of political Islam in Syria 47

held on the same day in Aleppo, Homs and Hama. Violent clashes resulted when security forces attempted to break up these demonstrations; three people were killed.

The religious community saw the article as sending an alarming message. That is, not only had the Ba'th leaders institutionalized state intervention in religious affairs and the economy, but now they were boldly moving to take away what control the religious class still had. This was accompanied by a public verbal attack by Khalid al-Jundi, head of the workers' military unit, who echoed Karl Marx in unequivocally stating that in his view, religion was indeed the opiate of the people.[47]

Two days later, the Syrian Ba'thi State chose to escalate matters by arresting Shaykh Habanka and 40 other opposition religious figures. When a number of Damascus businesses closed their shops in protest and demonstrations erupted in Homs, Aleppo and Hama, the regime retaliated by issuing a decree confiscating the shaykh's property and that of some 45 other Damascene merchants. Over almost three weeks, some 3,000 'ulama', merchants and notables were arrested, including for the first time Christian clergymen and merchants. Then on 15 May 1967, 300 people were arrested at the Aleppo mosque during clashes with security forces.[48]

At the same time as all these internal developments were affecting domestic stability within Syria, external events were also having an impact. These included the 1967 war with Israel, as well as overt attempts by neighbouring Arab states to incite the Syrian religious class and the Syrian people more generally against their government, by calling on them to overthrow the "Godless" Ba'th.[49]

Overall, the 1960s proved to be a period of profound crisis for the Islamic sector in Syria. Not only did President Nasser's crushing of the Egyptian Islamic movement weaken the Syrian Muslim Brothers by taking away the latter's ideological counterparts, but the Ba'th's decision to bar the Muslim Brothers from national political participation served to isolate them and thus keep them from playing any role in determining the country's direction at this crucial juncture. Moreover, without a concrete blueprint for moving ahead, they risked losing all their social standing over the course of a generation or two. Some maintain that it was as a result of the ban, and more importantly, the Ba'th's 1963 publication of *Ba'd al-Muntalaqat al-Nazariya*, that the radical wing of the Muslim Brothers emerged as an active opponent of the Ba'th Party leadership.

C Rise of Islamic militantism

Besides wrestling with the political and ideological measures taken by the revolutionary regime, the Muslim Brothers were also facing an internal crisis. On 3 November 1964, Mustafa al-Siba'i died, leaving the leadership of the Muslim

---

47 See Hinnebusch, "The Islamic Movement in Syria," p. 159.
48 See Bar-Siman-Tov, *Linkage Politics*, p. 159.
49 Olson, *The Ba'th and Syria, 1947 to 1982*, pp. 112–13.

48 The origins of the conflict

Brothers to his deputy, 'Isam al-'Attar. Al-'Attar was a Salafi Muslim who condemned the traditional schools of Islamic law for their alleged deviation from the Quran and the *Sunna*. These views alienated a majority of the Syrian religious 'ulama', who not only adhered to one of the traditional schools, but who were also Sufis rather than Salafis in their faith and practice.[50] At that time, Sufis generally felt that the Salafi current arriving from the Arabian peninsula was more of a threat than a potential ally.

Additionally, al-'Attar, who by December 1964 had been exiled and prohibited from returning to Syria, did not believe in armed struggle and for a while categorically refused to declare jihad against the Baʻth.[51] This caused a rift to form in the ranks of the Muslim Brotherhood's leaders. One faction under the leadership of Marwan Hadid, an agricultural engineer and philosophy graduate, became a fringe movement on the periphery of al-'Attar's political Muslim Brotherhood. It created a military wing that Hadid called "Muhammad's Battalions," which would later become known as "The Fighting Vanguard of the Muslim Brotherhood," and sometimes as "The Fighting Vanguard of the Party of God"[52] (hereafter referred to as "the Fighting Vanguard"). Despite the Muslim Brotherhood's Sufi roots, the Marwan Hadid faction had a Salafi outlook and believed in a radical Islamic *Sahwa* (awakening), which was in opposition to 'Issam al-'Attar's acquiescent *Salafiya* outlook. Juridically speaking, the Fighting Vanguard followed one of Ibn Taymiya's fatwas in advancing the proposition that Syria was a Muslim state ruled by a *Murtad* (heretical) *Batini* (inner, esoteric) sect, and thus that that there was no escape from violent confrontation. Effectively, therefore, a militant sort of jihad needed to be waged in order to guide the community back to Islam.[53] Perhaps unsurprisingly, Hadid's group would later become an important breeding ground for paramilitary cells.[54]

For its part, the state took measures to shrink the circle of social power left to the religious class by seizing control of the informal religious apparatus in Damascus. Repression through political de-liberalization forced the Muslim Brothers to choose between pre-emptively moving against the government or face a certain loss of all of its power. In April 1964, Marwan Hadid and his

---

50 Abd-Allah, *The Islamic Struggle in Syria*, p. 102.
51 Ibid., p. 103.
52 Daraj and Barut, *Al-ahzab wa al-harakat wa al-jama'at al-islamiya*, p. 268.
53 Although Ibn Taymiya's fatwa concerns the Isma'ili sect rather than the 'Alawis, according to the Salafi interpretation, the fatwa can be applied to any other *batini* sect in the Muslim world. It is important to add here that there are variances in Marwan Hadid's and Sa'id Hawwa's interpretations of who the *Murtaddun* are and how they are to be fought, yet in general, the *Mujahidun* did not have enough time to grasp or to follow the different formulations. The Syrian Salafis will be discussed further in Part III of this work. See Sa'id Hawwa, *Hadhihi Tajribati was Hadhihi Shahadati*, Cairo: 1987, p. 58; idem, *Jund Allah Thaqafa zu-Akhlaq*, 2nd edn, Beirut: n.d., pp. 380–7. See also Itzchak Weismann, "Sa'id Hawwa and Islamic Revivalism in Ba'thist Syria," *Studia Islamica* 85, 1997: 152.
54 Daraj and Barut, *Al-ahzab wa al-harakat wa al-jama'at al-islamiya*, p. 274.

colleague Sa'id Hawwa launched a widespread uprising in Hama that included the Communists and the Nasserites.[55] The uprising did not include the Damascus branch of the Muslim Brothers despite Hadid and Hawwa's impassioned pleas for support. Indeed, al-'Attar declared that he would rather gain power through a democratic election, even if to do so took him 500 years.[56] The uprising, which lasted 29 days, ultimately proved to be too small and too weak to present a real challenge to the new regime. It was not until 1976 that the Fighting Vanguard launched a so-called jihad against the Ba'th that truly threatened the regime's hold on power.

After the failure of the uprising, Marwan Hadid allied himself with Dr Ishaq al-Farhan, the general inspector of the Muslim Brothers in Jordan, this despite al-'Attar's explicit orders not to do so. He then formed a common *fida'i* cell with the Jordanian Muslim Brothers that was under the control of Fatah (the Palestinian movement led by Yasir Arafat, which later formed the Palestinian Authority).[57] A subsequent initiative launched by Hadid called for the abolition of al-'Attar's Damascus faction and Abu Ghudda's Aleppo faction, because of what he alleged was their willingness to form alliances with anyone willing to work with them, as well as because they had become mere *Tabligh* and *Da'wa* (preaching and missionary) groups. He followed up this initiative by issuing a letter demanding that true Muslims and Islamic groups wage war against the "heretic" Syrian regime.[58]

In 1975, weary of Hadid's actions, the Damascus Muslim Brotherhood leaders elected a new *shura* (advisory) council under the leadership of 'Adnan Sa'ed al-Din. Despite having the approval of the International Muslim Brotherhood, neither al-'Attar nor Hadid accepted the new group. But so as to distinguish itself from the new Muslim Brothers, Hadid's group changed its name to "The Fighting Vanguard of the Party of God" (*al-Tali'a al-Muqatila li-Hizb-illah*).

In addition to the organized groups of Muslim Brothers, it is important not to overlook the more loosely organized network built by the Muslim Brothers and the Fighting Vanguard around a number of shaykhs with large urban audiences. These religious leaders, all of whom effectively promoted and participated in city-based agitation, included Damascus's Shaykh Sa'id Ramadan, professor of Islamic law at the Shari'a faculty; Shaykh Muhammad 'Awwad, also based in Damascus, whose Friday sermons attracted a very attentive audience to al-Iman mosque; and Aleppo's Shaykh Khayrallah. As a result of the network and its actions, relations between the religious leaders and many others within the Muslim Brothers and the Fighting Vanguard went from overt hostility to clandestine collaboration. Indeed, it remains unclear whether the religious leaders at

---

55 The Nasserites were angry because they were not given any position within the new state.
56 Daraj and Barut, *Al-ahzab wa al-harakat wa al-jama'at al-islamiya*, p. 269.
57 Ibid., p. 272.
58 Ibid., p. 275.

times also negotiated the space for action with the regime or served as intermediaries for such negotiations. One thing that will become clear in later chapters is that state co-opted shaykhs helped put an end to political Islam in Syria, while also ensuring the survival and later expansion of a renewed politically quietist Islamic movement.

4 Conclusion of Part I

In the first part of this work, I traced the history of secularism in Syria and outlined the history, ideology and social background of the main players in the Ba'th and the Muslim Brothers. This makes it possible to understand the conflict that arose between the Ba'th regime and the Syrian Islamic movement in the 1970s and early 1980s, as well as its consequences (see Part II), but also to fully comprehend the reasons underlying today's complicated relations between Syria's various Islamic groups and the Syrian regime under President Bashar Asad (Part III). What this underlines is that the causes and consequences of the conflict between Syria's Islamic movement and the Ba'thist regime are more than simply of historical importance, since the manner in which the conflict was resolved was an experiment that has had a significant bearing on present-day Syria and on the country's Islamic movement.

In the following part of this work, the era of Hafez al-Asad is examined. The focus is on the roots of the Syrian Islamic movement's shift in the early 1970s from being an Islamic opposition movement to a militant or Islamist movement. This focus is contextualized by consideration being given to the beginning of the unravelling of the Syrian Ba'th ideology and of its secular model, as well as to the country's selective economic liberalization, which resulted in the resurgence of the traditional Syrian bourgeoisie and the re-stratification of Syrian society along class lines.

Part II
Hafez al-Asad's era and the conflict with the Muslim Brotherhood

Muting of Baʿthist secularism in Syria

4 Conflict with the Muslim Brotherhood

1 Introduction

The Islamic rebellion spearheaded by the Muslim Brotherhood that took place in the 1970s and early 1980s in secularly oriented Syria ended in defeat for Syrian Islamism, with the Muslim Brothers effectively excluded from the country's political system from then on. Yet this result should not overshadow the fact that it was the first, the largest and the richest instance of Islamic rebellion in the modern Arab world. Indeed, neither the Muslim Brothers in Egypt nor the FIS (Islamic Salvation Front) in Algeria were able to confront their respective regimes with the same intensity and for as long as the Syrian Islamic Front did. It is in light of this that the most important question that is addressed in Part II of this work is, how has this rebellion impacted upon Syrian society?

The main contentions in this section are the following: (1) while the rise of Islamic political activism in Syria during the era of Hafez al-Asad was very much contingent on the Ba'th's socio-economic and political policies, its fall was due to a mix of measures used by the regime to deal with the immediate and long-term threats to its rule; (2) that these survival measures redefined the Syrian regime's relationship to religion in general and to Islam in particular; (3) that the rebellion has deeply transformed Syrian politics and society, including the nation's secular culture; (4) that today's Islamic revival is very much rooted in the way the state chose to put an end to the Islamist threat.

Chapter 4 will describe the confrontations between the state and the Muslim Brothers (including the Fighting Vanguard) as a result of the latter's open challenge. It will also discuss existing theoretical approaches in the literature and will advance a new alternative approach for unpacking the reasons behind the transformation of the Syrian Islamic movement from a democratic political participant to a militant opposition. Chapter 5 will examine the regime's survival strategies and their enduring impact on both Syria's Islamic movement and secular environment. Ultimately, the manner in which the information is examined and organized in Part II offers insights that help explain the current mushrooming of Islamic groups in Syria and the extant command's strategy in dealing with them.

2 Hafez al-Asad's rise to power

Hafez al-Asad's rise to power in November 1970 was the outcome of a bloodless *coup d'état* called the Corrective Movement (*al-Haraka al-Tashihiya*),[1] and was soon followed by his election to the presidency of Syria in a popular referendum on 12 March 1971. In keeping with the programme of his Corrective Movement, al-Asad immediately proposed a policy of national unity based on reducing the scale of the country's social transformation, a selective economic liberalization and a retreat from the Ba'th system of single-party rule. He also sought to broaden the Ba'th's popular base through extensive recruitment from the public, something that the party's old guard had previously refused so as to ensure ideological integrity.[2]

These proposals were quickly translated into action. To expand the regime's social base and its ruling coalition, al-Asad created the National Progressive Front, a political corporatist grouping of willing leftist parties under the umbrella of the Ba'th. He also appointed a new People's Council that incorporated a broader spectrum of social actors. Another move was to initiate a controlled economic liberalization of the Syrian system, which required the acquiescence of the hitherto-hostile urban bourgeoisie and Damascene merchants, many of whom were either in alliance with, or part of, Syria's "religious class."[3]

Perhaps most important for this work is that al-Asad shifted the Ba'th away from its emphasis on revolution, secularism and atheism, and class warfare. This shift was subtle, and was only made apparent in certain overtly religious acts, although he continued to assert his pledge to serve as the president of all Syrians rather than in the name of one sect or of one religious group.[4] He thus began portraying himself as a privately pious president who respected Syria's religious 'ulama' and faith, something that previous leaders had not done. This public show of piety became more pronounced during the course of and following the regime's conflict with the Muslim Brothers.

Yet the changes initiated by al-Asad did not compromise the Ba'th Party's control over state and society. Quite the contrary, the Corrective Movement in fact reinforced the regime's rule and the president's control over a majority of

---

1 In the two years prior to the coup, the Ba'th had witnessed a power split which divided Ba'thists between Salah Jadid, who controlled the party, and Hafez al-Asad, who controlled the army. Jadid's attempts to oust Hafez al-Asad as defence minister during the Ba'th's Tenth Extraordinary National Congress failed, and Al-Asad retaliated the next day by occupying the offices of the party and the popular organizations, as well as by rounding up Jadid's supporters. Jadid himself was also arrested, and would spend most of the rest of his life in prison, only being released shortly before his death in 1993. See Tabitha Petran, *Syria*, New York: Praeger, 1972, pp. 239–49.
2 Bassel Salloukh, "Organizing Politics in the Arab World: State–Society Relations and Foreign Policy Choices in Jordan and Syria," McGill University: PhD thesis, 2000, p. 248.
3 Raymond A. Hinnebusch, "The Islamic Movement in Syria: Sectarian Conflict and Urban Rebellion in an Authoritarian-Populist Regime," in Ali E. Hillal Dessouki, ed., *Islamic Resurgence in the Arab World*, New York: Praeger, 1982, p. 161.
4 Nikolaos Van Dam, *The Struggle for Power in Syria: Politics and Society under Asad and the Ba'th Party*, London: I.B. Tauris, 1996, p. 94.

the political forces. Indeed, in the Constitution promulgated in 1973, an expanded Baʿth retained its role as the enforcer of executive policies, while the president took control of the party and the bureaucracy. New popular organizations were added to the long list of corporatist institutions that were created during President Nasser's rule over Syria and the pre-Asad Baʿth rule. This centralization of power, coupled with the expansion of the Baʿth social base that he orchestrated, allowed Hafez al-Asad to create a formidable system that can best be described as a "presidential monarchy."[5] As we will see in the next chapter, this presidential monarchical system allowed the government to enact a number of policies that both controlled and blurred the lines between the state and society.

One result of the ideological re-orientation undertaken by the al-Asad regime was a sort of doctrinal crisis for the Baʿth. Although the timing of this crisis is to some degree difficult to pinpoint, it seems clear that it arose because the Corrective Movement's pragmatic approach – which included imposition of a more hierarchical and centralized organizational structure, and the indiscriminate inflation of membership such that the party increasingly became a mere tool of mobilization[6] – undermined but was not able to replace the party's previously strong sense of ideological purpose.

Taken together, these various changes made the Baʿth susceptible to charges of oppression and sectarianism, since it was no longer able to hide behind the fig leaf of principled ideology. This made challenging the regime more easy in general. The most serious of the multiple challenges that it faced during its first 12 years in power came from the Syrian Muslim Brothers, whose military faction, the Fighting Vanguard, was very determined to topple it for allegedly being "heretical," "sectarian" and "corrupt."

The following section will review and expand upon the reasons behind the opposition to the Baʿth, as well as for the rise of Islamic militancy in Syria, through an examination of the theoretical literature on the subject. This literature can be grouped loosely into two schools: the sectarian school, which I consider to be part of the political culture school, and the socio-economic school. The section also considers a third theoretical school that has not yet been applied to the Syrian case: the Social Movement Theory school. The Social Movement approach adds significantly to attempts to understand the Syrian case, by virtue of its focus on explaining the *mechanisms* behind the shift from peaceful opposition to violent opposition (rather than simply focusing upon the reasons for that shift). It helps to answer such questions as: why does militancy occur when it does? And, how does a group shift from peaceful to violent forms of contention?

---

5 See Salloukh, "Organizing Politics in the Arab World," pp. 248–85; Raymond A. Hinnebusch, *Syria: Revolution from Above*, New York and London: Routledge 2001, p. 67; idem, *Authoritarian Power and State Formation in Baʿthist Syria: Army, Party and Peasant*, Boulder, CO: Westview Press, 1990, pp. 145–7.
6 Volker Perthes, *Syria under Bashar al-Asad: Modernisation and the Limits of Change*, London and New York: Routledge, 2004, p. 12.

56 *Hafez al-Asad's era*

Effectively, therefore, the following section aims to both review important scholarship as well as to shed light on past and present motivations. It will serve to demonstrate the driving forces and aspects of continuity between Hafez al-Asad's era and Bashar al-Asad's era when it comes to Islam and secularism.

3 Explanations of the violent contention: political and economic grievances, anomie and social alienation

A *The political culture school*

According to adherents of this school, political culture is key for a proper understanding of politics. In the case of the Middle East, it helps to explain such issues as the lack of democratic values, primordial and sectarian loyalties, patriarchal behaviour and gender biases.[7] Thus such things as ethno-sectarian divides – in terms of the kinship culture and political linkages that it gives rise to – are important reasons why violence is used to address new challenges and circumstances.

Dealing more specifically with Syrian politics: Nikolaos Van Dam's *The Struggle for Power in Syria* (1996) and Eberhard Kienle's "Entre jama'a et classe: le pouvoir politique en Syrie contemporaine" (1991) view Syrian politics as primarily primordial. Both authors focus on Syrian sectarian loyalties in their examination of the Ba'thist political era.

Kienle addresses the multi-faceted question "who holds the political power in Syria, and why?" In his answer, he gives priority to Michel Seurat's "Jama'a" (core group) concept (see Seurat's *L'État de barbarie*, 1989). This says that the new group in power is not an economic class in the sense of controlling the machinery of production, but a parasitic class that is connected by its primordial 'Alawite "group feeling" or "'asabiyya," and which uses its political power to extract funding from a collaborating Syrian bourgeoisie.[8]

Perhaps no work better addresses the influence of ethno-sectarian politics and

---

7 Daniel Pipes, *In the Path of God: Islam and Political Power*, New York: Basic Books, 1983; idem, *Greater Syria: The History of an Ambition*, New York: Oxford University Press, 1992; Amos Perlmutter, "Islam and Democracy Simply Aren't Compatible," *International Herald Tribune*, 21 January 1992; Elie Kedourie, *Democracy and Arab Political Culture*, Washington, DC: Washington Institute for Near East Policy, 1992; Bernard Lewis, "Islam and Liberal Democracy," *Atlantic Monthly*, February 1993; Su'ad Joseph, "Gender and Citizenship in Muslim Communities: Introduction," *Citizenship Studies* 3(3), 1999: 293–4.

8 Interestingly, it is this same "political culture" conceptual approach that has been mainly endorsed by certain Syrian Islamic thinkers to explain their fight whether against secularists in general or the Syrian regime, thinkers such as: Habanaka al-Midani's and 'Abd al-Rahman's *Sira' Ma' al-Malahida Hata al-'Azm* (1974); Mustafa al-Siba'i's *Asdaq al-Itijahat al-Fikriya fi al-sharq al-Arabi* (1998) and his *Islamuna* (2001); Sa'id Hawwa's *Fi Afaq al-Ta'lim* (1980), *Jund Allah Thaqafa Zu Akhlaq* (n.d.) and *Tarbiyatuna al-Ruhiya* (1979); Muhammad Sa'id Ramadan Al-Buti, *al-Ta'aruf 'ala al-Dhat Huwa al-Tariq ila al-Islam* (2009); and Abu Mus'ab al-Suri in his *Da'wat al-Muqawama al-Islamiyya*. In these writings, the core problem for Arab

Conflict with the Muslim Brotherhood   57

kinship culture in Syria than Nikolaos Van Dam's *The Struggle for Power in Syria*. In this influential work, Van Dam demonstrates that the Sunni urbanites whose prestige, influence and wealth were destroyed by the populist policies of the Ba'th effectively dismissed the Syrian regime's secularism and socialism as window-dressing for the transfer of power to minorities and to the rural sector.[9] Thus Van Dam's analysis tests the sectarian variable when examining the conflict between the Muslim Brothers and the Ba'th minority-led regime, in an attempt to determine the importance of sectarian motivations and kinship cultures in the parties' political behaviour between 1963 and 1996.[10] He notes that when socio-economic differences coincide with sectarian differences, they can give rise to class struggle. This explains how the so-called "historical revolution in the Syrian political elite" of 1963 had an immediate impact upon the composition and ideology of the country's political elite.

Although Van Dam's analysis hews to a political economy approach, he nonetheless contends that the struggle for political power in Syria has since 1963 been directed along sectarian channels and guided by a kinship ethos, this despite the fact that sectarian, regional, tribal and socio-economic factors are impossible to separate out when studying the relationship between urban Sunnis and rural compact religious minorities in the country.[11] He also asserts that prior to 1963, intra-elite conflicts over power occurred without the involvement of the rural and of the lower-class urban masses.[12] But following the 1963 Ba'th revolt, a new and upwardly mobile class of minority men and women emerged, as a result of their having received a higher education and having benefited from a focus on the empowerment of the long-forgotten rural periphery.[13]

Another important factor addressed by Van Dam is the Sunni/non-Sunni divide in the army. He shows that at the time of the Syrian–Egyptian union,

---

and Islamic societies is located within the people's abandonment of their true culture. According to this position, an Islamic resurgence will originate in the grievances of the masses, who view Islam as their "natural" salvation from both authoritarian regimes and the cultural domination of the West. See: Sa'id Hawwa, *Fi Afaq al-Ta'lim*, Cairo: Maktabat Wahaba, 1980; idem, *Tarbiyatuna al-Ruhiya*, Damascus and Beirut: dar al-Kutub, 1979; idem, *Hadhihi Tajribati wa-Hadhihi Shahadati*, Cairo: 1987; Abu Mus'ab al-Suri, *Da'wat al-Muqawama al-Islamiyya*; idem, "Mulahadhat Hawl al-Tajruba al-Jihadiya Fi Suriya" [Observations on the Jihadi Experience in Syria], in *Al-Thawra al-Islamiya al-Jihadiya Fi Suriya* [The Islamic Jihadi Revolution in Syria], extracts online: www.muslm.net/vb/archive/index.php/t-159953.html.

9 Alasdair Drysdale, "The Asad Regime and Its Troubles," *MERIP Reports*, November–December 1982, p. 3; Van Dam, *The Struggle for Power in Syria*.

10 This factional account has been endorsed by a number of observers other than Van Dam; Michel Seurat, *L'Etat de barbarie*; Paris: Collection Esprit/Seuil, 1989; Petran, *Syria*; Martin Seymour, "The Dynamics of Power in Syria since the Break with Egypt," *Middle Eastern Studies* 6(1), January 1970: 35–47; Muta' Safadi, *Hizb al-Ba'th: Ma'sat al-Mawlid, Ma'sat al-Nihaya* [The Ba'th Party: The Tragedy of Birth, the Tragedy of the End], Beirut: Dar al-Adab, 1964; Munif Razzaz, *al-tajriba al-murra* [The Bitter Experience], Beirut: Dar al-Nahar, 1969.

11 Van Dam, *The Struggle for Power in Syria*, pp. 13–14, 76–7.

12 Ibid., p. 77.

13 Federal Research Division, *Syria: A Country Study*, Washington, DC: Library of Congress, 1988, p. 72.

Sunni representation in the army was around 94 per cent, the highest it had ever been. But those numbers began to drop once the Ba'th came to power such that between 1966 and 1970, Sunni officers in fact accounted for only 45.1 per cent of the Regional Commands. As we have seen, during the rule of Salah Jadid and the dual rule of Jadid and Hafez al-Asad, power struggles among the Ba'thists resulted in a purge of top Druze, Isma'ili, Hawrani and Sunni officers. According to Van Dam, these purges meant that while the remaining Sunni military members slightly outnumbered their 'Alawi counterparts, they represented weaker army factions. Then in the period after November 1970, the number of Sunnis and of Syrian urbanites increased in the Regional Commands, at the expense of rural and religious minorities. Another development was that Orthodox Christian officers, who had almost always been represented in the cabinets but had never held military positions within the Syrian Regional Commands, now found themselves occupying very high positions in the Syrian Armed Forces.[14]

Van Dam interprets al-Asad's assumption of the presidency as representing both a concrete and a symbolic shift of power into the hands of a minority group. According to his account, rule in Syria had for centuries been monopolized by the Sunni Damascene elite, and thus the ascension of the 'Alawi Hafez al-Asad signalled the end of the monopoly on power previously enjoyed by the country's bourgeoisie and religious class. As we will see in the following section, this shift was also to blame for the "constitutional crisis" that erupted in 1973. Van Dam adds that under Asad, Sunni military officers continued to lack real power even though they constituted more than 50 per cent of the Regional Commands. He argues that this weakness was mainly due to their lack of cohesion and solidarity, and because they were often circumvented by lower-ranking 'Alawi commanders. This latter fact underlines the degree to which supremacy within the military remained mostly in the hands of reliable 'Alawi officers. Van Dam's general conclusion from this evidence is inescapable: that the increased political and military participation by religious minorities and the rural populace after March 1963, while perceived by many as a kind of national emancipation, was not seen as such by the traditional, mainly Sunni, urban elite. Their devastating loss of power and prestige ended up contributing strongly to the battle for supremacy between the Sunni-led Muslim Brotherhood and the 'Alawi-led Ba'th regime.[15]

While Van Dam's research is very solid, the manner in which he enmeshes all the class, geographical, ethnic and religious variables is both a strength and a weakness of his analysis, in that it renders it both comprehensive and convoluted. Moreover, his focus on the ethno-sectarian character of Syrian politics under the Ba'th is at best incomplete. In addition to his assumption that sectarian groups are unitary actors, he also fails to elaborate on his decision to focus upon the factional variable despite recognizing that other variables such as class and geographical background overlap with sectarian identity. Van Dam's argument is incomplete in

---

14 Van Dam, *The Struggle for Power in Syria*, p. 78.
15 Ibid.

other respects as well. He does not explain the parallel rise of Islamism in Egypt despite the Egyptian case's considerable variance from the Syrian case, especially in terms of the ethnic variable. Perhaps Alasdair Drysdale's observation, that "[t]he accuracy of those perceptions is irrelevant: what mattered was that a sufficient number of Syrians believed them. This ... made the sectarian issue an extremely sensitive one,"[16] can shed some light on Van Dam's choice of explanatory variable when accounting for the sudden resurgence of Islamism in Syria. Indeed, when considering the conflict that would later erupt, it becomes almost impossible to disentangle the sectarian argument from the political economy one, particularly given that perceptions and reality often became muddled together in the minds of those who took part in the conflict.

Indeed, although political culture approaches are "part of any effort to understand politics, whether in the Arab World or elsewhere,"[17] the focus of researchers on culture as a determining variable is believed by some to be a narrow reading of the complexities of Arab politics. As a result, despite the fact that culture has some role to play in politics, other structural variables need to be considered first.[18] More fervent critics argue that cultural behaviour is in itself determined by structural variables,[19] and hence should not be used as an explanatory tool. Furthermore, despite having the advantage of explaining the key discourse of Islamism and other Arab socio-cultural ethos, political culture explanations are ultimately incomplete when analysing Islamic revival and activism, as they do not explain why and how cultures or sub-cultures vary over time. In the case of this study, they fail to shed light on the heterogeneity of the Syrian Islamic movement. They also fail to explain the political flexibility of a movement whose doctrinal foundations are more or less fixed, do not elucidate the changing nature of state–society relations (including those of the Islamic society) and fail to explicate how and why the Syrian Islamic movement has re-emerged as an important player on the Syrian social and political scene when it had failed to do so some 30 years earlier.

B The socio-economic school

A second method for explaining the roots of the conflict between the Ba'th regime and the Muslim Brothers and the rise of political Islam in Syria is the socio-economic approach. This approach, whose main proponents include

---

16 Drysdale, "The Asad Regime and Its Troubles," p. 3.
17 Rex Brynen et al., *Political Liberalization and Democratization in the Arab World: Theoretical Perspectives*, Boulder, CO and London: Lynne Rienner Publishers, 1995, p. 9.
18 Anderson, Lisa. "Democracy in the Arab World: A Critique of the Political Culture Approach," in Rex Brynen et al., eds, *Political Liberalization and Democratization in the Arab World: Theoretical Perspectives*, Boulder, CO and London: Lynne Rienner Publishers, 1995.
19 Michael Collins Dunn, "Islamist Parties in Democratizing States: A Look at Jordan and Yemen," *Middle East Policy* 2(2), 1993; Augustus R. Norton, "Inclusion Can Deflate Islamic Populism?" *New Perspectives Quarterly* 10(3), Summer 1993; John L. Esposito, "Islamic Movements, Democratization and US Foreign Policy," in Phoebe Marr and William Lewis, eds, *Riding the Tiger: The Middle East Challenge after the Cold War*, Boulder, CO: Westview Press, 1993.

60 *Hafez al-Asad's era*

Raymond A. Hinnebusch and Hanna Batatu, contends that it is impossible to make sense of modern Syrian political developments without resorting to the class variable.[20] In considering the origins of the conflict, it argues that a majority of actors within the Islamic movement in Syria at the time were *not* motivated by confessionalism and religion, rather the conflict was over money. Proponents of the approach agree that as an ancient crossroads of world trade, it was no accident that the Syrian merchant class played an important role in the politics of the country.[21] In fact, a majority of the Muslim Brotherhood's members were tradesmen and craftsmen who had established themselves in the *suq*s (bazaars), such as the 'Asruniya, suq Saruja and the Midan in Damascus. In general, the country's merchant class tended to be hostile to the regime, who felt that it had deprived them of their wealth, as well as of power and prestige. This anti-regime sentiment was imported into the Brotherhood by its merchant members, and was the main reason for the organization's vigorous opposition to the regime.

According to Hinnebusch, under the *ancien régime*, the state acted as a mere executive committee of the landed commercial ruling class. But a continuation of the status quo was thought to be unworkable after the end of the French colonial period, and there was thus an expectation that there would have to be a change in the behaviour of the ruling class. At the time, the Ba'th offered the best medium for the middle class and the peasantry to form an alliance against an anti-reform ruling elite that had clearly aligned itself with landlords and business interests.[22] Given this, it is unsurprising that the Ba'th's politics once in power showed a clear bias against the notables and the *suq* culture. Large notables as well as small traders suffered from the Ba'th's social reforms, "especially the state takeover of foreign trade, restrictions on imports, and a growing state retail network which deprived merchants of business."[23]

---

20 The socio-economic school focuses in general on the impact of socio-economic grievances in alienating and transforming a given group into political activists. The members' demographic origins and profile, and their roots, educational level and economic context are often cited. Effectively therefore, their socio-economic grievances are examined and shown to be implicit factors, when not addressed by the state, in the shift towards militancy.
21 Richard T. Antoun, "Ethnicity, Citizenship and Class: Their Changing Meaning," in T. Richard Antoun and Donald Quataert, eds, *Syria*, Albany, NY: State University of New York Press, 1991, p. 1.
22 To cite a few works dealing with the crisis of the liberal system in Syria, see: Khodr Zakariya, *Some Peculiarities of the Class Construction in the Syrian Society*, Tokyo: Institute of Developing Economics, 1984; Petran, *Syria*; David Waldner, *State-Building and Late Development: Turkey, Syria, Korea and Taiwan*, Ithaca, NY: Cornell University Press, 1999; see also Jacques Weulersse, *Paysans de Syrie et du Proche Orient*, Paris: Gallimard, 1946.
23 Hinnebusch, *Syria: Revolution from Above*, p. 96; idem, "State and Islamism in Syria," in Abdul Salam Sidahmed and A. Ehteshami, eds, *Islamic Fundamentalism*, Boulder, CO: Westview Press, 1996, pp. 199–214. To learn more about the politics of the notables and Syria's liberal oligarchy, see: Albert Hourani, *Syria and Lebanon*, London: Oxford University Press, 1946; Philip S. Khoury, *Urban Notables and Arab Nationalism: The Politics of Damascus, 1860–1920*, Cambridge: Cambridge University Press, 1983; idem, *Syria and the French Mandate: The Politics of Arab Nationalism 1920–1945*, Princeton, NJ: Princeton University Press, 1987.

The implications of Hinnebusch's analysis are clear: the changes in the composition of the socio-economic elite that resulted from the Baʻth's rise to power had widespread economic repercussions, which included both threatening and weakening the status of members of the merchant class who opposed the government. These in turn failed to respond by re-organizing and galvanizing support through the traditional notable parties.[24]

More particularly, the urban traditional elite felt usurped by the rapid social and political changes that caused the cities to become dominated by new arrivals from the surrounding villages. This sense was further fanned by the fact that the new arrivals were for the most part minority group members – such as Isma'ilis and ʻAlawis – who were seen as being culturally insensitive to the socio-economic values that the Sunni urbanites held dear. Many feared that "urban culture" – understood to be a more sophisticated system of values and mores than its rural counterpart – was disappearing with the changes in the urban population, and indeed that the historicity of the city and of its urban residents were being threatened.[25]

In addition to changing the power dynamic and composition of the cities, the Baʻth's étatist and populist policies caused the merchant elite to lose power in the villages as well. In Hinnebusch's words,

> [t]he land reform and the efforts of the regime to substitute state and cooperative credit and marketing infrastructures for the old landlord–merchant networks deprived landlords and merchants (who usually also own modest amounts of land) of influence and wealth in the villages.

The Baʻth's populist policies also had very tangible economic impacts on the notable families. Policies such as increasing state control over foreign trade, restricting imports and putting in place a socialist fiscal policy, price regulations and a subsistence peasant policy all contributed to depriving the notable families of their usual sources of wealth. The nationalization of industries was particularly seen as an attack on business and property as a whole.

Another powerful group that felt assailed by the Baʻth's policies was the "men of religion." As Hanna Batatu explains, many of them could not live on the income that they earned from their religious service, and so frequently engaged in petty trade or handicrafts production.[26] As a result, they were dependent on the import–export capabilities of the big, traditional merchants.[27] Yet these merchants were pushed from their positions with the arrival of the Baʻth to

---

24 See Waldner, *State Building and Late Development*.
25 Today's Syrian television series such as *Layali al-Salihiya*, *Bab al-Hara* (all five parts) and *Ayam Shamiya* all attest to this deeply felt cultural difference. In these 30-episode series, the urban Sunni quarter had a specific culture that had dissipated by the 1950s.
26 Van Dam, *The Struggle for Power in Syria*, p. 102.
27 Batatu, "Syria's Muslim Brethren," pp. 15–16.

power, by large state-run organizations that were governed by technocrats, many of whom were of rural origin, were relatively hostile to the urban mercantile class and often lacked a basic understanding of trade. Batatu writes, "[t]he small-scale traders had clearly been more comfortable with the traditional big merchants who, in addition, were Muslim Sunni like themselves."[28] Indeed, consumer co-operatives were among the main establishments attacked during the Muslim Brotherhood demonstrations in the late 1970s in Aleppo and Hama.

For the disenchanted and disenfranchised great traditional notables, merchants and 'ulama', political Islam was appealing because it seemed to reflect their values while also holding out the possibility of uniting them with a big segment of the urban masses against their Baʿth antagonists.[29] Thus, unlike in Egypt or Iran, the strongest support for the Islamic movement in Syria came from the traditional urban quarters that had lost much of their power and capital during President Nasser's rule in Syria, and later felt politically and especially economically excluded by the Baʿth. Hinnebusch writes that "[t]he professional middle class frequently joined this coalition: Islamic protests against socialism were invariably linked with merchant and professional strikes. Thus Islam, interpreted to exclude socialism, became a natural vehicle of protest for the victims of the Baʿthist statism."[30]

According to the socio-economic paradigm, the 1970s saw an increase in the appeal of the Islamic movement due to the decision by a number of university students and urban upper-middle-class professionals to join the Muslim Brotherhood. They did so for a variety of reasons, though the most important was the widening criticism of Baʿthist rule during the period and the concomitant sense that the Islamists were the best vehicle for political protest. This criticism arose because of signs that the regime's populist policies were failing, and more generally that the regime had lost its dynamism and direction.[31] Specific problems included the fact that corruption was increasing economic and social disparities, inflation was rising and the rural exodus was continuing apace, all of which were strongly affecting the social and economic fabric of the principal cities.[32] The last point, about the rural exodus, was particularly significant, since the rapid growth in the population of many cities, and especially of Damascus, had produced a housing crisis. According to Hinnebusch, "[i]nflation hurt the state employed middle class while corruption, inequality and the enrichment of the power elite alienated many party members or sympathisers."[33] Drysdale's discussion of the Syrian economy of the 1970s is also informative:

> A parasitic new class, which feeds off of the public sector has come into existence. Fortunes have also been made in a booming real estate market,

---

28 Ibid.
29 Hinnebusch, "The Islamic Movement in Syria," p. 140.
30 Hinnebusch, *Syria: Revolution from Above*, pp. 93–6.
31 Drysdale, "The Asad Regime and Its Troubles," p. 4.
32 Hanna Batatu, "Syria's Muslim Brethren," *MERIP Reports* 110, November–December 1982: 19.
33 Hinnebusch, *Syria: Revolution from Above*, p. 97.

prices in some sections of Damascus rose tenfold between 1974 and 1976 ... Others have fared less well. For the substantial number of middle and lower level and government public sector employees, salaries have not kept pace with rapid inflation despite large periodic adjustments.[34]

The flight to political Islam as a vehicle of dissent by the urban middle classes was significant given that its members had once been drawn to the old notable parties and to other leftist parties. At the same time, it becomes understandable when one recalls that the authoritarian state had hindered other forms of organized dissent, such that there were few other viable political opposition movements.[35] It is also important to underline that this absence had a butterfly effect on the current growth of the Islamic movement in Syria, as will be argued in Part III of this work. Yet in spite of the pre-eminence enjoyed by the Muslim Brotherhood as a political opposition movement, it faced a number of barriers to recruiting in the 1970s. These included the fact that President al-Asad's cross-class, inter-sectarian ruling coalition included rural Sunnis who were not part of the established old elite, as well as Damascene Sunnis who were liberal-minded. They were generally unreceptive to the ideology of the Muslim Brotherhood, with the rural Sunnis particularly turned off by the Muslim Brotherhood's pro-business orientation and bias against rural migrants, and saw it as being in their best interest to support Asad's regime. Even within the Sunni urban lower strata, only traditional labour was clearly pro-Muslim Brothers.

What emerges, therefore, is that for the socio-economic school, large parts of the rural and urban masses were not attracted to the ideas of the Brothers because they depended on the state for work and feared the feudalist stance adopted by the group.[36] Support for the Brothers was also unevenly spread across the country, mainly due to the Asad regime's policies that favoured the capital at the expense of northern cities such as Aleppo and Hama.[37] These policies included agrarian reforms and the establishment of large state factories, which negatively impacted upon the traditional textile industries and agrarian bourgeoisie of Hama and Aleppo.[38] As will be shown in the following section, these two cities would later play leading roles in defining the Syrian regime's conflict with the Muslim Brotherhood, by virtue of the fact that the merchants backed the Muslim Brothers and carried out the longest strike in Syrian history during the March 1980 uprising. By contrast, it was the passivity of the Damascene merchants that played a key role in muting the Muslim Brotherhood's dynamism and perhaps even saved the regime.[39]

34 Drysdale, "The Asad Regime and Its Troubles," p. 6.
35 Hinnebusch, *Syria: Revolution from Above*, p. 97.
36 Ibid., pp. 97–8.
37 Ibid., p. 97.
38 Ibid.
39 Seurat, *L'Etat de barbarie*, p. 59. See also M.H. Van Dusen, "Political Integration and Regionalism in Syria," *Middle East Journal* 26, Spring 1972: 123–36.

Despite the undoubted strengths of the socio-economic school for explaining the reasons behind the emergence of the Islamic opposition in Syria, it is unable to satisfactorily account for why a number of Syrian Islamists later turned to violence as a radical tactic to express their discontent rather than to other, less risky means of collective action. As a result, there is a need to apply Social Movement Theory to the Syrian case.

C The Social Movement Theory school

Islamic activism in Syria has yet to be integrated into Social Movement Theory since such activism transcends the confines of Islam. Indeed, "social organization outside the auspices of the state is important because it counterweighs the power of the state, dilutes its control over society, and articulates and advances various societal interests vis-à-vis the dominant political elites."[40] In their attempts to apply Social Movement Theory to analysis of the Middle East, the following works try to come to terms with why actors risk joining Islamist movements under the hostile gaze of authoritarian states: *Islamic Activism: A Social Movement Theory Approach* (2004), edited by Quintan Wiktorowicz, addresses myriad case-studies of Sunni and Shi'i Islamic activism, though it remains silent on the Syrian case. In *Mobilizing Islam* (2002), Carrie Rossefsky Wickham examines the rise of Islamic activism in Egypt from 1984 to 1994 through the lens of the Social Movement model. Wickham answers very important questions related to why and how Islamic groups in Egypt were successful in attracting and galvanizing educated Egyptian youth, particularly in comparison with their secular rivals. These are very important questions to answer for the study of Syria today. Basing her analyses on Brysk's "symbolic politics" and Snow and Benford's analysis of framing, Wickham argues that a successful ideological outreach requires a resonant message, credible messengers and effective mechanisms of transmission, or in other words what she calls context specific "movement frames." She concludes that by introducing new values and developing new repertoires of personal and collective action, Islamist mobilization can contribute to more enduring forms of political change in the Muslim world as much as it may lay the foundation for new forms of authoritarian rule. The direction of this political change depends on the social and political forces with which those Islamic movements deal. In *Faith in Moderation: Islamist Parties in Jordan and Yemen* (2006), Jillian Schwedler examines the assumption that there is a causal relationship between the inclusion of Islamist parties in the political process and their moderation.[41] She focuses on

---

40 Brynen *et al.*, *Political Liberalization and Democratization*, p. 11.
41 F. Umar Abd-Allah, *The Islamic Struggle in Syria*, Berkeley, CA: Mizan Press, 1983; François Burgat and William Dowell, *The Islamic Movement in North-Africa*, Austin, TX: University of Texas at Austin, 1993; Gilles Kepel, *Muslim Extremism in Egypt: The Prophet and Pharaoh*, Berkeley and Los Angeles: University of California Press, 1986; Laura Guazzone, ed., *The Islamist Dilemma*, Reading: Ithaca Press, 1995; John Esposito, ed., *Political Islam: Revolution, Radicalism or Reform?* Boulder, CO: Lynne Rienner Publishers, 1997.

Conflict with the Muslim Brotherhood 65

"ideological commitments" rather than just behaviour. In so doing, she rejects the causal model based on institutional constraints, and instead adopts a process-model approach. Her approach combines three interconnected dimensions: political opportunity structures, internal group structures and boundaries of justifiable action.

The Social Movement Theory school has not been applied to the Syrian case of Islamic activism. And yet doing so is essential in order to explain the reasons behind the shift of the hitherto peaceful and democratic Islamic movement towards violent contention. It can help to explain this by shedding light on the operant mechanisms precipitating the shift, as well as the level and the timing of the outbreak of violence in the 1970s. It is also useful for assessing the possibility of violence today.[42]

According to this approach, violent conflict that results in the indiscriminate killing of non-combatants arises when actors rationally respond to a context of opportunities and constraints. Violence becomes the appropriate tactic when the political opportunity structure, characterized by repression, is accompanied by three conditions:

> (1) state repression creates a political environment of bifurcation and brutality; (2) insurgents create exclusive organizations to shield themselves from repression; and (3) rebels promote anti-system frames to motivate collective action to overthrow agents of repression ... where the regime is framed as fundamentally corrupt through anti-system frames, these radical, encapsulated organizations become further radicalized through a growing belief in total war.[43]

In the Syrian case, political exclusion of the Muslim Brotherhood, coupled with the regime's strong secularizing and populist measures that challenged the socio-economic basis of the group's leadership, resulted in the Brothers being denied their traditional space and independence. This likely gave credibility to those in the movement who maintained that the state targeted Islam and Muslims, and that it would use force to bring down the Islamic opposition.[44]

By virtue of how they were informally organized, as well as how Islam was generally practised and that Syrian city life was traditionally inaccessible to outsiders, the Muslim Brothers managed to shield themselves from the state as

---

42 For important works focusing on the nature of state repression, see Charles Tilly, *From Mobilization to Revolution*, Reading, MA: Addison-Wesley, 1978; Charles D. Brockett, "A Protest-Cycle Resolution of the Repression/Popular-Protest Paradox," in Mark Traugott, ed., *Repertoires and Cycles of Collective Action*, Durham, NC: Duke University Press, 1995; Christian Smith, *The Emergence of Liberation Theology: Radical Religion and Social Movement Theory*, Chicago: University of Chicago Press, 1991; and regarding the institutional strength of the state, see such authors as Hanspeter Kriesi, *New Social Movements in Western Europe*, Minneapolis: University of Minnesota Press, 1995.

43 Quintan Wiktorowicz, "Introduction," in Quintan Wiktorowicz (ed.), *Islamic Activism: A Social Movement Theory Approach*, Bloomington and Indianapolis: Indiana University Press, 2004, p. 21.

44 Ibid.

they spread their message. Thus they reached out to people in private houses, public and private prayer rooms, mosques, old *suq*s), at meetings of professional syndicates which were still autonomous from the political command (see Chapter 5), at shari'a schools and through social-welfare organizations. Social Movement Theory tells us that violent contention, whether Islamist or not, is a result of tactical considerations informed by the realities of repressive contexts and the shrinking pool of alternative actions. In the case of the Syrian Muslim Brothers, the Ba'th's crackdown on political parties involved the destruction of the Brothers' social and economic base. The regime also made strong efforts to control the political, economic and social order so as to successfully carry out its revolution, and excluded the religious class from playing any meaningful role in society, to the point of marginalizing it. These actions prompted a calculated response from proponents of violence within the general Islamist movement.

Here it is important to pinpoint the central role played by ideological framing, in this case the use of religion as a primordial element in turning the repressed opposition and its disaffected recruits into a violent movement.[45] If one looks closely, it becomes possible to discern that violent contention coincided with two important shifts within the Syrian political structure: the first was that an 'Alawi officer becoming president seemed to announce the end of the Sunni ideological and institutional monopoly on power, while the second was that the Asad regime excluded the Muslim Brothers from the National Progressive Front that it created in 1972 in order to accommodate other political parties. This exclusion forced the Muslim Brotherhood to choose between moving immediately to regain its formal access to power, or waiting until later and thus risking permanently losing all of its institutional and ideological influence.[46]

The present study is grounded in both the Social Movement Theory approach and the political economy approach. While the political economy school is best able to explain the resurgence of Islamism in the 1960s and 1970s in Syria, as well as the motivations behind the current resurgence of Islamic activism in the country, the Social Movement approach is best equipped to explain how that current resurgence has taken place.

Having examined the reasons behind the antagonism between the Ba'th and the Muslim Brotherhood, we now turn our attention to the bloody events of the conflict between them.

---

45 For the impact of state terrorism on Islamic movements, see also François Burgat, *Face to Face with Political Islam*, London and New York: I.B. Tauris, 2003.
46 However, because in the Syrian case, this grieving class was not numerous enough to recruit a large pool of members, the revolution from below failed to achieve its aim of bringing down the government. Moreover, the state, while authoritarian, was accessible to the remaining social groups, and hence posed a serious challenge to the formation of a large and effective opposition. In addition, despite the reactive nature of repression that the state deployed to quell the Islamist movement, mass mobilization was not possible given the sectarian, geographical and economic limits on the numbers of recruits at the time. For a comprehensive work incorporating the study of Islamic activism into Social Movement Theory, albeit one that does not specifically consider the Syrian case, see Wiktorowicz, *Islamic Activism*.

4 An open challenge, with emphasis on the secular element

In order to explain Islamic revivalism in Syrian society and the re-emergence of Islamist activity in the country after a 22-year absence, it is important to examine the past relationship between the Syrian state and the Muslim Brotherhood, as well as the ways in which the secular Baʿth regime dealt with the Islamic opposition between the early 1960s and the early 1980s. Doing so will also throw light upon the Syrian regime's current use of comparable domestic socio-political manipulations in the face of similar existential threats – such as the global economic crisis, the regime's own legitimacy crisis and the new regional reality – in order to contain religious discontent, eradicate the militant religious opposition and limit popular unrest while still maintaining the unity of the ruling coalition.

The next section of the chapter provides a history of the Baʿth regime's conflict with the religious class, and particularly focuses upon the state's clash with the Syrian Muslim Brotherhood and the Fighting Vanguard, which culminated in the decisive Hama battle of 1982. We will see how secularism played an important part in igniting the clash, as well as in subsequently bringing to an end the state's policy of muting secularism. During the course of the conflict, the role of Islam in shaping state policies and defining the culture was always in dispute, and indeed helped to delineate the contours of the confrontation. It is for this reason that the following discussion will pay particular attention to the conflict's underlying secular vs. religious aspect.

A Political Islam's ideology

The late 1970s saw the Fighting Vanguard declare the Baʿth Party to be an "atheist, sectarian and corrupt party that should be abolished."[47] It also chose to focus upon what it termed the "atheist" and "sectarian" (non-Sunni) aspects of the government in explaining its motivations:

> Three years ago, to be exact on 8 February 1976, the first bullet was fired for the sake of Allah, thereby opening the gate for the organized Jihad, which has now started to produce positive results. This first bullet, however, was the result of long and persistent suffering from oppression and terror. … The ordeal reached its climax, however, when oppression became concentrated against the Muslims and against the Islamic religion in particular: mosques were destroyed; religious scholars were arrested; educational programmes were banned; Islamic law schools were closed; atheist and disintegrative information and instruction were published; sectarian party domination increased steadily … the riches of the nation were plundered by way of corruption, embezzlement, illegal trade, doubtful transactions, and the unlawful enrichment of a handful of people at the cost of the overwhelming majority. … It is necessary, therefore, that the dead be resurrected

---
47 Van Dam, *The Struggle for Power in Syria*, p. 90.

from the sleep of non-being, that ambition and honour be activated, and that it be loudly acclaimed: "Allah is great; on to the Jihad": *Permission to take up arms is hereby given to those who are attacked, because they have been wronged, God has power to grant them victory.* ... The *Mujahidun* are young people who believe in Allah as their Lord, in Islam as their religion, and in our master Muhammad. ... They sacrifice themselves to liberate their religion and their nation from tyranny, infidelity, injustice and aggression; ... and to make the magnanimous *Shari'ah* the compassionate [Islamic] law for all peoples, and for the Syrian people in particular.[48]

As explained in Chapter 3, the Fighting Vanguard's ideology was marked by a radical Salafi discourse that relied heavily on the writings of Sayyed Qutb,[49] especially his book *Ma'alem fi al-Tariq*, as well as on the writings of Sa'id Hawwa and Marwan Hadid, though not on the books of Syrian Islamic pacifists such as al-Siba'i or Hasan al-Hadibi, the second superintendent general of the Muslim Brotherhood in Syria.[50] Hadid's works were marked by a dismissal of Syrian Sufism and by a belief in the radical *Sahwa* (awakening) of the Muslims, which he argued made it necessary to reinforce Islamic law. He also insisted upon the need for militant opposition to the Syrian regime. Hawwa by contrast considered preaching to be preferable to war, at least in theory. He was also more careful in defining the conditions under which jihad became a requirement, specifying that Syrian society must first be properly educated in the precepts of Islam. Meir Hatina explains that, in Hawwa's view,

The Sufi path of intensive prayer, fasting and discipline is important in an era in which materialism and hedonism are dominant, for it constitutes a necessary preparatory stage to the act of jihad. Such training must purify the Muslim soul of arrogance and block any possibility of the penetration of the winds of heresy and corruption. The training stage ends only when the readiness to die becomes the member's most desired ambition – the dividing line between those who truly aspire to jihad and those who seek to avoid it. As the hadith states: "The faith of he who died and did not fight or express willingness to die [for Allah] is tantamount to one who dies as a hypocrite."[51]

---

48 Quoted by Van Dam, ibid.
49 Qutb is widely regarded as the intellectual leader of the Egyptian Muslim Brotherhood.
50 See Sayyed Qutb, *Fi ma'alem al-Tariq*, Cairo: Dar al-Shuruq, n.d.; Hawwa, *Fi Afaq al-Ta'lim*, pp. 167–71; idem, *Hadhihi Tajribati was Hadhihi Shahadati*; idem, *Jund Allah Thaqafa zu Akhlaq*, 2nd edn, Beirut: n.d. See also Itzchak Weismann, "Sa'id Hawwa and Islamic Revivalism in Ba'thist Syria," *Studia Islamica* 85, 1997: 152. See also *idem*, "Sa'id Hawwa: The Making of a Radical Muslim Thinker in Modern Syria," *Middle Eastern Studies* 29, October 1993: 607–11. On the birth of radical thought within Islam, see also Meir Hatina, "Restoring a Lost Identity: Models of Education in Modern Islamic Thought," *British Journal of Middle Eastern Studies* 33(2), 2006: 179–97.
51 Meir Hatina, "Restoring a Lost Identity," p. 189.

Hawwa also insisted that the successes of the jihad had to be evaluated before engaging in militancy, and said that it was important to determine whether or not the Muslim regime to be fought against had truly abandoned Islam.[52] But notwithstanding these various conditions on how and when to deploy militancy, Hawwa's formulations, especially his concept of *ridda* (conversion), were ultimately no less radical than those of Qutb and Hadid. In fact, while Qutb delineated a world system of Islam and disbelief (*Jahiliyya*), Hawwa added an important distinction within the category of *Mushrikun* (non-believers). He said that jihad should first be waged against the *Murtaddun* (those who have abandoned Islam), and then against the rest of the *Mushrikun*. The latter includes the heterodox sects such as the Isma'ilis, the Baha'is, the Qadiyanis and undoubtedly the 'Alawis (who are not considered to be Muslim according to overall Salafi dogma), as well as adherents of the human-authored ideologies that oppose Islam openly such as the communists, the nationalists and those who preach the separation of religion and state. And while at an ideological level there were important differences between Hadid and Hawwa, these often did not matter in practice: "[f]or the *mujahidun*, who had neither the time nor the ability to follow his learned formulations, there was no real difference between him [Hawwa] and Hadid."[53]

B Political Islam confronts the state

As explained in the last chapter, Syria's "Islamic problem" first burst into the open in February 1964, with the so-called "Uprising of Hama." The uprising was marked by strong tensions between the Ba'th and the Muslim Brothers as well as a number of Hamawi imams who saw it as their moral duty to preach against the new regime.[54] It began with Marwan Hadid starting a student protest against the regime at one of the biggest high schools in Hama. The protest soon became a city-wide uprising led by the Muslim Brothers that lasted for 29 days and included elements from across the political spectrum, including the Nasserites and the Communists. This situation quickly degenerated into violent riots and demonstrations, with dozens of protestors killed by the army in the city's Sultan Mosque during attempts to quell the disturbance.[55]

---

52 See Weisman, "Sa'id Hawwa."
53 Ibid., p. 154.
54 Olson wrote that

> [t]he al-Asad regime, whether justifiable or not, began to be characterized by its opponents as a sectarian regime ... this charge against the Asad regime after 1975 weakened the regime's ability to use Ba'thist ideology as a legitimizing instrument for its main basis of power and, in fact after 1975 it became increasingly dependent on Alawite regional and family connections to maintain its hold on national power.

See Robert W. Olson, *The Ba'th and Syria, 1947 to 1982: The Evolution of Ideology, Party, and State*, Princeton, NJ: Kingston Press, 1982, p. 121.

55 Faysal Daraj and Jamal Barut, *Al-ahzab wa al-harakat wa al-jama'at al-islamiya* [The Islamic Parties, Movements and Groups], Damascus: The Arab Center for Strategic Studies, 2006, p. 268.

In their speeches, the demonstrators expressed dismay at what they perceived as rule by a minority "atheist" regime. At the same time, Zaki al-Arsuzi's articles that stressed the *Jahiliya* period (the pre-Islamic era) as being the golden age of the Arabs upset the Muslim Brothers.[56] Generally speaking, the fact that the regime's elites were both 'Alawi and Ba'thist made it possible for Islamic leaders to argue that the state's aggressive secularization polices were in fact aimed at making the Syrian people atheist as opposed to just secular, which would facilitate efforts by the allegedly atheist 'Alawis to control them.

The uprising can be seen as the point at which parts of the overall Islamic movement became radicalized, as well as when the new state's repressive response first crystallized. This response, which was due to the fact that the state was not strong enough to allow an emboldened Muslim Brotherhood, led to the uprising being swiftly crushed and a number of Brothers being put in prison.

In the 1970s, the Brotherhood's opposition grew even stronger. This was because the Ba'th lost the Sunni façade behind which it had sheltered since 1963, as a result of the 'Alawi Muslim Hafez al-Asad becoming the president and thus putting a tangible end to the tradition of having the country's commander-in-chief be a Sunni Muslim.[57] It was also because the draft constitution that was written in 1969 and adopted by the People's Council at the end of January 1973 omitted all references to Islam, other than a desultory mention that all religious practices would be protected by the state (see Chapter 2). Another provision in the draft constitution that incensed the Islamic movement and the opposition in general was the designation of the Ba'th as the leading party of the nation, which clearly indicated its ambition of shifting from being an instrument of class revolution and social levelling to a machinery of power in the service of *raison d'état* (which Islamists alleged served only 'Alawis). While large parts of the opposition lamented the seemingly certain end of democratic parliamentary politics in Syria, the Ba'th's monopolization of power also spelled the end of the traditional socio-political order. Moreover, the opposition's indignation was even stronger given their earlier expectation that al-Asad would dismantle the Ba'th's monopoly on power in an attempt to conciliate with, and win support from, the urban elite.

The draft constitution prompted the Syrian 'ulama', the Muslim Brothers and the untouchable Shaykh Habanka to stage a series of riots in February 1973 in the cities of Hama and Aleppo. These riots, which were said to be led by Marwan Hadid, Sa'id Hawwa and the Hama base of the Muslim Brotherhood, and which included the Nasserites and the Socialists under Hawrani,

---

56 Ibid. See also Olson, *The Ba'th and Syria, 1947 to 1982*, pp. 88–9.
57 As stated in Chapter 2, the 'Alawis, or Nusayris, were seen as an extreme sect of the Shi'a, and were considered infidels by Sunnis in general; moreover under the Ottomans they were heavily taxed. For a brief history of Ottoman Syria and Syria's heterogeneous population, see Moshe Ma'oz, "Society and State in Modern Syria," in Menahem Milson, ed., *Society and Political Structure in the Arab World*, New York: Humanities Press, 1973.

saw the militants attack a number of government centres as well as a few bars and cafes. Clashes with government soldiers resulted in the killing and wounding of a number of demonstrators and the arrest of Sa'id Hawwa and his followers.[58] But the mass protests also led to the draft constitution being amended, to include a new provision asserting that the president of Syria must be a Muslim, as well as changes to article 3 that made Islamic jurisprudence one of the main sources of legislation.[59] The draft was approved in a popular referendum in mid-March 1973, though the fact that sporadic demonstrations continued throughout April 1973 made al-Asad's compromises seem less than effective.

As mentioned in the last chapter, Marwan Hadid wrote an open letter calling for the abolition of al-'Attar's Damascus-based faction within the Brotherhood and Abu Ghudda's Aleppo-based factions. He accused them of allying themselves with anyone willing to work with them, even atheists, and of becoming mere *Tabligh* and *Da'wa* (preaching, proselytizing) groups. He also demanded that true Muslims and Islamic groups wage war against the "heretical" Syrian regime. As a result of these attacks, the main Islamic leadership decided to formally dismiss Marwan Hadid and others related to his group, such as 'Adnan 'Uqlah, from the Muslim Brotherhood.[60]

In 1975, a new *shura* council was elected under the leadership of 'Adnan Sa'ed al-Din. Despite having the approval of the International Brotherhood, neither al-'Attar (who had moved to Aachen in Germany) nor Hadid accepted the new group. To distinguish itself, Hadid's group began calling itself "The Fighting Vanguard of the Party of God" (*al-Tali'a al-Muqatila li-Hizb-illah*).[61] Hadid was arrested in Syria on 30 June 1975, and died in prison the following year; this led to 'Abd al-Satar al-Za'im (also from Hama) assuming the leadership of the Fighting Vanguard. The group's first anti-government operation was the assassination of the head of the military intelligence branch in Hama, Lieutenant Muhammad Ghaza, on 8 February 1976.[62]

In July 1976, the regime faced another challenge when Asad intervened in the Lebanese civil war by siding with the predominately Maronite Christian forces, and not with the predominately Muslim and secularly oriented Lebanese National Movement and its Palestinian allies. In the eyes of many in Syria, al-Asad had crossed a line and had betrayed the Ba'th's secular slogans. Nonetheless, the government made little effort to explain its decision to intervene against

---

58 Sa'id Hawwa would be released five years later in January 1978. Daraj and Barut, *Al-ahzab wa al-harakat wa al-jama'at al-islamiya*, p. 267.
59 See www.damascus-online.com/history/documents/constitution.htm. Nonetheless, article 83 of the draft constitution focuses upon eligibility, and says: "A candidate for the presidency must be an Arab Syrian, enjoying his civil and political rights, and be over 40 years of age." Significantly, it does not mention religion.
60 Daraj and Barut, *Al-ahzab wa al-harakat wa al-jama'at al-islamiya*, p. 273.
61 Ibid., p. 274.
62 Ibid., pp. 275–6.

72 Hafez al-Asad's era

Arabism. And while many Syrians were mystified by the decision, some viewed it as clear proof of the regime's anti-Sunni and pro-minority – in this case, Maronite Christian – biases.[63]

Relations between the regime and Syria's main professional syndicates (*al-Naqabat al-Mihaniya*) also began to sour at this time. These professional syndicates, who represent doctors, lawyers, pharmacists and engineers and who enjoy a substantial degree of autonomy, particularly compared to the labour unions, were outspoken in their condemnation of the intervention in Lebanon. Attempts by Ba'thist cadres to win leadership positions within the professional syndicates in the mid-1970s were in vain, and by 1978, "Islamist sympathies had spread in some syndicates, especially in the engineers' [syndicate]."[64]

Among the Islamists, the Lebanon intervention on the side of the predominately Christian Maronite forces was perceived as "anti-Islamic." It particularly angered the Fighting Vanguard's *mujahedin*,[65] many of whom had close ties with, and had trained under, the Palestinian faction Fateh in Jordan.[66] The Vanguard responded with a series of attacks on officers and party functionaries – most of whom were 'Alawis – as well as on government and military installations in the cities of Damascus, Aleppo, Hama, Homs, Latakia and Tartus. In concert with the professional syndicates (mainly the engineers), it also organized strikes in the bazaars, which are the locus of rich Sunni traders in many parts of Syria.[67] All of these actions prompted Hafez al-Asad to address the nation on 12 April 1976, where he reiterated the regime's commitment to secularism:

> Every person can recall when we were students, we used to say: religion is for God, and the homeland for all ... the Muslim and the Christian in this country both believe that the relationship between citizens is first and foremost the relationship of the homeland and Arabism ... the Muslim in this country takes an interest in the Arab citizen in Lebanon whether he is Christian or Muslim ... Christianity and Islam issued from our land. This is not a burden for us or a problem for us; it is a source of pride for all. These values emerged from our countries and our land ... we must be a nation worthy of these values, worthy of Christianity and Islam.[68]

---

63 See Hinnebusch, "The Islamic Movement in Syria," p. 162; Itamar Rabinovich, "The Islamic Wave," *Washington Quarterly*, Autumn 1979: 139–43.
64 Salloukh, "Organizing Politics in the Arab World," pp. 276–7. See also Seurat, *L'Etat de barbarie*, p. 76. In 1978, only three Ba'thist candidates were elected in the Damascus engineers' syndicate, one in the pharmacists' syndicate and none in that of the doctors.
65 Van Dam, *The Struggle for Power in Syria*, p. 71.
66 Daraj and Barut, *Al-ahzab wa al-harakat wa al-jama'at al-islamiya*, p. 272; Batatu, "Syria's Muslim Brethren," p. 19.
67 Hinnebusch, *Syria: Revolution from Above*, pp. 98–9.
68 Quoted in Olson, *The Ba'th and Syria, 1947 to 1982*, p. 170.

But al-Asad's address failed to quell the Islamists' furore, nor did it stop the professional syndicates increasingly gravitating towards the opposition. For example, in reaction to the death of two lawyers in prison, members of the lawyers' syndicate founded the Committee for Human Rights, which published accounts of human rights abuses perpetrated by the regime and demanded political reforms.[69] Meanwhile, the Fighting Vanguard continued their attacks on the regime. In February 1977, they killed the Rector of the University of Damascus, Dr Muhammad al-Fadel, and on 18 March 1978, they assassinated Dr Ibrahim Na'ama, the doyen of Syrian dentists and the Vice-President of the Syrio-Soviet Friendship Association.[70]

C Expansion and escalation of the confrontation

In addition to facing internal opposition, the Syrian Ba'th regime was also the focus of verbal broadsides by a number of neighbouring regimes, including that of Egypt.[71] According to Olson, "this development also seems to have been encouraged by Israel, to facilitate the negotiations for disengagement [after the 1973 war]," in order to discredit Syria given Syria's self-proclaimed pan-Arab stand.[72] Thus, following the 1973 disengagement between Egypt and Israel, Radio Cairo launched a number of verbal attacks insinuating that the Ba'th regime of al-Asad was a sectarian one. Egypt's signing of the Camp David peace agreements with Israel in 1978 served to further damage relations with Hafez al-Asad,[73] with Egyptian President Sadat accusing the Syrian regime of being "firstly Alawi, secondly Bathist and thirdly Syrian," and saying that President Asad "had the intention of setting up an Alawi state."[74] In 1979, Sadat insinuated that an 'Alawi regime is a heretical regime:

> I was prepared to talk on behalf of the Golan. But no. Let these dirty Alawis speak for it. These people who have lost all meaning of life. By God, let them face their people in Syria and let them solve it … we all know who the Alawis are in the eyes of the Syrian people.[75]

The verbal attacks on Syria were joined by the Saudi leadership. In a conversation between King Faysal and Sadat, both leaders agreed that "Hafiz al-Asad is Alawi and Ba'thist, and one is more evil than the other."[76] Olson explains that

---

69 Seurat, *L'Etat de barbarie*, p. 76.
70 Daraj and Barut, *Al-ahzab wa al-harakat wa al-jama'at al-islamiya*, p. 276. See also Patrick Seale, *Asad of Syria: The Struggle for the Middle East*, London: I.B. Tauris, 1988, p. 317.
71 Daraj and Barut, *Al-ahzab wa al-harakat wa al-jama'at al-islamiya*, pp. 280–1.
72 Olson, *The Ba'th and Syria, 1947 to 1982*, p. 121.
73 See Seale, *Asad of Syria*, pp. 303–15.
74 Quoted by Olson, *the Ba'th and Syria, 1947 to 1982*, p. 122; Van Dam, *The Struggle for Power in Syria*, p. 93.
75 Olson, *The Ba'th and Syria, 1947 to 1982*, p. 122.
76 Ibid.

While one has to interpret these remarks in light of al-Sadat's and Faysal's desire that Syria join in the step-by-step diplomacy [with Israel], the comments are also an indication of the Egyptian and Saudi Arabian leaders' condescending attitude toward the Alawites ... But ... it was not through the exploitation of sectarianism that the Alawites gained and maintained power.[77]

Meanwhile, in Syria the fighting had spread to Aleppo, Hama, Homs and Dayr al-Zawr. Baʻth Party and military installations were randomly attacked, and there were assassinations of military personnel and government civil servants, but also of doctors and university professors, most of whom were ʻAlawis.[78] Patrick Seale argues that this targeting of ʻAlawis suggested that "the assassinations had targeted the community and were deliberately setting out to sharpen sectarian differences, and in this they were successful."[79]

The conflict escalated even further after an incident at the Aleppo Artillery School on 16 June 1979, which marked a turning point in Syria's relationship with the Islamist movement. A captain in the Syrian military, Ibrahim al-Yusuf, summoned the school's cadets to an urgent meeting in the dining hall. Once assembled, the Sunni cadets were asked to leave, and large numbers of the remaining cadets were killed by a group of assassins that ʻAdnan Dabbagh, the minister of the interior at the time, accused of being a terrorist gang from the Muslim Brotherhood.[80] This represented the first time that the government had publicly accused the Muslim Brotherhood of militant activity. According to Patrick Seale, the regime considered the attack to be a declaration of war, and vowed to liquidate what it referred to as an "agent organization."[81]

The leadership of the Syrian Muslim Brotherhood denied any knowledge or involvement in the Aleppo incident, and reminded everyone that Captain Ibrahim al-Yusuf was a Baʻthist. Yet the group's stance was undermined to some degree by the Fighting Vanguard issuing a statement in June 1979 under the name "The Fighting Vanguard of the Muslim Brothers," which declared: "As to you Sunni intelligence officers, our fight was never with you, you embraced death while your ʻAlawi masters led the battles from behind the loudspeakers."[82]

The immediate result of the attack was the execution of 15 Muslim Brothers who were already in prison, and who were accused of taking part in previous

---

77 Ibid., pp. 122–3.
78 These assassinations included the President's personal physician, Colonel Khalil Shahada, in August 1979.
79 Seale, *Asad of Syria*, p. 317.
80 Estimates of the number killed vary between 32 and 83, depending on the source. See Drysdale, "The Asad Regime and Its Troubles," p. 8. See also Seurat, *L'Etat de barbarie*, p. 66. Seurat explains that 282 of the 300 cadets were ʻAlawi.
81 Thomas Mayer, "The Islamic Opposition in Syria, 1962–1982," *Orient* 24, 1983, p. 589.
82 Quoted in Daraj and Barut, *Al-ahzab wa al-harakat wa al-jamaʻat al-islamiya*, p. 280.

Conflict with the Muslim Brotherhood 75

attacks.[83] More generally, President Asad dealt with the situation in the country by attempting an oblique sort of reconciliation with the traditional Sunni class. That is, instead of heeding the calls from the major syndicates for an end to the state of emergency and for new elections, he played the Islamic card: he thus portrayed himself as a pious Muslim, he endorsed a few prominent 'ulama', and also launched a programme of selective economic liberalization that was aimed at revitalizing the private sector.[84] In addition, he made new appointments to various official posts so as to let more Sunnis into the national command of the Ba'th Party as well as the cabinet. He then undertook a limited *political* liberalization, introduced anti-corruption reforms and released a few Muslim Brothers from prison.[85] Yet these changes were not enough to overcome the regime's image of being corrupt and narrowly sectarian, and were seen as too little too late by its opponents.

One week after the minister of the interior commented on the Aleppo Artillery School attack and two weeks after the incident itself, President Hafez al-Asad spoke about it for the first time in public. According to Van Dam, his address aimed "to counter the sectarian propaganda and the unrest surrounding the Aleppo massacre, and to widen support for the Ba'th regime's campaign against the Muslim Brotherhood":

> The concept of "homeland" loses its meaning if its citizens are not equal. This equality is an integral part of Islam. We are leading the country in the name of the Arab Ba'th Socialist Party and as President of the Republic, not in the name of a religion or of a religious community, despite the fact that Islam is the religion of the majority. Ba'thists and those who believe in their homeland all believe in the principles of freedom, unity and socialism. ... Those who consider religion to be a matter of ritual and neglect its essence cause it to become an obstacle to progress. Since the start of the Corrective Movement [of November 1970], we have always affirmed that religion means love, work and achievement. What matters is the presence of moral values and ethics. We have always worked to strengthen religious values in the hearts of the citizens ... But now we are facing a conspiracy against our country, and a criminal act which was not committed by an individual which we can forgive, but by a political organization called the Muslim Brotherhood. ... This gang ... considers a third of the people to be non-Muslims [i.e. heterodox Muslims such as the Alawis, Druzes and Isma'ilis; and Christians]. Its members want to monopolize Islam for themselves, despite the fact that no party has the right to monopolize Islam or any other religion. ... Assassination attempts cannot overthrow this regime and we will not permit sectarian acts. ... The Arab Ba'th Socialist Party is a nationalist socialist party that does not differentiate between religions. As

---

83 Drysdale, "The Asad Regime and Its Troubles," p. 8.
84 Hinnebusch, *Syria: Revolution from Above*, p. 96.
85 Seale, *Asad of Syria*, pp. 323–32.

a faithful Muslim, I encourage everyone to have faith and to fight rigidity and fanaticism. ... If Syria had not always been above sectarianism, it would not now exist.[86]

While secularism permeated the message of Hafez al-Asad as he claimed to lead in the name of all Syrians, his message was also marked by his insistence that he was not just a Muslim, but a "faithful Muslim." Regarding Islam, al-Asad even ventured to describe the essence of the religion as being "love, work and achievement," so as to counter rival, radical interpretations.

Nonetheless, the attacks continued to escalate. In November 1979, militants entered a *mukhabarat* office and shot 14 of its staff members and security officers, to which the state responded by arresting Aleppo's Grand Imam Shaykh Zein al-Din Khayrallah, brother of the head of the militant Aleppo branch of the Muslim Brotherhood. The arrest prompted mass demonstrations in the city and, two days later, a shooting spree that ended in the deaths of dozens, including 18 members of the 'Alawite sect. A few days later, another assassination squad penetrated a school where Ba'thi cadres had gathered to prepare for an upcoming regional congress; here the death toll was 40.[87] Eventually, even Soviet personnel and property were targeted.[88]

By 1980, it is believed that the Islamists in Syria numbered around 30,000, including the vanguard of 'Adnan 'Uqla, al-'Attar's division within the Brotherhood, a number of Salafi activists, Sufis from the *Jama'at al-Huda* of Aleppo led by Abu al-Nasr Bayanuni, and a number of independent fighters trained by the Palestinian Fateh.[89]

In February 1980, the regime released about 500 members of the Muslim Brotherhood from prison, who had been detained since February and April 1979. In spite of this gesture, Syria's professional syndicates and associations took part in a nationwide strike at the end of March that had been initiated by the Muslim Brothers, who were feeling increasingly powerful. The strikes were largely concentrated in Aleppo, Hama, Homs and, to a lesser extent, Damascus, and unified two groups that opposed the regime: the Islamist militants led by 'Adnan 'Uqla's Vanguard and 'Isam al-'Attar, and the "Democratic National Bloc" made up of the Communists, the Arab Socialist Union (led by Jamal al-Atasi), the Worker's Party, the Old Ba'th and the Arab Socialists under Akram Hawrani.[90] Also supporting the strikes were a number of merchants who were angered by regime-imposed price controls, as well as representatives of the engineers', lawyers' and

---

86 Quoted by Van Dam, *The Struggle for Power in Syria*, pp. 94–5. For more of Hafez al-Asad's speeches regarding the conflict with the Muslim Brothers, see Ahmad Qurna, *Hafez al-Asad: Sane' Tarikh al-Umma wa Bani Majd al-Watan: 1970–1985*, Aleppo: Dar al-Sharq al-'Arabi, 1986, pp. 207–90.
87 Michel Seurat, "La Société syrienne contre son Etat," *le Monde Diplomatique*, April 1980.
88 Mayer, "The Islamic Opposition in Syria," p. 598.
89 Daraj and Barut, *Al-ahzab wa al-harakat wa al-jama'at al-islamiya*, p. 281.
90 Ibid., pp. 284–5.

physicians' professional associations. Manifestos were issued demanding an end to Syria's state of emergency, and "[e]xplicit anti-'Alawi overtones ran through the disturbances."[91]

Most analysts believe that the Democratic National Bloc was seeking a peaceful move towards democratic rule and wanted to pressure the regime through a general civil strike, while the Fighting Vanguard felt that a civil uprising and civil disturbances were necessary in order to topple the regime. The state's response to the so-called Uprising of March was a strategy known as "Necessary State Violence," also labelled "the Revolutionary Violence." It claimed that this response was necessary in order to stop the "Reactionary Violence."[92] Concretely, the state dispatched special commando units and the soldiers from Rif'at al-Asad's Defence Battalions (whose members were predominately 'Alawi, and were thus seen as being unswervingly loyal to the regime given the sectarian overtones of the whole conflict) to the cities of Hama and Aleppo. Massive search operations were carried out, and around 5,000 people were arrested.[93]

On 23 March 1980, Hafez al-Asad sought to court pious Syrians by declaring that the Ba'thist state supports anyone who upholds religious values.[94] At this point, he also tried to differentiate between "reactionary" (a word that was used by Ba'thists to indicate the religious in general) and "conservative" members of the Muslim Brotherhood, inviting the latter to join the National Progressive Front and to become part of the government coalition. These conciliatory gestures were backed up by more direct measures, due to state concerns about the potential for nationwide chaos. Thus on 14 April 1980, the government dissolved the executive councils of professional associations, dismissed their general congresses and detained an undetermined number of their leaders, members and human rights activists without trial, causing some to pre-emptively flee the country.[95]

On 26 June 1980, there was an attempt on the life of Hafez al-Asad that was attributed to the Muslim Brothers. After this incident, the hard-liners within the government such as Hafez al-Asad's brother Rif'at were given carte-blanche to bring down the opposition. Immediately, some 200 members of the Muslim Brotherhood who were already in prison were executed.[96] Troops were also sent into Syrian cities to track down, imprison or execute allegedly militant Muslim Brothers.[97] On 7 July 1980, Parliament made being a member of, or associating with, the Muslim Brotherhood a treasonous and capital offence. Law 49 reduced the sentence of anyone who renounced in writing their membership in the

---

91 Drysdale, "The Asad Regime and Its Troubles," p. 8.
92 Daraj and Barut, *Al-ahzab wa al-harakat wa al-jama'at al-islamiya*, p. 289.
93 Seurat, "La Société syrienne contre son état."
94 Van Dam, *The Struggle for Power in Syria*, p. 96, from Radio Damascus, 23 March 1980.
95 Drysdale, "The Asad Regime and Its Troubles," p. 8.
96 Ibid.; Umar F. Abd-Allah, *The Islamic Struggle in Syria*, Berkeley, CA: Mizan Press, 1983, pp. 84–5.
97 Van Dam, *The Struggle for Power in Syria*, p. 96.

Muslim Brotherhood to a maximum of five years in prison. This law led to a considerable shrinkage in the Brotherhood's membership – in Aleppo, for example, the Fighting Vanguard lost at least 600 of its members. Furthermore, Syria moved troops to its border with Jordan, in an attempt to dissuade its neighbour from supporting or giving refuge to Muslim Brothers. Asad's move discouraged Jordan only for a while, however. As for Iraq, 'Uqla had one permanent training camp and deputies in Baghdad, and was in direct talks with the Iraqi intelligence services.[98]

During this time, many members left the main Muslim Brotherhood and joined forces with smaller, apolitical Islamic groups in Syria (see Part III), while others fled the country entirely. The leaders of the Muslim Brotherhood, namely 'Adnan Sa'ed al-Din, Sa'id Hawwa and 'Ali Sadr al-Din al-Bayanuni, re-organized and formed the Syrian Islamic Front (SIF) in October–November 1980. The SIF allied itself fully with the Iraqi and Jordanian Brothers, and promised to continue fighting until the collapse of the Syrian regime:

> the present regime has reached the stage of no return ... it is now impossible for it to undergo a radical revision, we declare that there will be no truce, no laying down of arms, and no negotiation with those who are known for their deceit and for breaking their promises. We shall continue in our course, disregarding dangers and obstacles, until this oppressive regime has fallen and gone forever.[99]

The Islamic Front's plan was to create one unified military opposition coalition, and in the process to control 'Adnan 'Uqla and get him out of Aleppo. The Muslim Brotherhood's members and the Fighting and Islamic Vanguards agreed with the strategy, and thus re-assembled and united their military and political bases in December 1980.[100] But the coalition imploded when 'Uqla rejected the Muslim Brotherhood's negotiations to become part of the "National Alliance for the Liberation of Syria," which was to have included secular dissident groups such as the Nasserites and the Iraqi Ba'th, plus a number of individual dissidents. 'Uqla accused the Brotherhood's civilian leadership of treason, and of allying themselves with heretics and enemies of Islam. In January 1981, 'Uqla declared the total independence of the Fighting Vanguard (Marwan Hadid's battalion) from the Muslim Brotherhood, and claimed that he was continuing the fight for the sake of God.[101]

From March to September 1981, the armed struggle resumed. A number of car bombs exploded near and inside military bases and government buildings, killing and injuring many civilians and military personnel. In retaliation, the

---

98 Ibid., p. 293.
99 Translation in Abd-Allah, *The Islamic Struggle in Syria*, p. 212.
100 Ibid., p. 295.
101 Ibid., p. 298. It was only in April 1982, following the Hama massacre, that the Brotherhood dismissed 'Uqla officially from the coalition movement.

government security forces conducted large-scale search operations which eyewitnesses described as very brutal. The operations resulted in the deaths of at least 200–300 people, as well as the destruction of entire sections of Aleppo and Hama.[102] Tight security measures were also imposed, such as a ban on the use of motorcycles in some cities due to the fact that they had been used by the Muslim Brotherhood in hit-and-run attacks, as well as ordering all citizens aged 14 and older to obtain new identity cards.[103] More generally, efforts were made to improve the regime's image and to mobilize popular support through a series of ideological, political, economic and social measures, which will be discussed in the following chapter.

In January 1982, 'Uqla arrived in Hama anticipating the beginning of a war against the regime, and on 2 February 1982, the war actually broke out.[104] From the city's mosques, the Muslim Brothers urged the people of Hama to join in the fight against the regime. Meanwhile, several hundred men from the Islamic Front attacked police and the Ba'th Party headquarters in the city of Hama. They also ambushed government forces searching for dissidents in the narrow alleyways.[105] By the second day, the rebellion was spreading, with thousands taking to the streets.[106] The city seemed to be under the Mujahedin's control from 2 to 12 February.

The Syrian government was concerned that regional powers such as the Gulf states, Jordan, Iraq or even Israel might intervene on the side of the revolt, especially given that 'Adnan Sa'ed al-Din was in Saudi Arabia and Abu Ghudda was somewhere in the Arab Gulf, and were thus able to foment support for the opposition from there. Iraq had already involved itself by broadcasting a rebel plea by Front leaders Muhammad Abu Nasr al-Bayanuni, Sa'id Hawwa and 'Adnan Sa'ed al-Din, that called for a civil uprising against the Asad regime. The plea included a fatwa by the Islamic nation's 'ulama' to overthrow the Ba'th, and a demand that Damascenes close their stores, the universities, schools and all public establishments, in support of the rebels.[107] Yet as we will see later, these pleas failed to provoke any real reactions in the other cities, even within the Sunni areas.[108] The government's campaign against the Islamists included allegations that the United States and other countries were supporting them. More particularly, the Ba'thi state asserted that the Western powers and their "reactionary" Arab allies – namely Iraq and Jordan – were behind the Islamists' scheme. At the time, Syria was fighting against the Israelis

---

102 Mayer, "The Islamic Opposition in Syria," pp. 598–9.
103 Seale, *Asad of Syria*, pp. 326–32; Abd-Allah, *The Islamic Struggle in Syria*, p. 110.
104 Daraj and Barut, *Al-ahzab wa al-harakat wa al-jama'at al-islamiya*, p. 299.
105 Ibid., pp. 298–301; Mayer, "The Islamic Opposition in Syria," p. 604; Matthew S. Gordon, *Hafez al-Assad*, New York and Philadelphia: Chelsea House Publishers, 1989, p. 16.
106 Mayer, "The Islamic Opposition in Syria," p. 604.
107 See Gordon, *Hafez al-Assad*, p. 18; and Mayer, "The Islamic Opposition in Syria," p. 605.
108 Daraj and Barut, *Al-ahzab wa al-harakat wa al-jama'at al-islamiya*, p. 301; Mayer, "The Islamic Opposition in Syria," p. 605; Hinnebusch, *Syria: Revolution from Above*, p. 101.

80 Hafez al-Asad's era

in Lebanon, and thus also declared the attacks to be part of a wider "Zionist and imperialist strategy"[109] to weaken Syria from within.[110]

In response to the rebels' actions, Rif'at al-Asad's Defence Companies besieged Hama. Helicopter gunships and armoured units shelled the city from a distance. Then several thousand Syrian troops and Special Forces supported by armour and artillery moved into the city and crushed the insurgents during two weeks of bloodshed.[111] When the fighting was over, thousands were dead, many of whom were not part of the Islamic movement; this total included an estimated 1,000 soldiers.[112] In addition, large sections of Hama's old city were left entirely in ruins. Importantly, the army remained loyal to the regime – as Hinnebusch writes, "[it] did not, with few exceptions, split or unravel along sectarian lines, even under the pressures of near sectarian civil war."[113]

The Hama battle very clearly demonstrated that, whether out of fear[114] or simply lack of support for the rebels' goals, a majority of Syrians would not mobilize in support of the Islamic Front, as well as that the regime had good control over the country's security services. The defeat forced the Islamists to flee the country, and to officially declare an alliance with other secular parties and leaders. This led to the establishment of the National Alliance for the Liberation of Syria (*al-Tahaluf al-Watani li-Tahrir Suriya*), which included the Islamic Front, the pro-Iraqi wing of the Ba'th Party, and other independent political figures. The new Charter of the Alliance had only one paragraph directly referring to Syria's Islamic nature, which 'Adnan 'Uqla considered to be a betrayal of the Islamic struggle. Because the country's Islamic movement was already beginning to transform into a neo-fundamentalist movement focused upon bottom-up social change as the necessary precursor to eventual political

---

109 Daraj and Barut, *Al-ahzab wa al-harakat wa al-jama'at al-islamiya*, p. 280.
110 See Mayer, "The Islamic Opposition in Syria," pp. 604–5; Daraj and Barut, *Al-ahzab wa al-harakat wa al-jama'at al-islamiya*, p. 296; See also interview with Asad in the *Observer*, 7 March 1982. Although Israel approved Syria's intervention in Lebanon in 1976 under the indirect, US-brokered "Red Line Agreement," starting in April 1981 Israel actively worked against the Syrian presence in Lebanon by backing Bashir Jemayyel and the Lebanese Phalangists, who had turned against the Syrians. For more on the 1981 crisis, see Rashid Khalidi, *Under Siege: PLO Decision-making during the 1982 War*, New York: Columbia University Press, 1986; Itamar Rabinovich, *The War for Lebanon*, Ithaca, NY: Cornell University Press, 1985; and Seale, *Asad of Syria*, pp. 278–89.
111 Drysdale, "The Asad Regime and Its Troubles," p. 9; Mayer, "The Islamic Opposition in Syria," p. 604. See also Seale, *Asad of Syria*, pp. 332–8.
112 Estimates of the number of dead ran from as low as several hundred to as high as 40,000. For the official Syrian version, see *al-Thawra*, 3 March 1982. For the Muslim Brotherhood version, see *Al-Liwa'*, 31 March 1982. The *Observer*, 9 May 1982, mentioned around 10,000 dead.
113 Hinnebusch, *Syria: Revolution from Above*, p. 101.
114 Mayer writes that "fear of retaliation and, perhaps, inadequate countrywide planning on the part of the Islamic Front, are not adequate explanations for the Sunni community's failure to join the revolutionaries." He explains that the Ba'thi elite – composed of both minorities and Sunnis – as well as liberal-minded Syrians were not attracted to the idea of an Iranian-style Islamic revolution. See Mayer, "The Islamic Opposition in Syria," p. 606.

change, the Front dismissed 'Uqla, while also accusing him of being solely responsible for the Hama tragedy. 'Uqla was replaced by Sa'id Hawwa as the military wing commander.[115]

5 Conclusion

The destruction of Hama and the general ruthlessness of al-Asad's response had a chastening effect on Syria's estimated 30,000 Muslim Brotherhood sympathizers.[116] Nonetheless, the government's killing of many innocent civilians during the course of the Hama confrontation served to crystallize Syrians' discontent with the regime, while also helping to spark an increased willingness to integrate the Muslim Brotherhood's vision of the social order.[117] This latter development prompted the political command to modify its governing strategy, in an attempt to create a new legitimizing formula for itself, so as to maintain its rule. In essence, this new strategy aimed to replace the Islamic anti-regime movement with an effective Islamic alternative and to accommodate a powerful religious bourgeoisie. It is to this strategy that we now turn.

---

115 Ibid., pp. 606–8.
116 Daraj and Barut, *Al-ahzab wa al-harakat wa al-jama'at al-islamiya*, p. 281.
117 This will be discussed in the following chapter. See Seale, *Asad of Syria*, pp. 320–1.

5 Resurgence of neo-fundamentalism and decline of political Islam as a model for change (1982–2000)

1 Introduction

In the wake of the Hama events, the credibility of the Syrian Islamic Front (SIF) was greatly weakened by its perceived anti-rural and anti-minoritarian discourse and its foreign connections. The Ba'th, by contrast, was seen as having enough of an indigenous national character and a broad base of support, due to its secular discourse as well as its populist and socialist policies. These deprived political Islam of its nationalist *raison d'être* and a significant recruitment pool, and made it possible for the Ba'th to maintain control over the political scene. At the same time, however, the Hama events and the regime's response significantly eroded its popularity and legitimacy, by underlining just how far it was willing to go to remain in power. They also gave credence to the Muslim Brothers' accusations against the Ba'th regime, and ignited a grassroots-driven revival of religious sensibilities. Indeed, the 1980s were not an easy time for Hafez al-Asad and the Ba'th. The memory of the 1976 intervention in Lebanon and the bloody conflict with the SIF still haunted the command. Domestically, Syrians were indifferent about Syria's growing regional and international role, or that Israel decided unilaterally to evacuate Lebanon on 14 January 1985 while the Syrians stayed.

These factors prompted the political command to try to create a new legitimizing formula for itself, as well as to replace the tarnished Ba'thist dogma. This involved attempts to co-opt the opposition and to pre-empt future Islamic mobilization – and hence to quell the remnants of revolutionary Islam – all without resorting to political liberalization. More particularly, the regime moved to establish tighter state–society relations that encompassed both *control* and *co-optation* of the religious class. Thus, as the militant opposition was being quelled, the state was also creating a state that presided over a strong, centralized, regulatory government and bureaucracy which would provide the Ba'th with significant power.

The focus on generating a new legitimizing formula was mainly due to the political command's recognition that the traditional quarters' autonomous economic base and pervasive religious sensibility had proven very resistant to state penetration, this despite the state's outreach efforts and its various attempts to uproot the threat posed by the Islamic opposition. Thus the new approach aimed at blurring the borders between state and society, and thereby transforming the conflict from one between a corrupt and authoritarian clique and Sunni Islam to one between official moderate Islam and a revolutionary, de-stabilizing and radical Islam. For this strategy to be effective, it had to cover all aspects of state–society relations, that is, the ideological, institutional and economic components. More precisely, the new strategy would involve:

1   on an ideological level, increasing disregard for the secular principles of the Ba'th ideology and a re-appropriation of the religious message;
2   on a corporatist and institutional level, the creation of new alliances and institutions to broaden the regime's social base of support beyond its traditional core;
3   on an economic level, a relaxation of Syria's populist stance through selective economic liberalization;
4   the use of regional Islamist groups in order to assert Syria's Arabist and nationalist credentials while influencing regional realities.

In detailing and analysing these transformations over the following chapter, it will become clear that while they were aimed at controlling possible targets of outreach, they ended up creating a new dynamic of state–society relations and interactions.

2   Control and the blurring of borders between the state and society

Before the state could engage in its co-opting transformations, it had to first dismantle the institutions, or at least parts of certain institutions, which provided the opposition its organizational space and that shielded it from state control for as long as it did. Thus, the state unleashed a number of significant repressive measures against the institutions of the dissenting Islamic establishment. For instance, in September 1979, around 500 primary and secondary school teachers and dozens of university professors who were suspected of teaching pro-Muslim Brotherhood ideas in their classes were dismissed from their jobs.[1] At the same time, according to *al-Nadhir*, others were physically eliminated.[2]

The National Progressive Front was also affected by the regime's iron fist, as a result of a communiqué the Front published on 26 September 1979. The communiqué, which circulated throughout all of Syria, was a detailed indictment of the domestic situation in all its aspects. Thus it discussed the wave of corruption that had invaded the country, the inefficiency of the bureaucratic apparatus, the economic crisis, the absence of individual freedoms, the lack of justice in

---

1   Michel Seurat, *L'Etat de barbarie*, Paris: Collection Esprit/Seuil, 1989, pp. 78–9.
2   Umar F. Abd-Allah, *The Islamic Struggle in Syria*, Berkeley, CA: Mizan Press, 1983, pp. 112–13.

the justice system and the lack of a democratic political life. As explained by Michel Seurat, nothing was held back by the National Front, which even went so far as to demand the punishment of offenders and a reinforcement of vital institutions such as the People's Assembly and the Ministry Council. Following the publication of the communiqué, 52 bureaucrats were arrested. In the words of Seurat:

> It was a political event of considerable importance ... all of these events contributed to the maintenance of a strange, "end of an era" atmosphere in the capital's political circles ... people are acting as if the regime will be overthrown tomorrow.[3]

As a result of the general atmosphere of crisis surrounding the state, the Ba'th opted during its Extraordinary Seventh Regional Congress of December 1979 for "continuity" rather than a widening of the circle of power through an expansion of the National Progressive Front. At the same time, Rif'at al-Asad, the Commander of the Defence Companies and the leader of the Ba'th Party hardliners, vowed that he was ready to do anything that was necessary to restore peace.[4] It was to be less than six months later that Rif'at's assertions became concrete actions. As explained earlier, the summer of 1979 was anything but uneventful. The Syrian *Mukhabarat* often ventured into the smaller alleyways of Syria's northern cities accompanied by an impressive military armada, and it faced a number of armed attacks in the three major cities, including in Damascus. An autumn 1979 attack on an office of the *Mukhabarat* in which 14 members were killed prompted the government to arrest the shaykh of the Grand Mosque, Zeyn al-Din Khayrallah, whose brother was none other than Husni Abo, the military Commander of the Muslim Brothers in the Aleppo region who had recently been executed.[5] Later, following the attempt on Asad's life in July 1980, even Shadhili shaykhs were executed at the Palmyra prison.[6]

Yet the regime still felt that it needed to impose more state control over civil society. In particular, it targeted the professional syndicates, which it had failed to co-opt in the 1970s and which still enjoyed a large degree of independence compared to the rest of Syria's popular organizations. This targeting of the professional syndicates was due to their general defiance in Aleppo and Hama, and because of their calls for political reforms and their reporting of the regime's human rights abuses.[7] Thus the Professional Executive Councils were dissolved on 14 April 1980, despite the Muslim Brotherhood's negotiations with the Asad state and the government's promise to leave them intact. The state also detained a still undetermined number of the associations' leaders, executing a few of them

---

3 Ibid., p. 80.
4 Patrick Seale, *Asad of Syria: The Struggle for the Middle East*, London: I.B. Tauris, 1988, p. 327.
5 Ibid., p. 73.
6 Abd-Allah, *The Islamic Struggle in Syria*, pp. 84–5.
7 Bassel Salloukh, "Organizing Politics in the Arab World: State–Society Relations and Foreign Policy Choices in Jordan and Syria," McGill University: PhD thesis, 2000, p. 276.

without trial, while others fled the country.[8] Human rights activists from within the lawyers' syndicate were also detained without public trial, the closed in-camera trials were conducted with no one in the public sure of who was being detained and for how long. This marked the end of an autonomous civil society in Syria under the Baʿth.

The early 1980s also saw the state undertake a mass purging of religious associations, mosques and shari'a schools, eliminating these as training grounds for activism. Furthermore, a number of prominent Sufi *zawiya* shaykhs were found dead between 1980 and 1983 according to a number of people who witnessed the events first-hand (although no one was sure who was behind the assassinations).[9] The state even subjected all remaining religious institutions to state control and policing, thus depriving the Brotherhood of its main sites of outreach and ideological framing.

These serious efforts to uproot the threat posed by political Islam proved successful overall. Yet the traditional quarters' autonomous economic base and pervasive religious sensibility still proved resistant to state penetration.[10] Faced with this situation, aware of how the Muslim Brotherhood had created a new political space in Syrian society and unwilling to entertain the idea of making real political concessions, the regime was forced to re-visit its domestic stance towards Islam and the bourgeois class. This is the subject of the following section.

3 Co-optation, compromise and the muting of secularism

Motivated by a desire to control the public arena and an awareness of the nuance between the different Islamic actors, the Syrian state sought to replace the Muslim Brotherhood movement with an effective alternative that would close the void left by the state's dismantling intervention.[11] It also sought to extend its economic favours to a larger base, in an attempt to control possible sites and targets of outreach.[12] These objectives necessitated a shift away from a "statizing" or "étatist"

---

8 Alasdair Drysdale, "The Asad Regime and Its Troubles," *MERIP Reports*, November–December, 1982, p. 8.
9 Personal interviews, Damascus, April 2008.
10 Ibid., p. 231.
11 On Islamization from below, see Anabelle Böttcher, "Islamic Teaching among Sunni Women in Syria," in Donna Lee Bowen and Evelyn A. Early, eds, *Everyday Life in the Muslim Middle East*, Bloomington and Indianapolis: Indiana University Press, 2002; idem, *Official Sunni and Shi'i Islam in Syria*, Florence: European University Institute, 2002; see also Joshua Landis, "Islamic Education in Syria: Undoing Secularism?" in Eleanor Doumato and Gregory Starrett, eds, *Teaching Islam: Textbooks and Religion in the Middle East*, Boulder, CO: Lynne Rienner Publishers, 2007, pp. 177–96.
12 Sadowski analysed the use of patronage to co-opt elites and create a loyalty network in Yahya Sadowski, "Bathist Ethics and the Spirit of State Capitalism: Patronage in Contemporary Syria," in Peter J. Chelkowski and Robert Pranger, eds, *Ideology and Power in the Middle East*, Durham, NC: Duke University Press, 1988, pp. 160–84. Similarly, Heydemann explained how the co-optation of the social masses ensured the Baʿth's consolidation of power; see Steven Heydemann, *Authoritarianism in Syria: Institutions and Social Conflict*, Ithaca, NY: Cornell University Press, 1999.

approach to populist corporatism, in favour of a "privatist" approach that would involve economic, corporatist, institutional and ideological factors.[13] Concretely, this meant opening up the state's institutions to the private interests of the allies needed by the regime's coalition (economic factor), with the aim of inoculating the possible targets of the Islamic opposition against the Islamists' anti-regime message (corporatist factor), and also of initiating a political broadening of the regime's coalition to include the "religious class."[14] This latter point meant that there was a need to engage in "Muslim politics," which is explained by Piscatori and Eickelman as imagining politics in a way to compete and contest "over both the interpretation of symbols and the control of institutions, both formal and informal, that produce and sustain them"[15] (the institutional and ideological factors). The regime's action plan for incorporating the Islamic threat into its economic strategy and thereby contributing to the creation of a new legitimizing formula is examined more explicitly hereinafter.

A Tightening of state–society relations and creation of new alliances

The state's confrontation with the Islamists was made easier by changes to the various classes in Syrian society. By the late 1970s, the bourgeoisie had declined from 6.7 per cent to 1.3 per cent of the population, both because of the state's corporatist policies that stripped the class of its wealth and because of large numbers from the class exiting the country. At the same time, however, the salaried middle class and the state-dependent small-holding peasantry expanded significantly, from 42.4 per cent of the population in 1960 to 57.5 per cent in 1970. This allowed the political command to create an autonomous "Bonapartist state" capable of "balancing above Syria's fluidized classes and largely invulnerable to countervailing class power."[16]

In assuming a position above the classes, the state felt that it could recommence its efforts to shift from being an instrument of class revolution and social levelling to being a machinery of power concerned with the service of the *raison d'état*. In effecting this shift while guarding against possible challenges, the corporatist configuration in state–society relations had to be tightened. Nationalism was also to be accentuated, through increased indoctrination of the masses via the creation of youth brigades collectively called the Revolutionary Youth Federation (*Ittihad Shabibat al-Thawra*), whose main purpose was to "defend the revolution" and to

---

13 Guillermo O'Donnell, "Corporatism and the Question of the State," in James M. Malloy, ed., *Authoritarianism and Corporatism in Latin America*, Pittsburgh: University of Pittsburgh Press, 1977, p. 64.
14 These factors will be discussed in further detail in the following section.
15 Dale F. Eickelman and James P. Piscatori, *Muslim Politics*, Princeton, NJ: Princeton University Press, 1996, p. 5.
16 Raymond A. Hinnebusch, "Calculated Decompression as a Substitute for Democratization: Syria," in Bahgat Korany *et al.*, eds, *Political Liberalization and Democratization in the Arab World: Comparative Experiences*, vol. 2, Boulder, CO and London: Lynne Rienner Publishers, 1998, p. 226.

act as a special recruiting auxiliary to the party. At the same time, the general federation of the peasants (*al-Ittihad al-'Amm lil-Falahin*), as well as those of women, traders, artisans and students, were all re-organized and their organizations restructured and directly linked to the Ba'th Party.[17] According to Bassel Salloukh:

> The aims of attempts at organizing state–society relations, populist-corporatist or otherwise, then, is to blur, if not eliminate, "the horizon of options" available to opposition groups, and ensure in the words of Adam Przeworski, "the absence of preferable [or more accurately, viable] alternatives" to existing ruling regimes.[18]

These various efforts by the state meant that the 1963 configuration of organizations co-ordinating workers, peasants, youth, students, artisans and women (in addition to all public-sector employees), which had been aimed at indoctrinating, including and empowering these groups, was now being used to demobilize the masses to serve the raison d'état.[19] At the same time, the professionals and their associations remained very much autonomous from the regime, despite President Asad's commitment to their being centrally controlled This situation was an outgrowth of the Ba'th's lack of success at having its own members democratically penetrate the organizations in significant numbers, which underlined that before co-optation would be feasible, the syndicates' autonomy had to be curtailed.[20] The most effective way to accomplish this seemed to be to change their organizational structure – hence the regime launched a swift show of force and completely dismantled them, and then "corporatized [the syndicates] under the direct supervision of the Ba'th Party Professional Syndicates' Regional Bureau (*Maktab al-Naqabat al-Mihaniya al-Qutri*)."[21] Very soon afterwards, the National Progressive Front was expanded beyond the seven parties that initially made it up, to also include the leaders of the popular and professional organizations.[22]

In addition to now being in control of the professional organizations, the regime was also directly in control of a good proportion of the working population, by virtue of the fact that by the mid-1980s, almost 40 per cent of

---

17 Mahmud Sadeq, *Hiwar Hawla Suriya*, London: Dar 'Uqadh, 1993, pp. 111–12.
18 Salloukh, "Organizing Politics in the Arab World," p. 48. Also Adam Przewoski, "Some Problems in the Study of the Transition towards Democracy," in Guillermo O'Donnell *et al.*, eds, *Transition from Authoritarian Rule: Comparative Perspectives*, Baltimore: Johns Hopkins University Press, 1986, p. 52.
19 Sadeq, *Hiwar Hawla Suriya*, p. 112.
20 For more on the regime's dismantling of the Syrian civil society of the early 1960s and the creation of a *mujtama' mudad* (an opposing society), see Sadeq, *Hiwar Hawla Suriya*, pp. 83–90 and 111–12.
21 Salloukh, "Organizing Politics in the Arab World," p. 278.
22 Hafez al-Asad often addressed this issue of political democratization by stating that "anyone who wanted despotism would not have created a structure organizing peasants, women, youth, students, professionals, and expanding the trade unions." See Hinnebusch, "Calculated Decompression," p. 224.

Syrians worked for the state. This included large numbers who were part of the personal entourages of the regime's leaders and chief allies – for instance, the president alone had about 12,000 personal guards, while even such relatively minor figures as Faysal Dayub, dean of the dentistry school, and As'ad 'Ali, a literature professor at Damascus University and a Ba'th apologist, each had four guards.[23] To take another example, a small town called al-Hifa in the Latakia district had about 1,900 adult male residents, of whom around 550 were intelligence officers and Ba'thist informants. This meant that about one in four men were not just part of the Ba'th's political bureau, but were members of its security apparatus. Mahmud Sadeq explains that

> those working in the service of the [Ba'thist] apparatus are an essential instrument in the service of the "opposing civil society," [since] they occupy the lowest level of its pyramid, they form an important part of its political and social broad basis and are key intermediaries between society and the [Ba'thist] leadership.[24]

Sadeq concludes that these men and women have become stalwarts of the political class, and have forgotten that they were once at the heart of an active civil as well as political society.[25]

Yet while Hafez al-Asad's regime controlled all levels of institutional power – the army, the party and the state, as well as the many corporatist organizations – it nonetheless felt compelled to do more than simply tame the independent professional organizations. Indeed, it aimed for nothing less than to monitor and restrain all possible opposition. And a prominent part of this effort involved attracting the religious class by muting secularism.

B Manufacturing consent through the religious and the portrayal of the Muslim Brotherhood as an enemy of moderate Islam

Other than creating a broader social base of support, the regime's strategy for dealing with the Islamic threat involved a set of tactics that included a re-appropriation of religious institutions and messages, building of new Islamic institutions, muting of Ba'thist secularism, the mechanical inclusion of the 'Alawi sect under the rubric of Islam and a re-orientation of the conflict from one pitting the state against the religious class to one pitting moderate Muslims against radical Islamists. The regime now purportedly sat on the sidelines and appeared no longer to play a role in the conflict, as we will see hereinafter.

The earlier chapters of this work argued that the *suq*s (bazaars) and the urban quarters were still able to express themselves politically via Syria's traditional

---

23 Seurat, *L'Etat de barbarie*, p. 87.
24 Sadeq, *Hiwar hawla Suriya*, p. 112.
25 Ibid., p. 115.

Islamic movement, despite the fact that religious institutions and the commercial economy had been hurt by the Baʿth. Indeed, by using religious institutions such as the mosques and the *zawiyas*, the religious class had retained enough autonomy to pose a significant threat to the regime. It was with an eye to this that one of the first moves in the effort to blur the lines between the state apparatus and the traditional powerful institutions was to change the relationship between the state and Islam in the social public sphere. This involved the regime definitively moving away from aggressive secularization and promotion of atheism while simultaneously modernizing and constructing new religious institutions, which enabled it to gain a better grip over the community and to break down the barriers separating the state from the religious society.

Yet while these moves by the state were significant, it is nonetheless important to underline that it had been taking tentative steps away from its original articulation of secularism since the early 1970s. This involved a move from a version of secularism that is essentially anti-faith to one that accepts faith as part of its public space. It began with Hafez al-Asad's constitutional compromise in the early 1970s (see Chapter 2), and was concretely experienced as a muting of atheist and secular voices in the country, as well as a willingness to accept religiosity as being at the heart of self-definition, and also as part of the political sphere. This meant, for instance, that throughout the 1970s, Zaki al-Arsuzi's books that were critical of religion were taken off the shelves, and that self-declared atheist writers were asked to respect the sensibilities of Muslim believers. According to Hinnebusch, by "muting the secularism of his predecessors, he [Asad] tried to portray himself as a pious Muslim, re-introduced abolished religious formulas into public ceremonies, and cultivated the ulama' with honours and higher salaries."[26]

The regime's strong post-Hama interest in de-emphasizing secularism and atheism emerged very clearly in a symbolic letter by the leader of the Hama Baʿth Party that was published in the party's newspaper. The letter offered an account of the incidents of February 1982, and concluded by affirming the Baʿth's loyalty to Asad and to God. Lisa Wedeen writes that "[t]he avowedly secular regime, in the face of the Muslim Brotherhood's challenge, found that it too had to pay lip service to God. God, in turn, sided with the Baʿth."[27] By allying itself with God, the Baʿth was seeking to create a legitimizing formula for itself that would also build a bridge to the religious masses.

At the same time as it was linking itself to religion, the Asad regime worked to produce a new Islam that would be dependent on, and thus loyal to, the regime. This project involved re-framing the conflict in a manner that did not just take the regime out of the formula, but that in fact legitimized the state and helped to discredit any current or future Islamic group that was unwilling to join

---

26 Raymond A. Hinnebusch, "The Islamic Movement in Syria: Sectarian Conflict and Urban Rebellion in an Authoritarian-Populist Regime," in Ali E. Hillal Dessouki, ed., *Islamic Resurgence in the Arab World*, New York: Praeger, 1982, p. 161.
27 Lisa Wedeen, *Ambiguities of Domination*, Chicago: University of Chicago Press, 1999, p. 47.

the state–Islam alliance. Thus the Asad command began to actively court, sponsor and institutionalize alternative Islamic groups that were willing to play along with its political game. Over time, two groups emerged as particularly prominent: the Naqshbandi Kuftariya Sufi order under Shaykh Ahmad Kuftaro, and Shaykh Sa'id al-Buti's group, both of which expanded dramatically in the 1970s.[28]

Generally speaking, the Islamic groups that collaborated with the regime were encouraged to recruit members, to spread their religious message and to infiltrate the lives and minds of the masses through television programmes, the radio and the media in general. In return for this support, the shaykhs were expected to act as religious intermediaries between the state and the public and ensure that religious expression, teaching and practice were channelled through state-monitored institutions.[29] By co-opting Sunni shaykhs such as Ahmad Kuftaro and Sa'id al-Buti, the regime was effectively giving birth to its own Islamic revivalism, one that was meant to effect a rapprochement with Syria's religious masses and to fill the gap left by the destruction of the Muslim Brotherhood, all without resorting to political liberalization.[30] In order to make these goals possible, the government constructed around 8,000 new mosques throughout the 1970s, 1980s and 1990s, established around two dozen institutes of Islamic higher education and developed some 600 quasi-official religious institutions in all Syrian governorates and cities to replace those that had been used by the Muslim Brotherhood for recruitment. For instance, Shaykh Kuftaro's headquarters, Abu al-Nur mosque, was inaugurated in 1971. Within Abu al-Nur trust, *Ma'had al-Da'wa wa al-Irshad*, an Islamic reformist secondary school was founded in 1982 at the height of the Islamist uprising. Moreover, Abu al-Nur foundation has become part of a network of universities in the Muslim world such as in Libya, Pakistan and Sudan.

One of the most prominent institutions created by the regime was the Asad Institute for Memorizing the Quran, which had 120 branches in most Syrian cities and governorates, and was initially headed by then-State Mufti Muhammad Kuftaru and the minister of *Awqaf* (Religious Endowments).[31] The institute

---

28 The Naqshbandi Kuftariya order and the rest of Syria's Sufi Sunni orders, and their ideology and outreach methods, will be examined in Part III of this work. It is important to note here that Sufi orders are tightly knit networks due to the pyramidal structure of their chains of command.
29 See Böttcher, *Official Sunni and Shi'i Islam in Syria*, pp. 4–5.
30 Furthermore, the Damascus regime felt it important to face the rising religious influence from the Gulf region. It was in 1962 that the Muslim World League was created in Mecca to "wahhabize" Islam worldwide and to counter the influence of secular nationalistic movements in the Arab world, especially that of Nasser. One of the purposes of 9/11 was, according to Gilles Kepel, to mobilize the support of Muslims and to arouse emotional sympathy. As a result Syria has had a significant interest in creating Islamic alternatives to elsewhere in the Arab World. It has done so by creating around 600 Islamic institutes mainly in Damascus and Aleppo, where both Syrian and foreign students come to study. These institutes are mainly Sufi-oriented. The process of creation of an alternative to the radical Salafi trend is still operational today, as will be shown hereinafter.
31 *Al-Hayat*, 18 June 2005.

was staffed by government-appointed preachers and several shari'a professors from the universities of Damascus and Aleppo, who were in turn supervised by the authorities and in particular by the Ministry of *Awqaf* "to prevent radical infiltrations."[32] Other institutes such as the Faculty of Islamic Mission, the Lebanese Open Faculty of Islamic Studies, the Islamic University of Pakistan and the Sudanese Faculty of the Pillars of Faith were allowed to open in Syria during the period.[33]

The regime also sought to counter the effects of *al-Nadhir*, the clandestine newspaper published by the Muslim Brothers, by allowing religious scholars that were part of the country's Ministry of *Awqaf* to publish an Islamic newspaper, *Nahj al-Islam* (the Trail of Islam). This move away from enforcing an entirely secular media landscape as part of a sort of Islamic revivalism was not an isolated incident. For instance, a Quran recital show was allowed to air at 4 p.m. every day on the national channel, during which preachers would read passages from the Quran. Children who would tune in to watch their afternoon cartoons often caught the tail-end of this strategically scheduled programme. Popular Quranic shows were also aired on a weekly basis, of which the most prominent was Shaykh Sa'id al-Buti's programme. The fact that al-Buti was given the space to undertake this programme was a reflection of his service to the regime, as well as its approval of his stressing the apolitical and ethical nature of Islam, a stance that makes him the epitome of the neo-fundamentalist movement.[34] Al-Buti's service to the political command included intervening as an Islamic *'alim* and legitimator of it at key moments in the 1970s and 1980s, playing a vital role during the 1980s and 1990s in creating a religious Sunni community outside the traditional quarters of the cities and in allying it with the state, and helping to bridge the gap between the religious element in the Syrian Kurdish community and the state.[35] These various acts meant that he was the only Syrian preacher allowed to appear regularly on television and on radio, and was allowed to

32 Sami Moubayed, "The Islamic Revival in Syria," *Mideast Monitor* 1(3), September–October 2006. Online: www.mideastmonitor.org/issues/0609/0609_4.htm.
33 See Böttcher, *Official Sunni and Shi'i Islam in Syria*, p. 9. See also Leif Stenberg, "Naqshbandi-yya in Damascus: Strategies to Establish and Strengthen the Order in a Changing Society," in Elisabeth Özdalga, ed., *Naqshbandis in Western and Central Asia: Change and Continuity*, Istanbul: Swedish Research Institute in Istanbul, 1999, pp. 101–16.
34 See Muhammad Sa'id Ramadan al-Buti, *al-Ta'aruf 'ala al-Dhat Huwa al-Tariq ila al-Islam*, Damascus: Dar al-Fikr, 2009. Apoliticalism and a focus on the moral reform of the individual within Syria's current revivalist groups, including al-Buti's and Kuftaro's, are discussed in Chapter 7 of this study.
35 These interventions included opposing the attacks on government and Ba'th officials, as well as on 'Alawis, in the 1970s; condemning the killing of 83 'Alawi cadets on television, at the request of the Ministry of Information; giving a speech that was patronized by President Asad at the peak of the regime–Brotherhood violence in 1982; and thanking the "hidden hand" of President Asad for the repeal of censorship on Islamic publications and broadcasts, as well as the legalization of wearing the hijab in state institutions. See Andreas Christmann, "Islamic Scholar and Religious Leader: of Shaykh Muhammad Sai'd Ramadan al-Buti," *Islam and Christian Muslim Relations* 9(2), 1998, p. 149.

publish several dozen books and polemical pamphlets, as well as speak to hundreds of people at his Friday sermons in the Mawlana al-Rifaʻi Mosque and at his lectures held twice a week at the Tinjiz Mosque.[36]

In addition to allowing figures such as al-Buti and Ahmad Kuftaro their organizational and *da'wa* space, the Syrian political command also introduced profound changes to the relationship between Islamic groups and the state. There are a variety of reasons for why these Islamic groups – nearly all of which were Sufi – agreed to conform to this new relationship. Most obvious is the threat from, and destructive power of, the state in case of a refusal to conform. There was also the generalized fear in the country's Sufi communities of the rising star of Salafi Islam, which is considered foreign to *bilad al-Sham* (greater Syria) – and which would be easier to resist if they continued to exist on the one hand, and with the power of the state behind them on the other hand

At the same time, the regime's muting of its secularist discourse and its decision to allow the public expression of Islamic symbols and traditions such as the veil and going to the mosque for prayer made compromise much easier to rationalize. Indeed, the regime's acceptance of public religiosity was such that by the early 1990s, so many people would show up for Friday prayers that parked cars would entirely block the alleyways around mosques in Damascus. More directly, co-operative shaykhs received favours from the state that ranged from facilitating their official documentation to giving them permits to collect private donations, with the government even donating state land to build new religious buildings or mosques.[37]

The new alliances between the regime and certain Islamic groups made it possible for the former to achieve multiple goals at one time: first, it secured a larger base of support that included urban Syrians and Damascene Sunnis; second, it gained long-term political control over the messages of the shaykhs, and hence of the attendees at the *zawiyas* and mosques; third, the alliances created an environment of mutual suspicion and thus created some divisions between the religious shaykhs and businessmen, because of the fact that both were co-opted by the state; and finally, they helped to blur the borders between state and society.

The alliances also have had negative consequences for the political command. Most prominently, they created Islamized spaces that are largely devoid of clear organizational structures, a mix of formal and informal micro-societies that are very difficult to contain and control if infiltrated by radical elements (see Part III of this work for more on these Islamized spaces).

The 1990s were the peak of the regime's co-optation of, and compromises with, the religious community. Formal attempts at reconciliation included the release from prison of a number of members of the Islamic Front, i.e. the Muslim

---

36 Ibid., p. 149.
37 Paulo Pinto, "Dangerous Liaisons: Sufism and the State in Syria," in S. Jakelic and J. Varsoke, eds, *Crossing Boundaries: From Syria to Slovakia*, Vienna: IWM Junior Visiting Fellows' Conferences, Vol. 14, 2003, p. 7.

Brotherhood, as well as allowing some other members to return from exile, including 'Abdul Fatah Abu Ghudda and Abu Fateh Bayanuni.[38] Talhami explains that,

> [i]mmediately following his [Abu Fateh] return, it became clear that he was part of a move to create a Communist intellectual-Islamist front against the Asad government. Surprisingly, the administration cracked down on the Communist party, re-arresting its leader, Riyad al-Turk, but not on the Islamic leaders. According to some analysts, al-Bayanuni's return was a calculated move by the regime in order to deepen divisions within the Muslim Brotherhood resulting from this tactical shift favouring reconciliation with Syria's leftists and communists. The Muslim Brotherhood, it seems, is still incapable of mounting an exclusive campaign against the government.[39]

Another experiment at accommodation in the early 1990s saw the regime concede that *al-Ta'addudiya al-Siyasiya* (political pluralism) should be reinforced. This led to it experimenting with a tentative expansion of the political system to include "safety-valves." Thus the 1990 parliamentary elections were opened to independent candidates representing business people, religious leaders and professionals, and a number of prominent clerics and religious figures even won a few seats in the National Assembly (though these were not opponents of the regime). According to Hinnebusch, this opening "signified the legitimation of interests outside the regime's original coalition and the government's desire to incorporate the more complex social coalition it [was] putting together."[40]

While some observers argued that this represented a relaxation of state control over society, it is important to also recognize its usefulness as a co-optation tactic. Indeed the limited *Ta'addudiya* (pluralism) and the new array of corporatist associations that it gave birth to linked the Ba'th even more closely to Syrian society, putting around 60 per cent of the population under the party's direct control and within its zone of influence. It also gave these Syrians a tangible measure of social power and state access and thus an interest in maintaining the status quo, which would prove to be a major block on the Muslim Brothers' ability to effectively practise mass recruitment.

A final element in the political command's efforts to control the Sunni religious community was to bring the country's 'Alawis closer to the Islamic mainstream, by strengthening the ties that linked them religiously to the Shi'i sect, and hence dismiss accusations that 'Alawis are heretics. Thus hundreds of *Hawzas* and *Husseiniyats* were built, financed and supervised by Iran,[41] and

---

38 He was allowed to return to Aleppo from Saudi Arabia and resume his religious activities.
39 Ghada Hashem Talhami, "Syria: Islam, Arab Nationalism and the Military in Syria," *Middle East Policy* 8(4), December 2001: 125.
40 Hinnebusch, "Calculated Decompression," p. 225.
41 Iran has the biggest Shi'i population in the Muslim world.

thousands of Iranian clerics were allowed into Syria to act as teachers and guides to the 'Alawi community. Although this did not seem to convince pious Sunnis that the 'Alawis were Muslims, it did at least serve one main political purpose: the creation of a Shi'i axis stretching from Lebanon to the Pakistani border that had the potential, in the long term, to help maintain the regime's power against foreign foes such as Saudi Arabia, and to maintain its superiority over any resurgent form of Islamist activity, given its powerful regional alliances.[42]

C Reaching a modus vivendi with the bourgeoisie: economically rewarding patronage networks and re-invigoration of the private sector

The regime did not stop at re-creating loyal popular and professional associations, improving its image with the religious class and re-making Islam to fit its own modernizing agenda. It also aspired to reach an economic *modus vivendi* with the Syrian bourgeoisie, in light of the latter's traditional rapport with the religious class and the fact that they had maintained their economic power despite the regime's populist policies that aimed to reduce it.

Generally speaking, the 1970s were a period of sustained economic growth. The decade also saw the public sector become the core of the economy, which gave the state a reasonable amount of independence from the bourgeoisie. Yet, as Hinnebusch explains, the public sector did not become an engine of capital accumulation powerful enough to uphold the state's many commitments. Moreover, public investment efficiency worsened throughout the 1970s, such that public sector surpluses were able to finance only 54 per cent of the ambitious fourth five year plan (1976–1980).[43] The impacts of this economic shortfall were compounded by the fact that the solidarities of religious and traditional merchant families had survived the regime's populist mobilization and its tight social control, which meant that they were able to continue to support the Muslim Brothers' actions against the political apparatus. As a result, a relaxation of Syria's populist authoritarianism and a selective re-invigoration of the private sector were necessary, particularly once the 1980s economic recession began to bite. This meant that in addition to the regime's deployment of corporatist programmes aimed at securing the support of the rural masses and the salaried middle class, there was a need to expand the use

---

42 Regionally, it allowed Asad to re-negotiate Syria's role and her relations to neighbouring Gulf States, but this is outside the scope of this study.
43 Raymond A. Hinnebusch, "The Political Economy of Economic Liberalization in Syria," *International Journal of Middle East Studies* 27(3), August 1995: 305–10. See also *idem*, "Syria: The Politics of Economic Liberalization," *Third World Quarterly* 18(2), 1997: 249–65; and Steven Heydemann, "The Political Logic of Economic Rationality: Selective Stabilization in Syria," in Henri J. Barkey, ed., *The Politics of Economic Reform in the Middle East*, New York: St Martin's Press, 1992, pp. 11–39.

of patronage networks so as to bind businessmen and the ever-increasing number of small merchants to the Asad regime and thereby to tame the opposition once and for all.[44]

To accomplish this while maintaining the support of the rural and salaried classes, a sort of precocious Keynesianism was deployed. In 1980, the fifth five year plan allocated 30 per cent of all government investments to rural services; government employees were given pay raises ranging from 10 to 75 per cent; there was a tightening of the system of price controls; more land was distributed to peasants; food and medical subsidies were increased; and grants to university students were increased to US$150 per capita, a sum equivalent to all revenues earned from oil exports that year broken down on a per capita basis.[45] Rural programmes such as the building of the Tabaqa Dam, improvement of farm technology and the extension of electricity and credit facilities to rural areas proved to be not only economically sound, but politically sound as well given that the support of the rural masses was crucial in the fight against the Muslim Brotherhood.

Another area of concern for the regime was the ongoing discontent of the Sunni old bourgeoisie, who had lost their power to the new emerging classes. As stated in the previous two chapters, these groups' main political expression was through the Islamic movement, which they supported faithfully. Yet the regime's ability to address their concerns with state investments was severely limited by the austerity measures that were introduced in the late 1970s and early 1980s. It thus had to tame the potential Islamic opposition by retreating its protracted class war with the bourgeoisie. This involved a two-pronged action plan: détente through the formation of clientelistic business alliances with the Sunni Damascene elite,[46] and the integration of Syria's Sufi shaykhs into this clientelistic network controlled by the state.

It was during the Eighth Regional Congress of the Syrian Ba'th that the first part of the plan took shape, in the form of a tentative and selective economic liberalization. But the relaxation of state controls over the economy was not matched by political liberalization.[47] This meant that patronage networks, bribery, fraud and other related illegal, informal practices became even more widespread under the Asad regime. Sadowski explains that "[e]xtensive abuse of

---

44 Important to say here that, while products such as sugar and rice were efficiently subsidized by the state, powerful Ba'thist members would buy large amounts of these low-priced goods and sell them at much higher prices in the free market of Lebanon. Of course, access to Lebanese market and getting these products across the Syrian–Lebanese border was sanctioned by the military lords that governed these borders. Meanwhile, the middle class and the impoverished in Syria often struggled to have access to certain products due to the resulting shortages in the Syrian market – otherwise more than self-sufficient.
45 David Waldner, *State Building and Late Development*, Ithaca, NY: Cornell University Press, 1999, p. 121.
46 See Volker Perthes, *Political Economy of Syria under Asad*, London: I.B. Tauris, 1995.
47 Yahya M. Sadowski, "Cadres, Guns, and Money: The Eight Regional Congress of the Syrian Ba'th," *MERIP Reports* 134, July–August 1985: 3–8.

patronage helped the Muslim Brotherhood to build a following, lending credibility to its charge that national resources were being squandered to benefit a privileged 'Alawi' minority."[48] Interestingly, the attempts in the mid-1970s to quell some of the patronage abuses and to limit corruption were actually reversed in the late 1970s and early 1980s, in an effort to secure the regime's broad base of support in the face of the Muslim Brotherhood's escalated attacks.[49] This led to the creation of a "state bourgeoisie," which took shape through the tendering of state contracts that were offered to anyone willing to join the military–mercantile nexus of power. As a result, "the former antagonism between the state and the private bourgeoisie gradually declined."[50]

The 1980s and 1990s proved to be a challenge financially for Syria. It suffered from an over-inflated bureaucracy that could not be supported by the country's economic base, widespread corruption and a growing population, set against a backdrop of declining Arab aid and petro-money, which taken together led to a combination of stagflation and a shrinking economy. As a result, the populist Ba'th that had once pledged to liquidate the old societal values of a "backward bourgeois society"[51] by encouraging developmental programmes could no longer uphold its statist ideology. Law 186 was approved in 1986, and provided for the creation of financial institutions as well as for tax and border control exemptions for tourist projects. That same year, legislative decree number 10 allowed for the creation of private companies, to help the government deal with the agricultural crisis. In 1991, Laws 10 and 20 made it easier to privately invest in nearly all sectors of the Syrian economy, offered a number of fiscal incentives to private companies and new entrepreneurs, reduced business taxes and removed provisions that penalized business profit.[52] International companies jumped at the opportunity to invest in Syria, with Adidas, Benetton and Naf Naf (to name only a few) opening their first shops in the country's bigger cities. This trend continued right to the end of President Hafez al-Asad's reign, with his final significant economic measure in April 2000 involving the dilution of the Economic Security Court (*Mahkamat al-Amn al-Iqtisadiya*), which is responsible for looking into economic crimes "against the people."

48 Ibid., p. 7.
49 Ibid.
50 Hinnebusch, "Calculated Decompression," p. 233.
51 See *Barnamaj Itihad Shabab al-Thawra* (Program of the Union of the Revolution's Youth), Damascus, 1985; See also Hinnebusch, "The Political Economy of Political Liberalization in Syria."
52 *Al-Iktisad Wal-Aamal*, pp. 18–19, 30–44. Law 10 opened the way to economic *infitah* by allowing private investments regardless of nationality to undertake projects in all fields on the condition that the project's fixed assets are higher than 25 million Syrian liras (which would then have equalled US$200,000). Law 10's most important decrees exempted all imports related to the functioning of businesses from trade taxes and tariffs. Companies in which the state contributes over 25 per cent are exempt from income and property taxes for the first seven years. Companies not benefiting from the state contribution are exempt from income and property taxes for the first five years. Two additional years of exemption are allowed in certain conditions. Law 10 allowed investors to open up accounts with the Syrian commercial bank in foreign capital.

Syria's move in the 1980s and 1990s away from economic re-distributive reforms and towards a selective economic liberalization[53] was based upon its need to have the private sector serve as an engine of economic growth. And given that the private sector was still dependent on the state, this process would simultaneously help to consolidate the state's political power. This resulting neo-mercantilist logic is an inevitable result of Populist Authoritarian (PA) regimes' logic.

By October 2000, 1,598 projects had been approved, with a total working budget of over 327 billion Syrian liras (US$6.54 billion).[54] A few individuals profited as a result of the new *modus vivendi* between the state and the newly embourgeoisied elite (*al-Tabaqa al-Jadida*), as well as due to the amalgamation of a number of 'Alawi military and bureaucratic elites with the Sunni, mainly Damascene, old bourgeoisie. As Hinnebusch explains,

> The regime's dual public-private sector strategy protected its populist constituency – co-operatized peasants, public sector-workers – from bourgeois encroachment thereby limiting the possibilities of surplus extraction by private capital. But it also co-opted others who benefited from trade liberalization, state contracts, or work abroad. The state was able to avoid any decisive choice between statism and private capitalism.[55]

Yet although the regime of Hafez al-Asad did succeed in balancing its populist and liberalizing economic agendas, there were repercussions from the policy. Most important among these was the creation of a complex bourgeois class composed of an old "revitalized bourgeoisie" and an "embourgeoisied elite," which will continue to grow in size unless there is a reversal of the economic liberalization measures taken by the state.[56] The significance of this cannot be underestimated, since as was discussed earlier, free enterprise and the Islamic sector are closely intertwined in the Syrian context, and thus the faith and power of one group are inevitably linked to the other. Furthermore, the redeployment of an economic elite gives rise to a difficult-to-resolve contradiction that is inherent to

---

53 The need to accommodate the business religious class arose from a number of economic challenges including the un-success of the state's Import Substitution Industrialization (ISI) measures, balance of payments difficulties and the collapse of Syria's patron, the Soviet Union. Perthes explains that the solutions adopted by the regime in the 1980s to address the economic crisis, which included austerity for the workers and the salaried middle class, private-sector revival accompanied with some export promotion, but not privatization, served the interests of the state elites and their private-sector partners. Volker Perthes, *Political Economy of Syria under Asad*; idem, "The Bourgeoisie and the Ba'th," *Middle East Report* 21(170), May–June 1991: 31–7; idem, "The Syrian Private Industrial and Commercial Sectors and the State," *International Journal of Middle East Studies* 24(2), May 1992: 207–30. See also Eberhard Kienle, ed., *Contemporary Syria: Liberalization between Cold War and Cold Peace*, London: British Academic Press, 1994.
54 *Al-Iktisad Wal-Aamal* (Syrian economic journal), p. 30.
55 Hinnebusch, "The Political Economy of Economic Liberalization in Syria," pp. 311–14.
56 Ibid.

98 Hafez al-Asad's era

PA regimes: they need to control the rising socio-economic group while simultaneously ensuring its co-optation by granting it the freedom to make money. As will be discussed in the following chapter, this is exactly what happens when, by the end of the 1990s, the targeted liberalization initiated by the regime could no longer satisfy the growing economic and political aspirations of the state elite.[57]

D The tacit gender pact

An important aspect of state–Islamist relations under the regime of Hafez al-Asad was the changing status of women and state policies towards women. In this section, it is argued that the Syrian government used the issue of women's rights as a way to accommodate the traditional classes' vision of the societal order. And though the Baʿthist regime did not adopt, and thus did not actively reinforce, patriarchal religious principles, it did appeal to the religious sensibilities and economic interests of Syria's traditional bourgeoisie and religious class on the issue. Thus, by the early 1980s, it had become clear to most Syrians that the equality-oriented secularizing policy of the Baʿth and its targeting of the Personal Status Law (the only body of law that differentiates between the rights of women and of men, as opposed to the Syrian Constitution, which does not) was no longer on the state's to-do list.

It is not unusual for states in the Middle East to give way on gender-related issues in order to appease and co-opt a dissenting religious class, whether Christian, Muslim or Jewish. In explaining Arab state policies, Kandiyoti writes:

> Islamist tendencies and movements enter this equation in ways specific to each context, which does not invite easy generalizations. A conclusion that does seem permissible however is that when they do become a factor, tighter control over women and restrictions of their rights constitute the lowest common denominator of their policies.[58]

This conclusion underlines the importance of the evolution of gender relations in Syria from the 1970s to the 1990s.[59] It is a subject that has been largely ignored by students of contemporary Syrian politics, despite the fact that it ties in with both the economic liberalization and the co-optation of the religious class by the state.

As was described previously, the Syrian government's effort to co-opt the religious and business classes meant that it had to give in to at least some of their demands. This led to the muting of secularism, as well as a halt to the enforcement of a secular statutory code and the institutional empowerment of

---

57 The changing neo-liberal market-driven policy and the growing influence of the Islamic sector will be further discussed in Part III of this work.
58 Deniz Kandiyoti, "Women, Islam and the State," *Middle East Report* 173, *Gender and Politics*, November–December, 1991: 9–14.
59 The same trends apply to the period under Bashar al-Asad. The role of women shaykhas in Syria's Islamic revivalism is discussed in Chapters 7 and 8 of this work.

Syrian women. It also led to major amendments being made to the Syrian Law of Personal Status, especially the drafting of Law 34, which dated from 1975. That law was meant to replace Law 59 of 1953, and marked the high-water mark of secularization particularly concerning such familial issues as polygamy, dowry, custody of children and guardianship, while its drafters promised more secularization to come.[60] Nevertheless, further amendments to Syria's penal, naturalization and the personal status codes, all of which treated women as legal dependents, were since dropped by the state.[61]

The reality of such a halt was crystallized in women's overall status at work, which was greatly worsened by their being limited in terms of work opportunities in the revitalized private sector. More particularly, although the total number of women in the work force increased in the 1980s and beyond, this increase was concentrated in the government-controlled public economic sector. Meanwhile in the revitalized private sector, their numbers actually decreased without the government intervening, as a concession to the urban traders' class. Effectively, therefore, the country's employment situation for women came to reflect the prevailing gender bias in Syrian society. In other words, the uncontrolled private sector mirrored better the prevailing patriarchy of Syrian society, which, starting in the early 1980s, the once-feminist state chose to overlook.

To illustrate this point, it is useful to consider female labour statistics from the 1970s to 1995.[62] The percentage of women working in industry in the public and private sectors increased from 13.4 per cent in 1971 to 23 per cent in 1981, but then decreased drastically during the 1980s and 1990s, reaching a level of 9.8 per cent in 1995. The same was true in the services sector. There, the percentage of women workers was 18.7 per cent in 1970, and had reached 47.2 per cent by 1981. Yet by 1995, the number of women workers had decreased to 30.2 per cent.[63] In general, there were more women who were employed in 1981 than in 1970, and more women who were employers in 1981 than in 1970. Yet between 1981 and 1995, the proportion of women that earned wages decreased, more women became unpaid family workers, and a smaller percentage of women were employers.[64]

---

60 Faysal Daraj and Jamul Barut, *Al-ahzab wa al-harakat wa al-jama'at al-islamiya* [The Islamic Parties, Movements and Groups], Damascus: The Arab Center for Strategic Studies, 2006, p. 268.
61 Annika Rabo, "Gender, State and Civil Society," in Chris Hann and Elizabeth Dunn, eds, *Civil Society: Challenging Western Models*, London and New York: Routledge, 1996, p. 170.
62 I choose the bracket 1970–1995 because the major socio-economic shifts happened during these years. Not much has changed in terms of gender relations since the mid-1990s. I mainly use the ESCWA's 1995 study on "Women and Men in Syria" because it is one of the few locally conducted, reliable and consistent studies that include Syrian labour statistics all the way from the 1970s to 1995. I then compared the ESCWA's numbers with the Syrian state's statistical studies on employment and gender, and found that they mostly match.
63 ESCWA, "Women and Men in Syria," pp. 72–3.
64 Ibid., p. 78. It is important to note that the same patterns, although much less pronounced, were registered in the case of men, except that the number of men being employers has increased from 1981 to 1995, unlike that of women. This is partly due to the economic crisis in the late 1970s and early 1980s, and men's switch to the re-energized private sector.

If one looks exclusively at the government-controlled public sector, the picture is drastically different from that which prevailed in the private sector. In the former, the number of women employees kept on increasing between 1970 and 1995: in 1981, around 30 per cent of active public sector workers were women, while by 1995, around 40 per cent were women. Meanwhile in the private sector, the number of women decreased by around 10 percentage points from 1981 to 1995,[65] this is at a time when the private sector was increasing in size in Syria and when its contribution to Syria's GDP was higher than that of the public sector (the ratio was 70/30). And those trends continued into the 2000s: by the year 2006, 25 per cent of workers in the public sector were women, while in the private sector, only 8 per cent were women.[66]

These numbers reveal three main trends: first, from the 1980s onwards, the participation of women in the economic sphere receded in many areas, although overall it was rather more positive due to an inflated public sector. Second, regardless of what progress has been made in the areas of education and overall employment for women, there does not seem to have been a strong impact on perceptions about gender relations and roles, as measured through the prism of the employment market. Finally, there is an interesting dichotomy between the private sector and the public sector when it comes to gender. More specifically, the public sector controlled by the state has remained relatively favourable to women, while the private sector, which was revitalized by the state in the early 1980s in order to accommodate certain elite interests, has not been especially favourable to them.

As the numbers show, the employment status of women has become a symbol of the differences between the private and public sectors in Syria: one controlled by a "freer" patriarchal society allowed to dominate and define its own economic scene, the other by the state. It also underlines that the revitalization of the private sector was achieved at the expense of the economic situation of Syrian women, and that it was part of the gender pact between the regime and the co-opted bourgeoisie. Deniz Kandiyoti explains this tendency to compromise on gender issues by arguing that whenever the state negotiates with Islamist and Islamic groups, women become another negotiating tool, a card in the hand that any state or leader can play in order to tip the scale in the negotiation.[67] In this context, gender relations become increasingly politicized.

On the social level, the state sought to alleviate the anxiety of the religious class in Syria by both muting Ba'thist secularism and by dropping its feminist agenda at the institutional and legal levels. The retreat from secularism was clear in Hafez al-Asad's speeches from the early 1980s, which suddenly began to feature religious allusions and quotations from the Quran to justify various

---

65 Ibid., p. 79.
66 Syria's Labour Force Survey, 2006. Online: www.ilo.org/public/english/employment/gems/eeo/download/syria.pdf (accessed 10 July 2008).
67 See Valentine M. Moghadam, *Modernizing Women: Gender and Social Change in the Middle East*, 2nd edn, London and Boulder, CO: Lynne Rienner Publishers, 2003, p. 151.

arguments.[68] Al-Asad also stepped back from his initial support for the 1982 decree forbidding the wearing of headscarves in the educational sector and in public-service buildings (although the decree itself was not revoked), by affirming in one of his rare presidential addresses that "In Syria, dress is a matter of private and personal choice ... customs and traditions cannot be overcome by violence."[69]

This speech followed an incident in which young women from the Youth Organization supported by the Syrian state attacked veiled women by forcibly removing their veils in Damascus's al Hamidiya bazaar. The regime's reaction to the incident made it clear that Ba'thist secularism was no longer merely muted. Rather, it was mutating from seeing religion as a private matter that should be kept outside the state's institutions to tolerating religious symbols and practices. This showed the regime's strategic pursuit of a partnership with "moderates" within the religious class, as well as its acquiescence to the desire of pious Syrians to reassert their practices within the various public spheres.[70]

In making this change to Syria's secular model, Hafez al-Asad's regime was also publicly stepping away from having the state contribute to mediating the roles and rights of women. According to one civil rights activist, while religiosity was resurging within the public sphere, there was no concomitant right to be free from religious obligations. Moreover, the whole debate about whether religion as practised is truly the word of God or rather simply a patriarchal innovation was no longer possible, especially for women. Effectively, the state would no longer provide protection for those women who want to emancipate themselves from the normative prevailing practices in society and the family.[71]

The regime's goal of co-opting the religious class also meant that its policies of secularization and of equal rights for men and women were no longer possible. This was especially so in light of the growing importance of the Islamized spaces, the growing number of supporters of the Islamic groups and the increasing pervasiveness of their message. Indeed, these factors meant that efforts by secularists to put forward a non-patriarchal Family Law, to ban polygamy for men and to give equal inheritance rights to men and women were in vain.[72]

Generally speaking, the 1980s saw women become embroiled as symbols in the struggle over religious identity and the legitimacy of the regime. For those

---

68 Nikolaos Van Dam, *The Struggle for Power in Syria: Politics and Society under Asad and the Ba'th Party*, London and New York: I.B. Tauris, 1996, p. 96.
69 Oral sources; quoted in Rabo, "Gender, State and Civil Society," p. 170. In 1982, the regime had issued a decree prohibiting the wearing of headscarves anywhere in the educational system. In one conversation I had with a school director whose school received in the early 1980s clear orders forbidding veiling in her school, she admitted being shocked and confused by the speech.
70 In Asad's speech, the dress acted as a socio-political symbol rather than a traditional cloth.
71 It is important to say here that, in addition to impacting the trajectory of women's rights in Syria, the resulting Islamized micro-societies have also developed a gendered aspect to them as they focus heavily on women to transmit social behaviour and conventions. That's where the role of shaykhas and sisters comes into play, as will be shown in later chapters of this work.
72 Rabo, "Gender, State and Civil Society," p. 170.

concerned with salvaging the threatened Islamic identity, women's behaviour, dress and appearance had to reflect certain interpretations of religious texts and mores.[73] Thus the veil reappeared en masse, and became not just a symbol of lack of choice – as it had been proclaimed less than 50 years earlier by the Ba'th among other leftist groups – but rather a distinguishing mark of the anti-Ba'thist Sunni woman.[74] Both President Asad and most Syrians understood that the veil was no longer just a religious garment, but was also a political statement as well as a sign of a suppressed civil society that wished to reveal itself.[75] And as the veil reappeared, harassment of the liberally clothed became more frequent.

The regime's strategy left many women to fend for themselves in defining and demanding respect for their civic rights. This was evident in the fact that while the government was encouraging women to take on a wider array of roles in education and in the civil service, it had not put in place laws that protected women's right to so challenge social conventions. This legal vacuum made the predictability and consistency of compensatory and conservative normative ideologies more attractive, and soon would become an ideological vacuum as well – given the overall defeat of secular discourse (see Part III).

E The regional factor

We have seen that the dramatic economic and social changes wrought by the Ba'thist revolution and by the authoritarian regime of Hafez al-Asad led to the rise in the late 1970s of Islamist militant activity in Syria. Over the next few chapters, it will be shown that while the policy of co-optation and compromise with the business and religious classes put a stop to the anti-regime violence, it also made possible the Islamic revival that Syria is witnessing today. At the same time, this revival was aided by the regime's regional policy and by Syria's strategic relations with its neighbouring Islamists. It is to this topic that we now turn.

States typically sponsor proxy groups for ideological, domestic, strategic and leverage reasons.[76] Throughout its history, the Ba'th state has sought to expand its regional support network in order to extend its pan-Arab ideology, to strengthen and legitimize its domestic hold on power, to influence its neighbours and more importantly to reduce Israeli and American influence in the region. Ironically given the regime's strong secular commitments during its first years in power, Asad's efforts to build support regionally found a receptive audience with Islamist movements in neighbouring states. The regime's willingness to work with these groups underlines Hafez al-Asad's use of *realpolitik* in order to play a major role in the region. It also speaks to the depth of Syrian existential fears of Israel. The Syrian

---

73 Moghadam, *Modernizing Women*, p. 154.
74 For more on the topic, see Saba Mahmood, *The Politics of Piety*, Princeton, NJ and Oxford: Princeton University Press, 2005.
75 This was clear in Asad's speech concerning the veil (above).
76 See Daniel Byman, *Deadly Connections: States that Sponsor Terrorism*, Cambridge: Cambridge University Press, 2005.

Golan Heights were occupied by Israel in 1967 and annexed in 1981 albeit UN resolution 497 against the annexation. These were deepened by the 1978 peace accords between Egypt and Israel, which removed a strong Arab ally in resisting the Zionist state, and which drove Syria to seek strategic parity with Israel. In the absence of a credible Arab military option to balance Israeli power, and because it was surrounded by hostile regimes in Jordan and Iraq, Syria chose to do so by fortifying its alliance with Iran and by acting as an intermediary between the Islamic Republic and the Arab states. Syria also established a much-needed patron–client relationship with the Soviet Union.

Yet the collapse of the Soviet Union and the subsequent relative strengthening of the United States and of its ally Israel increased Syria's regional worries significantly. It was thus forced to pursue politics by other means.[77] This led to Hafez al-Asad choosing a realist path and overlooking ideological differences in entering into a number of complex, controversial and yet powerful patron–client relationships with multiple organizations in the region, including the Palestinian Front for the Liberation of Palestine-General Command (PFLP-GC). Indeed, seeking to re-order Syria's geo-political environment, and in an attempt to counter-balance Israel's steady expanded front, the 1990s witnessed the Damascus regime moving closer towards becoming a patron of the Palestinian Muslim Brothers, and other Islamist movements. It also forged regional alliances with such groups as Hizbullah in Lebanon, Hamas, and the Palestinian Islamic Jihad (PIJ) in Palestine. And despite the strong ideological differences between the Ba'th and its new allies,[78] Hamas and the PIJ were allowed permanent bases and offices in Syria. In response to international censure for doing so, Syria has argued that the groups are legitimate armed resistance movements rather than terrorist organizations, and has claimed that their Syrian headquarters are merely civilian offices. This has not stopped Israel and the United States from insisting that they constitute a mechanism through which Palestinian Islamists are trained, given logistical assistance and funded by the Syrians.[79]

Regarding the Palestinian organizations, Islamic Jihad is a smaller ally to Hamas, and was formed in the 1980s as a guerrilla organization with no overt political ideology. It claims to receive its orders from a secret council that is in continuous contact with the leadership in Damascus. Hamas, which was allowed to open a new office in Damascus in March 2000, was created during the first

---

77 Syria had signed on 8 October 1980 a 20-year Treaty of Friendship and Cooperation with the Soviet Union.

78 For instance, the PIJ's ideology is stated as the following:

> Our clear and strategic goal is the mobilization of the Muslim public on our occupied soil and its direction towards a war of jihad against the thieving Zionist entity. The armed struggle is the only way to defeat the Jewish entity on the soil of Palestine.

See *Yediot Ahronot*, 18 November 1994.

79 See the Israeli military intelligence report at: www.mfa.gov.il/MFA. "Iran and Syria as Strategic Support for Palestinian Terrorism (Based on Interrogations of Arrested Palestinian Terrorists and Captured Palestinian Authority Documents)," Document number TR6-548-02, Israel Defence Forces, Military Intelligence, September 2002.

104 *Hafez al-Asad's era*

Palestinian Intifada in 1987 by Palestinian Muslim Brothers.[80] It is alleged that in 2002, some 10 per cent of its budget came from Iran via Syria and Hizbullah.[81] According to the Israeli Mossad, Iranian funds are transferred to the Palestinian territories through the PIJ and Hamas, and via the Syrian banking system.[82] Interrogation of Hamas and PIJ activists captured by Israeli intelligence has allegedly revealed that Syria in fact provides training camps to the activists and professional instruction on the preparation of explosives.[83]

President Asad's efforts to expand Syria's regional influence so as to avoid diplomatic marginalization have also focused upon Lebanon. Since its independence from French occupation, Lebanon has been perceived by Damascus as Syria's political and security backyard, and thus organically connected to the Syrian political environment. It is with this in mind that Syria has intervened repeatedly in the domestic political affairs of its neighbour. In the late 1970s and 1980s, there was a convergence between Syrian interests and those of the Lebanese Shi'i resistance movement. The mainstream Shi'i movement AMAL moved to ally itself with Asad first,[84] followed by the more religiously inspired Hizbullah.

Although Hafez al-Asad's domestic struggles with Islamist groups might make it seem as if he would be wary of allying with an Islamist group in nearby Lebanon, the pragmatism driving his policies caused his regime to use every asset at its disposal.[85] Concretely, the Ba'th regime's patron–client relationship with Amal has served three purposes: (1) Amal passively backed Syrian intervention in Lebanon in 1976; (2) the relationship allowed Asad to cement his ties with Iran; and (3) it provided the Syrian regime with an ally that was strongly opposed to Israel during its 1982–1983 struggle with the Jewish state.[86]

The regime also benefited from its relationship with the other Lebanese Shi'i resistance movement, Hizbullah (the Party of God). Founded in the mid-1980s, Hizbullah is not the creation of Syria but rather of Iran, and has considered the Iranian Islamic Revolution as an inspiration to action.[87] Although initially wary

---

80 Kenneth Katzman, *Terrorism, Near Eastern Groups and State Sponsors* (Report for Congress), Washington, DC: Library of Congress, 2002, p. 35.
81 Katzman, *Terrorism, Near Eastern Groups and State Sponsors*, p. 11.
82 See www.mfa.gov.il/MFA/The+Iranian+Threat/Support+of+terror/Iran.
83 Katzman, *Terrorism, Near Eastern Groups and State Sponsors*, p. 45.
84 The AMAL movement was established in 1975 by Imam Musa al-Sadr. In Arabic the name means hope, but it is also the acronym for *Afwaj al-Muqawama al-Lubnaniyya* (Lebanese Resistance Detachments). Patrick Seale notes that the Lebanese Shi'a in the south had welcomed Israel's invasion of Lebanon in the hope that the Israelis would deliver them from "the high-handed Palestinians, but ... Israel's attempt to impose Maronite rule drove the Shi'a into outright opposition." See Seale, *Asad of Syria*, p. 396.
85 Ibid.
86 Ibid., pp. 396–7. For instance, the AMAL militia proved to be a powerful ally as it fought alongside other Syrian proxies such as Walid Jumblat' Druze forces for control of West Beirut against Israel in August–September 1983. The mainstream Shi'i movement had also successfully seized control over West Beirut in February 1984. See Seale, *Asad of Syria*, pp. 414–15 and 468.
87 Augustus R. Norton, *Hezbollah: A Short History*, Princeton, NJ: Princeton University Press, 2007, pp. 34 and 36.

of the movement in the 1980s, Syria soon made Hizbullah its most important surrogate and proxy in Lebanon.[88] It used Hizbullah to bolster its claim to be an important regional player, one that should not be easily dismissed and whose interests and grievances needed to be listened to. Syria's ability to vector the relationship into a greater regional role flowed from the fact that Hizbullah became the only non-Palestinian movement still waging an armed struggle against Israel in the 1990s. Syria was often accused of allowing Iran to operate training camps in the Beka' Valley when Syrian forces were present in Lebanon.[89] Moreover, Israel claims that Syria transfers equipment and weapons sent by Iran to the Palestinian and Lebanese territories through Hizbullah. Implicit within this claim is that Syria has had to develop and maintain a very close relationship with Iran, which is a major sponsor and political patron of Islamist groups in the region.

Overall, Syria's patron–client relationships with the Shi'i movement serve a number of purposes: (1) they are a general mechanism for wielding influence in Lebanon and for helping to control other parties in that country; (2) they are deployed as pressure instruments against Israel in a balance of terror tactics; (3) they provide domestic and regional legitimacy through these attacks, since the Islamist movement's fight against Israel is popular with most Arabs in the region; (4) and they help to control Saudi Arabia's Wahhabi web of influence in Syria.[90]

Similarly, Syria's patron–client relationships and alliances with the Sunni Islamist resistance groups have helped to propagate the Syrian regime's vision, which is rooted in nationalism and Arabism, and which transcends regionality and territoriality. They have thus made the country appear to be the region's populist power par excellence.[91] Such alliances not only helped polish the Syrian regime's pan-Arab resistance credentials (domestically as well as regionally), they also demonstrated Syria's strength to regional foes as well as its willingness to defend its interests, and have underlined its view that Israel's policies towards the Palestinians cannot be isolated from the region as a whole.

Syria's use of such alliances has served one other purpose crucial to a regime that relies at least partly on its foreign policy for survival and influence: it has allowed the regime to keep a tight control over Arab Islamist activity at home. This policy, which is still being practised by the Ba'thi regime under President Bashar al-Asad, will be examined more closely in Part III of this work. Yet it is important to underline here that the policy has not been entirely successful, since the country's use of Islamist groups has also made it possible for certain groups to become stronger. This has made it harder for the regime to exploit the

---

88 Norton, *Hezbollah*, p. 35.
89 Seale, *Asad of Syria*, p. 396.
90 Points 1 and 2 from Norton, *Hezbollah*, p. 35.
91 Syria's direct involvement with those Islamist groups is defended by Syrians on the basis that the movements Damascus hosts and consolidates are legitimate resistance movements against Israeli occupation.

empowered groups while still controlling them, particularly given Syria's domestic Islamic revivalism and the covert sectarian tension that underlies its socio-political foundations. Furthermore, a number of Syria experts claim that many Syrians oppose the regime's support of the Lebanese Shi'i movement and its alliance with Iran at the expense of its good relations with the Lebanese Sunni constituency and its leaders, and accuse the regime of supporting the Shi'i group for sectarian reasons rather than nationalistic ones.[92] This feeling, if harnessed by Islamic counter-elites, could ultimately contribute to the possibility of radical Sunni collective action against the regime.[93]

4 Conclusion

Part II of the book has surveyed the reasons behind the decline of political Islam and Islamism as a model for political change in Syria. It has explicated the policies of Hafez al-Asad's regime regarding containing and co-opting the Syrian Islamic bourgeoisie, and has underlined the results of these policies – namely, muting of the Ba'th's secular agenda, the re-appropriation of Islam as an ideology and sponsorship of Islamic shaykhs considered "moderate" and essentially pro-regime, the shaping of a new socio-economic order that is removed from the populist Ba'thi doctrine in order to co-opt Syria's bourgeois class, and the use of regional Islamist groups in order to assert Syria's Arabist and nationalist stance while influencing regional realities.

The changing status of women both in society and in the law reflects the changes that have flowed from the Islamic trend's expanded social and political profile in Syria. With regard to gender relations and public morality, religious leaders have once more assumed positions of authority. As such, Ba'thist secularism has been de-emphasized in favour of conservative social convention.

Ultimately, the strategy of Hafez al-Asad's regime of shifting the conflict from one between the Muslim Brothers and a corrupt ruling clique to one between "moderate good Muslims" and "radical terrorist Muslims" was successful. Moreover co-optation and economic liberalization extended the regime's coalition to the bourgeois and religious class, thus helping to ensure the regime's survival. Yet this socially and politically engineered reinforcement of Islamic shaykhs, groups and institutions caused a vital transformation in the *form* of the Syrian Islamic movement, such that it was no longer a political entity competing for power and the state. In order to survive the 1970s, Islamic groups became strategically quiescent, pro-regime and apolitical. In return, they were provided a space in which to organize, funding and a platform from which to spread their message and recruit new members that they had not had prior to the conflict. This platform included the educational system and extended to the radio, television and the media.

92 Interviews conducted during the months of March and April 2008.
93 See Islamist websites at http://almaqdese.com/e?i=98 and www.alsunah.net (accessed 13 August 2008).

As part of its re-organization of the Syrian Islamic scene, the regime felt sufficiently secure domestically to use regional Islamist militants to influence Syria's transforming geo-political environment without the fear of this policy encouraging militantism inside the country. Regional policy successes no doubt added to the stability of the regime during the 1980s and 1990s.

Part III of this work will show that the Ba'th's survival measures have been fraught with inherent paradoxes and dangers. The regime's legitimizing formula has resulted in the re-invigoration of a large and influential Islamic sector, one that is outgrowing the government's ability to control it. Indeed, the regime's balancing act between the different social forces, which was so successful in the 1980s and early 1990s, became more tenuous in the late 1990s and, as we will see, increasingly so under the new presidency of Bashar al-Asad. The old alliance between the socio-economic elite – in both its older and newer forms – and the religious class is re-emerging, again at the expense of supporting socially and economically marginalized groups. Syria's foreign policy, which includes relying on and supporting Islamic groups operating in the region, is adding to the authoritarian regime's troubles, as Syrian society is further Islamizing from below.

We will see that the unintended consequences of the state's policies included the eventual assertion of religiosity and the rise of Islamist activism concomitant with the demise of the Ba'thist secular model in Syria. In an attempt to understand the consequences of the Hafez al-Asad regime's choices in maintaining its rule and controlling the Syrian domestic scene, the following part explores the implications of the fact that Asad's strategies underlie his son's policies and alignment choices.

Part III
Bashar al-Asad's era
Fundamentalist and Islamist revivalism

6 Bashar al-Asad following in his father's footsteps

The promotion of moderate Islam from above in the name of de-radicalization

1 Introduction

The preceding chapters delineated the Islamic aspect of the domestic context inherited by the extant command when it took power in July 2000. In so doing, they illustrated the ways in which an avowedly *laïque* secular Baʿthist command dealt with the Islamic militant opposition from its emergence in 1963 to its seeming demise at the beginning of the 1980s. It was demonstrated that Populist Authoritarian (PA) survival strategies that were meant to consolidate regime control of the political arena in fact paved the way for the emergence of a new "reformed" and "moderate" Islamic movement as a significant player on the Syrian domestic scene.[1]

Part III of this work examines the period since Bashar al-Asad took power, and considers the development of state–Islamic relations and their impacts on Syrian society by focusing upon the following questions: how has the Islamic movement evolved under the current regime in Syria? In what ways have President Bashar al-Asad's policies regarding Syria's Islamic revivalism differed from/been similar to those of his father? To what extent has the Bashar regime been able to successfully co-opt the Islamic and Islamist movements, and what does this tell us in terms of the larger analytical questions driving this study (which are, what are the roots of Islamic activism in a secular authoritarian state, how has such activism evolved, and how has it impacted upon the Baʿthist secular model)?

In answering Part III's questions, the elements of both continuity and change in the Syrian state's relationship with an increasingly autonomous and powerful

---

1 As shown in previous chapters, this socially engineered reinforcement and empowerment from above of Syria's Islamic movement included a vital transformation in its *form*. That is, the Syrian regime not only promoted a strategically quiescent, although still large and powerful, parallel Islamic sector, it also sought to re-orient it from being a largely anti-Baʿthist regime Islamic/Islamist movement to a semi-autonomous, pro-regime, apolitical fundamentalist movement focused upon the reform of the Syrian individual. Furthermore, as part of its re-organization of the Syrian Islamic scene, the regime felt sufficiently secure domestically to use regional Islamist militants to influence Syria's larger geo-political environment without the fear of this policy encouraging militantism inside the country.

Islamic movement are examined. It is suggested that the president is facing similar challenges to those faced by his predecessor in the early stages of his command, namely an economic crisis exacerbated by strong demographic growth, Islamist activity at the domestic level and a new geo-political reality as a result of war in the region. But an important *difference* in the situation facing Bashar's government is that his response options are narrowing. This is because of the previous command's economic, social and regional policies discussed in the last chapter, which have led to an ongoing re-configuration of state–society relations such that these relations are no longer entirely under the current leadership's control.

The new political command thus stands at a critical juncture, which is the natural outcome of the built-in structural limitations of the PA regime created by the Ba'th in 1963.[2] Ultimately, the regime's survival strategies, while successful in postponing the need for larger structural adjustments during Hafez al-Asad's presidency, are no longer sufficient to tame the opposition or to secure the loyalty of strategic sectors. The reason for this is that economic development without political liberalization is "bound to deepen civil society, and continuing social mobilization in this context will generate stronger, more autonomous social forces that cannot readily be controlled except through greater political liberalization."[3] More specifically, Hafez al-Asad's regime succeeded in maintaining its control over the mobilized Islamic groups, but the regime of his son is no longer able to do so, for a number of intertwined reasons: in the non-democratic setting of Syrian politics, the social engineering from above that is aimed at inhibiting the emergence of a viable political alternative to the regime, and thus at consolidating the latter's control, has constrained the set of options available to it. On one hand, the co-opted Islamic sector that was allowed to develop and recruit members under the previous presidency has today become a significant organizational force that, thanks to its outreach methods,[4] is growing increasingly independent of the regime's control. On the other hand, the bourgeois class that Hafez al-Asad co-opted through selective economic liberalization has also become an important force, and is successfully pushing the state for further economic liberalization. The predicament, therefore, is that although selective economic liberalization addresses the desires of the powerful capitalist and *arriviste* elements linked to the regime, it also forces the state to abandon its

---

2 PA regimes do not remain popular or representative of popular interests; they suffer from built-in contradictions between their attempts to mobilize yet control popular participation and the rise of a new bourgeoisie who have a vested interest in economic liberalization. See Raymond A. Hinnebusch, *Syria: Revolution from Above*, London and New York: Routledge, 2001.
3 This is not to say that a deepened civil society will inevitably lead to political democratization. Indeed, this assumption has been discredited for a while now in the scholarship; as Hinnebusch puts it, "it could simply mean more power for the 'haves.'" See Raymond A. Hinnebusch "Calculated Decompression as a Substitute for Democratization: Syria," in Bahgat Korany *et al.*, eds, *Political Liberalization and Democratization in the Arab World: Comparative Experiences*, Boulder, CO: Lynn Rienner Press, 1998, pp. 238–9.
4 These will be examined in Chapter 7 of this work.

social-welfare programmes and thus to widen the gap between the impoverished classes and the economic elite. A widened gap means that the state can no longer maintain its balancing act of satisfying its base of support – the middle and lower classes – and the new capitalistic class. In this sense, the strategic choices available to the leadership in Damascus have been altered, and generally narrowed.

It is at this juncture that the link between the economic and the Islamic factors emerges: the impoverished class can no longer rely on the regime's populist policies for support, and feels abandoned. Thus its members are shifting their attention and allegiance towards the only sector that was allowed to prosper under the previous political command and that can help to fill their needs through its proficient welfare network, the Islamic sector.

A critical examination of the current government's social, economic and regional policies will serve to validate the above arguments, and is presented in this first chapter of Part III. Chapter 6 will thus survey the ongoing de-Ba'thization and de-laïcization of the Syrian social system, the regime's renewed alliance with the Islamic sector, as well as the regime's economic policies, particularly its abandonment of a large part of Ba'thist populist reforms and its encouragement of private enterprise. Also surveyed are the regime's regional policies, which have focused on deepening patron–client relations with Islamist groups in neighbouring countries, a step believed to be aimed at maintaining Syria's political standing and influence in the region.[5]

This tripartite focus – on the social, economic and regional elements – will help to illustrate both why and how the current command is failing in its efforts at maintaining control over Syria's active groups. It will become clear that its deepening alliance with Syria's Islamic sector and with regional Islamists has become a threat to both the Syrian political order and to Syria's overall social harmony. And as will be shown in the last part of Chapter 6 and in subsequent chapters, the social, economic and regional survival strategies once used by the elder Asad are no longer able to control Syria's increasingly autonomous Islamic civil society, nor to prevent the resurgence of underground Islamist activity in the country.

2 Islamization from above: how is today's Ba'thist regime further empowering Syria's Islamic sector?

This section will discuss the social, economic and foreign policy measures deployed by the current administration to bolster its legitimacy in the eyes of the now powerful and increasingly independent Islamic sector, as well as to maintain the coalitions it inherited from the previous command. The section thus illustrates the growing strength of the Islamic sector in light of the limitations of these survival strategies within the current political context.

---

5 A dubious region where Iraq – now deemed to be a friendly neighbour after the collapse of the competing Ba'th regime – is no longer capable of providing Syria with the military weight and strategic depth it needs to sustain its military balance with its regional foes (regional policy).

A Islamization from above and the new state's social policies

Upon assuming power in July 2000, the new President Bashar al-Asad appeared to be committed to the secular core of Ba'thism.[6] When asked about Syria's Islamic question, Bashar made comments similar to those that his father would have made a few years earlier. For instance, in one of his earliest interviews after becoming president, Bashar al-Asad discussed the possibility of having an Islamic party within the confines of the National Progressive Front.[7] He explained that the country's existing stability must not be compromised, and that religious and ethnic structures should not feel under attack as this would be too explosive for Syria. The president added that he feared de-stabilizing developments like those that took place in Algeria in 1991 might also occur in Syria: "[a]t that time, the [Algerian] government misjudged the people, and the Islamists threatened to assume power. To this day, the Algerians are paying the price for this miscalculation." When asked how he proposed to prevent such an eventuality in Syria, or in the words of the journalist, to prevent "the formation of religious parties that are democratically elected, but then act undemocratically," the Syrian president explained that one cannot apply German or Western standards to developments in the Middle East:

> In Germany, you may have a religious Christian party, the CDU [Christian Democratic Union], but it has effectively assimilated itself into the fabric of the country. In return, your history prevents you from having any large nationalist parties. Our experience has shown us that the situation in Syria became stable because the entire society is secular. We must preserve that.[8]

Despite making this verbal commitment to Syria's secular heritage and expressing concern about the potential outcomes of religious politicization, Bashar al-Asad's first decisions as president seemed clearly supportive of the increasingly influential and autonomous Syrian Islamic sector. Indeed, while expressing its loyalty to secularism, the new political command chose to further dismiss the Ba'thist understanding of secularism (the weakening of religion in the public sphere) by increasingly flirting with Syria's religious groups. This was based on the rationale that it was important to build on previous accommodationist policies (see Chapter 5) in order to impede the advance of Islamist radicalization.[9]

---

6 The rise of Bashar al-Asad to power was not surprising to Syrians. Following the death of his brother, Bashar was quite clearly being groomed to take on his father's position, and within six weeks of his father's death, Bashar was elected in a referendum with 97.3 per cent of the votes.
7 *Der Spiegel*, 9 July 2001.
8 Ibid.
9 Addressed during Bashar al-Asad's inaugural speech and the Tenth Ba'th Conference in June 2005. See *Teshreen*, 6 June 2005; *Al-Hayat*, 19 June 2005. A number of Syrian observers agree that Ba'thist ideology no longer guides the regime's moves. See also David Lesch, *The New Lion of Damascus: Bashar al-Asad and Modern Syria*, New Haven, CT: Yale University Press, 2005 and Flynt Leverett, *Inheriting Syria: Bashar's Trial by Fire*, Washington, DC: Brookings Institute Press, 2005.

The new command also underlined the importance of "democratic thinking" and "the principle of accepting the opinion of the other," and moved to concretize these pronouncements through a series of social measures that served to both theoretically and tangibly further integrate the country's religious and Islamic element into the wider society.[10] Thus the regime promulgated a bill allowing those in political exile to return safely to Syria, including opposition figures who were prominent members of Syria's Islamic movement living abroad such as Islamist leader Abu Fateh al-Bayanuni, a Muslim Brother himself and the sibling of the Muslim Brotherhood's current leader 'Ali Sadr al-Din al-Bayanuni. It also released long-serving prisoners accused of belonging to the Islamist movement, and released a further 700 Muslim Brotherhood political prisoners a year into Bashar's presidency, among them senior Islamic leaders such as Khalid al-Shami, who was one of the leaders of the Islamic rebellion and had been in prison since 1982. Another 112 prisoners were released in December 2004. President Bashar al-Asad also closed down the notorious Mezza political prison, which had become a symbol of the regime's repression and was strongly feared by political dissidents in general and Islamic activists in particular. Indeed, within the first years of Bashar's rule, the number of detainees fell to between 300 and 1,000 people, which was a significant drop in light of the 4,000 political prisoners held by Syria in 1993.[11]

Another early measure taken by President Bashar al-Asad was to repeal his father's 1982 decree prohibiting the wearing of headscarves by girls in any part of the educational system in Syria.[12] This move was seen as symbolically significant in spite of the fact that the decree had not been enforced since Hafez al-Asad's 1982 speech declaring dress to be a personal matter, since it made official the shift in the state's model of secularism in Syria, away from *laïcité* and towards a religiously friendlier form of secularism, the Anglo-Saxon model.[13]

10 Bashar al-Asad's inaugural speech saw him pledge allegiance to his father's legacy and continuity of his policies, while also stressing the importance of domestic development, technical modernization and integration into the global system, all previously neglected by his father in favour of maintaining steady foreign policy. He pledged to reform the education and administrative systems and to encourage the evolution of civil society in Syria. Accordingly, despite relying on a few advisors from his father's circle, Bashar made some very significant changes in the course of consolidating his power. Ultimately, a new generational guard took over at almost all levels of government. In the same vein, in July 2003, Bashar al-Asad issued a decree separating the party and state; appointments to government offices would henceforth be based solely on merit rather than party affiliation. See *Syria Times*, 18 July 2000; Volker Perthes, *Syria under Bashar al-Asad: Modernisation and the Limits of Change*, London and New York: Routledge, 2004, pp. 9–10. See also Sami Moubayed, "The Islamic Revival in Syria," *Mideast Monitor* 1(3), September–October 2006.
11 Joshua Landis and Joe Pace, "The Syrian Opposition," *Washington Quarterly* 30(1), Winter 2006–2007: 47.
12 Eyal Zisser, "Syria, the Ba'th Regime and the Islamic Movement: Stepping on a New Path?" *Muslim World* 95, January 2005: 43; idem, *Commanding Syria: Bashar al-Asad and the First Years in Power*, New York: I.B. Tauris, 2007, p. 93.
13 See Chapter 2 for an explanation of the differences between the two models.

116 Bashar al-Asad's era

Ahmad Salkini, the political advisor and spokesman of the Syrian government in Washington, explains today's Syrian secularism:

> Secularism is often defined as "indifference to or rejection or exclusion of religion and religious considerations." Syria defines it differently – not in terms of "rejection," or even "tolerance," but in terms of "embracing" all religions and "taking pride" in a diverse heritage. While some countries in the Middle East tout themselves as a state for one religion (the Jewish State), Syria prides itself on being a state for all religions – and no religion. It is this formula that defines the true Syrian identity. The Syria I grew up in embraced everyone. My own father is a decorated veteran of the 1973 war against Israel. Yet, when his first child was born after the war – and after four previous heartbreaking miscarriages – it was a Syrian Jewish doctor in whose hands he entrusted my life. I owe my life to that doctor, who saved me after a complication during infancy that nearly resulted in my death.[14]

This sort of official speech is different from the one advanced in the 1960s and 1970s, where there was an understanding that state officials are to avoid discussing religion and focus instead on how the new generations of Syrians have rejected "reactionary ideologies" in favour of "science" and "reason" (see Chapter 2).

Damascus's placating of the increasingly influential Islamic sector was also extended to both the party and the military. For instance, the year 2003 saw Asad lift a long-standing ban on religious practice in Syria's military barracks, while at the Ba'th Party Conference of June 2005, the political command declared that it would be a grave mistake not to give Islamic groups a platform to express their views since frustration only leads to fundamentalism.[15] In 2007, the military academy invited religious authorities to lecture cadets for the first time since the Ba'th rise to power. The invitees, who included Syria's Mufti Ahmad Hassoun, MP Shaykh Ahmad Habash and Christian Patriarch Isidor Batikha, addressed the topic of the role of religion in confronting the new geo-political challenges facing the Syrian nation.[16] This choice of topic by the state once again made clear its backing for a new sort of Syrian secularism, one that does not observe a strict separation between religion, the state and of the private activities of Syrians when it comes to religion.

In February 2004, the Syrian state went further by organizing the country's first religious conference in 40 years. The conference was entitled *Tajdeed al-Khitab al-Dini* (Renewal of the Religious Message), and attracted a large number of globally known Islamic thinkers and leaders. Even more striking was the regime's reaction to the Danish cartoons ridiculing the Prophet Muhammad that

---

14 Ahmad Salkini, "Syrian Secularism: A Model for the Middle East," *Christian Science Monitor*, 13 July 2010.
15 Zisser, "Syria, the Ba'th Regime and the Islamic Movement," pp. 61–2.
16 *Al-Hayat*, 29 March 2006; Cham Press: www.champress.net (accessed 30 March 2006).

were published in early 2006. While the protests in Egypt and Jordan were spearheaded by the Islamic civil society, those in Syria were organized by the state and thus put the state into a position of being the protector of Islam.[17]

That same year, the state issued a decree expanding the number of official Islamic institutions in Syria – that number in the thousands – by endorsing the creation of a Shari'a faculty at the University of Aleppo. This was in addition to the existing Shari'a faculty at the University of Damascus, whose enrolment numbers about 7,600 students, half of whom are women, and that graduates around 600 students a year.[18] A high-ranking official argued that the opening of such institutions helps to fill an important need given the increasing number of applicants wanting to study Islamic theology and Islamic Law in Syria, whether from Syria or from abroad. He also asserted that such a move would serve to promote moderate Islam, because of the academic commitments of the teachers involved.[19]

Another high-ranking official told me that the Syrian *Tajdeed* (Renewal) Islamic Movement is led by "mindful shaykhs who are constantly communicating with the state," and other "moderate" 'ulama' within the Syrian Ministry of *Awqaf* (Endowments). Accordingly, these religious scholars are constantly working to counter the radical (Islamic) regional and global elements, and to ensure that moderate as well as modern interpretations of Islam are made available to the public.[20] The rationale that is at work here is hard to escape: the state is no longer concerned with asserting Syria's hitherto secular culture, but rather is focused on containing religious radicalization – which would allow it to maintain its authoritarian power. Thus Syrian secularism has moved from asserting an anti-religious ideal to accepting religious difference and different religious identities in mediating state–citizen relations.

Other significant moves made by the government include letting the public enter mosques outside prayer times and allowing them to organize public festivals and to post religious banners in the streets in celebration of the Prophet Muhammad's birthday, something that had not been seen in the country for decades.[21] For someone who has not visited the country for a few years, the number of religious banners on the streets of Damascus is almost a surreal experience given the once implicit prohibition on such religious manifestations. Indeed, the once imposing Ba'thist banners fade into the background relative to the numerous colourful religious ones.

The state's accommodation of Syria's Islamic society did not extend to political accommodation, in the sense of allowing Islamic political parties to join the National Progressive Front. Yet it did allow some prominent Islamic figures, whether religious leaders or business leaders associated with a religious leader,

---

17 *Times of London*, 31 January 2006; *Gulf News*, 11 February 2006.
18 Syrian Ministry of *Awqaf*, 31 December 2007.
19 *As-Safir*, 6 April 2006.
20 Personal interview, Damascus, March 2008. Methods of outreach used by these shaykhs are discussed in Chapter 7 of this work.
21 Moubayed, "Islamic Revival in Syria." See also *New York Times*, 6 April 2006.

to participate in elections as independents. For example, in the 2007 legislative elections, "Muhammad Hamshu, a nouveau-riche Sunni and crony of the Asad family, and 'Abd al-Salam Rajih, dean of Kaftaru Academy's Shari'a faculty, came out on top with about 80,000 votes each."[22] The regime's decision to allow such participation could very well be due to the exigencies of maintaining domestic stability in the face of external challenges, particularly the war and subsequent unrest in neighbouring Iraq, as well as the withdrawal of Syria's troops from Lebanon following strong American and international pressure related to the assassination of Lebanese Prime Minister Rafiq al-Hariri in 2005. This suggests that Syria's foreign policy is newly linked with its domestic policy, which is a distinct change from the time of President Hafez al-Asad, when the country's corporatist structure meant that its foreign policy was kept strictly separate from its domestic policy.[23] In light of the Islamic extremism witnessed in neighbouring Iraq, this can explain the extant command's decision to seriously accommodate the religious sensibilities of Syria's Islamic groups (this will be further discussed hereinafter).

While the Syrian state has up to now allowed only Islamic figures to participate in elections as independents, some observers think that President Bashar al-Asad is seriously considering allowing a Syrian Islamic party to participate in the traditionally leftist National Progressive Front, as a way of co-opting ascendant Islamic groups and Islamist militants.[24] These observers say that such an action is supported by members of the new government, such as Shaykh Muhammad Habash, the preacher Muhammad Kamil al-Husayni and the new Grand Mufti Ahmad Hassoun. Their support is predicated on the notion that the regime's promotion of moderate Islam within the confines of the Syrian political system is important for diffusing Islamic discourse and thus neutralizing Islamist contention in the country. The import of such a move would clearly be significant, since it would end the Ba'th's long-standing separation of religion and the state. And whether or not it ultimately goes ahead, the mere fact that it is being considered underlines the extent of the regime's desire to appear open to Islamic actors in the country.[25]

In 2009, the state's accommodationist stance was broadened when it released a statement saying that it does not hold a "negative view" of Shaykh Hadi al-Bani's Islamic group.[26] The move was contentious for Syrian secularists – and more

---

22 Thomas Pierret and Kjetil Selvik, "Limits of Authoritarian Upgrading in Syria: Private Welfare, Islamic Charities, and the Rise of the Zayd Movement," *International Journal of Middle Eastern Studies* 41, 2009: 600–1.
23 For more on this, see Bassel Salloukh, "Organizing Politics in the Arab World: State–Society Relations and Foreign Policy Choices in Jordan and Syria," McGill University: PhD thesis, 2000.
24 Interviews with high-ranking government officials, Damascus, March–April 2008.
25 As was noted earlier, certain religious figures have been allowed to stand for parliamentary elections, and have even been successful at winning several seats since the early 1990s; but they were not standing as part of an Islamic party, or even as independent Islamic figures.
26 See Chapter 7 for more on Shaykh al-Bani.

specifically, for Baʿthist secularists – because the state had previously only extended inclusion to Islamic groups that were respectful of the country's secularism. Now it appeared to be moving towards accommodating a group that advocates the creation of an Islamic state in Syria, is opposed to women's equality with men and is considered by many to be one of the most radical neo-fundamentalist groups functioning in the country. The statement shattered the idea that only "moderate" religious ideas were tolerated by the state, and caused a number of Baʿth members to declare that the Baʿth is no longer a party that upholds secularism. Indeed, some members reacted to the state's recognition of al-Bani's group and to the various other measures aimed at compromise with, and accommodation of, Syria's resurgent Islamic movement by saying that the party should be re-named "the Islamic Baʿth Party" in light of the infiltration of conservative elements within its ranks.[27]

While this latter reaction was perhaps a bit over-heated, it is clear that the new command was pushing the political system's secular boundaries when it committed the Syrian state to supporting religious moderation. It is also clear that the regime's policies signalled the end of Baʿthist secularism as it had been known and practised, and a move towards articulating a new ideal for secularism in the country.

B Islamization from above and economic liberalization (infitah)

The economic choices made by the current command, which are a significant factor in understanding its declining legitimacy among the populace (see hereinafter and Chapter 9), are largely the result of the previous command's economic policies during the 1980s and 1990s.

We have seen that by the end of the 1990s, the state could no longer contain the contradictions inherent in the PA political model, particularly the growing economic aspirations of the state elite. This is because the PA regime's co-optation measures and the limited nature of the liberalization process that it deployed were contradictory and hence unsustainable in the longer run. As Hinnebusch explains:

> The investment environment was arguably not liberalised enough to attract sustained productive investment. Significant constraints remained built into the political system … Private sector industrial growth took the form of a further proliferation of small enterprises owing to fear of government regulation, populist labour law and the absence of financial markets to finance expansion.[28]

As a result, while the previous command's targeted liberalization was successful in postponing larger structural adjustments, it is no longer sufficient to secure the loyalty of strategic constituencies such as the business and the religious classes.

---

27 See Baʿthist website All4Syria at: http://all4syria.info/content/view/16751/96 (accessed 12 November 2009).
28 Hinnebusch, *Syria: Revolution from Above*, p. 135. See also pp. 136–7.

Furthermore, rapid depletion of oil reserves and a low rate of economic growth since the mid-1990s, coupled with significant demographic growth and soaring unemployment, meant that the country was heading towards a number of new economic challenges.[29]

In the face of these challenges, the Bashar al-Asad command chose to deploy further liberalizing measures. This was based on the idea that the private sector has become "a second engine of growth,"[30] and was also informed by global economic trends in favour of economic openness. Yet while the relaxation of economic control initiated by his father was neo-mercantilist, in the sense that it was designed to further state power formation and accumulation of wealth rather than to encourage the growth of private capital,[31] Bashar al-Asad's new economic formula has included a significant shift towards private capital development. Leverett explains, "the president wants to build up a real private sector, able to create jobs, before proceeding with large-scale privatizations."[32]

The state's shift to a new economic formula is the result of genuine "new thinking."[33] Bashar's alleged new thinking was underlined when he, upon assuming power in 2000, chose to place a higher importance upon dealing with growing economic pressures rather than the struggle with Israel. Indeed, while asserting his loyalty to Ba'thism, Bashar al-Asad's inaugural address in July 2000[34] emphasized the importance of a number of concepts not usually acknowledged in Ba'thist parlance, most notably free enterprise and Syrian integration into the global economy:[35]

> it has become necessary to move in steady, though gradual, steps, towards performing economic changes through the modernization of laws, the erosion of bureaucratic obstacles standing in the way of internal and external investment flow, the recruitment of both private and public capital, and the activation of the private sector and granting it better opportunities to work. ... We have also to put into place a wise economic policy that bridges gaps between sources and expenditure, between export and the rehabilitation of the private and public economic sectors, to face the increasing

---

29 These economic challenges are examined hereinafter.
30 Hinnebusch, "Calculated Decompression," p. 233.
31 See Chapter 5. See also Raymond A. Hinnebusch, "The Political Economy of Economic Liberalization in Syria," *International Journal of Middle East Studies* 27(3), August 1995: 311–14; Volker Perthes, "The Bourgeoisie and the Ba'th," *Middle East Report* 21(170), May–June 1991: 31–7.
32 Leverett, *Inheriting Syria*, p. 71.
33 Ibid., p. 30. Indeed, Hafez al-Asad's economic policies had two major goals: to undercut the potential opposition of the Sunni bourgeoisie and the Syrian Islamists, and to utilize strategic rents and aid from Arab Gulf states to confront the Israeli state.
34 See the Arab Gateway website: www.al-bab.com/arab/countries/syria/bashar00a.htm (accessed 12 April 2009).
35 See *Teshreen*, 6 June 2005; *Al-Hayat*, 19 June 2005; Lesch, *The New Lion of Damascus*; and Leverett, *Inheriting Syria*.

dangers resulting from the challenges of globalization. In this way our economy may well assume a respectable place in regional and international economic blocs.[36]

With this speech, Bashar al-Asad was clearly deviating from the original populist discourse, by incorporating a more liberal understanding of politics and by avoiding any mention of Ba'thist ideological cornerstones such as state interventionism, economic justice and social welfare, thereby drawing nearer to the common and contract law traditions of the Anglo-Saxon world.[37]

As a result of this intentional move away from state capitalism and towards a market economy, fiscal, monetary and trade reforms in line with International Monetary Fund (IMF) recommendations and adjustments were initiated. Measures towards structural changes (such as trade liberalization, tax policy reforms and liberalization of interest rates) aimed at creating new "sources of growth," with the main driver being both domestic and foreign private investment.[38] Investment Law 10 was also amended twice, once in 2000 and again in 2003. These revisions were aimed at modernizing the Syrian legislative and financial systems in the economic sphere and relaxing importation laws. They resulted in the opening of private banks and insurance companies starting in 2004,[39] and in general, credit to the private sector rose from around 7 per cent of overall credit in 2002 to some 46 per cent in 2005.[40]

Thus, the state decided to expand its economic patronage network by granting permits to four Islamic banks in 2006. These are the Syrian National Islamic Bank, Bank al-Sham, the Baraka Bank of Syria and the Nur Islamic Bank.[41] Their capitalization is allowed to reach US$100 million, three times larger than the capitalization permitted to the non-Islamic private banks.[42] Commenting on

36 See www.al-bab.com/arab/countries/syria/bashar00a.htm.
37 See also Leverett, *Inheriting Syria*, pp. 69–70. Here, one has to recognize the importance of economic liberalism in the production of a vision of society. See: Olivier Roy, *Secularism Confronts Islam*, New York: Columbia University Press, 2007. It will be argued later that this new turn towards a market economy contributed to the increasing popularity of the Islamist movement in Syria. While the role of ideology and regional factors played a key role, changes in the country's social and economic landscape led to the expansion of an Islamic economic sector and contributed to the appeal of the Islamist opposition.
38 IMF, "Staff Report for the 2006 Article IV Consultation," prepared by the Staff Representatives for the 2006 Consultation with the Syrian Arab Republic, 13 July 2006. IMF Country Report No. 06/294, p. 38. Online: www.imf.org/external/pubs/ft/scr/2006/cr06294.pdf.
39 See news.bbc.co.uk/2/hi/business/7934644.stm and www.syria-bourse.com. For a view of the economic challenges facing Syria, as well as of economic needs from a Syrian perspective, see Nabil Sikkar (the executive director of the Syrian Bureau for development and investment), *al-Islah al-Iqtisadi fi Suriya*, al-Rayes Books: Damascus, 2000; idem, "Hatmiyat al-Islah al-Iqtisadi fi Suriya" [The Inevitability of Economic Reform in Syria], *Al-Iktissad Wal-Aamal* 247, July 2000: 28–32; see also *Al-Iktissad Wal-Aamal*, special issue on investment in Syria (November 2000).
40 IMF, "Staff Report for the 2006 Article IV Consultation," p. 10.
41 *Al-Sharq al-Awsat*, 28 August 2007.
42 *As-Safir*, 6 April 2006; *Al-Watan*, 27 August 2007.

the inauguration of Bank al-Sham, the Grand Mufti of Syria, Badr al-Din Hassoun, asserted that studies show that 47 per cent of Syrians dealing with the banking system prefer dealing with Islamic institutions, "especially in light of Syria's move towards a market economy."[43]

In another liberalizing move, the Damascus Securities Exchange was launched in March 2009 with six companies listed, and in May 2010, as many as 14 stocks were listed, with a total worth of US$1.2 billion. The market includes ten banks and insurers; other companies deal in logistics, media, food and agricultural sectors.[44] Indeed, in December 2010, the Minister of Finance explained that the new 2011 budget foresees that as much as half of the expected 4,000 billion Syrian liras poured within the economy are expected to be made by the private sector. This is a precedent in Syria's budgeting plans.[45]

Another initiative that is indicative of the Ba'th's new direction is a programme called "Start Your Project," which teaches young entrepreneurs how to launch their own business, and ultimately to transform their ideas into fully fledged enterprises. Once the programme was approved, accords were signed between the government and the private and public banks to fund the trainees' projects and to provide the necessary capital for their start-up companies.[46]

A commercial sort of economic *infitah* (opening) was also introduced in 2000, and a number of bilateral free-trade accords were concluded in an attempt to create a free-trade zone within the Arab world. The Greater Arab Free Trade Agreement (GAFTA), under the tutelage of the Arab League, came into effect in January 2005, and led to customs duties being eliminated between Syria and all other members of GAFTA,[47] thus marking the end of Syria's Ba'thist protectionist measures for its domestic market and for its fledgling industries. In 2004–2005, the last remaining boycotts based on the Arab League Black List of companies dealing with Israel were lifted in Syria. As a result, Coca Cola and Pepsi were allowed into the Syrian market.[48] And in January 2007, Syria's free-trade agreement with yet another neighbouring country, Turkey, came into force.

In addition to these economic reforms, the government also launched a number of changes related to the agrarian sector that can best be described as "counter-reforms." Thus between December 2000 and January 2005, the Ba'thist

---

43 Ibid. [Author's translation.]
44 See Wharton website: http://knowledge.wharton.upenn.edu/arabic/article.cfm?articleid=2459&language_id=6 (accessed May 2010). Trading takes place from 10:30a.m. to 1:00p.m., Monday, Tuesday and Thursday. In a move designed to foster stability, the Syrian Commission for Financial Markets has kept a tight grip on share trading: daily share movements are limited to 2 per cent, for example, and investors cannot deal in a single stock more than once a day.
45 Syrian TV, "Interview with the Minister of Finance," 28 December 2010.
46 *SANA News*: www.sana.sy/ara/7/2008/07/25/185541.htm.
47 The other GAFTA member states are: Jordan, United Arab Emirates, Bahrain, Saudi Arabia, Oman, Qatar, Morocco, Lebanon, Iraq, Egypt, Palestine, Kuwait, Tunisia, Libya, Sudan and Yemen.
48 Leila Vigual, "La 'nouvelle consommation' et les transformations des paysages urbains à la lumière de l'ouverture économique: l'exemple de Damas," *Revue des mondes musulmans et de la Méditerranée* 115–16, December 2006: 23–5.

government promulgated a number of political decrees to bring about the privatization of state farms in Syria. Myriam Ababsa explains that

> [t]he principal decree, decision number 83, promulgated on December 16, 2000, allocates land in shares of 3 ha for irrigated land and 8 ha for non-irrigated land. Decision 83 called for land to be distributed by order of priority, to landholders expropriated in the agrarian reforms of 1958, 1963 and 1966, to farm workers and to employees of the General Administration of the Euphrates Basin (GADEB). In January 2005, 12,500 beneficiaries received 38,500 ha. Half of them were former landowners or beneficiaries of the earlier land reforms, a third were sharecroppers with leaseholds and a fifth were workers and GADEB employees.

According to Ababsa, these moves marked the end of the socialist side of Ba'thist ideology, since "[t[he primary beneficiaries of the reform process are not the traditional rural constituents of the Ba'th party, but a re-emergent class of latifundists tied to the central state and to traditional power structures."[49]

Other "counter-reforms" launched by the Syrian government were related to its subsidization of products such as sugar, electricity and transportation. These subsidies, which had been in place since 1963, were cancelled for everything except staples like bread over the course of several years. This led to the prices of such important commodities as gasoline and cement rising by 23 and 55 per cent, respectively, in 2006.[50] One report explains that

> [d]iesel subsidies alone have cost between US$1 billion and US$1.5 billion annually over the last five years. According to Dr. Nabil Sukkar ... the government has managed to postpone this difficult decision for some time, but can no longer afford to do so and likely will continue along the path it has already begun to embark on.[51]

In an interview in December 2010 on Syrian TV, the Minister of Finance explained that the state continues to take upon it the livelihood of Syrian citizens but that it also needs to move towards more economic liberalization and can no longer act as a welfare state in today's global reality.[52]

In retrospect, it can be seen that the amendment of Investment Law No. 10 in 2003 marked the government's definitive move towards the private sector. Indeed, this relaxation of economic controls and the accompanying increase in domestic investment and private-sector growth was a strong factor in the Syrian economy's expansion at an average rate of 7 to 8 per cent per annum from 2003

---

49 Myriam Ababsa, "Contre-réforme agraire et conflits fonciers en Jazîra syrienne (2000–2005)", *Revue des mondes musulmans et de la Méditerranée* 115–16, December 2006: 211.
50 IMF, "Staff Report for the 2006 Article IV Consultation," p. 11.
51 See the Syria Report, 23 June 2008. Online: www.syria-report.com/article.asp?id=2897&rub=24.
52 Syrian TV, "Interview with the Minister of Finance," 28 December 2010.

to 2007.[53] Yet at the same time, this encouragement of the private sector has created other sources of worry for the regime.[54] First, it is causing the sharp re-stratification of Syrian society along class lines, and a widening gap between the rich and the poor. This gap highlights the degree to which the poor have failed to benefit from the economic growth that paralleled the country's *infitah* policies. Indeed, while the period 1997–2004 was marked by strong economic growth, it also saw inequality rise by 11 per cent.[55] This trend has been further accentuated by the fact that about two-thirds of its exports are oil-related (since profits from the oil sector disproportionately benefit the upper classes).[56] The second major worry for the political command arising from its selective encouragement of the private sector is that the market-oriented measures are leading to an abandonment of the populist reformist policies that had assured it of the support of the middle and lower classes (see Part I of this work).

The last few years have also witnessed the emergence of powerful businessmen who have become members of the People's Assembly and ultimately powerful opposition activists. Unlike the Sunni merchant class, who mainly hail from Damascus and were under the patronage of Hafez al-Asad's command, these businessmen are growing independent of the government's "special arrangements." In their demands for modernization, they are pushing for more structural changes and greater privatization measures, and are calling for the creation of an overall system based on liberalized markets.[57] The mere fact that they are able to make these demands shows the degree to which economic liberalization has become an indispensable engine of growth for the state, albeit one that is testing the regime's ability to balance Syria's various social groups, from the increasingly marginalized to the newly emerging business elite.

Islamic revivalism cannot of course be solely explained through reference to the economic liberalization deployed by the current political command and discussed above. Nonetheless, the country's Islamic and Islamist movements have a clear opportunity to benefit from the present economic situation, and to be supported by the economic elite – through elite extension – in doing so.[58] This

53 See www.fedcommsyr.org/economy.html.
54 This topic will be discussed in more detail in Chapters 8 and 9.
55 Heba al-Laithy, *Poverty in Syria*, UNDP Report (June 2005), pp. 9 and 12. See also Eyal Zisser, *Commanding Syria: Bashar al-Asad and the First Years in Power*, New York: I.B. Tauris, 2007, pp. 111–18; the CIA World Factbook (accessed 16 September 2008); Syrian Central Bureau of Statistics Reports, online: www.cbssyr.org [Arabic]; UNICEF and the Syrian Central Bureau of Statistics, *al-Maseh al-'Unqudi Muta'aded al-Mu'ashirat*, Damascus 2006, online: www.cbssyr.org/people%20statistics/Final_Report_Syria_ARB.pdf; United Nations Development Programme Syria, online: www.undp.org.sy.
56 Al-Laithy, *Poverty in Syria*, p. 9. Although this has not yet been fully documented, oil revenues are said to be monopolized by the few in the country rather than re-distributed.
57 Zisser, *Commanding Syria*, pp. 83 and 92.
58 As we will see in subsequent chapters, this is especially so because having espoused a free market ideology in the 1970s and 1980s, the Islamic sector is re-adapting its ideology, incorporating populist elements within its agenda and therefore appealing to those who were opposed to the movement a few years earlier, namely the lower classes and the rural constituency.

situation is in many ways dire: there has been an influx of some 1.5 million Iraqi refugees into Syria since the beginning of the war there, who benefit from the same advantages enjoyed by Syrian citizens such as schooling and healthcare;[59] unemployment has risen to approximately 25 per cent and has reduced some 10 per cent of the population to poverty in certain regions of the country; there has been an enormous loss of revenue as a result of Syria's withdrawal from Lebanese territory in 2005;[60] and the Syrian welfare system has largely collapsed due to the move away from state capitalism and towards greater privatization. Moreover, the impact of these factors has been magnified by the country's significant demographic expansion and the accelerating rural exodus. Taken together, this situation has caused the poor in Syria to feel abandoned by the state, and for lack of any other viable ideological and institutional alternative, to begin turning their eyes towards the rising parallel Islamic sector, which ironically is the only alternative that was permitted to prosper under the Ba'th regime.[61] Effectively, therefore, economic liberalization within the context of the economic recession that the country has been experiencing since the late 1990s is providing Syria's Islamic groups with an important platform for mobilization, something it did not have 30 years ago when a majority of the Syrian populace supported the secular, populist programmes of the Ba'th.

C Islamization from above and the regime's foreign policy

The following section discusses the current regime's foreign policy in terms of its use of regional Islamist militant groups. It considers the consequences of these policies in light of the domestic and regional contexts, as well as with an eye to the larger arguments, thereby linking the state's current foreign policy to the revivalism in the Islamic sector domestically and to the creation of an Islamist sub-sector that is gaining in strength and is increasingly beyond the Syrian state's control.

While domestic social and economic factors have partially determined Bashar al-Asad's policy of carefully cultivating an Islamic profile in domestic affairs, another key reason for the Syrian state's policy of Islamization from above has been as a direct outcome of the American-led intervention in Iraq and the

---

59 See Ashraf al-Khalidi et al., *Project on Internal Displacement Iraqi Refugees in the Syrian Arab Republic: A Field-Based Snapshot*, Bern: The Brookings Institution, University of Bern, June 2007.
60 See Gary C. Gambill, "Syria after Lebanon: Hooked on Lebanon," *Middle East Quarterly*, Fall 2005: 35–42; "Syria, President Bush, and Drugs: The Administration's Next Iraqgate," Subcommittee Staff Report, House Judiciary Committee's Subcommittee on Crime and Criminal Justice, 28 October 1992; Ziad K. Abdelnour, "The Revival of Lebanon's Drug Trade," *Middle East Intelligence Bulletin*, June 2001.
61 The impact of the relationship between economic liberalization and economic crisis on Syrian society will be further discussed in Chapter 7 of this work. See UNDP, *Poverty in Syria: 1996–2004*, New York: UNDP, 2005; Zisser, *Commanding Syria*, pp. 111–18. See also Nabil Marzuq, *al-Faqr wa al-Batala fi Suriya* [Poverty and Unemployment in Syria], Damascus: Arab Centre for Strategic Studies, 2004.

ensuing rise of Islamist militancy in the region.[62] This rise has been both a blessing and a challenge to the Damascus administration. On one hand, the permeation of these Islamist groups in the region can be used to reinforce Syria's influence and position as a regional power, given the patron–client relationships established by Hafez al-Asad with these regional Islamist groups (see Chapter 5). Indeed, a state that has the ability to wield the trans-national "weapon" of Islamism can clearly make an impact upon regional events. On the other hand, however, Syria is a secular state and its political command is still perceived by certain Islamists as an 'Alawi heretic command, which makes it a potential target of the ascendant jihadist activity.[63]

As will be detailed below, Bashar al-Asad's continuation of Hafez al-Asad's pragmatic foreign policy of engaging with Islamist groups – so as to use them for Syria's own purposes and regional concerns – is causing the further Islamization of the Syrian domestic scene.

Continuing his father's pragmatic approach to the region

Many political observers, and especially those from the "West," anticipated that President Bashar al-Asad would pursue a different foreign policy than that of his father. This was because of his relatively young age when he assumed the presidency, as well as the amount of time that he had spent living in Europe prior to becoming president. In particular, many observers expected Bashar al-Asad to step away from the previous regime's championing of Arab and Syrian nationalism, and to initiate an ideological and strategic rapprochement with the powers of the West.[64] These expectations were quickly dashed, however, as Bashar laid out policies that were in line with those of his father, and indeed seemed at times even more hard line according to critics of the Syrian policies, especially when it came to Syria's regional policy. This was especially evident in his approach to the Palestinian question and to the American intervention in Iraq.[65] And while the policy orientations of Bashar al-Asad's command may have been opaque to many Western observers, they were arguably quite understandable in light of the country's regional concerns.[66] For the United States, "Syria maintains the capac-

---

62 It is important to note here that the Syrian existential fears that ensued from the American-led intervention in Iraq and the resulting chaos of the neighbouring country Iraq have led the Bashar al-Asad administration to further work with and appease regional Islamists. American-imposed sanctions on Syria following the Hariri assassination in Lebanon have reinforced these policy choices.
63 For some within the religious groups, Syrian secularism is "an atheist cover up" fashioned by Syrian 'Alawis in order to restrict Syria's Muslim practices and law and confine them to the private sphere.
64 See Eyal Zisser, "Syria and the War in Iraq," *Meria* 7(2), June 2003. Online: http://meria.idc.ac.il/journal/2003/issue2/jv7n2a4.html (accessed 14 October 2008).
65 The information on Syria's links to regional Islamist groups is necessarily fragmented given the lack of corroborating sources. Thus what is important to take away from these allegations is the general trend of Syria's involvement in the region.
66 Mona Yacoubian and Scott Lazensky, *Dealing with Damascus: Seeking a Greater Return on U.S. Syria Relations*, New York: Council on Foreign Relations, 2008, p. 2.

ity to obstruct U.S. interests if it feels its own interests are threatened." In the words of Volker Perthes, "Syria's leaders may not always act wisely, but they have rational and legitimate security concerns."[67]

Syria's regional influence and pragmatic approach were tested within the first year of Bashar's rule, during which two foreign policy crises broke out. The first was the Palestinian intifada in September 2000, which resulted in renewed Syrian backing for Palestinian Islamists both within Syria and in the Palestinian territories, as well as renewed skirmishes between Hizbullah and Israel. The second crisis was the "war on terror" declared by the United States in the wake of the 11 September 2001 al-Qaeda attacks on New York City and Washington, and the ensuing American-led intervention in Afghanistan and Iraq.

Resistance to Israel and its repercussions

The Palestinian Intifada prompted a pragmatic response from the new Syrian administration. Eyal Zisser writes:

> The outbreak of the intifada caught Damascus completely by surprise, and it may be assumed that the Syrians did not initiate the renewed Hizballah activities against Israel that occurred in early October 2000. At most they had been informed of no more than the organization's general intentions, an expression of the new balance of power created between Damascus and the organization following the death of Hafiz al-Asad. Nevertheless, from the moment the intifada broke out, Bashar tried to exploit the new realities emerging in the region to promote his personal status as well as Syria's standing as a regional power. These new regional realities provided a golden opportunity for him to establish his personal and political status as the head of the Arab rejectionist camp, or at least as the head of a camp whose opposition to Israel was staunch and uncompromising. The mood of the public on the streets of Damascus as well as in the other Arab capitals substantially contributed to Bashar's increasingly tough policy. He wanted to create the image of being close to the heart of the Arab man [and woman]-on-the-street and willing to do his bidding.[68]

Continued Syrian support for the Palestinian and the Lebanese resistance to Israel have prompted the Israelis and the American administration under George W. Bush to accuse the Bashar al-Asad command of de-stabilizing the region by enabling Islamist groups, namely Hamas and the Lebanese Hizbullah.[69] Indeed, an Israeli military intelligence report alleged that Syria was putting the Lebanese territory at the disposal of the Palestinian Islamic resistance (by allowing arms to

---
67 Perthes, *Syria under Bashar al-Asad*, p. 6.
68 Zisser, "Syria and the War in Iraq."
69 See Yacoubian and Lazensky, *Dealing with Damascus*, p. 3; *International Herald Tribune*, 20 December 2007.

be provided to the resistance, as well as by allowing money transfers and training to take place), and was also enabling Hizbullah to pressure Israel along the Israeli–Lebanese border, in support of the Palestinian resistance.[70] The Israeli security services also alleged that its interrogations of senior operational activists had determined that the Palestinian Islamic Jihad (PIJ) commanders in the Hebron area were in contact with senior PIJ activists in Damascus such as Akram al-Ajuri, and that these activists were helping to direct operations in the Palestinian territories, and were also transferring money for the fight against Israel through the Syrian national banking system.[71] Another allegation was that of the more than 20 Hamas activists arrested by Israel in the second half of 2001, almost all had been trained in Syria, and were receiving operational instructions from Syria. The activists, originally students at Arab universities, were allegedly contacted by the Hamas headquarters in Damascus and were sent for training in Syria and in Lebanon's Beqaa Valley. At these training camps, the students received instruction on the use of arms, explosive charges and explosive belts, as well as in intelligence activities.[72] Whether these specific allegations are truthful or not, the Syrian command has appeared more supportive of Islamist groups than the previous one. Not only did it continue to play host to Hamas and the PIJ leaders, and express the need to keep supporting both the Palestinian and the Lebanese resistance, be it Islamist or secular, it has also invited Hamas and Hizbullah leaders to speak in Damascus. This is a new event in the life of Syrians. It speaks to the depth of Syrian existential fears of Israel and the new regional reality.

Regarding Syria's relations with Hizbullah, the withdrawal from Lebanon in April 2005 following the still-unsolved assassination of Lebanon's Prime Minister Rafiq al-Hariri[73] led to a decline in direct Syrian control over the Shi'i movement. Nonetheless, the Syrian intelligence apparatus remains active underground in Lebanon.[74] Generally speaking, Israeli sources claim that Bashar al-Asad has lent relatively more support to the resistance movement compared to his father:

---

70 "Iran and Syria as Strategic Support for Palestinian Terrorism (Based on Interrogations of Arrested Palestinian Terrorists and Captured Palestinian Authority Documents)," document no. TR6-548-02, Israel Defence Forces, Military Intelligence, September 2002. Online: www.mfa.gov.il/MFA.
71 Ibid.
72 Ibid. According to Syrians, the Palestinians' acts are mere resistance to Israeli occupation rather than terrorism. That being said, the Syrian administration has also denied the Israeli allegations.
73 The Hariri assassination was initially thought to be the fault of Syria rather than of Israel. Accordingly, it sparked a further downward spiral in Syria's relations with the Western powers, and ended in Washington's withdrawal of its ambassador from Damascus. Leverett, *Inheriting Syria*, p. 17. In 2010, a controversial UN report and the Hariri Future Movement exonerated the Syrian administration of the Hariri assassination, although recent reports have put the blame on Hizbullah agents while the investigation is still ongoing.
74 See Gambill, "Syria after Lebanon"; Sami G. Hajjar, "Hizballah: Terrorism, National Liberation, or Menace?" Strategic Studies Institute, US Army War College, August 2002.

[t]he Bashar Assad regime not only allows Hizbullah to carry out terrorist attacks from Lebanese territory, as one of the expressions of its support for the Intifada, but also provides direct aid to the Hizbullah, a step from which Assad Sr. refrained.[75]

For instance, Bashar al-Asad's command has been blamed for Hizbullah's use of anti-aircraft guns, as well as for its use of mortar and rocket barrages targeting Israeli outposts in the disputed Shebaa Farms, a 15-square-mile strip of mountainous territory running along Lebanon's south-east border with the Golan Heights. Blanford points to three occasions since December 2002 when Syria wielded its influence in Lebanon to "exact revenge, although not always claiming responsibility, upon Israeli troops on the border for assassinations of its personnel presumably ordered by Israel."[76]

Whether or not these Hizbullah measures were directly sanctioned by the Syrian president, it is clear that he has stepped up certain kinds of assistance that mark a strengthening of the relationship between the resistance group and Syria. This stronger relationship has led to Hizbullah's leader Hasan Nasrallah appearing more frequently on Syrian television, and being represented as a close friend of Bashar al-Asad. Some observers have also claimed that Bashar has drawn upon the shaykh's rhetoric and strategizing to counter regional and international pressures. On the domestic front, Bashar's ties with Hizbullah's Nasrallah have allowed the Syrian president to demonstrate ideological loyalty to the Palestinian-Arab cause, which is strategically important since such an anti-Western stance helps to further legitimize his rule.

Yet despite the undoubted advantage of such legitimization, Syria's closer ties with Islamic groups have also proven to be a challenge to the country's secular political culture. Thus official speeches by the president and by civil servants, as well as the state media in general, make reference to the legitimacy of the Islamic resistance while ignoring the previous "secularizing" agenda (notwithstanding the two logics are not necessarily mutually exclusive). Effectively, therefore, the secular message has lost its impetus, clarity and vibrancy at precisely the moment that support for religious groups was bolstered. To give a concrete example, Syrian patriotic flags and pendants used to have only secular Ba'thist symbols on them, with Mao Tse Dong and Fidel Castro featured when representations of international personalities were called for. Yet today, Shaykh Hassan Nasrallah appears on such patriotic accessories more often than leftist leaders do. It reinforces the idea that the Syrian state has reached a turning point in terms of balancing ideological commitments with political action.

---

75 "Iran and Syria as Strategic Support for Palestinian Terrorism," Israeli Defence Forces.
76 Nicholas Blanford, "Hizballah and Syria's 'Lebanese Card'," *MERIP Reports*, 14 September 2004. Online: www.merip.org/mero/mero091404.html.

The 9/11 attacks and the Iraq crisis

The other crisis that broke out in the first year of Bashar's rule was the 9/11 attacks. These produced a new regional and international reality that culminated in the American-led invasions of both Afghanistan and Iraq, which have certainly impacted Syrian domestic and foreign policy.

Syria immediately denounced the 9/11 attacks, and recognized the American right to self-defence. The Syrian regime even allowed American FBI agents to enter Syrian territory in search of al-Qaeda activists who were thought to be hiding in the country.[77] This strong stance against al-Qaeda was in line with Damascus's position even before the US-led invasions of Afghanistan and Iraq, notwithstanding Syria's clear disapproval of the American invasion. Syria's relatively pro-American stance took a beating, however, in the summer of 2002, when reports emerged that the Syrian command had defied UN-imposed sanctions on Iraq by turning a blind eye to the smuggling of weapons from Eastern Europe into Iraq via Syria, which involved Firas Talas, son of former Syrian Defence Minister Mustafa Talas, and Rami Makhlouf, a cousin of Bashar al-Asad and a well-known businessman in Damascus.[78] Also in 2002, Jordanian and American intelligence reported that Islamist fighters linked to al-Zarqawi's Jund al-Sham organization were operating out of Syria. The fighters were believed to be receiving both funding and training in the country.[79] In late 2002, it was reported that the Bashar al-Asad command had allowed the Iraqi Ba'th to hide some of its weapons in Syria, and had even assisted in the transfer of Iraqi weapons to Hizbullah.[80] April 2003 saw the US administration accuse the Syrians of transferring dual-use items to the Iraqi resistance, of smuggling night-vision goggles into Iraqi territory[81] and of turning a blind eye to pan-Arab and Islamist volunteer fighters who were crossing the Syrian border into Iraq.[82]

---

77 Zisser, "Syria and the War in Iraq."
78 For more on Rami Makhlouf from the US Treasury point of view, see www.treas.gov/press/releases/hp834.htm (accessed 31 October 2009).
79 Alon Ben-David, "Jordanian Indictment Reveals Operations of Jund al-Sham Terror Network," *Jane's Intelligence Review*, 16 June 2003.
80 Leverett, *Inheriting Syria*, p. 16. See also Anthony H. Cordesman, "The Department of Defense Quarterly Report on Stability and Security in Iraq: The Warning Indicators," Center for Strategic and International Studies, Washington, DC, 22 December 2006.
81 See *As-safir*, 15 April 2006; See also Leverett, *Inheriting Syria*, pp. 16–17; Barbara Slavin, "U.S. Warns Syria; Next Step Uncertain," *USA Today*, 17 September 2003; Gary C. Gambill, "Syria Rearms Iraq," *Middle East Intelligence Bulletin* 4(9), September 2002, online: www.meforum.org/meib/articles/0209_s2.htm; and Hans Greimel, "Foreign Fighters Remain Threat in Iraq," *Associated Press*, 15 April 2003; Zisser, "Syria and the War on Terror." Syria's defiance in 2002–2003 of the US-imposed sanctions on Iraq, particularly by allowing the movement of "foreign fighters" across its border into Iraq in the early days of the war, was met with increasing international rhetorical pressure on the regime to modify its economic and political system. The pressure culminated in the American enactment of the Syria Accountability Act in November–December 2003. Additional economic sanctions on Syria were issued by the Bush administration in May 2004. See Leverett, *Inheriting Syria*, pp. 16–17.

In 2004, the US Treasury labelled the Commercial Bank of Syria a rogue financial institution, and accused it of backing "terrorist" activities in Iraq.[83]

The Syrian administration denied these accusations.[84] Still, as a result of both mounting international pressure and voices within the Syrian state apparatus, further measures were put in place in early 2004 to hinder the movement of fighters in and out of the country (particularly from Iraq). A spokesperson of the Syrian state explained that Syria has placed 530 inspection centres on the Syrian–Iraqi border in order to control Islamist fighters entering and leaving Syria.[85] One unintended consequence of these tightening measures was the eruption of a number of spill-over Islamist attacks inside Syria, despite the state's best efforts to quash such internal disturbances.

Syria's role as a transit corridor for militants heading to Iraq might have served two purposes for the Syrian state: it possibly provided an outlet for Syrian jihadists to be active while remaining relatively unthreatening to the Syrian domestic scene, and it also allowed Syrian intelligence to monitor the flow of fighters and collect information on them, as well as to recruit Islamist collaborators (see Ghuraba' al-Sham section in Chapter 8).

Syria's relations with Iran

Syria and Iran have become increasingly close under Bashar's presidency. This is the result of a number of factors, most importantly the chill that has affected Syria's relations with its Arab neighbours beginning in the early 2000s. Since the 2003 war on Iraq, the Syrian administration has often expressed its disenchantment with the pro-American Arab states, mainly Saudi Arabia, Kuwait and Egypt. Damascus has also repeatedly confirmed its alliance with the Islamic Republic of Iran. For instance, in one of his most recent interviews on the subject, President Bashar al-Asad reiterated that "the strategic relations between Iran and Syria are based on shared principles and interests affirming that as long as their ideologies intersect on foreign policies, they would remain allies."[86] He also said that Iran's support for Syria's opposition to the Zionist regime is of

---

82 See the previous footnote. See also "Akthar Min Ra'i," Al-Jazeera TV, 18 September 2009. Syria has since repeatedly denied the accusations that it is deliberately allowing weapons and militants into Iraq, arguing that it is simply unable to completely control such a long border. They point to the similar American inability to control the flow of immigrants from Mexico into the United States. In other words, Syria is willing, although not completely able, to stop all infiltrations from its territory into Iraq. On where the jihadists came from, see Joseph Felter and Brian Fishman, *Al-Qaida's Foreign Fighters in Iraq: A First Look at the Sinjar Records*, West Point, NY: Combating Terrorism Center, 2007. Online: http://ctc.usma.edu/harmony/pdf/CTCForeignFighter.19.Dec07.pdf.
83 US Treasury, "Treasury Designates Commercial Bank of Syria as Financial Institution of Primary Money Laundering Concern," 11 May 2004. Online: www.ustreas.gov/press/releases/js1538.htm.
84 See "Hiwar Maftuh," Al-Jazeera TV, 30 June 2007.
85 "Akthar Min Ra'i," Al-Jazeera TV, 18 September 2009.
86 *Press TV*, "No effort can distance Syria from Iran," 18 September 2008. Online: www.presstv.ir/detail.aspx?id=69800&sectionid=351020101.

132 *Bashar al-Asad's era*

great importance, and reconfirmed Tehran and Damascus' shared stance in support of the Islamic resistance in Lebanon and Palestine. According to al-Asad, "The achievements of the resistance over the past decade and its victory over the Israeli regime are the result of Tehran–Damascus strategic relations."[87]

Syria's relations with Iran are central to this work for two main reasons. The first is the manner in which they are contributing to the shifting role of secularism in Syria, as was explained in the previous paragraphs. The second reason flows from Iran's Shi'i identity, which some say has been a spur to Shi'ism in Syria, a development that is an unwelcome one for many Syrians (see Chapter 8). Indeed, a number of Sunni shaykhs and observers have alleged that the government is actually promoting the conversion of Syrians to Shi'ism in an attempt to shift the country's demographic balance in favour of the sect, since the regime is itself overwhelmingly composed of Shi'i (of the 'Alawi sect).[88] And despite denials by a number of Sunni members of the Syrian regime, including MP and Sunni Shaykh Muhammad Habash, the belief that Shi'ism is growing in the country is fuelled by the fact that there are now around 500 Shi'i *Hawzas* and *Husseiniyat* that accommodate thousands of Iranian clerics, all financed, built and supervised by the Iranian embassy.[89] The belief is also fuelled by such developments as the upcoming inauguration of the country's fifth Islamic bank by the Syrian *Ahl al-Bayt* Shi'i society, as well as the impending launch of a television channel and an Islamic financial institution to promote multi-lateral relations among Islamic countries. Regarding the activities of the *Ahl al-Bayt* society, the Syrian Muslim Brotherhood leader at the time, 'Ali Sadr al-Din al-Bayanuni, said that

> The real problem is not that a number of people have become Shii, but that Shiism has been disseminated and caused problems within Syrian society. When people convert from being Sunni to Shia, it provokes Sunni scholars and individuals and creates problems within the fabric of the Syrian society. I know that significant divisions have occurred in some villages due to the dissemination of Shiism. Many reports have declared unlimited Iranian support to Shiism in Syria. There is an attempt to establish cultural centers for disseminating Shiism in Syria in different governorates and cities that have never known this before.

Al-Bayanuni then elaborated on the reasons behind the spread of Shi'ism in Syria:

> There is a religious doctrinal reason and a political one. The wave of Iranian progress in Syria hasn't been limited to Shiism. There is cultural, charitable

---

87 Ibid.
88 See Hamida Hamid, "A Study on Conversion to Shiism in Syria," *Elaph* 7 January 2007; "Religious Leaders Reject the Dissemination of Iranian Shiism in Syria," online: www.aljaml.com/node/9168 (accessed 5 November 2008); See also CNN website: www.arabic.cnn.com/2007/middle_east/4/2/shiite.syria/index.html.
89 Hamid, "A Study on Conversion to Shiism in Syria."

and even military Iranian activity. Iranian influence in Syria is not only doctrinal, but also political, social and military. Husseiniyats are being built for the Shia minority in Aleppo, Idlib and the new Shia villages in Jaser Ashour and others. On the radio in Damascus, the call to prayer is broadcast at times from the shrine of Sayyeda Zainab or Sayyeda Ruqayah according to the Shia method; that is, they add "come to the good deed" after saying "come to prayer and come to success." This wasn't the case before in Syria.[90]

It is claimed that the *Ahl al-Bayt* society in Damascus is directly linked to the Iranian embassy in the Syrian capital, and is not subject to the supervision of Syrian authorities. In the National Salvation Front's[91] statement following their June 2008 annual meeting, there was a warning to Syrians of further Iranian activity, "[w]hat [has] made things worse is the Iranian incursion that is spending money in the country without any supervision in order to increase the tension and threaten the national harmony."[92] In a discussion with a secular 'Alawi journalist, he asserted that even the otherwise secular 'Alawi community has started to feel the impact of society's Islamization: "Whether this is due to a general emulating of the Sunni piety movement, or to an Iranian Shi'i intervention in Syria, it is unclear," though it has meant that "a number of 'Alawi women have started to wear headscarves, in a clear divergence from 'Alawi norms. Men have also been going to the Friday prayer and signing up for economic and miscellaneous social benefits in nearby Shi'i mosques."[93]

The true extent of this alleged Shi'i Islamization of Syrians is not yet clear. Yet what is clear is that the current administration has continued to endorse both the Lebanese Shi'i Party and Iran while at the same time encouraging the country's de-secularization, this despite the public's awareness of increasing Sunni–Shi'i sensitivities regionally. This endorsement has, for instance, led to 'Imad Mughniya – Hizbullah's head of external operations who was allegedly involved in the attack on the American military base in Lebanon during the Lebanese civil war, as well as in the bombing of the Israeli embassy and the Jewish community centre in Buenos Aires – being made to feel welcome in Syria, and often residing in the country until his mysterious assassination on 12 February 2008.[94] It has also led to Syria allowing Iran to resupply Hizbullah with weapons through the Damascus airport, despite the efforts of the United States to control the Shi'i group by providing military and law enforcement assistance to the Hariri coalition in Lebanon. Syria has also allowed visiting Iranian officials to meet with Palestinian organizations based in Syria.[95]

90 *Asharq al-Awsat*, 16 July 2008.
91 The National Salvation Front is an opposition group composed mainly of Muslim Brothers, in alliance with the now-exiled ex-Vice President Abdul Halim Khaddam, although this alliance ended in June 2009. For more on this alliance, see Chapters 6 and 7.
92 The National Salvation Front at www.free-syria.com, 2 July 2008.
93 Private communication, January 2009.
94 Zisser, "Syria and the War in Iraq."
95 Kenneth Katzman, *Terrorism, Near Eastern Groups and State Sponsors*, Report for Congress, Washington, DC: The Library of Congress, 2002, p. 35.

Syria's animosity towards al-Qaeda and Fath al-Islam

Syria does not have any direct relations with al-Qaeda, and seems to view the al-Qaeda regional cells (based mainly in Iraq) and the pro al-Qaeda groups such as the Lebanese Fatah al-Islam (FAI) as having the potential to become threats to Syrian political stability.

The FAI is an Islamist group that gained support among the very poor residents of the Palestinian refugee camp of Naher al-Bared, near Tripoli in Lebanon. The group was accused by the Syrian government of staging the so-called "Damascus bombing" in September 2008 that caused the death of 17 Syrians and injuries to dozens more.[96] The organization and its leader Shaker al-'Absi have been under intense pressure by the Lebanese government since March 2008 to cease their activity. 'Absi, who was born in a refugee camp near Jericho, joined Yaser Arafat's Fatah movement as a teenager, but then associated himself with the international militant movement by becoming a follower of Abu Mus'ab al-Zarqawi. Along with al-Zarqawi, he was sentenced to death in absentia by the Jordanian authorities for the 2002 murder of US diplomat Laurence Foley in Amman. In his description of 'Absi, Michael Radu writes:

> The organization [the Fatah movement] sent him to study medicine, but he dropped out in favor of becoming a pilot, receiving training in Libya and later serving as an instructor in South Yemen. Later he participated in combat, on the winning Sandinista side in Nicaragua and on the losing Libyan side in that country's conflict with Chad. Disappointed with Arafat's corruption, he joined dissident, pro-Syrian factions and moved to Damascus, where he discovered religion and became a fervent believer. Afterward he became associated with Al Zarqawi's group in Iraq and Jordan. ... This, then, is a case of a rebel in search of a global ideological and strategic anchor to articulate and justify his fight for a particular cause. Associating with Al Qaeda satisfied both needs.[97]

Radu alleges that, in addition to being a supporter of al-Qaeda, 'Absi and his FAI organization have links with the Syrian regime. He claims that "[t]he fact that Fatah al-Islam is seen as both an al-Qaeda spin-off and a Syrian tool should not be confusing, not in light of the organization's pattern of tactically piggy-backing other causes."[98]

Prominent among those making these accusations was the Lebanese administration led by Sa'ed al-Hariri, al-Hariri's *Tayar al-Mustaqbal* (Future

---

96 Naser Qandeel in "Ma wara' al-Khabar," Al-Jazeera, 30 September 2008. This incident and its relation to FAI will be further discussed in the next section of this chapter.
97 Michael Radu, "Al-Qaeda Confusion: How to Think about Jihad," *Foreign Policy Research Institute*, July 2007: 4. Online: www.fpri.org/enotes/200707.radu.alqaedajihad.html.
98 Ibid. For more on Syria's relation with the FAI, see the next section of this chapter.

Movement),[99] as well as the Syrian opposition abroad (at least according to Israeli and American intelligence reports). This opposition movement, which includes prominent Lebanese Sunni Muslim clerics such as Shaykh Bilal al-Baroudi, went so far as to claim that FAI is the "fabrication" of the Syrian *Mukhabarat*.[100] In defending this position, they point to the fact that Shukri al-'Absi – who was first captured in Syria in November 2002 for illegal Islamist activity – was released by Syrian intelligence less than three years after his capture in June 2005, while far less militant dissidents such as Michel Kilo and 'Aref Balila remain in prison.[101] They also reference the *al-Mustaqbal* newspaper report from 15 November 2008, in which it was reported that captured members of FAI had confessed that the group is controlled by the Syrian *Mukhabarat*. Ahmad Merhi, one of the principal sources for the story, explained that the head of the Syrian Intelligence Counter Terrorism Bureau, Brigadier General Jawdat al-Hasan, knew about the role of the Syrian *Mukhabarat* in the formation and subsequent actions of FAI.[102] The rationale is that the militant Islamist incidents which the Syrian state blamed on Salafi groups (such as Jund al-Sham, discussed in Chapter 8) were in fact staged by the Syrian command, to help create the impression that both Lebanon and Syria were being threatened by militant Islamists and thus that the Syrian regime's Emergency Law domestically and presence in Lebanon regionally were still justified.[103]

Yet despite the fact that this sort of analysis has received considerable attention in the Arabic and Western media, it remains unproven and rather improbable. Indeed, in terms of defeating al-Qaeda, both Syria and the United States share the same goal.[104] When questions about the state's alleged links with FAI were put to a number of Syrian officials, they insisted that there was no relationship with the group.[105] According to a high-ranking security official, the George W. Bush administration became such a committed enemy of Syria that it brought together a coalition of Sunni Arab states, including Saudi Arabia, in order to fight Syrian and pan-Arab influence in Lebanon with false accusations. The official added that not only do Saudi nationals constitute 30 per cent of the members of FAI, but around 1,000 Saudis were rounded up in Syria's al-Yarmuk refugee

---

99 Lebanese authorities' statement concerning the explosions in 'Ayn 'Alaq in Lebanon; see *al-Mustaqbal* (Future) TV, 12 March 2007. Since September 2010, this is no longer the stance taken by the *Mustaqbal* movement, which has exonerated Syria in the death of Rafiq al-Hariri, and has reconciled with Damascus.
100 See LBC TV and Al-Jazeera TV, 12 October 2008; Al-Jazeera TV, 30 September 2008.
101 See www.ahrarsuria.com, 12 November 2008; Reuters, 17 October 2008.
102 Although knowing about the task does not necessarily imply complicity. *Al-Mustaqbal*, 15 November 2008. Also, in September 2010, the Future Movement exonerated Syria of these allegations and reconciled with Damascus.
103 See Al-Jazeera, 30 September, 12 and 13 October 2008; LBC, 12 October 2008.
104 Yacoubian and Lazensky, *Dealing with Damascus*, p. 5. See also the analysis of Naser Qindeel on "Ma wara' al-khabar," Al-Jazeera TV, 30 September 2008.
105 Private communication. See also Syrian analyst and spokesperson 'Imad Fawzi al-Shu'aybi on "Akthar min Ra'i," Al-Jazeera TV, 18 September 2009.

camp on suspicion of belonging to al-Qaeda and of funding Sunni radical movements such as al-Zarqawi's Jund al-Sham and FAI.[106] This, it seems, is an ongoing concern to the Syrian intelligence units.

The same denial of a relationship between the Syrian regime and al-Qaeda sympathizers has been repeatedly put forward in the Syrian media by official government spokesmen.[107] They assert that groups such as Jund al-Sham and FAI are a threat to Syria because they can empower the radical Salafi element in the country and in the region. The spokesmen point to the state's past battles with Islamist radicals, and its attempts at containing this radical dogma by bolstering the "moderate" local Islamic groups. They also point to the most recent Damascus bombing – which as was noted earlier, is blamed on FAI by Syrian intelligence – as proof of the dangers of such empowerment.[108]

Domestic impact of Syria's regional policy

While these accusations and statements underline that the Syrian state is at loggerheads with FAI, they do not necessarily offer a strong explanation for the rise in militant activity in Syria. Instead, that rise is most probably the result of so-called blowback, in which anyone wanting to directly fight against the American intervention in Iraq was once allowed to cross the border from Syria.[109] Now that the Iraq infiltration routes have been shut down, however, these militants are becoming active in Syria.[110]

The Syrian state's policy of supporting Shi'i and Sunni Islamist groups regionally and its role as a transit corridor and thus a supporter of Islamist militants headed to Iraq and to Lebanon help to polish its pan-Arab resistance credentials, despite seeming to be at odds with its pan-Arab stance and ideology. This is because from the point of view of the Arab public, the message being sent by the regime is quite clear: Israel's policies towards the Palestinians cannot be considered in isolation from the regional context, and in fact colour that entire context. Furthermore, the Syrian regime's moves are in line with its long-standing pragmatic prioritization of foreign policy over domestic policy, notwithstanding the new president's commitment to paying more attention than his father to the domestic scene, and make it clear to regional and international foes that they must take Damascus into account when making decisions regarding the Middle East.

At the same time, however, this regional empowerment of Islamists is occurring at the expense of Syria's secularism and indeed of its longer-term domestic

---

106 Private communication. See also Al-Jazeera, 2 June 2006; *Al-Hayat*, 3 June 2006; *al-Akhbar*, 7 November 2008; *Al-Sharq al-Awsat*, 9 July 2007.
107 See for example *Teshrin*, 3 June 2006; *Syrian TV*, 6 November 2008.
108 Private communication, March 2008.
109 See Alon Ben-David, "Jordanian Indictment Reveals Operations of Jund al-Sham Terror Network."
110 *Time*, 27 September 2008; Moubayed, "The Islamic Revival in Syria."

stability, particularly because domestic Shi'i and Sunni neo-fundamentalist groups have been greatly revitalized with the blessing of the regime.[111] What emerges, therefore, is that for both domestic and regional reasons, Syria is being increasingly Islamized, particularly since the accession of Bashar al-Asad to the presidency, and moreover that this Islamization can no longer be controlled by the current regime. This latter point will be examined in greater detail in the following section of this chapter, and more explicitly in the following chapters of this work.

3 The resulting above-board and underground activity

Of 584 charitable organizations in Syria, 290 are registered Islamic organizations, of which most are active in Damascus and its suburbs. They are based in local mosques and poor neighbourhoods. Of the more than 100 charitable organizations in the capital, approximately 80 per cent are Sunni Islamic; these operate a network that serves about 73,000 families, with a budget of around US$18 million per year.[112] The country also has 976 Islamic schools and institutes and over 9,000 active mosques, which together offer over 400,000 lessons a week. Since the mid-1990s, Islamic groups have managed to ally themselves with Syria's influential and affluent, mainly its traditional business class, though also with religious Syrians who became wealthy through their time working in the Gulf states.[113] As a result, the groups are more able to provide services in both well-off and less well-off districts (see Tables 6.1, 6.2 and 6.3).

Table 6.1 Permeation of Islamic organisations in Syria

Syria	Islamic organizations (including charitable)	Islamic schools and Islamic institutes	Active mosques	Secular cultural institutes and forums[1]
Total	584 (290)	976	Over 9,000	84
Members	72,751 families	Women: 72,000 (active)		Several thousand
Outcome	842 million Syrian Liras distributed		416,000 lessons/ week	Fewer than 100 performances per year

Source: Table based on numbers provided by *al-Hayat*, 18 June 2005 and 5 January 2006; and the Syrian Ministry of *Awqaf*, studies and statistics 31 December 2007 and 31 December 2008.

Note
1 Secular institutes such as the Goethe Cultural Centre and the Adham Isma'il Arts Centre, although not including the public schools and government organizations.

111 This will be discussed in detail in Chapter 7.
112 See *Al-Hayat*, 5 January 2006 and 18 June 2005.
113 See *Al-Hayat*, 3 May 2006 and 5 January 2006.

138 *Bashar al-Asad's era*

Regarding education, almost 200 of the country's 400 (approximately) private educational institutions[114] are said to be influenced by Islamic groups, despite the fact that the curriculum is set by the Ministry of Education, and is hence secular. In Damascus, this means that as many as 25 per cent of students are taught by teachers with an overtly religious agenda, and moreover must take extra-curricular classes about Islam (extra-curricular classes are not controlled

Table 6.2 Number of Mosques according to governorate in 2007

Governorates	Number of mosques		Under construction	Permits in process	Not constructed with permits
	Formal	Informal			
Damascus	371	122	11	17	7
Damascus suburbs	182	591	95	15	18
Aleppo	450	1,280	36	7	2
Lataquieh	85	195	3	6	–
Tartus	8	109	10	2	2
Homs	150	421	–	–	–
Hama	91	670	23	15	–
Idleb	74	960	34	114	–
Dayr al-Zor	27	1,225	30	25	20
Al-Raqqal	19	435	23	6	5
Al-Hasaka	53	850	10	5	4
Quneitra	–	73	7	4	2
Dar'a	61	230	42	25	20
Total	1,569	7,162	324	241	80

Source: Table from Syrian *Awqaf* Ministry, 31 December 2007.

Table 6.3 Al-Asad Islamic Institutes in 2007

Governorate	Number of al-Asad Islamic institutes
Damascus and suburbs	414
Homs	60
Hama	51
Aleppo	3
Lattaquieh	43
Tartus	6
Al-Raqqa	11
Dayr al-Zur	71
Al-Hasaka	16
Dar'a and Suweyda	81
Quneitra	14
Idleb	70
Total	840

Source: Syrian *Awqaf* Ministry, based on a survey published on 31 December 2007.

114 Numbers reported by Syrian government in 2004.

by the state).[115] Even as they follow the curriculum, some of these teachers avoid certain classes about evolution theory, for instance, or add their own comments to the lessons. In general, they are said to be directly linked to both official and non-official Islamic groups. Furthermore, a number of religious groups have managed to acquire permits to open private schools and institutes all over Syria, by exploiting administrative loopholes and their good relations with sympathetic officials within the Syrian bureaucracy. To give an example, al-Bawader school, now led by an Islamic group, was originally composed of ten sections and located in the old Mezzeh district. Today, the school has expanded to as many as 40 classes and has relocated to the Kafer Suseh area. These schools have managed to bypass the Syrian education ministry's several controls over the curriculum and more importantly over teachers, and thus have successfully avoided conforming to the ministry's secular impositions.[116]

The state has also proven to be directly affected by the Islamic revival. Indeed, the surfacing of draft legislation in June 2009 that was expected to amend and further secularize the Personal Status Law in Syria not only showed that certain state officials lacked an affinity for the secular ideology of the Ba'th, but also gave rise to the suggestion that "radical Islamic elements" had assumed high-ranking positions within the secular political apparatus. The draft was seen as an attempt by Sunni radicals to strike a blow against demands for identical rights for men and women in Syria (as already stipulated within the Syrian Constitution), and as an attempt to generate a split between Sunnis and non-Sunni minorities in the country, given that it allowed a specific Sunni religious vision to define family rights. According to critics, it disregarded the concept of citizenship as articulated in the Syrian Constitution and consolidated the power of Islamic courts and other religious courts over all matters related to marriage, divorce and inheritance. It also maintained so-called Islamic clauses that have been under attack by secular lobbyists in the country since 1953. Other contentious clauses included continuing to allow polygamy for men, legalizing the marriage of children under the age of 18 (15 for boys and 13 for girls), requiring women to get their husband's permission before being able to travel outside the country and requiring women who have divorced and kept custody of the children to seek the approval of their husbands for what sort of work they do. The draft legislation ignored the recommendations of (secular) civil rights experts and committees. In fact, even "moderate" interpretations of Islamic law endorsed by prominent Syrian shaykhs such as Muhammad Habash and Mahmood Akkam were dismissed.[117] In parliament, the speaker

---

115 See All4Syria Website: http://all4syria.info/content/view/29490/80 (accessed 19 July 2010).
116 Ibid.
117 For instance, in his Islamic *Tajdeed* (Renewal) programme, Shaykh Muhammad Habash asserts the right of the woman to state the conditions of her marriage in her marriage contract. He rejects the marriage of children under the age of 18, and states that women have the right to divorce their husbands with or without the man's approval (the *Tajdeed* programme, pp. 18–20). For a brief overview of the draft and reactions to it, see Syria Briefing, IWPR Report, 12 June 2009; *Gulf News*, 23 June 2009.

responded to the outcry by issuing a very brief statement to the effect that the leaked document was just a draft. The legislation was not subsequently re-visited by either the president or the parliament. Yet the mere fact that it was drafted clearly proved startling to secularists, minority groups, Syrian women's groups and Ba'thi loyalists within the state.

This snapshot of the Syrian Islamic sector makes it clear that it has become significantly more influential than the country's secular sector, which is represented by fewer than 100 active institutes[118] whose memberships number in the mere thousands. The increased influence of the Islamic sector comes at a time when the Syrian state's hegemonic domestic control is in relative decline. Indeed, while the authoritarian Syrian command has been able to cultivate the loyalty of many Islamic shaykhs and regional Islamists in order to consolidate its rule in the face of domestic, regional and international challenges, it has not been as successful as the previous command at suppressing Islamic groups and militant Islamist activity at the domestic level.[119]

The net result of this situation is the emergence of a number of Islamist groups demanding the abolition of Syria's secular political system (this will be thoroughly examined in Chapter 8), as well as a resurgence in the number of militant Islamist attacks, which seems to herald the possible revival of militant Islamism in Syria after some 22 years of quietude. Examples of these new attacks are many – for instance, in April 2004, an "al-Qaeda linked group" composed of Islamists returning from Iraq launched the so-called Mezzeh Attack from an empty UN building in Damascus;[120] in early 2005, an attack in Damascus on behalf of Jund al-Sham, an al-Qaeda-inspired jihadist organization reportedly linked to al-Qaeda ideologue Abu Mus'ab al-Suri, was barely thwarted;[121] in the summer of 2005, a group of gunmen were apprehended after a shooting in Mount Qasyun;[122] in June 2006, there was heavy gunfire in the heart of Damascus as security forces clashed with ten masked gunmen that were said to be preparing to stage an attack on governmental buildings, resulting in the death of two Syrian security personnel and four militants, as well as the capture of the remaining militants.[123] In February 2008, a car exploded in the Damascus suburbs killing one person.[124]

These various armed incidents and the possibility of wider unrest that they seemed to threaten were likely a contributing factor in the severity of the regime's response to the July 2008 protest by prisoners at the Sednaya political

---

118 Secular institutes such as the Goethe Cultural Centre and the Adham Isma'il Arts centre, not including state organizations.
119 This is due to the state's domestic accommodationist policies and economic liberalization, as well as its use of Islamists as a mechanism to wield influence regionally, all discussed previously. The state has been more successful at suppressing pro-democracy secular groups (see chapter 9).
120 *Al-Ba'th* newspaper, 11 April 2004; *SANA*, 11 April 2004.
121 *Al-Ba'th* newspaper, 4 July 2004. For more on Abu Mus'ab al-Suri, see Chapter 8 of this work.
122 *SANA*, 6 July 2005; *Al-Hayat*, 10 July 2005.
123 *Al-Ahram*, 8 June 2006.
124 *Al-Akhbar*, 13 February 2008.

prison, a facility that holds approximately 4,000 political prisoners, most of whom are said to be Islamists and Muslim Brothers.[125] This response saw hundreds of political detainees injured, and dozens of Islamic prisoners killed.[126] According to the Syrian Islamic Front, the incident was very much reminiscent of the bloody massacres committed by the Syrian authorities against political prisoners in Hama in 1982.[127] Moreover, the July events at Sednaya prison followed on the heels of another violent confrontation there only a few months earlier, during which several detainees were killed.[128] This confrontation was blamed on prisoners serving sentences for terrorist activities, who according to the regime initiated the clashes with the prison's guards during an inspection.[129]

The Islamic National Salvation Front reacted to the Sednaya confrontations by issuing a statement calling on Arab and international human rights organizations to establish an independent investigation committee:

> in order to probe the authorities' actions in Sednaya prison, where almost four thousand political detainees are held, and to submit the investigation's conclusions to the International Criminal Court. It is time for the ruling regime in Syria to pay for its crimes in this prison, as in all other situations where torture and mistreatment are causing the death of prisoners and detainees ... the world should no longer ignore the desperate call of the political detainees in Syria's prisons. The disobedience action that happened in Sednaya today is only the first episode in the comprehensive disobedience movement that the Syrian population is today preparing, to show the regime that its criminal policies are no longer bearable. And if Syria's political detainees are today once again ignored [by the international community], then this will show how alone the Syrian population is in its struggle against tyranny and injustice.[130]

The Kurdish Coordination Committee, an umbrella group of Kurdish opposition parties in Syria, also reacted to the Sednaya confrontations by saying that the prisoners were only demanding better living conditions. Meanwhile, the regime insisted through the Syrian state news agency that "[s]everal prisoners convicted of extremism and terror crimes created chaos. ... The issue required the interference of anti-riot units to restore calm."[131]

125 *SANA*, 6 July 2008; Al-Arabiya news channel, 6 July 2008.
126 *Al-Marsad al-Suri li-Huquq al-Insan* [Syrian Observatory for Human Rights], 5 July 2008. Online: www.syriahr.com.
127 Ahrar Suria, 7 July 2008. Online: www.free-syria.com/en/print.php?articleid=29516.
128 Ibid.
129 *Kuwait Times Daily*, 5 July 2008; *Haaretz*, 5 July 2008; *SANA*, 6 July 2008; see also Reuters, online: http://uk.reuters.com/article/latestCrisis/idUKL0659890120080706.
130 www.free-syria.com (accessed 7 July 2008). Online: www.free-syria.com/en/print.php?articleid =29516.
131 *SANA*, 6 July 2008.

The Sednaya incident was not the last Islamist-related episode in Syria. On 27 September 2008, a car packed with 200 kg of explosives detonated along the Damascus International Airport road near the area's intelligence headquarters and the important Shi'i shrine *al-Sayida Zeynab*, killing 17 civilians and wounding dozens more. Some accounts claimed that Syrian intelligence officer George Ibrahim al-Gharbi, who was known to observe Islamist groups in Syria, was also killed in the attack. The death toll could have been much worse had the attack taken place on a school day, when hundreds of students would have been in class at an adjacent school.[132] The attack was characterized as the biggest in Syria since the Hama battle some 16 years earlier, because of the high number of civilian deaths and the large quantity of explosives used.[133] According to the Syrian *Mukhabarat*, the attack was carried out by a suicidal *Takfiri* "jihadist" who entered the country from Lebanon,[134] while an investigative report aired on Syrian TV later blamed the Salafis of the Lebanon-based Islamist organization FAI.[135] A few days after the attack, in an allegedly related incident, the Yarmuk Palestinian camp witnessed clashes between Syrian security forces and an Islamist group taking cover in the camp.[136]

These many examples of Islamist militancy show a clear weakening in the state's control over the Syrian domestic sphere, an impression that is added to by reports in *al-Akhbar* newspaper that ten other terrorist attacks were thwarted by the Syrian security forces in the same period. The increased number of such incidents also underlines the growing strength and boldness of Syria's Islamist underground movement.

4 Conclusion

Hafez al-Asad's strategy of co-optation and compromise with the Syrian bourgeoisie and with the bourgeois-backed religious class weakened the Ba'th's secular and étatist hold on power. It also created a bourgeois class that has agitated for more economic privatization, and a growing neo-fundamentalist Islamic movement, both of which are crowding out the regime's originally populist policies. It is this situation that confronted Bashar al-Asad upon assuming the presidency in June 2000.

The preceding analysis has shown how, in order to consolidate power, Bashar's new command sought to reinforce the government's alliances with society's powerful groups, namely the Islamic sector and Syria's old and new entrepreneurial class (all at the expense of the secular, mainly leftist, opposition). It has also shown how this reinforcement was effected by continuing the economic liberalization and social accommodation initiated by the Hafez

---

132 Syrian TV, 29 March 2008; *SANA*, 30 March 2008; Syria News at www.syria-news.com/readnews.php?sy_seq=83046.
133 Al-Jazeera net, 30 March 2008; *Al-Hayat*, 30 March 2008; *ASP*, 29 March 2008.
134 Syria's role as a transit corridor for jihadists headed to Iraq discussed above.
135 The organization FAI discussed above. Syrian TV, 6 November 2007; *Al-Akhbar*, 7 November 2008.
136 *Al-Akhbar*, 13 October 2008.

command, thereby moving even further away from the Baʿth's populist-socialist roots and closer to an economic *infitah*. As we have seen, the impetus for this policy was the inherent contradictions within the PA political model, particularly its aim of balancing populist inclusive policies with authoritarian control. The net effect is that the remnants of Baʿthi statism are dissolving, leaving the current command with an eroding base of social support and the country with a corrupt elite – albeit one that is in alliance with the regime – that is greedy for further selective economic liberalization, along with a continuation of the regime's protection from domestic competition in the marketplace.

Another act of regime compromise, one that was aimed at accommodating the increasing manifestations of religiosity on the street and among the elite, saw Bashar al-Asad begin to more openly support religion in general and "moderate" Islam in particular, thereby raising expectations that the era of a Baʿthist monopoly on power was drawing to a close. This move by Bashar's regime has its roots in Hafez al-Asad's de-secularization strategy, which had been at least partly aimed at preventing his regime from being accused of practising sectarian and "atheist" politics. That strategy, which included allowing Syria's Islamic movement to Islamize the country's masses at a popular level, has meant that new generations of Syrians no longer tend to see secularism as the normative good that older generations see it as. Hence the current regime's decision that they needed to begin advocating the cause of moderate Islam as part of a move away from Baʿthist secularism and towards the Anglo-Saxon secular model, so as to get in line with the prevailing mood in large parts of society.[137]

Importantly, however, while Hafez al-Asad's regime managed to successfully co-opt and control Islamic groups, the current regime's socio-economic policies and manoeuvres are increasingly empowering the country's Islamic movement by giving such groups the opportunity to transform themselves from communal welfare organizations into socio-political actors in the public sphere.

The preceding chapter also showed that the link between Syria's Islamic revivalism and the possibility of political Islamic outreach falls within the reality of the rising impoverished class. In other words, the facilitating condition of Islamism in Syria is structural economic inequalities. The argument is that the economic liberalization policies are widening the gap between the rich and poor in Syria; since the regime is deliberately promoting these policies, it is simultaneously being forced to relinquish its populist policies that once ensured it a significant and committed base of support among the lower classes. As a result, the poor feel abandoned by the regime, at the same time that they feel welcomed by the only socio-political alternative that was allowed to grow under the Baʿth: the Islamic sector. It is this dynamic that is driving the growth in Syria's Islamic revivalism (as will be further discussed hereinafter).

---

137 For more on Syria's civil society in general, see Sylvia Chiffoleau, "La Syrie au quotidien: cultures et pratiques du changement Présentation", *Revue des mondes musulmans et de la Méditerranée* 115–16, December 2006. Online: http://remmm.revues.org/document3008.html (accessed 16 October 2008).

Moreover, the war in Iraq has added another ingredient to the mix. This is because regional Islamist groups that had been co-opted by the Syrian regime as a mechanism for wielding influence in the region have shown that they can turn against the "atheist" regime once the war in Iraq is over (this will be further discussed in Chapter 8). Given the increasing Islamization of Syria on one hand and, on the other, the economic crisis that many Syrians are facing as a result of the regime's turn towards a market economy, such groups are finding it relatively easy to mobilize and recruit members among the general populace.

Ultimately, the increasing empowerment of neo-fundamentalist groups within Syria and of Islamists at a regional level will have a two-fold effect: it will give rise to a significant challenge to the regime's political stability, and will also stir up conflict in Syria's ideologically, religiously and ethnically diverse society. This latter development is because of fears that having a regime that is overly influenced by Islamic figures could very well result in political tension and factionalism within the country.

The following two chapters provide a typology and a description of the emerging Islamic (Chapter 7) and Islamist (Chapter 8) groups, while also examining their ideological, communal and political outreach methods within the current Syrian context. The robustness of these groups, their legitimacy and the effectiveness of their growth outside the scope of the regime's control are especially addressed, all within the larger framework of this work's main concerns with how Ba'thist secularism is weakening from above and Islamic revivalism is permeating Syrian society from below.

7 Islamization from below

Islamic revivalism as a model for social change and the erosion of Ba'thist secularism

1 Introduction

The Syrian regime's survival policies in the last phase of Hafez al-Asad's rule and under Bashar al-Asad's new rule led to the erosion of Ba'thist secular dogma within Syrian society, as well as to the formation and strengthening of a variety of fundamentalist Islamic groups. These micro-groups both benefited the Syrian state and benefited from it; while they were accommodated and empowered from above, they have also proven to be successful outreach agents from below.

The success of the Islamic sector in attracting members and in asserting itself as a domestic actor in Syria prompts a variety of questions: what groups and individuals make up today's Syrian Islamic movement? Is this movement different from the one that challenged the Ba'th in the 1960s and 1970s? If yes, in what ways? Beyond a state-level of analysis, what are the internal reasons behind the Islamic sector's success in expanding its membership? And, what sort(s) of outreach (ideological, political, economic) is the Islamic sector deploying?

The intention of this chapter is not to provide a comprehensive account of the Islamic parties' dogma or their interpretation of Islamic precepts. Rather it is to help elaborate this work's core theoretical and empirical concerns by highlighting the different key groups that make up Syria's Islamic movement, as well as by unpacking the movement's overall discourse and methods of outreach in order to explain the reasons behind its increasing membership and rising influence (beyond the role played by the actions of the state, discussed in previous chapters).

In contrast to most analyses, which have routinely grouped all of Syria's Islamic groups together and portrayed the country's Islamic sector as homogeneous, it is argued here that today's Syrian Islamic sector is not composed of the same groups that challenged the Ba'th in the 1960s and 1970s. It also is different from the one that was allowed to emerge in the aftermath of Hama. Indeed, it is growing increasingly robust and powerful to the point that it is no longer just a simple client to the patron-regime but is instead moving towards becoming an equal ally or partner with it. More particularly, while a majority of the various Islamic groups are still co-opted and accommodate the ruling coalition, there are some that have the capacity to circumvent the state's mechanisms of control. This is because of the groups' informal and de-institutionalized nature and their methods of outreach.

These various analyses are in line with the work's larger argument, that Syria's Islamic groups were empowered from above and then later invigorated from below by the contradictions inherent to the country's populist authoritarian political model. As we have seen, this invigoration gathered speed as a result of liberalizing policies adopted by the government, which led to a gradual re-emergence of Syria's private sector.[1]

2 The dawn of an Islamic renaissance: general discourse

A Ethical renaissance and apoliticalism

Syria is witnessing an Islamic renaissance that is evident in the emergence of a plethora of apolitical Islamic organizations and charitable associations, as well as Islamic bookstores, institutes and forums that are supposedly supported by, and functioning under the patronage of, the Syrian political elite.[2] This Islamic renaissance is the result of the Syrian command's attempts at power consolidation.

---

1 This liberalization and the instability in Iraq have led to a debate over identity among many Syrians. This will be examined in Chapter 9. See Yahya Sadowski, "The Evolution of Political Identity in Syria," in Shibley Telhami and Michael Barnett, eds, *Identity and Foreign Policy in the Middle East*, Ithaca, NY: Cornell University Press, 2002, pp. 137–54; and Yasseen Haj Saleh, "Political Reform and the Reconfiguration of National Identity in Syria," *Arab Reform Brief*, 14 June 2006. Online.

2 While the Syrian Muslim Brotherhood has attracted much of the attention from scholars, this is due to its earlier militant activity and violent conflict with the state. Indeed, other Islamic Sufi organizations, pietistic in nature rather than politically oriented, have since the Hama incidents of 1982 played a very important role in Syrian society, and have impacted significantly upon society and upon the Syrian state. In other words, the political activities of the Muslim Brethren have tended to overshadow the apolitical activities of the other Sufi groups, such as the Naqshbandiya, the Shadhiliya and the Rifa'iya among others. This is all the more important given that since the Hama massacre in 1982 and the downfall of the Muslim Brotherhood, Syria has witnessed the resurgence en masse of these less well-known Islamic populist groups. To cite a few of the works expanding scholarship on Syria's apolitical Islamic organizations and their leaders' dogma: Annabelle Böttcher, "Islamic Teaching among Sunni Women in Syria," in Donna Lee Bowen and Evelyn A. Early, eds, *Everyday Life in the Muslim Middle East*, Bloomington and Indianapolis: Indiana University Press, 2002; idem, *Official Sunni and Shi'i Islam in Syria*, Florence: European University Institute, 2002; Andreas Christmann, "'The Form is Permanent, but the Content Moves': The Qur'anic Text and its Interpretation(s) in Mohamad Shahrour's *Al-Kitab wa l-Quran*," *Die Welt des Islam* 43, 2003: 143–72; idem, "73 Proofs of Dilettantism: The Construction of Norm and Deviancy in the Responses to *'al-Kitab wa'l-Qur'an: Qira'a Mu'asira'* by Mohamad Shahrour," *Die Welt des Islam* 45, 2005: 20–73; Leif Stenberg, "Naqshbandiyya in Damascus: Strategies to Establish and Strengthen the Order in a Changing Society," in Elisabeth Özdalga, ed., *Naqshbandis in Western and Central Asia: Change and Continuity*, Istanbul: Swedish Research Institute in Istanbul, 1999, pp. 101–16; idem, "Young, Male and Sufi Muslim in the City of Damascus," in Jørgen Bæck Simonsen, ed., *Youth and Youth Culture in the Contemporary Middle East*, Aarhus: Aarhus University Press, 2005, pp. 68–91.

Thus the context in which today's Islamic groups are functioning is different from the one in which the Muslim Brothers operated. At the same time, the groups' agenda is also different from the agenda that was previously advanced by the Muslim Brotherhood. An examination of these differences can explain the success of the current Islamic sector at building up the movement and the failure of the earlier Islamic movement to effectively build itself up within the authoritarian and supposedly *laïque* context of Syrian politics.

A key factor in the failure of the Syrian Islamic movement of the 1970s was its inability to recruit the public masses, whose imagination was instead captured by the populist Baʿth and other leftist parties. This failure was largely because the movement was perceived as defending the traditional, urban political order and the morality of the economic status quo in which its members had established their powerful alliances. Meanwhile, the socialist Baʿth Party advanced a programme aimed at changing society's socio-economic stratification, and that promised an end to parochialism and the onset of social mobility for those members of society who had up to then been excluded. Today, the regime has abandoned most of its populist policies, while Islamic groups are in their majority no longer seen as part of the traditional political Islamic network that once pushed for an unpopular status quo.

Importantly, these orders have chosen a different path from that trod by the Muslim Brotherhood, by focusing on surviving *within* the existing political establishment. This focus has caused them to work at building a discreet and gradual kind of Islamic revivalism, one that aims to create a renewed Islamic society by focusing upon change at the individual level rather than upon macro political reforms or the re-organization of society by wielding the powers of the state. In other words, their agenda is socially oriented, and aims at the moral regeneration of individuals and of small sub-communities.[3] They underline that Islam is essentially about fairness, human compassion and morality.[4] Virtues such as *Sabr* (patience), *Hikma* (wisdom), *Tasamuh* (compassion), *Hiwar* (dialogue), *Khayr* (virtue), *Musawat* (equality) and *'Adel* (justice) are presented as the bases for true belief. In an interview conducted in Damascus, an Islamic *Da'iya* noted that

> the individual and his family is what matters to us, the question of control over the state is an irrelevant question; the state is an extension and a reflection of the family and on that basis, one need not worry about the state, we are not in a hurry. Our goal is to defend Islam and the *Shari'a*, the state's role is to allow us to do so.[5]

---

3 See, for instance, Muhammad Sa'id Ramadan al-Buti, *al-Ta'aruf 'ala al-Dhat Huwa al-Tariq ila al-Islam*, Damascus: Dar al-Fikr, n.d. See also Muhammad 'Abd al-Satar, "Al-Tajdid fi al-Fikr al-Islami," delivered on 7 March 2009. Online: www.syrianawkaf.org.

4 The state's vision of Islam is outlined on two websites, that of the Ministry of *Awqaf* and the site of the Ministry of Culture. For a prominent shaykh's understanding of the Syrian state, see Muhammad Shahrur, *Tajfif Manabi' al-Irhab* [Draining the Sources of Terrorism in the Islamic Culture], Damascus: al-Ahali, 2008, pp. 140–1.

5 Personal interview, Damascus, March 2008.

The shaykhs with whom I spoke asserted that Islam is a state of mind (*Hala*) that must be grounded in every Muslim mind and heart. A Muslim *Da'yia* should concentrate on teaching monotheism (*Tawhid*) and purifying the heart of doubts, sins and distractions, so that it becomes the nucleus of the correct Islamic way of life. It is only when a person commits themselves to complete obedience to God that they will be able to cultivate the seeds of righteous politics and justice.

Prominent and recurring themes in their discourse include "moderation in Islam," "the dialectic of compassion and tolerance" and "the Islamic right to ideological difference." Generally speaking, members of these Islamic microcommunities are asked to re-invent themselves as part of a new "Islamic" sub-community, through an emphasis on the "formation of the Spiritual Muslim" (*al-Islam wa Bina' al-Insan al-Rabbani*) – an emphasis which underlines the argument that these modern groups have turned fundamentalist rather than Islamist. At the same time, shaykhs criticize the politicization of the Islamic *Da'wa* in search of the utilitarian need to control the political apparatus. According to Al-Buti:

> The success of such an endeavor is assured by raising the activities of Islamic *Da'wa* above the political, and by elevating oneself above the political ambitions inherent in the search for power ... and this is what many Muslims cannot yet agree on, unfortunately!... As a result, the concept of Islamic *da'wa* in their activities only means the resurgence of political movements whose purpose is to reach the seat of power. This is what I mean by politicizing Islam, and maybe the more precise expression is: the politicization of the Islamic *da'wa*.[6]

In pursuing this particular brand of Islamic revivalism, official Islamic groups in Syria have achieved a status and strength that is greater than that achieved by the Muslim Brothers before them, or by their secular counterparts during the same period, so much so that one Sufi apprentice explained to me that "1982 [the Hama battle] was a blessing in disguise [for Syria's religious orders and religious life]."

The Islamic groups' focus on the ethical rather than the social or the politico-economic is proving effective in terms of popularizing their Islamic discourse within Syria. This is because their ethical discourse is helping to create a moral synthesis that joins together a number of overlapping, sub-national cleavages among Syrians. For instance, out of ten "Intellectual Principles" outlined by the late Mufti Kuftaro as a guide to Syria's Muslims, three stress the importance of co-existence between Muslims and non-Muslims, and between the different Muslim sects. In the same vein, Shaykh al-Buti, the current Mufti Badr al-Din and the Syrian Minister of Endowments, Muhammad 'Abd al-Satar, have often lectured on the common moral roots shared by

---

6 Stated in one of al-Buti's lectures entitled "Tawdhif al-Din fi al-Sira' al-Siyasi" [the employment of religion in the struggle for power], delivered in March 2000. Author's translation.

Islamization from below 149

all religious denominations.[7] Shaykh Hassoun has regularly given lectures and speeches praising Syrians for living as one "human family" able to come together over shared religious, legal and spiritual notions.[8] In a country where politics have often meant trouble and division, focusing on the ethical *da'wa* in religion instead of on its political discourse is certainly understandable, especially within the authoritarian context of Syrian politics. Perhaps more importantly, doing so is also amenable to the public.

It is worth remembering that groups willing to acquiesce to the political order were effectively empowered by the state, which was determined to get rid of contentious Islamic groups in the country (see Chapters 5 and 6).[9] Thus the Islamic groups' tactical move away from political outreach and towards ideological communal outreach can partly be attributed to moves made by the Syrian state. That being said, the movement's success also points to the internal capabilities of the Islamic groups, particularly their effective reading of, and tactical response to, the shifting, non-political opportunity structures available within the Syrian context.

The flexibility and innovation displayed by the Islamic groups is perhaps unsurprising when we consider their previously successful transformation in the face of modernity. More specifically, we can point to their adaptation to the pressures from the rising Salafi movement that came to Syria from the Gulf region and from Egypt in the early twentieth century, which saw them switch to promoting a pietist, orthodox version of Sufism.[10] This version of Sufism was upheld and promoted by

---

7 Kuftaro explains,

> All the *mujtahid imams* used to say, if the following *hadith* is sound, then it is my school: "if Sunna means following the prophet, peace be upon him, then we are all Sunna. And if Shi'ism means the love for the prophet's family, then we are all Shi'a." [author's translation]

"كل الأئمة المجتهدين كانوا يقولون إذا صح الحديث فهو مذهبي" "إذا كانت السنة إتباع رسول الله صلى الله عليه وسلم فكلنا سنة، وإذا كانت الشيعة حب آل بيت رسول الله صلى الله عليه وسلم فكلنا شيعة"

See "Mabadi' Fikriya," at www.kuftaro.org. See also lecture given by the current Mufti of Syria, Shaykh Ahmad Badr al-Din Hassoun, "Suriya: Madrasat al-'Aysh al-Mushtarak," given in Homs on 22 July 2009. Recording available online: www.drhassoun.com/news/news_details.php?news_id=750. See also a lecture delivered at the Asad Library in Damascus by Shaykh Muhammad 'Abd al-Satar, "Al-'Alaqat al-Insaniya fi al-Islam," online: www.syrianawkaf.org.

8 See Dr Hassoun's lecture in Hama entitled "Syria: An Example for National Unity," given at the Arab Cultural Centre in Damascus, 28 June 2010.

9 In this deployment, the regime transformed the confrontation, from one between Islam and a political actor that was widely seen as secular, corrupt and minoritarian, to one between "moderate Islam" (as shaped by political realities inside Syria) and "radical Islam" (see Chapters 5 and 6).

10 Given that Sunni Syrians are, in the majority, Sufis, and given that the division between Salafi and Sufi currents in Islam is less clear-cut than it appears on the surface – at least in Syria – it is important to understand Sufism in this case as simply meaning historical traditionalism. In fact, populist Sufi orders of the early twentieth century, to which the Syrian Muslim Brotherhood also belongs, accepted the Salafi interpretations and adopted its modernizing outlooks of promoting the advancement of an overtly modernist Islam. It is modernist in the sense that it is shedding the mystical and ritualistic aspect that had developed in the previous centuries, in an attempt to meet the changing demands of modernity.

shaykhs such as Amin Kuftaro (father of the Kuftariya movement in Syria), 'Abd al-Karim al-Rifa'i and the late Mufti of Syria, Shaykh Ahmad Kuftaro. Ahmad Kuftaro was particularly notable for his downplaying of Sufism's mystical aspects in favour of a more orthodox interpretation, based at least partly on a view that the Islamic world is needlessly divided into a Sufi mystic camp and a rigid Sunni camp.[11] This interpretation turned out to be more appealing than traditional Sufism to a majority of the educated Sunni populace in Syria. A similar degree of flexibility and pragmatic innovation can be seen in the decision by a majority of Syria's Sufi orders to eschew the confrontational route chosen by the Muslim Brotherhood and to embrace political quietism. Doing so allowed them to survive the political changes that spelled the end of the "politics of the notables," by accommodating the new political elites and their revolution from above.

B Accommodation of the state

Although it is politically quietist and focused on ethical regeneration, the religious discourse propagated by the Islamic groups is not ontologically apolitical. Keeping in mind the Islamic groups' ongoing need to ensure that they are accommodated by the state, their messages do tend to promote a vision that endorses the actions of the Syrian political command and, more importantly for this work, the separation of the state from religion.[12] Indeed, the ostensibly orthodox discourse that these modern social movements advance masks a truly innovative element within that discourse, that is, their imbuing of popular religion in the country with certain political assumptions that could very well be read as promoting secularism. Thus we see them asserting that the politicization of religion is a modern phenomenon in the region. We also see them affirming the importance within the Islamic tradition of working with the governments of existing nation states, in order to best serve the nation's interests – sometimes expressed as the Syrian nation, other times as the Arab nation – while also helping to spread *Da'wa* and Islamic civilization.[13] In so

---

11 Kuftaro explains: "الإسلام كل لا يتجزأ، فهو علم القرآن والحكمة والتزكية" [Islam is indivisible, it is the science of the Quran, the science of Wisdom and the science of Purification][author's translation]. See www.kuftaro.org. See also Muti' al-Hafez and Nizar Abaza, *Tarikh Ulama Dimashq*, 3 vols, Damascus: Dar al-Fikr, 1991. To examine the complexity of the Salafi–Sufi relations and continuity in Syria, see Itzchak Weisman, *Taste of Modernity: Sufism, Salafiyya, and Arabism in Late Ottoman Damascus*, Leiden: Brill, 2000; idem, "The Politics of Popular Religion: Sufis, Salafis, and Muslim brothers in 20th-Century Hamah," *International Journal of Middle East Studies* 37, 2005: 37–58.

12 See speech delivered in November 2007 at the German Bundestag by Syria's Grand Mufti, Ahmad Hassoun, "al-Ilmaniya laysat did al-Din wa ana Muslim Ilmani" [secularism is not against religion and I am a secularist Muslim], online: www.dw-world.de/dw/article/0,,2851007,00.html; see also Muhammad Shahrur, *Tajfif Manabi'al-Irhab*, pp. 140–1. See also section discussing Kuftaro's order next.

13 Ibid. It is claimed that Shaykh al-Rifa'i always sought to reform the state, its laws and rules, in a calm manner, by working towards what he wanted "with little noise or clamour": "He would 'move' the sincere representatives to whom he gave his support, and hold them responsible for correcting mistakes. These representatives [ultimately] had a significant impact, in that many matters finally returned to their original [traditional, religious] course" [author's translation].

doing, the locus of the mosque is frequently imbued with a politicized meaning. It is often described as a symbol of unity and of the elective ties of affinity that bind the individual to the *Umma* (nation), as well as, more importantly, the *Umma* to the rulers of the country. Indeed, the political stability of the nation-state is stressed and celebrated as a requirement for the rebirth of an Islamic civilization, hence the political importance of the president's presence – documented in pictures that all Syrians can see – within the mosque environment. Effectively, therefore, the discourse seeks to create a direct correlation between two supposedly distinct aspects of Syrian society: the secular and the religious. The current Grand Mufti in Syria has more recently asserted, "*ana Muslim 'Ilmani*" (I am a secularist Muslim).[14]

Furthermore, Syria's official shaykhs are very reluctant to condemn the country's rulers, despite their view that the rulers' actions are misguided or deplorable and that they neglect Islamic Law (the *Shari'a*). The shaykhs consequently emphasize virtues such as *Sabr* (patience), *Hikma* (wisdom), passive resistance, gradual change and "true beliefs rather than militant actions."[15] There is also an oft-expressed desire to avoid repeating the mistakes of the past, in which "a minority of radicals took over Syria's Islamic movement," and an insistence that doctrinal education is required before any form of change is undertaken.[16] The following passage from the Zayd movement sheds light on the overall opinion concerning the state and Islamic education:

> A number of young men from the different Islamic movements would seek out the shaykh [al-Rifa'i] every now and then, feeling disgusted with a certain [political] party or side. You [would] see them keenly talking to the shaykh, filled with disgust, requesting his backing for their position, and the shaykh [would] listen to them silently and calmly. As they finished, he would turn to them and say: "My sons, isn't our obligation before we undertake what you want to do that we unite the mantle of Islamic groups so that their allegiance is one? Isn't it a duty to thoroughly prepare for what you are undertaking, and learn from the lessons and experiences of others, which caused what they caused. By God, if I found the time, I would take up arms despite my incapacity and old age. I would lead you to first open the house of al-Maqdes, whose abandonment taints all capable Muslims with sin. My sons, be wary of the enemies of Islam who promise you help and incite you to take up arms in the face of the regime so that you and your idea are destroyed.[17] [author's translation]

14 Speech made by Ahmad Hassoun in November 2007, online: www.dw-world.de/dw/article/0,,2851007,00.html.
15 See also Muhammad Habash's definition of the Islamic *Futuhat* in his *Tajdeed* (Renewal) programme: www.tajdeed.org. Habash states that current times demand that political action be led by a (secular) national state, and war by a modern professional army. Habash's programme is discussed hereinafter.
16 Personal interview, Damascus, 10 April 2008; Shahrur, *Tajfif Manabe' al-Irhab*, p. 139; Ahmad Muhammad Zayed, "Ida'at fi tariq al-A'imma wa al-khutaba' 1," online: www.sadazaid.com (accessed 19 July 2010).
17 See "Mawqef al-Shaykh min al-Siyasa" and Ahmad Muhammad Zayed, "Ida'at fi tariq al-A'imma wa al-khutaba' 1," online: www.sadazaid.com (accessed 19 July 2010).

152 Bashar al-Asad's era

The need for "correct education" before change has been endorsed by a number of prominent 'ulama', such as the previous and current Muftis of Syria.[18] Al-Buti notes that *al-'Atifa al-Islamiya* (the Islamic feeling) is not enough on its own, but should be guided by Islam's restrictions and its methodical markers.[19] Their resolve to avoid radicalization causes the shaykhs to assert that the notion of "Jihad" is a complex one and that violence is not lawful in Islam. They insist that jihad is not synonymous with *Qital* (battle), more particularly that it is not a violent struggle against the ruler and should not be used to justify the goal of shifting the balance of power within a socio-political order.[20] Shaykh Muhammad Shahrur writes, "All Arab regimes, no matter their kind, are wiser than the people they govern…"[21] Shaykh Muhammad Habash goes the furthest in his analysis. He writes in his Renewal Program:

> We request the revision of the creeds [*Ahkam*] of Jihad. And we deny that Jihad is fighting [*Qital*] in order to have people enter Islam, instead it is the deployment of what is available of might in order to terrorize the enemy of God. And it is the organization of the formal and trained armies and the people's armies, under the supervision of the state, in order to protect the nation and defend land and honour. We believe that today's Jihad is Jihad *al-Dafi'* [defensive jihad], as for Jihad *al-Talab* [offensive jihad, or pre-emptive jihad], it is a matter of the past, it was meant to allow preachers to

18 This is part of Kuftaro's own "Intellectual Principles." The first and fourth principles stress the importance of knowing the Quran in order to create a true Islamic community. The first principle states:

> The early Muslims conquered half of the old world with one book and one teacher. [author's translation]

> المسلمون الأول بكتاب واحد ومعلم واحد فتحوا نصف العالم القديم

See www.kuftaro.org. Interestingly, doctrinal education has also been encouraged by others, who were, however, anti-regime, such as: the Muslim Brotherhood's ideologue Sa'id Hawwa, Sayyid Qutb, Fathi Yakan and even Abu Mus'ab al-Suri. The last of these asserts that the lack of doctrinal training was a major reason for the defeat of the Fighting Vanguard and the Muslim Brothers in the early 1980s, and he concludes that the need to establish an environment of conflict against the status quo and the ideological setting is as a result a necessity. See Sa'id Hawwa, *Fi Afaq al-Ta'lim*, Cairo: Maktabat Wahaba, 1980, pp. 65–72; idem, *Al-Madkhal ila Da'wat al-Ikhwan al-Muslimin*, Amman: Dar al-Arqam, n.d., pp. 308–9; Fathi Yakan, *Kayfa Nad'u ila al-Islam?* [The Way to Preach Islam], Beirut: Mu'assasat al-Risala, 1977; idem, *Al-Isti'ab fi Hayat al-Da'wa wa al-Da'iya* [Awareness in the life of the *Da'wa* and the *Da'iya*], Beirut: Mu'asasat al-Risala, 1997, pp. 9–15, 62–70; for extracts of Abu Mus'ab al-Suri's Da'wat al-Muqawama al-Islamiya, see: www.muslm.net/vb/archive/index.php/t-159953.html (accessed 10 November 2008).
19 Al-Buti, "Min al-Tataruf ila al-Hiwar" in *Mushkilat fi Tariq al-Nuhud*, p. 14; Muhammad 'Adnan Salem, "Awaliyat al-Qira'a fi Hayat al-Insan," in *Mushkilat fi Tariq al-Nuhud*, pp. 33–51.
20 See, for example, the work of Sa'id al-Buti, *Jihad in Islam: How We Understand It and How We Apply It*, Damascus: n.d. See Shahrur, *Tajfif Manabi' al-Irhab*, especially pp. 55–141. See also a number of lectures given to the public at the Ummayad Mosque and at the Abu al-Nur foundation, for instance, Ahmad Kuftaro, "Tawdih li-Ma'ani al-Jihad" (16 April 2004); "al-Islam wa al-Salam" (12 September 2003); "al-Islam wa al-Irhab" (15 August 2003). Online: www.kuftaro.org.
21 Shahrur, *Tajfif Manabi' al-Irhab*, pp. 138–9.

present their message freely and is hence not justified today, given today's advanced communication technology.[22]

Habash continues,

> We also assert that many of the wars that happened over the course of Islamic history were not legitimate [religiously driven] Islamic conquests, many of them involved looting, aggression, and fighting for power. And these are facts that should be studied within the logic of history, and without the religious sanctimony attributed to [Islamic] fighters.[23]

Grand Mufti Ahmad Hassoun is in agreement with Habash's latter statements.

These shaykhs contend that Salafi *Takfiri* Islamists are a by-product of the present crisis in religious education, and are not evidence of a religious renaissance. According to the shaykhs, true Muslims following true Islam (*Risalat al-Islam al-Haqqa*) not only *adapt* to changing circumstances, they are the leaders of "progress" and know how to remain true Muslims while accepting change.[24] In the Syrian 'ulama's' main teachings and throughout their lectures, they challenge anyone who assumes that he or she knows the whole truth, accusing them of forgetting that their idiosyncratic understandings of the religious texts are no more than human interpretations, inductions and mere hypotheses.[25] Hassoun writes, "Do not teach people hatred and bitterness, your interpretations are not sacred."[26]

In general, the Syrian shaykhs' pronouncements are threaded through with an emphasis on the ethical aspect of life rather than its political aspect. Individual piety and adherence to daily religiosity by being ethically aware of one's actions, attending mosque and partaking in weekly religious lessons and *Zikr* sessions are put forward as social as well as religious acts, and are claimed to be at the heart of the Islamic state.[27]

3 Outreach methods and Islamization from below

I have stressed both the state's strategies to control Syria's Islamic movement and ensure its apoliticalism, and the Islamic groups' responses to the shifting

---

22 Author's translation. This is in contradistinction to a number of (mainly Salafi) religious scholars who argue that the order of Jihad has not been abrogated, and that Defensive Jihad is not a concern of the modern sovereign state.
23 Author's translation. See "Risalat al-Tajdeed," online: http://altajdeed.org [Arabic] (accessed 19 July 2010).
24 Shahrur, *Tajfif Manabi'al-Irhab*, pp. 25–6; see also Muhammad Sa'id Ramadan al-Buti, *al-La Madhhabiya: Akhtar Bid'a Tuhadid al-Shari'a al-Islamiya*, Damascus: Furat, n.d.
25 Shahrur, *Tajfif Manabi'al-Irhab*, pp. 21 and 239–41. Also, observation based on weekly lessons delivered by prominent shaykhs such as Abd al-Fatah al-Buzum, Usama al-Rifa'i and Tawfiq Ramadan, under the tutelage of the Ministry of *Awqaf* at the Umayad mosque, addressing *Fiqh*, *Hadith* and *Usul al-Fiqh and al-'Ibadat*.
26 Author's translation. Speech delivered at the German Bundestag, 1 November 2007.
27 Ibid.

political environment in order to explain the dynamic Islamic and Islamist resurgence in Syria. Yet no explanation would be complete without an examination of the movement's outreach methods: the material and psychological incentives, as well as the constitutive role that ideological framing has played in the flourishing process from below.

A Ideological framing and the conversion of difficulties into problems

A powerful recruiting method used by the Islamic movement consists of ideological framing. This form of cultural outreach has allowed the different Islamic groups to strategically and successfully popularize their message, and thus to promote religious revivalism. In Syria, ideological framing consists of elevating the religious and moral consciousness of society, and of stimulating or "renewing" a much-needed social repertoire of "ethical" habits and behaviours. The goal is to achieve an organically "stronger" (homogeneous) and "healthier" (religious and God-fearing) society.

The underlying rationale for the ideological framing is that the socio-economic difficulties and challenges faced by Syrians are rooted in the ethical sphere, and thus are problems that can be overcome. While certain groups, such as the Kuftariya and the Tajdeed movements, tend to advance essentialist "moral" and "spiritual" arguments, other groups, such as Zayd movement and al-Buti's group, focus on the specificity of the "Islamic" aspect of their *da'wa*.[28] In general, these groups have efficiently used the organizational and institutional space that the state has left open to them. Carrie Wickham explains this process by reference to the Egyptian example: "[t]he dissemination of the Islamist *da'wa* through print and audio technologies at the micro-level was intricately related to the institutional developments at the macro-level."[29] In many ways, what was occurring in Syria during the 1990s was comparable to what happened in Egypt in the 1970s, in the sense that this new sort of cultural production was accelerated and resulted in the creation of a network of independent Islamic currents that sought to promote a new Islamic ethos and to fine-tune Syria's Islamic revival.

Since that time, increasingly efficient outreach methods have been employed, such as regular appearances on Syrian television and radio by the most prominent religious authorities (though admittedly still not to the same extent as their Egyptian and Jordanian counterparts).[30] Advertised lectures and lessons at

---

28 These groups are examined hereinafter.
29 Carrie Rossefsky Wickham, *Mobilizing Islam: Religion, Activism, and Political Challenge in Egypt*, New York: Columbia University Press, 2002, p. 134.
30 One prominent name is Shaykh Marwan Shaykhu, a senior officer in the Ministry of *Awqaf*. Marwan Shaykhu gives sermons every Friday on the radio and weekly *Fatawa*. He also presents religious programmes on Syrian national television, as well as daily *Iftar* speeches during Ramadan.

mosques and Islamic institutes are used as a means of disseminating Islamic ideas. Other methods of ideological outreach include Friday sermons and prayers, books, pamphlets and CDs, distributed at mosques and in local neighbourhoods' mushrooming Islamic bookstores – the most famous of which is al-Salam Baramka bookstore – as well as via very sophisticated Islamic websites.[31]

The content of the community outreach tends to focus upon a variety of fairly typical themes that resonate with the public, from youth education to what it means to be pious. Books written by Mustafa al-Siba'i, the Muslim Brothers' first Superintendent, Muhammad Ratib al-Nabulsi, Muhammad Sa'id al-Buti, the late Ahmad Kuftaro, Ahmad Badr al-Din Hassoun, Muhammad Habash and Syria's Minister of *Awqaf*, Muhammad 'Abd al-Satar, among others, inundate bookstores' shelves and give the strong impression that Syria is a religious country.[32] Articles published in magazines and pamphlets distributed in mosques underline that the duty of every Muslim to promote the "right Islam" begins with a change from within, rendered as a *Fard 'Ayn* (religious obligation incumbent upon the individual in Islam).

At the same time, secular publishing houses in Syria such as al-Tali'a (New Vanguard), al-Hiwar and al-Ahali, which were very popular in the 1970s and 1980s, are today seeing their sales decline:

> New Vanguard is facing growing financial problems and last year [2007] published a mere 10 titles, of which only one was an economic text. It's a far cry from the early 1990s when the publishing house was releasing upwards of 40 titles a year and was one of the country's largest book publishers.[33]

The larger issue hinted at in this decline of secular publishing houses is that, notwithstanding the rise of overt religiosity worldwide, the regime's empowerment of Syria's Islamic sector has come at the expense of the country's secular public space. Moreover, while mainstream (secular) publishers are facing financial hardship and have therefore decreased their overall activity, publishers of religious texts (whether Muslim or Christian) are well funded and are finding a highly receptive audience. This is allowing them to expand their distribution

---

31 Websites that are remarkably better than those of any secular organization in Syria. For instance, see www.taghrib.org, www.sheikhrajab.org, www.kuftaro.org, www.drhassoun.com, www.zuhayli.net, www.bouti.com, www.syrianawkkaf.org.
32 See, for instance, Mustafa al-Siba'i, *Asdaq al-Itijahat al-Fikriya fi al-sharq al-Arabi* [The Sincerest Intellectual Directions in the Arab East], Damascus: Dar al-Waraq, 1998; idem, *Islamuna* [Our Islam], Damascus: Dar al-Waraq, 2001; Muhammad Sa'id Ramadan al-Buti, *Kalimat fi Munasabat* [Words on Occasions], Damascus: Dar al-Fikr, 2002; Muhammad Umar al-Haji, *'Alamiyat al-Da'wa ila allah ta'ala* [The Global Call to Allah], Damascus: Dar al-Maktabi, 2007; Sadek Nahyoum, *Islam Didd al-Islam* [Islam versus Islam], London: Riyad al-Rayes Books, 1994; Muhammad Ratib al-Nabusli, *Muqawimat al-Taklif*, Damascus: Dar al-Maktabi, 2005.
33 *Syria Today*, October 2008.

networks and thus to attract more readers, concretely leading to a doubling in sales over the last few years: "It's an economic fact that religious books are at the heart of publishing in Syria," said 'Adan Salem, owner of Syria's largest religious publishing house al-Fikr (The Thought), which has branches in a number of Arab countries including Algeria, Yemen, Egypt and the Gulf states.[34] "Ninety percent of books we publish are religious, but they are moderate in their views," Salem stressed. Hussein 'Odat, owner of al-Ahali (The People) publishing house and also a political commentator, said that religious publishing houses have a considerable commercial advantage over their mainstream rivals, because they are supported by religious institutions. "The religious text publishers are funded from institutions which order advance copies of books and agree to distribute them in a way that small secular authors and publishers cannot hope to match," he said. "There has been a definite increase in religious books published over the last decade."[35]

At the 2008 Damascus International Book Fair – which for the last 26 years has been Syria's literary event par excellence, featuring international authors and many of the country's most liberal writers – Syrian secular intellectuals became suspicious of religiously motivated interference from the Ministry of *Awqaf*. These intellectuals claimed that books with overt sexual content were removed from the shelves, something that was denied by the organizers of the fair. In an investigation into the incident, *Syria Today* added that

> The Fair, held at the Assad National Library from 1 to 15 August and featuring 35,000 titles from 400 publishing houses from 23 foreign and Arab countries, also highlighted the growing trend among Syrian readers for religious texts. This growth in religious publications is having a profound impact on the industry, with Islamic publishing houses pushing aside their one-time large mainstream publishing rivals to dominate the sector.[36]

What is made clear in this report is how the country's Islamic sector is growing at the expense of the country's secular public space.

Nahj al-Islam, which is the Ministry of *Awqaf*'s official Islamic magazine, and which often features the words of the Syrian president on the first page followed by a *Hadith* or a Quranic *Sura* on the second, has certainly taken on a tone of *Da'wa*. The magazine routinely addresses the state's concerns regarding issues such as the meaning of respect and tolerance for the rights of others and the importance of education. But it also reflects the realities of Islamic revival in Syria, and hints at the manner in which such revivalism will likely influence Syria in the face of new domestic and international challenges. For instance, influenced by their belief in the need to harness the energy of the country's

---

34 Ibid.
35 Ibid.
36 Ibid.

young people, the journal recently dedicated a whole section to issues faced by young Syrians, ranging from intellectual challenges, law, the economy, astronomy, the social sciences, sex and gender issues and other moral and behavioural dilemmas. All of these diverse topics were addressed through references to the Quran, the *Hadith* and the Sunna. The journal emphasized the need for Islamic knowledge and Islamic integration within the socio-political structure, in order to wage a successful struggle against macro- and micro-level ills.[37]

A final important point related to ideological outreach concerns the subject of fear. Fear has repeatedly come up in my discussions with recruits and prospective recruits, and it is therefore important to consider its role in this sort of ideological framing. Generally speaking, it seems that male Syrian shaykhs try to avoid the subject of hell, while female preachers use it when they encounter resistance from recruits or prospective recruits. In one of the conversations that I had with an Islamic activist, she noted that women refusing to wear a veil and a long, dark blue coat because of their impracticality, especially during summer, they are reminded of the "heat of hell." In other words, they are told that enduring the summer heat for the sake of pious modesty is better than refusing to wear the coat and ultimately suffering the heat of hell. In other conversations, unveiled women told me that they are sometimes stopped on the street and accused of being heretical. One shaykh I talked to said that this is not the way preaching is usually done, and that if anything it is the exception to the rule. He said that certain over-zealous recruiters who do not know how to approach the subject of piety sometimes do not properly carry out their role. More generally, the movement is attempting to make sure that guilt is not used to ensure religious compliance. Some of my interviewees said that the use of fear made the movement less appealing to them, while other recruits had not encountered it.

The fact of trying to entice women and men to dress and talk in a certain manner tends to be a polarizing issue, appealing to some and objectionable to others. The conformity that is demanded and the sense of belonging to a spiritual community are often appealing to younger women. One older woman noted:

> Sometimes, it is almost a rebellious act against their families and societies. Some women need to belong, and they [religious groups] do make it easy to belong, it's almost a sorority of some sort. Once you are accepted in, you have all the love and privileges in the world, but resist and they will show you a different face ... they justify their aggression in the name of God. To me, they sound angry and frustrated more than God-loving.

When I introduced the topic of fear and conformity to a Qubaysi shaykha, she said that they follow state-approved lessons and a specific curriculum. The promotion of piety through fear is not part of the curriculum at all, and if anything, the message being propagated is that Islam is about respect, love and tolerance.

---

37 See, for example, *Nahj al-Islam*, December 2007, March 2008, May 2009, July 2009.

She added that some women believe mentioning heaven and hell, particularly the beauty of heaven and the fire of hell, can lead recruits to make up their mind. "We are not extremists ... we believe that once [a woman] is part of the movement, she will follow our lead [the path of good] on her own." The Qubaysi shaykha did, however, admit that the content of sessions ultimately depends on the teacher rather than being simply a literal presentation of the curriculum.[38]

B Material incentives

Beyond the use of ideological framing, the groups' activities include offering material and social-welfare benefits and aid. In particular, they offer Islamic reconciliation services that help to solve family issues by providing interpretations of Islamic law, distribute clothing and food during religious holidays and help to cover medical expenses when these are not fully covered by the state. The organizations also invite many youth to private educational lectures. Indeed, it is clear that the financial factor, of directly and indirectly providing charitable and social services, has played one of the most important roles in helping to ideologically recruit the public. This is not to discount the importance of the prayer groups, but rather to situate them as part of a larger Islamic framework that imparts a feeling of confidence and of security upon which members can rely while still retaining their dignity when in need of financial aid.

Ultimately then, the method that has attracted the most recruits to Syria's Islamic movement is the provision of social aid and charity.[39] Indeed, the movement has, since the mid-1990s, grown ever more efficient at providing social-welfare services to the increasing number of impoverished Syrians in urban and rural communities. In 2005, out of 584 registered charitable organizations operating in poor neighbourhoods and out of local mosques, 290 were Islamic, and it is estimated that some 80 per cent of the 100 charitable organizations in Damascus are Sunni Islamic. Moreover, in the early 2000s, some 72,000 Syrian families received help from charitable Islamic associations (see Table 6.1).[40] Concretely, this has often meant that groups develop their own saving associations based on *Zakat* money, *Sadaqa Jariya* (recurring charity) and other public contributions. These then act as a formal and an informal source of credit.

---

38 One thing was clear during my research, both in the literature and during conversations with informed observers: whether a group is perceived as extremist is *not* based on how it expects women to behave. That is, the group can be radical when it comes to women and still be considered moderate because it holds flexible views otherwise.

39 This was claimed by a number of Syrian intellectuals. In an attempt to verify this claim, I asked 45 members of Islamic networks to rank their reasons for adhering to the Islamic network of which they are a part. Four choices were given: (1) spiritual/religious betterment; (2) family tradition; (3) social obligation; (4) the social services the network provides. Out of the 20 members who agreed to answer, 13 stated that the network's social services were the most important reason they initially joined.

40 *Al-Hayat*, 18 June 2005. For more on the poverty element, see Chapter 9.

Furthermore, a number of groups are heavily funded and supported by both domestic and international actors, including Saudi and Kuwaiti shaykhs and Syrians whose wealth was made in the Arabian Peninsula. They use the money to build mosques, primary schools and housing for students, to sponsor students of Islamic Studies, to pay for marriages and to build medical clinics as well as to help cover medical expenses. The money is also used for aid to orphans, and to supply additional allowances and identity cards to the handicapped so that they can secure special privileges or in case of their arrest or harassment. The collected money is also distributed cyclically and in turn to the registered members of a particular group, through a parallel financial sector that operates beyond the government's watchful eye. According to Leif Stenberg, members of the Abu al-Nur foundation "can obtain an education, find employment, purchase a house or car, and get married ... Abu Nur provides the option of social mobility."[41]

Beyond reaching out to the impoverished in Syria, these Islamic groups have, since the mid-1990s, succeeded in attracting members from an influential and affluent constituency, mainly the traditional Syrian business class. This has in turn given them an increased capacity to provide food and medical assistance to the poor in less well-off neighbourhoods, such as the al-Qanawat neighbourhood. But what are the motivations for the middle and upper-middle classes to participate in the organizations, since presumably they do not require financial aid to the same degree? Part of the answer is that the traditional merchants who form a significant part of the upper class have never been truly pro-regime, and have always been a natural ally of Islamic associations (see Chapters 3 and 4). But when I put the question to my interviewees, they all answered that it was also very "prestigious" to be part of certain prayer groups. The response was particularly emphatic from the girls attending the Islamic meetings. One girl noted that "they [shaykhs and shaykhas] are actively recruiting the wealthy and the influential. They are preparing the best women and men to lead the nation." When I asked how she could tell that these women and men come from the "best" families, the consistent answer was that their last names are well known as belonging to influential families. And indeed, the participants at certain meetings are often a veritable who's who of the Damascene elite. Thus it is a prestigious and powerful network to join precisely because of the alleged exclusivity of certain home meetings (some meetings are open to all), where membership is apparently not open to all but rather one has to be invited to join. Young middle- and upper-class girls are especially attracted to the exclusivity that characterizes the meetings, and tend to compete regarding who from within a particular group of friends was asked to attend first.

This trend of attracting influential women is certainly new in Syria. In the early twentieth century and until very recently, influential Syrian women tended to join the secular movement rather than the Islamic one. The new tendency is partly a testimony to the success of the new Islamic leaders in framing their

---

41 Stenberg, "Young, Male and Sufi Muslim in the City of Damascus," pp. 84–5.

ideology to attract this kind of constituency. But it also testifies to the intersection of two other important realities: (1) that the secular movement – embodied by the Ba'th – has failed to meet Syrian women's psychological and socio-economic needs; and more importantly, (2) that the Islamic movement has no real competitor. That is, the Syrian Islamic society is the only ideological group that has been allowed to prosper under the secular authoritarian Ba'th.[42]

C Dispersed, personal and informal aspect of the Islamic network

Part of the success of Syria's Islamic network in recruiting members and spreading all across Syria is due to its operating in seemingly non-political settings, which makes it possible to keep the state at relative arm's length and to attract the Syrian masses. Yet it is important not to overlook the network's success at cultivating an informal, flexibly organized, personalized nature, in parallel to its official public face. Indeed, the institutions governed by the new Islamic groups such as mosques, Islamic *Nadwat* (Quranic study groups) and Islamic *Jam'at* (gatherings) rely on personal relationships, careful word-of-mouth invitations and a nexus of informal and associational networks embedded in personal interactions and social relationships to connect with people. Ultimately then, it is the informal, with its ability to engender a foundation of both trust and social pressure, that gives these associations their power.

According to a large number of my pious interviewees, shaykhas feel comfortable enough to disregard the invisible line between the private and public spheres by sometimes recruiting women in the streets. As one woman put it, "women are allowed to cross these lines [between the private and the public spheres] because of the assumed non-violent aspect of their message." Maya was approached by a shaykha in her neighbourhood, who insisted that she attend a few lectures taking place in the same neighbourhood. Maya at first refused, but the shaykha insisted, and after a few more chance meetings, Maya finally felt pressured enough to attend, "I thought I would not lose anything by going." Many lessons later, Maya was still not on board with becoming a member of the group. It is at that point that the shaykha's older sister got involved, and Maya was finally recruited. A friend of Maya was also pursued by the shaykha's committed apprentices who often "wandered" in the neighbourhood. She was eventually banned from attending lectures for not conforming to their teachings. When I asked Maya if she still saw her friend, she said that the group's pressure is strong, and so she sees her mostly indoors in order to avoid being reprimanded.[43]

---

42 Although it is important to add here that a detailed study regarding what percentage of the elite are members of these groups has yet to be conducted.
43 When I asked her why she is telling me all of this – given her dedication to the group – she explained that because I was not veiled myself, she felt encouraged to criticize the shaykhs' ways. She would not have had this conversation had I been a practising Muslim.

The fact that the piety sessions are dispersed all over the city is also a strength of the movement's outreach. In a conversation with a number of the regular members of a prayer group, Ola and Suzanne explained that if the group did not hold sessions all over the city at a variety of times, they would not be able to attend. Ola's work with the group involves her travelling from one end of the city to the other, and she does not have a routine schedule at work. She added that the only reason she trusts her several prayer teams (in terms of confiding in them) is because only the truly pious are accepted to join.

> It took a couple of months before I was approved [as a regular member] … This one [the group] was not penetrated by the snooping regime informants … We are not discussing politics at all. I just don't want to feel watched because I pray and attend lessons a few times a week. With terrorism, you never know when being pious will become a problem. I don't want my children to have problems because their mother is committed to learning more about her religion.

The personalized nature of the fundamentalist groups has also ensured that ideational framing is as effective as it can be. Individuals feel relevant to the group, which seems continually engaged not only in their cultic piety but in their diverse mundane endeavours as well. And while the groups have a power structure that relies on shared interests and superimposed layers of command, their leaders are also imbued with an aura of religious sacredness that renders the relationship between the members and the shaykh one of *Ihtiram Kamil wa Ta'a Kamila* (total respect and absolute obedience). As an Islamic *da'iya* explained to me during an interview in Damascus, "A direct relationship with the shaykh is essential for the transformation of the heart to happen."[44]

One of my pious interviewees, Husam, explained to me that he enjoys going to the nearby mosque every Friday, but that it is the informal *Jam'at* held at the house of one of the shaykhs that he enjoys the most: "These visits are friendly, include one on one discussions, and the hours are very flexible. He is often home, and receives us whenever we have time in between prayers." When I asked about how he chose that particular shaykh, his answer was that the shaykh's house is next to his, and the man is very moderate in his interpretations of the Islamic texts. Moreover, he treats Husam as a friend. The fact that the network's shaykhs can be reached in their homes for consultations shows how they have effectively re-created the Islamic network's local ties with communities, de-institutionalized ties that were once lost under the secular political order of the Ba'thi state.

The *Nadwat* and *Jam'at* allow Islamic leaders to construct micro-mobilization contexts and macro-collective identities of shared meaning, connecting members

---

44 Personal communication.

162 *Bashar al-Asad's era*

to potential recruits and *da'wa* activists. And importantly for our analysis, the Syrian government is well aware of this quasi-underground movement building, which operates in parallel to the registered formal institution building. Indeed, the government's toleration of it can be seen in the fact that the Ministry of *Awqaf* recognizes that some 7,000 mosques are considered "uncontrolled" by the Ministry (see Table 6.2).

From a macro-perspective, these Islamic groups are becoming ever more omnipresent and closely identified with the local character of the neighbourhoods in which they operate. This makes it possible for them to gain an informal advantage – relative to their secular counterparts – and to more effectively intervene in individuals' lives whether the individuals are part of the movement or not. In this regard, the activities of the organizations are reminiscent of the early-twentieth-century social-welfare *Jam'iyat* that gave birth to the Muslim Brotherhood in the 1940s, a fact that has not been lost on the government – in the words of one of my interviewees, who works for the Syrian military intelligence service: "We know that they can decide to act at any moment, but there is nothing we can do at this point, suffice it to say that they are here as much as we are here."[45]

Yet in seeking to understand the present circumstances of Syrian revivalist Islamic groups, it is important to remember that they are not the simple product of Arab authoritarian co-optation measures, as many would likely argue. Rather, they have capitalized on the regime's structurally induced political weaknesses to achieve a commanding position of relative independence within society, one that nearly all secular social institutions have failed to achieve.

In order to better contextualize the Islamic sector's growing membership and outreach, the following section surveys the most important groups and briefly outlines their dogmas.[46]

4 Syria's fundamentalist groups

A number of Islamic orders and groups have become very influential within Syria's Islamic revivalist movement:[47] the Kuftariya Naqshbandiya order, which

---

45 Personal interview conducted in Damascus April 2008. On the study of Islamic activism as part of the overall Social Movement Theory, see Diane Singerman, *Avenues of Participation: Family, Politics, and Networks in Urban Quarters of Cairo*, Princeton, NJ: Princeton University Press, 1996; Jillian Schwedler, *Faith in Moderation: Parties in Jordan and Yemen*, University of Maryland, 2006; and Quintan Wiktorowicz, ed., *Islamic Activism: A Social Movement Approach*, Bloomington and Indianapolis: Indiana University Press, 2004.
46 It is important to note that the Syrian Islamic discourse is nuanced, complex and sometimes ambiguous, depending on the group studied, but also on the shaykh or shaykha being examined within a particular group. Therefore, it is important to stress that the points presented above are general ones, meant to form a basis for the study of Syria's "official" or "legal" Islamic movement.
47 There are at least 20 active Islamic groups in Syria at the time of this writing. Due to the large areas of overlap in their discourses, only the areas of difference will be examined hereinafter.

includes prominent shaykhs such as Salah Kuftaro and Wafa' Kuftaro, among others;[48] Munira al-Qubaysi's "sisters," which was officially recognized by the state in May 2006; the late 'Abd al-Karim al-Rifa'i's group of the Rifa'i order, also known as the Zayd movement;[49] 'Abd al-Hadi al-Bani's *Jama'a*; Sa'id al-Buti's "Middle Path" movement;[50] Al-Khaznawi's group; Huda Habash and her followers;[51] and her brother Muhammad Habash's *Tajdeed* (Renewal) group.[52]

A Focus on humanity's shared ethics

The Kuftariya Naqshbandiya

Probably the most prominent group in Syria is the Kuftariya Naqshbandiya order.[53] Originally led by Shaykh Amin Kuftaro, the Kuftariya is a branch of the prominent Naqshbandi Sufi order. Like other orders that chose political quietism in order to survive the Ba'th era, the Kuftariya preaches a version of Islam that focuses on ethical renewal and a shared sense of human spirituality, tradition rather than textualism and on the transformation of society through the changed

---

48 The most prominent order in Syria is the Naqshbandiya order. Other prominent orders are the Shadhiliya and the Rifa'iya. The Naqshbandiya includes the teachings of the late Amin Kuftaro, the late Ahmad Kuftaro, the late Amin Shaykho, Salah Kuftaro and Wafa' Kuftaro. See Stenberg, "Young, Male and Sufi Muslim in the City of Damascus," pp. 68–91.

The Shadhiliya order draws on the teachings of shaykhs 'Abd al-Rahman al-Shaghuri, Shukri al-Luhafi, Shaykh Saleh al-Hamawee and Muhammad Hisham al-Burhani. Their *Zikr* sessions are held at the Nuriya Mosque, al-Sadat Mosque and al-Tawba Mosque in Damascus.

The Rifa'iya order includes the teaching of Ahmad al-Habbal at the Mosque of Badr al-Din in Damascus and Sariya al-Rifa'i at Thabit al-Ansari and al-Rifa'i mosques also in Damascus.

49 'Abd al-Karim al-Rifa'i's *da'wa* team includes shaykhs such as Sariya al-Rifa'i, Usama al-Rifa'i, Na'im Iriksusa and Nadhir al-Maktabi, among others.

50 See Chapter 5. Also see Andreas Christmann, "Ascetic Passivity in Times of Extreme Activism: The Theme of Seclusion in a Biography by al-Buti," in Philip S. Alexander *et al.*, eds, *Studia Semitica: The Journal of Semitic Studies Jubilee Volume*, Oxford: Oxford University Press, 2005, pp. 279–303. See also Fred de Jong, "Les confréries mystiques musulmanes au Machreq arabe," in Alexandre Popovic and Gilles Veinstein, eds., *Les Ordres mystiques dans l'Islam: Cheminements et situation actuelle*, Paris: Editions de l'EHESS, 1986.

51 Al-Khaznawi and Huda Habash's groups and dogma will not be discussed below because I did not get to talk to any of their members. But for information on Khaznawi, see Chapter 8, and the movement's website at www.khaznawi.de. For more on Huda Habash, see Hilary Kalmbach, "Social and Religious Change in Damascus: One Case of Female Religious Authority," *British Journal of Middle Eastern Studies* 35, 2008: 37–57.

52 Dr Habash has published 31 books in Arabic. For an introductory article with Dr Habash discussing his revivalist movement, see *Asharq Al-Awsat*, 3 February 2006. For Western works, see Paul L. Heck, "Religious Renewal in Syria: The Case of Muhammad al-Habash," *Islam and Christian–Muslim Relations* 15(2), April 2004: 185–207; idem, "Muhammad al-Habash and Inter-religious Dialogue" [Muhammad al-Habach et le dialogue interreligieux], in Baudouin Dupret, ed., *La Syrie au Présent*, Paris: Sinbad/Actes Sud, 2007.

53 The Naqshbandiya order has impacted upon most of Syria's most influential shaykhs examined in this work.

individual.[54] Stenberg writes: "The idea of cleansing the heart is ... considered important because it constitutes a base from which a new Muslim can be created – the heart being the center of 'religion' within the body."[55] The group is composed of around 10,000 front-line members who are regular attendees at the al-Nur Mosque in the Rukn al-Din district, *al-Thanawiya al-Shar'iya* for girls, and the mixed Faculty of Islamic *Da'wa*. It stresses the importance of inter-faith dialogue and acceptance, including ecumenism – rather than just inter-faith co-operation – and a de facto separation of religion and the state.[56]

The late Ahmad Kuftaro and his daughter Wafa' Kuftaro have issued a large number of female teaching permits, and the group claims that most of the female teachers working in Damascus and its suburbs are products of their *Jama'a*. The families of these women, especially their husbands, are also very involved in the group's activities. Indeed, the contacts and relationships of the husbands assist the women in distributing much-needed help to families in need. More generally, the group's members are encouraged to engage with both welfare organizations and with Syrian businessmen. The group has also built a strong alliance with the state through the efforts of the late Shaykh Ahmad Kuftaro, whose whole family is considered part of the state's patronage network.

The Tajdeed *movement*

Shaykh Muhammad Habash is another religious scholar who advocates for renewal (*Tajdid*). His manifest attempts at bridging the supposed gap between classical Muslim thought and modernity have marked him out as perhaps the boldest of all Sunni clerics in Syria today, and have resulted in him being seen as the heir to Ahmad Kuftaro by many Syrians. Habash's mission since the late 1980s has been to lead a campaign of Islamic renewal, while also learning what the West has to offer in terms of intellectual, scientific and ethical insights.[57] This mission has been effected in his capacities as director of the Center of Islamic Studies in Damascus and as a teacher with the prominent Abu al-Nur

---

54 See www.kuftaro.org; Paulo Pinto, "Dangerous Liaisons: Sufism and the State in Syria," in S. Jakelic and J. Varsoke, eds, *Crossing Boundaries: From Syria to Slovakia*, Vienna: IWM Junior Visiting Fellows' Conferences, Vol. 14, 2003, p. 7.
55 Stenberg, "Young, Male and Sufi Muslim in the City of Damascus," p. 73.
56 Although on this point, Kuftaro understands secularism to be *'Imaniya*, not *'Almaniya*. He perceives the word as stemming from *'Ilm* (science). *'Ilm*, he says, is entirely in line with Islam's teachings, since *Talab al-'Ilm* (the right to one's education) is an obligation (*Farida*) on all Muslims and hence is an intrinsic part of Muslim culture: "إن العلمانية التي تعتمد العلم التجريبي، هي حلقة صغيرة من حلقات الإسلام"
George Tarabishi, one of Syria's main secular academics and intellectuals, explains that secularism in Arabic comes from the word *'Almana*, i.e. to make part of this world, which is in opposition to *Rahbana* (to become part of the spiritual). This view is not shared by all secular academics in Syria. One wonders whether Kuftaro can reconcile Muslim ideology with secularism based on this understanding of secularism.
57 See his article in *al-Thawra*, 29 May 2009.

Foundation, as well as in his position as a member of the *Majlis al-Sha'b* (Syrian Parliament) since 2003. Unlike al-Buti, he has deliberately shed the conservative leanings of Syria's religious education. Indeed, one of his paramount statements in his *Risalat al-Tajdeed* (Mission of Renewal) is: "We believe that to every nation its laws and methods, and that to every generation its time and place."[58] He also says that there is no such thing as East and West, asserting that "the Earth is round and keeps on turning."[59]

One of Habash's most interesting intellectual contributions is his counter-Salafi teachings regarding Islam's outward obligations, and his clear rejection of the monopolizing Salafi claim to salvation and authenticity.[60] Habash's 31 books and dozens of articles are all based upon one main premise: that there is more than one path to God and salvation, and Islam recognizes and confirms the validity of them all. His teachings stress that no one has a monopoly over *Akhlaqiyat* (morals) and *Fiqh* or *al-Haqiqa* (truth), and that all religions are effective avenues to prosperity in this world and salvation in the next, a claim that ultimately aims to strip Islamist leaders of their religious power and influence. In his inter-religious debates and discussions with secularists, Habash argues that as much as 80 per cent of the general populace – and of Muslims more specifically – are conservative, that approximately 20 per cent are reformists, and that less than 1 per cent are extremists.[61]

Habash believes that the state is ultimately responsible for issuing laws and regulating society, a view that is reflected in his vision of women's rights and his views on adultery. His interpretation of "Jihad" leaves space for a new understanding of many of the so-called *Futuhat*, or Islamic conquests. He rejects the rightfulness of the traditional definition of jihad as a fight to spread Islam, and believes that today's jihad is one that ought to be directed by the state and its regular army.[62]

Habash's election to the Syrian parliament in the 2003 elections attests to the regime's overall approval of his work, and the votes he won underlie the success of his calls for renewal in most religious matters on the Syrian national scene.

---

58 Author's translation. From Dr Habash's *Risalat al-Tajdeed*, p. 7. Available at *al-Tajdeed* website: http://altajdeed.org/web/index.php?option=com_remository&Itemid=40&func=fileinfo&id=215 (accessed 23 December 2009).
59 See *al-Thawra*, 29 May 2009: فالأرض كروية، وهي تدور باستمرار
60 For instance, concerning the wearing of the *Hijab* by women, Habash asserts that veiling is a matter on which no consensus has been reached among the religious clerics; he also explains that ultimately it is a matter to be decided by the woman herself since she alone is impacted by it. See his Renewal Programme, pp. 21–2. Concerning the appropriate punishment for adultery, which a large number of Salafis believe to be stoning or flagellation, Habash explains that stoning is not Islamic and contradicts Islamic creeds and the spirit of the Quran. According to him, it is a matter for the modern state to look into. For more quotes from Habash's programme, see above and Chapter 5 of this work, particularly the section on gender relations.
61 See, for instance, Muhammad Habash, "al-I'tiraf bi al-Akhar Mas'ala Siyasiya Aydan," in Adeeb Khoury, ed., *Ishkaliyat al-I'tiraf bi al-Akhar*, Damascus, 2007, pp. 141–5; *Asharq Al-Awsat*, 3 February 2006; see also his TV appearance on BBC World News, "The Qatar Debates," 7 June 2009.
62 An interesting article to read is his "Qira'a li-al-mashru' al-Siyasi li al-Rasul al-Akram" [a reading of the political programme of the Prophet], in *al-Thawra*, 6 March 2009. Also, Habash's Renewal Programme, p. 25.

166 *Bashar al-Asad's era*

Paul Heck notes that "Islam, as he [Shaykh Habash] represents it, is not a force to be subdued but a partner in building human society."[63] Indeed, Habash goes the furthest among Syria's religious 'ulama' in endorsing a vision of society that is reminiscent of the *Mu'tazila* doctrine[64] in accepting the secular as part of the larger Islamic civilization.

B *Focus on the specificity of the Islamic message*

The Zayd movement

The Zayd group, which was originally led by the late Shaykh 'Abd al-Karim al-Rifa'i, and which resumed its work in Syria in the early 1990s after an earlier pause, due to its members' involvement in the Islamic rebellion of the 1970s and early 1980s, is today one of the largest and most influential (maybe even most independent) Islamic networks within the country's revivalist movement.[65] The network includes a main centre and mosque (*Markaz wa Masjed* Zayd Bin Thabet), as well as a number of affiliated mosques, libraries and powerful charitable organizations such as Jam'iyat Hifz al-Ni'ma al-Khayriya. It has a programme entitled *Nahwa Da'wa 'Alamiya* (Towards a Global *Da'wa*), and offers a variety of services, including prayer groups, summer camps, night lessons and courses teaching *Fiqh, Akhlaq, Nahu, Tafseer, Hadith* and *al-Sira al-Nabawiya*.[66] The groups and courses are for both adults and children.

The network's most prominent leading members include shaykhs Na'im Iriksusa, Nadhir Maktabi, Sariya and Usama al-Rifa'i. They lecture at the Zayd Bin Thabit al-Ansari Mosque and the 'Abd al-Karim al-Rifa'i Mosque in Damascus. Their *da'wa*-oriented teachings downplay Sufism's traditional practices in favour of renewal (*Tajdid*) of Islam, without, however, dismissing the virtues of the Sufi Rifa'i way. The group advances that "the present is not a time of *turuq* [Sufi paths to God], but of science,"[67] meaning that a focus on modern sciences rather than mystic traditions is a better way to interpret or perform piety and proselytize Islam in this time and era. Thus, knowledge of *Tawhid* (the principle of the oneness of God), *Fiqh, Tafseer* and *Hadith* is characterized as being vital for Muslims, yet emphasis is primarily placed on the reality of moral change and on the need to

---

63 In the late 1980s, supported by the Abu al-Nur Foundation, Habash became the first director of the Center of Islamic Studies in Damascus, which works for religious renewal via publications, lectures and conferences. In his election to parliament, Habash received the highest number of votes after the government-sponsored Ba'th candidates, and was subsequently chosen by his fellow parliamentarians to represent them in the six-member office of parliament.
64 Doctrine that sought to ground the Islamic creedal system in reason and logic.
65 See Sada Zayd website: www.sadazaid.com, section on "manhajahu al-tarrbawi." For more on the Zayd group, see Thomas Pierret and Kjetil Selvik, "Limits of Authoritarian Upgrading in Syria: Private Welfare, Islamic Charities, and the Rise of the Zayd Movement," *International Journal of Middle Eastern Studies* 41, 2009: 595–614.
66 Article on the curriculum of Zayd Bin Thabet Mosque online: www.sadazaid.com/play.php?catsmktba=3163.
67 "الحاضر ليس وقت طرق إنما هو وقت العلم"

re-interpret (*Ta'wil*) parts of the Islamic texts so that they can be made to serve new times and contexts. To accomplish this latter goal, questions regarding the universality and particularity of various interpretations are raised during lessons. These are often held at night so that members can attend after work hours. If renewal is conducted properly, the Rifaʻi *da'wa* programme envisions that the *Nahda Masjidiya* (Mosque Revival) that is witnessed today will eventually lead to a *Nahda Ilamiya Shamila* (an all-encompassing Islamic revival).[68]

The Middle Path Islam: Tajdeed *not* Tabdeel *(renewal not replacement)*

Another important group within the Syrian revivalist movement is led by Shaykh Sai'd Ramadan al-Buti, one of the country's most renowned Islamic preachers (see Chapter 5). Of Kurdish origin, al-Buti started his academic career in 1961 as an assistant professor at the newly founded Islamic Law Faculty at Damascus University.[69] Although he does not condone secularism, he has been willing to accommodate and comply with the ideals of the secular political setting. During the 1970s, al-Buti opposed the attacks on government and Baʻth Party officials, and the assassinations of prominent ʻAlawis by Muslim Brothers and members of smaller Islamic groups. His agreeing to intervene as an Islamic *'alim* and legitimator of the Syrian state at a much-needed moment made al-Buti a public and influential religious figure.[70]

A believer in a gradual Islamic awakening, he advanced a programme called "the Middle Path Islam," which is described as being situated "between the current realities of a secular state and an ideal Islamic society."[71] According to Shaykh al-Buti, his Middle Path programme has helped to guide Muslims who wish to resist the secularizing tendencies of the Syria's political culture, as well as the radicalization of Islamic thought at the hands of the so-called "Kharijites of this era" (Khawarej Haza al-'Asr).[72] Al-Buti himself is very critical of the emerging radical and textual-literalist tendencies within Islamic thought, particularly literalists' attempts to negate the "other."

---

68 See Zayd movement website: www.sadazaid.com.
69 After completing his doctorate at al-Azhar in Cairo in 1965, he became a lecturer in comparative Islamic jurisprudence and religious studies at Damascus University, and then a professor of comparative law and Islamic doctrine (*al-Fiqh al-Islami wa Madhahibihi*) at the Department of Islamic Law.
70 These interventions included opposing the attacks on Baʻth officials, as well as on ʻAlawis, in the 1970s; condemning on television, at the request of the Ministry of Information, the killing of 83 ʻAlawi cadets; giving a speech that was patronized by President Asad at the peak of the regime–Brotherhood violence in 1982; and thanking the "hidden hand" of President Asad for the repeal of censorship on Islamic publications and broadcasts, as well as the legalization of wearing of the hijab in state institutions. See Andreas Christmann, "Islamic Scholar and Religious Leader: A Portrait of Shaykh Muhammad Sai'd Ramadan al-Buti," *Islam and Christian Muslim Relations* 9(2), 1998: 149.
71 Christmann, "Islamic Scholar and Religious Leader," p. 149.
72 See www.bouti.com, "Kitab Maftuh ila Jaridat al-Khaleej," in the "Kalimat al-Shahr" section (accessed 15 July 2010). The Kharijites were an early community of zealous Muslims who believed that they alone were destined for salvation. They had a very strict Islamic ideal, and tried to force their vision on the Muslim community, ostracizing anyone whom they perceived to be a sinner.

168 *Bashar al-Asad's era*

Thus a number of his major works are dedicated to attacking the radical positions of the Salafiya movement, by using textual analysis and criticism to correct their efforts to uncover an authentic Islam free from traditional accretions.[73] Although al-Buti does not condemn all Salafi adherents, he is harsh in his criticism of Salafiya as a *Mazhab* (school of Islamic Law). He is also harsh in his critique of certain young modernists who believe that they can legitimately designate others as *Kuffar* (un-believers), this despite their limited and relatively superficial understanding of *Usul al-Fiqh*.[74] Indeed, his writings and sermons against these young modernists have caused him to be "excommunicated" by a number of radical groups, as well as by a Syrian Salafi Islamist living abroad.[75]

Al-Buti addresses hundreds of people at his Friday sermons in the Mawlana al-Rifa'i mosque and during his lectures at the Tanjiz Mosque. As a professor at the University of Damascus, he has had – and continues to have – considerable influence on generations of teachers during their formative years, many of whom have gone on to teach religion and shari'a in Syria's state primary and secondary schools. Despite his old age, he continues to capture the imagination of millions of young Muslims all over the Islamic world, and has certainly played a major role in Syria's resurgent Islamic movement.

When one considers Sai'd al-Buti's fatwas, sermons and lectures of today in relation to those from his past, it is clear that he has become more overtly critical of Syria's secular political position over time, and moreover has become increasingly committed to orthodoxy and tradition as part of his call to hold on to the fundamental Islamic principles (*al-Tamasuk fi al-Thawabet*). These fundamentals, according to al-Buti, are timeless and universal; they cannot be altered or dismissed, hence one of his slogans is "renewal, not replacement" (*Tajdeed, wa laysa Tabdeel*).[76]

'Abd al-Hadi al-Bani's group

Another group in the Islamic movement, and arguably the one whose behaviours are the most unusual, is Shaykh 'Abd al-Hadi al-Bani's Sufi organization. Al-Bani has built a mosque for his *Jama'a* in the Muhajerin district, called the Kinani mosque. The mosque's gate has four guards, apparently so as to ensure that only those who belong to the group enter. It is said that once inside the mosque, no talking or praying is allowed unless Shaykh al-Bani is there to lead it. Importantly, his disciples are not allowed to participate in any other shaykh's sessions, nor even in the Muslim pilgrimage to Mecca, so that their souls remain pure.[77]

---

73 See, for instance, al-Buti and Muhammad al-Habib al-Marzuki, *al-La Mazhabiya Akhtar Bid'a Tuhadid al-Shari'a al-Islamiya*, Damascus: Dar al-Farabi, n.d; al-Buti, *al-Salafiya Marhala Zamaniya Mubaraka La Mazhab Islami*, Damascus: Dar al-Fikr, 2006.
74 Christmann, "Islamic Scholar and Religious Leader," pp. 156–7.
75 Al-Buti was excommunicated by Al-Tartusi. He was also criticized by other Salafi preachers such as Shaykh Salman al-'Awda.
76 See al-Buti, *al-Mazaheb al-Tawhidiya wa al-Falsafat al-Mu'asira*, Damascus: Dar al-Fikr, 2008.
77 Private communication, Damascus, April 2008.

Islamization from below   169

Unfortunately, beyond the fact that al-Bani's teachings have a Naqshbandi grounding, very little is known about what sort of Islamic discourse he advances. What is known is that the group aims to establish "an Islamic *Umma*, rather than an Arab one."[78] Al-Bani's group also takes a stand against women mixing with men, and against women working outside the confines of their homes. Al-Bani additionally prohibits his followers from watching television and engaging with new technologies such as the Internet. Syrian intelligence keeps a close eye on the activities of the Kinani mosque and of its regular members. The Bani group was recognized as part of Syria's official Islamic groups in 2009, which caused a great stir in Syria's political environment.[79] By 2010, the state had issued a new ban on the group's activity.

C The women's piety power

In Syria, the revivalist movement is not only led by male shaykhs, but also by very influential shaykhas (female religious leaders).[80] Most discussions of the role of women in Islamic movements focus on their status within the context of state policy or Muslim patriarchal society, but very few analyse the significant role of women in the upper ranks of the leadership within the Islamic community itself. Syria offers a different perspective in our understanding of the role of women and Islamic activism. Indeed, it is not possible to explain the success and growing autonomy of Syria's revivalist movement and of its most important constituent groups without reference to the role of its women leaders in this process. Shaykhas have been much more successful than men in bridging the divide between the public and private spheres, a conceptual divide that often limits male shaykhs' access to women and the family unit overall. More importantly, as women have come to increasingly participate in public life, albeit within patriarchal structures, the status of women has become a key issue in the mobilization arsenal of Islamic groups and in their ideological "framing."[81]

Syrian shaykhas as muftis

The increased role of women in Syria's Islamic revivalist movement could explain why the country's current Grand Mufti, Shaykh Ahmad Hassoun, declared on 10 June 2008 that shaykhas are indeed being prepared to become

---

78 See Ba'thist website All4Syria at: http://all4syria.info/content/view/16751/96 (accessed 12 November 2009).
79 A number of Ba'thists were outraged by a notice issued by the regime on 23 August 2009, stating that the Ba'th does not hold a "negative view" of al-Bani's group, despite the group's aim of creating an Islamic Syrian state. A number of Ba'thi members went so far as to say that the Ba'th is no longer a party that upholds secularism, and should be re-named "the Islamic Ba'th Party."
80 It is important to note here that female shaykhas are leaders within the above-mentioned groups.
81 Wickham explains the act of framing as "the creation of motives for movement participation." See Wickham, *Mobilizing Islam*, p. 120.

170 *Bashar al-Asad's era*

muftis. This would mean that, in addition to their already-achieved teacher positions, they will be able to issue Islamic religious opinions and rulings, a role that has generally been monopolized by men.[82] It seems that Shaykh Hassoun would like to see these female muftis take on official positions within the Islamic sector in order to promulgate and teach what he calls the "correct Islam" to women. However, some secularists argue that the goal of this educational project is manifestly not to empower female scholars, but rather to increase the visibility of conservative women, to promote formal Islamic practices and to Islamize the family unit. Regardless of which of these two views is more accurate, there is no doubt that female religious education has been a successful method for forging and sustaining ties with potential recruits, and thus promoting Islamic revival in secular Syria.[83]

Ultimately, the entry en masse of Syrian women into the Islamic movement testifies to the important role played by shaykhas in the process of Islamizing society. In fact, the number of girls attending the lessons of shaykhas has increased to such an extent that many observers believe that there are now more girls receiving an Islamic education than boys – one reliable estimate is that there are more than 75,000 women attending these schools. Similarly, though it is unclear how many of the country's 700 Islamic schools are for girls, most observers believe that schools for girls outnumber those for boys.[84]

The Qubaysi sisters

In addition to Shaykha Wafa' Kuftaro and Shaykha Huda Habash, both mentioned earlier, a prominent example of an Islamic female leader is Munira al-Qubaysi, who was also once a disciple of the late Shaykh Ahmad Kuftaro. Although Qubaysi was imprisoned a few times in the early 1960s, she has since become Syria's most prominent shaykha. This might be due to the fact that she has never been seen as a clear *'Alemat al-Sulta* (religious scholar who has been co-opted by the state), but rather has retained a low public profile while still being allowed to continue her work. Indeed, her group is not clearly pro- or anti-state, and its main focus appears to be first and foremost the revivalism of Islamic piety in Syria and the Arab world. Thus Qubaysi and her followers have preached an apolitical Islam mainly to girls and young women, focusing on *Hadith*, *Fiqh*, *Tafseer* and *Akhlaq* (disciplines usually addressed by male scholars only) while seemingly attempting to recruit those who were most socially "liberal."[85]

One woman explained to me that the more defiant she was in one of Qubaysi's class (in terms of being more socially liberal), the more the shaykha praised her and presented her as an example of someone who is outwardly lost and yet inwardly

---

82 Al-Arabiya net, 10 June 2008.
83 See Annabelle Böttcher, "Islamic Teaching among Sunni Women in Syria," in Donna Lee Bowen and Evelyn A. Early, eds, *Everyday Life in the Muslim Middle East*, Bloomington and Indianapolis: Indiana University Press, 2002, p. 290.
84 See *Al-Hayat*, 3 May 2006; See also *New York Times*, 29 August 2006.
85 Private communication with a group of Qubaysiat women, December 2007 and September 2010.

pious, who would eventually come to understand God's calling and adhere to the group's dictates.[86] But a couple of weeks later, she was asked to quit the sessions because she was corrupting the other girls with her interlocutions and doubt. Qubaysis, it seems, often ask their students to pledge allegiance and obey only the shaykhas even if this goes against the wishes of their parents. This has caused some parents to object and retrieve their daughters from the Qubaysi-led schools.

In another conversation, an atheist woman told me that she was explaining to a couple of Qubaysiat ladies that she enjoys life and would never follow their lead. The next day, they visited her unannounced, and had musical instruments with them. They started chanting and playing music. The point being made was that "they are not Wahhabis, and religion can be fun." The atheist woman then continued, explaining that they had originally approached her because,

> they saw me cry at a funeral [with the Quran being recited in the background] and thought I am going to be an easy recruit. When they mentioned this to me [crying while the Quran was being recited], I told them I was sad, I hadn't even noticed the recital ... it had nothing to do with God.

The Qubaysi Sisters meet in their private homes and private schools that the sisters have invested in, some of which are better known than others, such as the Farah house.[87] They began doing this in the aftermath of the 1982 Hama Battle. Interestingly, their recruitment of affluent and influential followers has allowed the sisters to successfully lobby the government of President Bashar al-Asad for licences to teach in private schools such as the 'Umar Ibn al-Khattab school, al-Basha'ir school and al-Na'im school in Mazzeh, the Dawhat al-Majd school in the Malki district and al-Bawader school in Kafer Suseh.[88] Qubaysi's group is now led by two shaykhas, Su'ad Bakdunes, who is the director of the Dar al-Na'im school in al-Rawda area, and Haifa' Quweidar, the director of 'Umar Ibn al-Khattab school in the Mazzeh District.[89] Other renowned shaykhas within the movement are shaykhas Khayr Juha, Muna Quweyder, Dalal al-Shishakl, Nahidah Taraqji, Fa'izah al-Tabba', Fatima Ghabbaz, Nabilah al-Kuzbari and Raja Tsabihji.

While the Qubaysiat sisters were only recognized by the Syrian state in 2003, they had been working semi-openly as religious preachers and teachers since the early 1960s. At least half of the 75,000 women taking religious lessons in Syria are followers of Qubaysi.

5 Conclusion

In the 1970s and early 1980s, the Islamic opposition in Syria did not enjoy a broad social base of support. The minorities, the peasants, the salaried middle

86 Ibid.
87 See *Al-Hayat*, 3 May 2006. See also Al-Arabiya news: www.alarabiya.net/articles/2006/05/03/23408.htm.
88 Ibid. See also Sami Moubayed, "The Islamic Revival in Syria," *Mideast Monitor* 1(3), September–October 2006. Online: www.mideastmonitor.org/issues/0609/0609_4.htm.
89 Private communication, April 2008.

class, the professionals and academics, and even the Sunni elite of Damascus, were not attracted to an Islamic nationalist alternative that was in league with the traditional rich landlords and merchants. As a result, the political Islamic movement was believed to have failed in its efforts to seriously impact upon Syria's political and social scenes.

This chapter has argued that although the Muslim Brotherhood-led political movement of decades past was significantly curtailed, the rest of Syria's Islamic movement has continued to have a presence on the country's domestic scene. In so doing, it has accumulated enough power and importance to effectively impact upon today's status quo. In essence, the Syrian Islamic movement has proven to be a very adaptable *realpolitik* player. In order to survive the Ba'th era, it has chosen to become a tacit ally of the political elite. As a result, the different orders and shaykhs developed a seemingly apolitical programme that focused on Islamic change from below. Thus the movement shifted its focus from the broader meta-narratives of politics to the ethical regeneration of individuals and political quietism.

Certainly the accommodation orchestrated by the regime is a priori an essential part of the relationship between the Islamic orders and the Ba'thi political command. That is, the willingness of the state to tolerate and to co-opt the Islamic orders has provided Syria's Islamic movement with an important space for organizing.[90] Yet within the space provided by the state, effective outreach and communication methods and the organizational composition of the Islamic groups – marked as it is by increasing decentralization, and a small-clustered profile – have allowed them to have an increased level of social outreach.

Indeed, the personal, informal and de-institutionalized nature of the orders greatly enhances their ability to practise effective ideological framing and social outreach, especially because the orders' members have direct access to the leading shaykh at the top of the Sufi pyramid and feel overall relevant to the congregation's spiritual and mundane existence. Furthermore, the ethical discourse of the Syrian Islamic orders has been moulded to appeal to different social backgrounds and sub-national cleavages, thereby ensuring that a diverse public embraces it. Finally, the orders' growing strength also stems from their re-creation of a large Islamic network through social action from below, particularly the organization of charitable services, the development of closer ties with the local communities that the orders are gradually being left to service (in light of the state's liberalization policies), a focus on youth, the collection of donations and the organization of weekly get-togethers.

---

90 In so doing, the regime has been moving closer to re-creating the political environment that prevailed in the early twentieth century, in which the politics of the notables (who were in favour of classical economic liberalism) dominated in Syria. Indeed, to counter the influence of the radical elements within the Syrian Islamic movement, the Ba'th regime has provided Islamic groups who are willing to compromise with some organizational space. This compromise has not involved the groups making dogmatic concessions. The results are reminiscent of that earlier era, in which the religious orders and the political leaders agreed to serve each other's purposes rather than to fight over power. This will be discussed further in Chapter 9.

As a result of these outreach measures, the movement has succeeded in re-creating a large network of neo-fundamentalist organizations and charitable associations that are effectively operating within – and providing services within – the available legal space. While doing this, the co-opted Syrian Islamic network seems to be supplementing and perhaps even to some degree supplanting the once-populist Ba'th, which used to draw support from the disadvantaged rural and urban classes. In other words, Syria is effectively witnessing the resurgence of a very powerful, semi-autonomous, Islamic network.

Having examined the concrete results of the regime's co-optation measures, as well as the success of the Islamic movement at using the space provided in order to effectively advance its discourse, we now move to a discussion of a resurgent and rising opposition movement: Syria's opposition Islamic groups.

8 Re-emergence of political Islam
Syria's Islamist groups

1 Introduction: opposition pacifism and opposition activism in the search for systemic change

We have seen that Syria's official Islamic groups and formal networks – such as the Naqshbandiya Kuftariya order, the Qubaysiyat, the Zayd empire and the *Tajdeed* movement – have been more or less open to state co-optation because of their inherent political quietism, and that since 1982, they have become more influential while growing ever more autonomous from the state. But there are other Islamic groups in Syria (albeit still very small in numbers and recruits) that have been less willing to work within the confines imposed by the state's policy of political pacification. These latter groups are part of Syria's political Islamist opposition, which is resurfacing in the country. It consists of a number of groups who share the conviction that a formal Islamization of political power, whether from above or from below, is an essential element in order to achieve a God-fearing and pious society.[1]

The Syrian Islamist opposition movement can be divided into two streams: the pacifist Islamists and the militant Islamists.[2] Groups in both streams are gaining in influence and strength, especially since the war in Iraq (see Chapter 6).

An examination of this nascent movement's nature and agenda, as well as its leaders and outreach methods, will help to complete drawing the map of Syria's Islamic revivalism. It will also help to advance our understanding of political Islam more generally, and of the possibility of Islamist militancy within Syria and in the region in the absence of political liberalization.

---

1 See Yahya Sadowski, "Political Islam: Asking the Wrong Questions," *Annual Review of Political Science* 9, 2006: 219.
2 As stated in the introductory chapter of this work: an "Islamist" party leans towards political action through the state. It aims at struggling to change the political regime and then imposing – from above – Islamic values on society. A "fundamentalist" party may also have counter-hegemonic political aims; yet it is mainly concerned with the restoration of an Islamic ethical model through the re-establishment of Muslim law and customs, and the re-Islamization of each individual with the aim of creating a perfect Muslim society.

2 Ideology: Islamists vs. fundamentalists

Political Islam in its pacifist and militant versions emerged at least partly in response to the perceived shortcomings of Islamic fundamentalism. Because of this, as well as the long-established link between fundamentalism and Islamic schools, Islamists developed an anti-clerical stance, with their lay movement usually existing outside the body of the 'ulama'. There are a number of reasons for this: first, Islamists insist that the 'ulama's' traditional education has left them ill-equipped to defend Islam against the new ideas that have swept in from the West and pushed aside the political ideal of the Islamic *Khilafa* (Caliphate).[3] They also claim that fundamentalists have failed to interpret, portray and defend Islam in a way that would allow it to address the problems of modernity while still maintaining its authentic essence and message.[4] This concern is not new and indeed has been voiced since the early twentieth century by Islamic ideologues all over the Islamicate world, including Syrian Salafis such as Sa'id al-Jabi and Sa'id Hawwa.[5] In his explanation of the Islamists' intellectual inclinations, Sadowski writes,

> Islamists, with their cosmopolitan backgrounds, introduced various tools they had borrowed from the West into their organizational arsenal ... they drew on anti-modernist philosophies that embodied Western dissatisfaction with the consequences of industrialization and positivism: Spengler, Althusser, and Feyerabend supplied some of their favourite texts.[6]

Another issue over which Islamists differ with fundamentalists is regarding apolitical understandings of Islam, something that the former firmly reject because they see it as sheer falsification of knowledge and a corruption of Islam that flows from an urge to please the holders of political power. According to Islamists, in opting for political quietism, fundamentalist clerics have not only failed in their efforts at convincing the modern masses of the virtues of religiosity beyond *Fiqh* (jurisprudence) and *'Ibadat* (practices), but have been co-opted and corrupted by secular authorities, to the point of ending up on the secular regime's payroll.[7]

---

3 It is important to note here that not all Islamists perceive democracy as a Western ideal. Some view the *Khilafa* system as a democratic organization of rule. See Sadek Nahyoum, *Islam Didd al-Islam*, London and Beirut: Riad el-Rayyes Books, 1994, pp. 15–8.
4 This fear about the Muslims' intellectual decline is not a new concern. Indeed the concept of "renewal" through a cleansing return to the purity of Islam's Golden Age has been a recurring theme throughout Islam's 14 centuries of history.
5 See Chapter 3.
6 Sadowski, "Political Islam," p. 222.
7 It is important to say here that, similar to Islamists, certain Islamic intellectuals also criticize the *Faqih* in an aim to free Muslim societies from the burdens of the past, and to advance systems of governance that shift power from the *Fuqaha'* and the rulers to the peoples.

3 Syria's pacifist Islamists: *al-Tayar al-Islami al-Dimuqrati* and the Syrian Islamic Front

The majority of the members of Syria's current Islamist opposition movement were once part of, or linked to, the Syrian Muslim Brothers. After the 1982 Hama Battle, some of the remaining members of the Muslim Brothers chose to take the quietist path by pursuing pacifist politics, and have thus shifted their focus towards encouraging a peaceful revolution from below. These individuals are mainly traditionalist and orthodox Sufi in their outlook, which is different from other countries, where counter-hegemonic[8] Islamists have been mainly Salafi, such as the *al-Takfir wa al-Hijra* groups and the *I'adat al-Da'wa wa al-Tabligh* groups.[9] In general, pacifist Islamists are competing for doctrinal control of Syrian society with both the state-sanctioned factions, i.e. the fundamentalists whom they believe to be controlled by the state, and with the Syrian militant Islamists, whose Salafi outlook they claim is counter-productive to achieving an Islamic state (as will be elaborated in the examination of the groups' particular doctrinal statements later in the chapter).

Ideologically, leaders within this opposition movement believe that the 'ulama' can engender an Islamic consciousness from below, or what is called "the consciousness of unification," but only once they have recruited enough supporters willing to closely follow their religious teachings. According to their understanding, *al-Hala al-Islamiya* (the Islamic state) is the most important platform for the transformation and purification of society. And the only safe way to advance this goal within Syria's authoritarian political context is through invitation-only organizing, word-of-mouth gatherings, private meetings and informal lessons. Thus inconspicuous, often unregistered mosques and urban *zawiyas* are developing beyond being simply places for *da'wa* and prayer, to

---

8 One explanation of counter-hegemony is advanced by Nicola Pratt as "a creation of an alternative hegemony on the terrain of civil society in preparation for political change." See Nicola Pratt, "Bringing Politics Back In: Examining the Link between Globalization and Democratization," *Review of International Political Economy* 11(2), 2004: 331–6. Online: www.jstor.org/pss/4177500.

9 Despite these groups' radical outlook, they claim to have no involvement in politics. The *Takfiri* groups agree that contemporary societies are similar to the state of the *Jahili* and *Kafir* (apostate) society in Mecca in the period between the emergence of the prophetic message and the Prophet's migration to Medina. The members of these societies are hence un-believers, or at best ignorant of the true meaning of the Islamic message. However, this group does not believe it is time just yet to declare Jihad or to initiate the active construction of the Islamic state, as this had not been ordered in Mecca when Muslims were few in numbers and weak. The *Da'wa wa al-Tabligh* groups agree with the *Takfiri* groups that the members of these Islamic societies ignore the meaning of true Islam, yet it is important that there are some who do take it upon themselves to re-enlighten Muslims to the main Islamic precepts, implications and its various practices without abandoning those societies or isolating themselves from them. For a typology of these groups, see Dia' Rashwan, "al-Juzur al-Fikriya lil-tayar al-salafi wa ta'biratihi al-mukhtalifa" [the intellectual roots of the Salafi movement and its diverse expressions], in Muhammad Salim al-'Awa *et al.*, eds, *Al-Irhab, Juzuruhu, Ana'uuhu, Subul 'lajihi*, Cairo: 2005, pp. 92–4.

now also being centres of political activity.[10] As such, these centres are seen as being "liberated zones." When I asked about the meaning of this expression, my interviewee explained, "It means being liberated from one's own corruption, bitterness and need whether psychological or material." It also means "being liberated from the interference of the corrupt and the cynical."

Although their meetings are secretive, their political message is known to most Syrians since it is similar to the one once advanced by the Syrian Muslim Brothers. These groups call for "democratic rule,"[11] and are very critical of the Syrian political order and particularly of the state's domestic and regional policies. While the regime's domestic policies are said to be corrupt and corrupting of the public masses, its regional policies are seen as anti-Islamic notwithstanding their pro-Islamic façade, and ultimately as destructive of Syria's Arab heritage and undermining of the country's Islamic pride. Syria's alliance with the Shi'i Iranian Republic is particularly looked down upon; an alliance with Saudi Arabia would be much preferred. When I asked a high-ranking officer whether the state was concerned about the re-emergence of these domestic groups, he replied:

> aren't we concerned that if one day their leaders tell them to attack, they might? Aren't we worried about a domino effect given our knowledge of their existence and growing influence? Of course we are, but there is no way around it at this point.[12]

The two non-militant Islamist groups in Syria are *al-Tayar al-Islami al-Dimuqrati* (the Islamic Democratic Current) and the Syrian Islamic Front (SIF). They are both overtly against the existing Syrian regime.

A The Islamic Democratic Current

Membership

The Islamic Democratic Current is a new outspoken, self-proclaimed pro-democracy Islamic group functioning within Syria. It is believed to be an offshoot of the Syrian Muslim Brotherhood, more particularly of the group's remaining loyalists inside the country (the group's leadership has been exiled from Syria since the early 1980s). There are no detailed analyses of the Islamic Democratic Current's membership currently available. But Syrian observers with whom I spoke insisted that the group mainly attracts members of the traditional Sunni religious class, small merchants and traditional artisans still living

---

10 Private communication.
11 The exact meaning of the term "democracy" (the word used by Syrian groups is *dimuqratiya* rather than *Shura*) varies depending on the opposition group, as will be shown hereinafter.
12 Private communication.

178 *Bashar al-Asad's era*

in old quarters of the cities. These members tend to be older than the individuals joining the multi-national militant Islamist groups, and to have maintained a traditional way of life.[13]

Although the work of the group is not clearly defined and the movement is often seen as being "unstructured" and "too loose" to attract significant numbers of members, its leadership issues regular statements in Syrian newspapers which are reminiscent of messages issued by the SIF in Europe.[14] In these statements, the Islamic Democratic Movement alleges that it is not allowed to undertake the outreach that apolitical Islamic groups are able to undertake. The group claims that it is prevented from giving religious lessons or from delivering sermons in mosques, while other clerics that focus on religious matters instead of on Syrian politics are offered organizational and recruiting space, and are given platforms on state radio and television from which to promote their views.[15] The group also complains about the state's constant harassment of its members. Indeed, known members of the Current, such as Ghassan al-Najar (an engineer), Dr Yasser al-'Iti, a poet and an academic from Damascus and Dr Ahmad Tu'ma, a dentist from Dayr al-Zur, have served prison sentences for speaking out against the current political apparatus, and for supporting the dissenting movement under the "Damascus Declaration."[16]

Discourse

In a statement published in 2008, the Islamic Democratic Current calls on *abna' al-watan al-wahed min kafat al-adyan wa al-a'raq* (the sons of the nation from all religions and ethnicities) ... *ahiba'ana fi al-'aqida wa shuraka'ana fi al-watan* (our friends in faith, and our partners in the homeland), to support the Islamic Democratic Current: "we promise you citizenship and complete equality in rights and duties in return for your support, in war and in peace" [author's translation]. The statement then details a number of issues for which it condemns the Syrian political order, including the continued Israeli occupation of the Golan Heights, the regime's empty claims of resisting the Israeli occupier and the continued existence of Law 49, which makes membership in the Muslim Brothers a crime punishable by death in Syria.

In terms of economic policy, the Current alludes to its populist programme by highlighting the state's economic and social failures, as well as Syria's deteriorating living conditions:

> poverty levels have affected as much as one-third of the country's populace, and we are moving from the devastations of a socialist system towards the

---

13 Ibid.
14 These messages will be examined hereinafter. A number of Syrian observers argue that the Islamic Democratic Current is but the domestic branch of the exiled SIF.
15 Private communication. See also Kuluna Shuraka' website: http://all4syria.info/content/view/140/65 (accessed 12 August 2009).
16 Ibid. See also al-Marfa' website: www.almarfaa.net/?p=243 (accessed 7 September 2008).

Re-emergence of political Islam 179

corruption of a market economy, both systems serving to steal our wealth
and our resources. Years have passed, yet illiteracy and ignorance are rising,
and children are not attending their schools to provide for their families.
[author's translation]

The Current notes that people are reaching out to private organizations for aid
and support, and asserts that a universal social insurance and health-care system
are the responsibility of the state (*Mas'uliyat al-Dawla*).[17]

The group's political ideas were summarized in a more recent statement published on a number of Syrian websites. In it, the Current expresses its commitment to "democratic rule" and the need for political change, and denounces the existing government's corrupt and authoritarian ways. Even more, it openly rejects secularism and describes the supporters of secularism as the enemies of Islam. Secularism is said to be a disguise for the enemies of Islam who are hiding within the regime. The statement reads:

> The people have the right to choose their leaders and their representatives
> ... within a transparent and an honest parliamentary system ... the enemies
> of Islam have shown their teeth, and some of them hide under the bitter disguise of secularism in order to uproot religion from society and life ...
> holding up positions from within the regime in order to attack Islam ... all
> with the knowledge and awareness of those within the Ministry of Endowment [*Awqaf*], the *ifta'* authorities and the National Assembly, who hold no
> real power ... this minority of people attacks Islam ... in the name of
> modernity, renewal, women's rights and Westernization.[18]

The statement also addresses the Syrian Islamic movement more generally. It encourages the members of the movement to continue in their non-militant ways, and emphasizes the Current's dedication to peaceful persuasion. It also criticizes the co-opted leaders of Syria's Islamic movement, and calls on them to change their ways:

> To our beloved people and to the Islamic Current everywhere, we will continue to call for justice and a return to the right path using dialogue and persuasive wisdom ... As for you, members of the Islamic Current, you are not
> a political party, although preaching for democracy and shura [consensus] is
> part of our call. You are not a welfare organization, although backing
> welfare associations and civil society is part of our program, and you are not
> a purpose-specific association meant to serve a narrow purpose. You are the
> beating heart of this nation, nurtured by the Quran.

17 See www.almarfaa.net/?p=243 (accessed 7 September 2008).
18 Author's translation. Statement published on Kuluna Shuraka': http://all4syria.info/content/view/13055/39 (accessed 23 August 2009).

180 *Bashar al-Asad's era*

The Islamic Democratic Current implicitly denounces the Kuftariya and Muhammad Habash's Renewal Programmes, and more specifically one of Habash's main principles ("We believe that to every nation its law and method, and that to every generation its time and place"),[19] saying that the programmes serve those in power rather than Islam. It asserts:

> As to you members of the Islamic Current, if asked about your call, say: we call to an all-encompassing Islam, pertinent to all sectors of life, and true to every place and time. The government is part of it, as freedom is part of its obligations. If told, this is part of the political, say, this is Islam as it should be, uncategorized.[20]

This last statement clearly contradicts the declarations made by the Grand Mufti Ahmad Hassoun and prominent shaykhs such as Dr Muhammad Habash, Sa'id al-Buti and Dr Muhammad Shahrur, who claim that the politicization of religion can only lead to radicalization and is, theologically speaking, wrong. In this sense, Syria's Islamists have very little in common with Syria's fundamentalists; their interpretations of the Islamic creeds are, in certain issue areas, very far apart.

B The Syrian Islamic Front

From militantism to pacifist Islamism

In the aftermath of the 1982 Hama Battle, the SIF – also known as the Syrian Muslim Brothers (see Chapter 4) – gradually moved to modify its tactics. Thus it has rejected its militant wing and has again expressed its willingness to work, and has indeed worked, alongside the other secular opposition parties. In so doing, it has shown itself to be a pragmatic and tactically flexible party, and has also transformed itself from being an Islamist group actively working to topple the Syrian regime from above into an opposition faction committed to gradual, pacifist change from below. The group's previous Superintendent[21] (or Secretary General) explains:

> We think that the great active Syrian people are the ones capable of toppling this regime, God willing. The role of the ... Front is to educate and mobilize people, and working for explaining the Syrian issue in international forums and working for raising the international blockade on it.[22]

---

19 See section on Muhammad Habash in previous section of this chapter.
20 Author's translation. See Kuluna Shuraka' website: http://all4syria.info/content/view/13055/39 (accessed 23 August 2009).
21 In August 2010, the Shura Council of the Syrian Muslim Brothers elected Muhammad Riyad Shaqfa (Abu Hazem) as new Secretary General and Hatem al-Tabsha as the Shura Council's chairman. Shaqfa is a civil engineer and had graduated from the Damascus University in 1968. Shaqfa survived an assassination attempt in Baghdad in 2003 after the fall of the Iraqi regime. His car was allegedly riddled with bullets.
22 Al-Ikhwan website: www.ikhwanweb.com/article.php?id=3222 (accessed 5 January 2010).

Furthermore, the SIF has expressed its willingness to work under the umbrella of a secular political system, a commitment that sets it apart from the Islamic Democratic Current discussed above.[23] The SIF is therefore currently fully committed to change from below if necessary, or to gradual change from within if allowed to become part of the Syrian parliament.

As a result of this transformation, the SIF is presently the only Syrian political Islamic *party* (the Islamic Democratic Current has not yet called itself a political party) that overtly opposes the regime, doing so from within the pacifist constellation of Syria's opposition groups, known as *al-Tajamu' al-Watani al-Dimucrati* (the National Democratic Grouping). Al-Bayanuni explains, "We denounce and condemn the extremist religious trends and the killing of innocent people. Endorsing bloodshed is against the Brotherhood's methodology."[24] The Muslim Brotherhood's transformation into a non-militant group is due to a number of factors, most importantly the annihilation of its armed wing during and after the Hama Battle.[25] Thus, the Muslim Brotherhood (today the SIF) survived the 1980s by virtue of the fact that its most prominent leaders, such as 'Ali Sadr al-Din al-Bayanuni, 'Issam al-'Attar and 'Adnan Sa'ad al-Din, among many others, fled from Syria at a time when Syrian Muslim Brothers were being imprisoned and sentenced to death by the Ba'thi political command. These shaykhs have, since the group's defeat by the Ba'th, upheld an alliance with Syrian secular and left-wing parties such as the Communist Party, the Nasserites and most recently 'Abd al-Halim Khaddam's provisional Ba'th.[26]

The SIF's resurgent presence in Syria

Despite its rather faint voice and the fact that its members are scattered across the country, the SIF is still quite well-known to Syrians. One reason for this is the regular appearances by the group's previous superintendent, Sadr al-Din al-Bayanuni, on Arab TV channels such as Al-Jazeera and Al-Arabiya, during which he often argues that the end of Syrian authoritarianism is imminent.

---

23 Secularism according to the SIF would have Islam as the source of legislation within a system that separates between faith and politics, recognizes the complexity of the Syrian context and the right for every Syrian to have his or her political say. The previous Secretary-General of the SIF, al-Bayanuni, has in fact criticized the Egyptian Muslim Brothers' new programme (October 2007) for stating that women and non-Muslims cannot become president of Islamic nations. Al-Bayanuni explained that there shouldn't be second- and third-class citizens in Islamic nations. See *Asharq al-Awsat*, 29 October 2007; Ikhwan website: www.ikhwanweb.com/article.php?id=2507 (accessed 5 February 2007), about establishing a political party that is open for all regardless of race, religion or ideology.
24 See Ikhwan website: www.ikhwanweb.com/article.php?id=18638.
25 Private communication, November 2008.
26 Although this odd alliance named the National Salvation Front (NSF) was terminated by the Islamic Front in April 2009. Khaddam was Syria's long-time Ba'thist vice-president turned dissident following the unresolved assassination of Rafiq al-Hariri in Lebanon.

Another reason for the group's continued profile in the country has to do with its joining in on some of the activism undertaken by the secular opposition (the secular opposition will be further discussed in Chapter 9 of the work). In particular, it signed up to the "Damascus Declaration for Democratic and National Change," which was an initiative launched by most of Syria's intellectuals and civil society groups. Yasin al-Haj Saleh, a Syrian journalist known for his secular opposition to the Baʿth, underlined the importance of the Damascus Declaration:

> The main importance of the declaration derived from the identity of the parties that signed it. The original document was signed by five parties and gatherings ... No sooner had the declaration been issued than the Syrian Muslim Brotherhood also joined in and called on others to sign it. The Brotherhood described it as a starting point for a new national consensus. Soon other smaller groups and individuals, both within Syria and outside, joined – the most problematic of them being the Reform Party of Syria headed by Farid Ghadry, which is based in the United States. The Damascus Declaration was a historic initiative. For the first time since the Ba'ath Party seized power in 1963, a broad understanding was reached between the main body of the Syrian opposition and a majority of Kurdish parties, between secular parties and the Muslim Brotherhood.[27]

According to political observers, the resurgence of the Syrian Muslim Brothers in the last few years can also be linked to its relationship with former Vice-President ʿAbd al-Halim Khaddam. In 2005, a new opposition coalition – known as the National Salvation Front (NSF) – that included the Muslim Brotherhood was formed under the leadership of Khaddam, who had defected from the Syrian regime and was living in exile in Paris. According to Landis and Pace:

> The alliance has bolstered the positions of Khaddam and the Muslim Brotherhood. By linking up with the secular Khaddam, the Muslim Brotherhood has showcased its eagerness to prioritize political pragmatism over narrow ideology. It may have alleviated the anxieties of Alawites and military leaders who believed that the Muslim Brotherhood's first move in power would be to purge old regime loyalists. Khaddam can appeal to the international audience in a way Bayanuni never could.[28]

Indeed, more insight is provided by Sami Moubayed:

---

[27] See SyriaComment: http://faculty-staff.ou.edu/L/Joshua.M.Landis-1/syriablog/2005/10/yasin-haj-salih-sn-appeal-for.htm (accessed 20 February 2008).

[28] Joshua Landis and Joe Pace, "The Syrian Opposition," *Washington Quarterly* 30(1), Winter 2006–2007: 58.

although Khaddam, who defected ... after decades of loyalty to the regime, is a public relations liability for the NSF ... his personal wealth and close ties to the Saudis and the Harriri family in Lebanon could give the Brotherhood a new lease on life.[29]

The same idea is expressed by Badran:

The Brotherhood's alliance with Khaddam opened the way for diplomatic breakthroughs, most notably in Lebanon, where Bayanouni's emissaries were warmly received by Druze leader Walid Junblatt and (more discreetly) other undisclosed members of the ruling March 14 coalition. They also visited Turkey (this time receiving substantial media coverage).[30]

Although Syrians generally tend to dismiss opposition movements that are based outside the country, the regime sees the SIF as a threat to Syria's political stability, whether on its own or as part of the secular NSF. This is because the SIF is the most overtly political Syrian Islamic opposition, as well as because the long-standing movement still has a following among Syrians despite the command's many attempts to crush it.[31] That the state still perceives the SIF to be a threat is shown by the fact that Law 41 – which makes it a crime to be a member of the Muslim Brotherhood – is still in force, even though there have been a number of requests from within the Syrian parliament to abolish it. It is also made clear by the state consistently denying the Brotherhood's attempts to regain the right to operate legally in Syria.[32]

The reappearance of the SIF as a player in Syrian politics is linked to the admixture of economic and political restrictions that are inherent to Populist Authoritarian regimes, which have created an unstable social context that renders Islamic groups relatively more attractive – due to the services and monetary advantages they offer.[33] At the same time, it can also be linked to the fact that the Ba'th Party has kept any viable secular alternative from developing over the last 30 years, while also mobilizing the Islamic one. A third factor is that the Syrian Islamic movement overall has abandoned the elitist orientation that characterized its earlier iteration, and has demonstrated a much greater flexibility and awareness of the grievances of the public masses within its re-invigorated ideology. Thus the movement's ideas (and thus the SIF's ideas) have become increasingly attractive just at the moment when the secular Ba'th regime is stagnating.

---

29 Sami Moubayed, "The Islamic Revival in Syria" *Mideast Monitor* 1(3), September–October 2006. Online.
30 Tony Badran, "Divided They Stand," *Mideast Monitor* 31 October 2006.
31 Although there are no data that can attest to such a statement, it is believed to be the case by a number of Syrian experts with whom I talked.
32 *Al-Hayat*, 16 January 2001.
33 *Al-Hayat*, 5 January 2006.

Current discourse

The Secretariat General of the SIF has softened its message in order to attract the same constituency that the Ba'th once galvanized. This clear shift in positions between the Syrian state and the Islamic opposition reinforces the explanation put forward by the "geo-political school" for understanding the popularity and present dimensions of neo-fundamentalism and Islamism.[34] This school argues that in its populist thrust, political Islam has taken on a trans-national character that has caused it to become as important as communism and Third Worldism were in the 1960s.[35] The shift in positions also reflects the SIF's recognition of something that Raymond Hinnebusch once observed, that the Islamic opposition would have to mobilize the rural public to have any chance at de-stabilizing the Ba'th regime, something that the Muslim Brotherhood failed to accomplish in the 1970s and 1980s.

Thus it is clear that today's SIF is changing. The movement has shifted its focus from the urban Sunni bourgeoisie to the periphery and to the rural and socially marginalized groups, with the ultimate aim of effecting change from below. This shift is increasingly evident in the movement's latest proclamations. For instance, the Front held its annual meeting in Brussels in February 2008, during which the Muslim Brothers (or the SIF) and 'Abd al-Halim Khaddam (whose alliance is the NSF) discussed the situation in Syria and the Arab region, and considered the possibility of re-activating the internal Syrian front, or in other words re-deploying within Syria in order to effect political changes. According to the final statement published after the meeting:

> the Front put in place a complete plan for the coming stage ... in early 2008 Bachar al-Assad's regime hid its anxiety by escalating its oppressive actions under the state of emergency imposed since 45 years. This is the practical proof of the imminent end of the tyrants. The regime keeps issuing death sentences against its political opponents under the law number 49; it is closing down on peaceful political activism, strengthening its security grip, terrorizing citizens by arresting activists and intellectuals randomly and with no reasons.

In addition to criticizing the regime for disregarding human rights, the statement highlighted the country's difficult socio-economic conditions, particularly the deteriorating living situation of Syrian citizens. It said that these have been aggravated by "the dangerous increase of prices that has doubled the suffering of the Syrians to an extent that basic needs have become a far-fetched dream."[36]

---

34 Discussed in the introductory chapter of this work.
35 See, for example, Olivier Roy, *L'Echec de l'islam politique*, Paris: Le Seuil, 1992; François Burgat, *Face to Face with Political Islam*, London and New York: I.B. Taurus, 2003; and Gilles Kepel's *Jihad: the Trail of Political Islam*, Cambridge, MA: Belknap Press, 2003.
36 Statement by the general secretariat of the NSF in Syria after the meeting on 28 and 29 June 2008. Online: www.free-syria.com/en/loadarticle.php?articleid=29423 (accessed 10 December 2008).

And in a bald attempt at attracting the support of the small, peasant holding class, the statement argued that the regime's new economic policies have hurt Syrian farmers by focusing on pleasing a narrow elite:

> The bad and hesitant economic policies of the regime have inflicted more daily suffering on the Syrian citizens. The catastrophe is getting worse and affecting the agricultural season which forced thousands of farmers from Jazeera, Deir al-Zour, and Rikka to leave their lands and move to the edges of the cities in other districts. The regime did not present any support for these regions as was the case in the neighboring countries affected by the catastrophe, to make it worse the regime confiscated the crops and made the crisis even harder. The regime has transformed from being the protector of the country to becoming a servant of a narrow corrupted elite that control the national wealth. The regime was not satisfied by stepping on the honor of the majority of its citizens but also deprived them of bread with its neglectful policies amid the international price crisis.[37]

The SIF has also taken steps to form alliances with the Kurdish community in Syria. With the Kurdish minority becoming an increasingly important social force, especially since the 2003 invasion of Iraq, the Islamic Front decided in March 2005 to open up a dialogue with them and to declare a unified front with the Syrian Kurds against the injustices of the Ba'th.[38]

The Syrian Kurds have a slightly more complicated political history in Syria. Since the Ba'th's 1963 rise to power, all regional, ethnic or religious parties have been banned. The Ba'th reasoned that these kinds of political parties fall outside the scope of Arab nationalism and thus hurt Syria's unity and sovereignty.[39] Despite these limitations, however, Syrians of Kurdish origin have continued to be part of the state apparatus, and have positively contributed to the Syrian political scene, often by mediating between the state and the socially peripheral Kurdish populace.[40] At the same time, Kurdish opposition to the Syrian state has never disappeared – the preservation of Kurdish parties, although they exist outside the legal political scene, can be viewed as a manifestation of a Kurdish identity that wants itself outside the scope of the Syrian nation-state and is a clear disagreement with the national Ba'thist order.

---

37 Brussels, June 2008. Online: www.free-syria.com/en/loadarticle.php?articleid=27470 (accessed 10 December 2008).
38 A few months later, Bashar al-Asad ended one of his speeches with clear religious invocations.
39 Elizabeth Picard, "Fin des partis en Syrie," *Revue des Mondes Musulmans de la Méditerranée* 81–2, 1996: 223.
40 Although they remained un-recognized as a national ethnic category, the Kurdish elite was co-opted by the state either through the redistribution of funds or through political co-optation. The Kurdish community structures, however, were kept intact in order for the co-opted elites to mediate between the state and the Kurdish population.

186 *Bashar al-Asad's era*

The Kurdish question has become more prominent and the "nationalist" Kurds more outspoken since the arrival of Bashar to power, particularly following the 2003 American-led intervention in Iraq and the resulting uncertainty regarding the autonomy of Iraqi Kurds. Since the 2003 invasion, Syrian Kurds have cultivated an increasingly autonomous political space, which has changed from one characterized by "dissimulation" to one characterized by "defiant visibility."[41] While skirmishes between the Kurds and state security forces have taken place in Syrian Kurdish areas since 2000, these have intensified in the last few years. For instance, an incident between Kurdish dissidents and the Syrian security forces in Qamishli prompted the following statement by a number of Syrian Kurdish parties (the Kurdish Democratic Front in Syria, the Kurdish Democratic Alliance in Syria, the Kurdish Coordination Committee and the Kurdish Democratic Party of Syria):

> To our Kurdish citizens in Syria, to the Syrian public opinion – all national and democratic forces, and to all those who believe in world peace and welfare: The Syrian regime has once again targeted the Syrian Kurds, as part of the series of racist and chauvinist policies undertaken against them since the Baath took over power several years ago. The Syrian regime is resorting to more oppression, terrorism and killing against the Syrian Kurds in order to impose its discriminative policies and drive the Kurds to abandon their national rights and cultural identity. On the 20th of March 2008 and during the celebrations of the Niroz day in Qamishli, the regime's ruthless security agents opened fire against Kurdish citizens, who went down the streets to dance and rejoice this cultural occasion. Three young citizens were killed: Mohamed Zaki Ramadan, Mohamed Yehya Khalil and Mohamed Mahmoud Hussein. Several others were severely injured, among which: Riad Chaykhi, Karam Ibrahim al-Youssef, Mohamed Mohyi al-Din Issa and Mohamed Kheir Khalaf. While we strongly condemn the killing of our Kurdish citizens, we hold the Syrian authority responsible for this bloodshed and we declare a national state of mourning. Niroz celebrations will be cancelled this year in all regions inside Syria and abroad as a protest against this heinous crime. We also reassure that despite the threats, the killings and the sacrifices, the Syrian Kurds will never give up on their national rights and will struggle for their freedoms by all pacific and democratic means, for the ruling authority's terrorism will never succeed in discouraging the Kurds in their battle for freedom and justice.[42]

Because of the importance of the Kurdish component in the definition of the national political culture, it seems certain that the Kurdish "vote" (or at least

---

41 Jordi Tejel Gorgas, "Les Kurdes de Syrie, de la 'dissimulation' à la 'visibilité'?" *Revue des mondes musulmans et de la Méditerranée* 115–16, December 2006, p. 117.
42 Free Syria: www.free-syria.com/en/loadarticle.php?articleid=27172 (accessed 10 December 2008).

Kurdish support) is being fought over by the Syrian command and the Islamic opposition. Since 1991, the state has promoted an increasing number of candidates of Kurdish origin (15) to stand in parliamentary elections. Three of them also appeared on the list presented by Syria's Kurd organizations: Kamal Ahmad, President of the Kurdish Democratic Party; Haj Darwish, President of the Progressive Democratic Kurdish Party; and Fu'ad Ekko, representative of the Kurdish Popular Party. The Syrian command's decision to encourage their standing for election was meant both to court and co-opt the Kurdish opposition, as well as the Sunni Islamic one.[43]

As stated earlier in this work, shaykhs such as Ahmad Kuftaro and Sa'id Ramadan al-Buti are of Kurdish origin, and their prominent position within the state apparatus is at least partly meant to demonstrate the regime's interest in both the Kurds and the religious class. Importantly, the political co-optation of the Kurdish elite is also aimed at blocking any rapprochement between the Kurdish forces and the Islamic movement, particularly the Islamic Front – since they are both opposition groups. And indeed dissident Kurds do tend to see themselves, in terms of identity, as Sunni Muslims more than anything else.

For its part, the Islamic Front has been adamant in stressing that political change will soon engulf Syria:

> [T]he regime has become obsessed with controlling the Syrian people and containing the general state of protest among the citizens. The last arrest campaign against ... the Islamists and the Kurds, added to the last few years' arrests, have summed [added] up to thousands of arrested citizens. The racist policy against our Kurdish brethren continues and the whole population is now under a political and a security siege. Meanwhile the regime blames its people for its own failure.[44]

In another statement, the Front elaborated on the assassination of the Kurdish opposition Shaykh Mashuq al-Khaznawi in May 2005 (for more on the assassination, see Chapter 9). The SIF's statement seemed aimed at linking the Kurdish (Sunni) grievances to the Iranian (Shi'i) presence in Syria, thus implicitly alluding to the Sunni identity of Kurds and the Shi'i identity of the Iranians as a front to attack the regime:

> Every year, the majority of the region's populations, Kurds, Iranians, and Egyptian Arabs joyfully celebrate the Niroz day. Except that this year, the ruthless Syrian regime not only violated our Kurdish brothers' freedoms, denying them the right to celebrate this cultural occasion in different cities like Damascus and Aleppo, but Bachar al-Assad's oppressive security agents also perpetrated a new bloodshed, killing three young Kurd citizens.

---

43 Gorgas, "Les Kurdes de Syrie," p. 123.
44 See Free Syria: www.free-syria.com/en/print.php?articleid=25890 (accessed January 2009).

And while the Iranian community was given the chance to celebrate the Niroz day this year, as it happens every year, next to the shrine of Sayyida Zeinab, Kurds are being brutally killed. Why are these Syrian citizens denied the right to rejoice this occasion in their own country, while the Iranian community is given a total free hand in Damascus and its suburbs? This Iranian community that today owns most of Damascus' lands, mosques and shrines ... This same community that undertakes development plans, not to help the Syrians improve their living standards, but to exploit each and every one of them in order to establish a powerful religious Iranian lobby that would sow sectarian discord every time it is offered the chance too. But despite all this, the Syrian security agents would of course not undermine any of the Iranians' religious celebrations, but would on the contrary kill our Kurdish brothers who wanted to passively rejoice the Niroz day. This deadly regime is therefore to be held responsible for our dear citizens' slaughter, for it is constantly violating the Syrians' basic freedoms and liberties.[45]

The above-quoted SIF statement points towards the Front's attempts to destabilize the current political command. It has done so by playing on Sunni sensitivities and concerns regarding the Shi'i influence in Syria, and by stoking fears among the general Syrian populace about factional politics within the country as a result of the state's alliances and Iranian interventions. For instance, in a statement issued following their June 2008 annual meeting, the SIF (under the umbrella of the NSF) endorsed the opposition activity taking place in Syria and warned of further activities that would affect the whole population:

What made things worse is the Iranian incursion that is spending money in the country without any supervision in order to increase the tension and threaten the national harmony. ... The conspiracy of the regime against our people has reached its peak and the popular tension is expressed in different regions of the nation. The late [recent] events in Kamishly, Deir el-Zour, Jisr al-Shaghour and al-Zabadany are only a fraction of what is actually taking place and will spread further until the volcano of popular anger explodes and all the people will participate in making their future and defining their destiny. The arrests that led thousands of our people into prisons in the last months and the torture in the dark dungeons is making new victims to be added to the thousands of missing and arrested people; these measures will not stop the march to freedom and dignity. The regime's policies are still contributing to the destruction of the national unity and spreading sectarianism and racism that present great dangers to the nation. The regime is still undertaking its oppressive and

---

45 See Free Syria: www.free-syria.com/en/loadarticle.php?articleid=27172 (accessed 10 December 2008).

unjust policy in adopting the law number 49 that sentences to death all members of the Muslim Brotherhood and oppresses the Kurdish people who are our brothers in nation and destiny.[46]

Although this message appears quite scattershot, mentioning as it does Iranian interventionism in Syria, Syrian factionalism, the regime's "elitist" economic policies and its "racist" and "oppressive" nature, it is clearly playing on all sorts of fears currently felt by the Syrian public. At the same time, the Front's inclusive new message is aimed at presenting its agenda as a non-"racist," non-"elitist" alternative to that of the existing Syrian command.

The Internet and other new communications tools have given Syria's *al-Tayar al-Islami al-Dimuqrati* (the Islamic Democratic Current) and the SIF a platform from which to express their agendas. Indeed, while the Brotherhood was once willing to accommodate the regime in exchange for a general amnesty and the repeal of Law 49, it is no longer interested in doing so.

4 Islamist militant groups and the call to Islamic resistance

The militant Syrian Islamist groups are an increasingly important element in the country's political opposition movement.[47] Their re-emergence over the last six years has been marked by increased activity levels, and can be largely explained by referring to regional factors, particularly the war in Iraq and the Syrian regime's regional policy. This situation gives a new impetus to efforts aimed at understanding Syrian Islamists, particularly the nature of their beliefs and the sort of recruiting strategies and mechanisms they are deploying.

A A topography of Syria's militant Islamists

Membership and overall ideology

Generally speaking, the members of militant Islamist groups are of rural rather than urban origins. They are much younger than their counterparts in the pacifist opposition groups (some 8,000 fighters in Syria, most between the ages of 18 and 30).[48] As a result, they did not witness the conflict between the Muslim Brothers and the state during the 1970s and early 1980s, and in fact some with whom I spoke were not even aware of the essentials of that conflict. This generational gap marks them as part of a global "revisionist" and "modernizing" movement rather than the traditionalist movement epitomized by Syria's Muslim Brothers (also known as the SIF) and the Democratic Islamic Current.

---

46 Brussels, 29 June 2008. General Secretariat of the NSF in Syria. See Free Syria: www.free-syria.com/en/loadarticle.php?articleid=27470.
47 Here I am following the definition of "Islamism" outlined in the introductory chapter of this work, which called it the wish to impose religiosity from above, either peacefully or through militant means.
48 See *Al-Hayat*, 5 January 2006.

The militant Islamists are part of the Salafi movement, and believe that the phase of history presently being experienced by the Islamic world can be compared to the one experienced by the first Muslims during and immediately after their migration from Mecca to Medina, a period in which the political and social aspects of Islam first meshed together. According to this view, today's Muslim societies and their political leaders have returned to a state of *Jahiliya* (ignorance) regarding Islam. It is thus not the time for a calm *da'wa* and *tablighi* movement, nor for pacifist political activities; instead, the present situation calls for a militant re-Islamization of the community, to re-establish a society that adheres to the norms that they believe were in place in Medina after the Prophet Muhammad set up the first Muslim polity there.

Many Syrian neo-fundamentalist shaykhs and pacifist Islamists are largely in agreement with the notion of joining the government, regardless of its ideological orientation, in order to have an opportunity to promote Islamic hegemony. This pragmatic viewpoint is not shared by militant Islamists, who insist that the shari'a prohibits them from becoming part of a non-Muslim governing regime[49] or from "join[ing] the governing apparatus under the pretext of 'peaceful resistance' and service to the faith."[50] Thus militants believe in the need for political rupture and socio-political change from above when the *Umma* or its leaders are going astray, actions that they call *Hakimiyat Allah* (the Rule of God).[51] They also charge the fundamentalists and pacifist Islamists with being servile to the current holders of political power on their numerous websites, though this charge is blunted somewhat by the fact that the Muslim Brotherhood has itself become a pacifist Islamist group – as we saw earlier – albeit one that is very critical of the government. The militant Islamists emphatically shun ideas advanced by prominent Syrian shaykhs such as Ahmad Hassoun, Ratib al-Nabulsi, Muhammad Shahrur, Muhammad Habash and Ahmad Kuftaro, and that promote peaceful coexistence, the truth of all religions and inter-civilizational exchange.[52] In other words, present-day Syrian militants condemn other Islamic opposition groups for their adoption of "pragmatic politics," their "false" understanding of Islam, their alliance with the secularists and their endorsement of what they perceive as a Western-style political system. The militants also accuse them of being scholars of evil (*'Ulama' al-Su'*), and denounce them as infidels because of their refusal to indict the regime under which they serve. As an aside, it is interesting to note that this position is

---

49 Although there is disagreement on which regimes are Islamic and which ones are not. For example, there is an Islamist divergence on whether the Jordanian Kingdom is an Islamic establishment or not. This sort of disagreement does not, however, include the Syrian order. For a justification of Syria's political system, see Muhammad Shahrur, *Tajfif Manabi'al-Irhab* [Draining the Sources of Terrorism in the Islamic Culture], Damascus and Beirut: al-Ahali, 2008, pp. 139–41.
50 Al-Suri, "The Call to Global Islamic Resistance," translated in Jim Lacey, ed., *The Canons of Jihad*, Annapolis, MD: Naval Institute Press, 2008, p. 169.
51 Shahrur, *Tajfif Manabi'al-Irhab*, p. 140.
52 See ibid., especially pp. 55–198.

strongly reminiscent of the manner in which 'Adnan 'Uqla's Fighting Vanguard opposed the Muslim Brotherhood's compromises and alliances with other opposition groups in the 1970s.

For the militants, even the mosques of the fundamentalist 'ulama', such as al-Nur Mosque, the Mosque of Badr al-Din, al-Tawba Mosque in Damascus and al-Tawhid Mosque in Aleppo where many prominent scholars preach and teach, are considered to be tainted institutions that true Muslims should shun. Such mosques are dubbed *Masajid al-Dirar* (The Mosques of Detriment). According to prominent Syrian Islamist Abu Mus'ab al-Suri, the worst part is that considerable segments of Islamic societies have unconsciously become part of the enemy's apostate culture.[53]

What is clear from these Islamist positions is that it is not enough to simply be a pious Muslim. Rather, it is imperative to be militant when the Muslim *Umma* is threatened.[54] In taking this stance, they are ideologically contrasting Islam with *Kufr* (heresy). They are also accusing their opponents within the Islamic movement of abandoning one of Islam's core precepts, namely the compulsory duty of every individual (*Fard 'Ayn*) to engage in jihad,[55] which they interpret as meaning *Qital* (fight) and as a *Fard 'Ayn* (duty that falls upon the individual) rather than as a *Fard Kifaya* (obligation that falls upon the whole community; the individual is not required to perform it as long as a sufficient number of community members fulfils it). *Qital* is argued to be a *Fard 'Ayn* in light of the fight's *defensive* nature against the West's so-called "Third Crusader Campaign."[56]

Doctrinally speaking, nearly all the militant Islamists can be categorized as radical Salafis rather than as orthodox Sufis. They adhere to a blend of Sayyed Qutb's ideas (politically) and the official teachings of the Wahhabi school (socially). In general, they share many of al-Qaeda's core teachings on Islam, and take it upon themselves to spread the ideas of al-Qaeda when recruiting activists. They believe that promoting jihad will free Islam from the "defeatists" and the "hypocrites" among the Islamic leaders.[57] As a result, Islam will awaken the masses to their neglected Islamic essence. Their most prominent leaders, such as Mus'ab al-Suri, who is considered to be al-Qaeda's foremost strategic

---

53 Al-Tartusi, *Haza Huwa al-Buti Fa-ihzaruh* [This Is al-Buti So Beware of Him]; Al-Tartusi, *Sifat Masajed al-Dirar al-Lati Yajeb I'tizaliha* [Description of the Mosques of Detriment That Are to Be Shunned]; Abu Qutada, *Hijran Masajed al-Dirar* [Avoidance of the Mosques of Detriment]; available at the Tawhed website at www.tawhed.ws (accessed 20 September 2008).
54 See E-prism at http://e-prism.org/images/Zarqawi_-_Mujahidin_road_map_-_July_04.doc (accessed 10 September 2008).
55 Jihad is considered to have become a *Fard 'Ayn* rather than a *Fard Kifaya* (if performed by some, then the duty falls from the rest) due to the fact that Muslims are acting defensively. See Islamist websites such as Minbar Suriya al-Islami; Al-Tajdeed Forum; Minbar al-Tawhid wal Jihad; al-Sunnah Forum: www.tawhed.ws; www.almaqdese.com; www.alsunnah.info; www.nnuu.com.
56 Al-Suri, "The Call to Global Islamic Resistance," p. 164.
57 See al-Zawahiri to *AFP*, 21 August 1997; also, Sayed Qutb, *Fi Ma'alem al-Tariq*, Cairo: Dar al-Shuquq, n.d., p. 71.

thinker, have adapted to living by the sword. They have also retained ties with the leaders of the Global Jihadist group, especially the Afghani and the "Mesopotamian" (i.e. Iraqi) al-Qaeda, as well as with other Syrian Islamists that fled the country to Europe (such as Muhammad Haydar Zamar, also known as the Syrian Bear) in the aftermath of Hama.[58]

Outreach methods

Islamists have advanced their own methods of outreach in their war against various political and religious enemies, in the form of a multi-faceted programme that links the internal front to the external one. According to Mus'ab al-Suri, the programme has a religio-cultural component, a political-intellectual component and a military component. He writes that, "without military resistance, the influence of all peaceful work – however important – will be scattered to the winds."[59] Importantly, women are assigned an educational role in terms of communal outreach and ideological framing, though one that is confined to the private sphere of the family and the home.[60]

Syria's militant Islamist leaders initially promote their religio-cultural, political and military programme to potential recruits through informal lessons in private homes. People who join the movement then take part in inconspicuous "prayer rooms" and learn in unregistered "school rooms" – which are advertised

---

58 Al-Suri was born and grew up in Aleppo in Syria, and spent four years in the University of Aleppo's Department of Mechanical Engineering. He was a member of the Muslim Brotherhood in the late 1970s, and joined the radical militant off-shoot of the Muslim Brotherhood, the Fighting Vanguard (al-Tali'a al-Muqatila) in the early 1980s. In 1980, he allegedly fled Syria and joined the Syrian Muslim Brotherhood in exile, receiving training in Iraq and Jordan. He then moved to France and Spain where he has lived since the mid-1980s. His Syrian network included Islamists such as 'Uthman Abu 'Umar (Abu Qutada), who is today considered to be al-Qaeda's spiritual leader in Europe. Abu Qutada was the chief editor of the Al-Ansar magazine, for which al-Suri was editor and a frequent contributor. Al-Suri also knows Riyad 'Uqla (Abu Nabil), the top representative of the Jordan-based al-Tali'a al-Muqatila, and the Syrian businessman Ma'mun Darkanzali, based in the Hamburg district of Uhlenhorst. Darkanzali was indicted by Spain and the United States on charges of being a key al-Qaeda financier in Europe, and of assisting the Hamburg cell believed to have planned and carried out the 9/11 attacks. One of al-Suri's principal associates was Muhammad Bahayah (Abu Khalid al-Suri), who was variously described as a "mid-level" activist, "courier" and a "member of Usama Bin Laden's structures in Europe." He operated mostly out of Turkey, until he fled to Iran and Afghanistan in 1999. Al-Suri is reportedly an al-Qaeda member. What is known is that he has nurtured contacts with at least two jihadists in Denmark, one of whom is Abu Rashid al-Halabi, a Syrian Muslim Brotherhood activist who had obtained permanent residence in Denmark, and who was considered to be a member of Abu Dahdah's Spanish al-Qaeda cell. Nasar was reportedly captured by Pakistani security in Quetta, Pakistan in late October 2005, handed over to American custody and then sent to the notorious Guantanamo Bay detention camp. It is now reported that he has been secretly transferred back to Syria for indefinite detention in the Fir' Filastin (Palestine Branch) detention centre in Damascus.
59 Al-Suri, "The Call to Global Islamic Resistance," pp. 167–8.
60 Ibid., p. 168.

by word-of-mouth – and then later in one-on-one private meetings. It can take as much as a year to recruit one member, particularly since the process relies on carefully checked recommendations and family ties.[61]

I interviewed a father whose son – here called "H" – had become part of the Syrian Islamist movement and wanted to join the Islamist militancy in Iraq. I was particularly interested in learning about the ideological transformation of his son and his wife, especially as I knew that the family had been much more atheist than religious. The father eventually said the following:

> I don't know why, after all, H had a secular upbringing and was not a religious man until his mid-20s. No one is veiled in our family, Ramadan is not that big of a deal, and most of us don't even pray ... when I asked H, he said that God was not bestowing his *Baraka* (blessing, gift) on him and his family because he was not a true believer ... maybe we should have helped him more with his financial troubles ... we made him feel isolated and with no backing ... he was never a smart student and failed at everything he did, we never thought it would come to this though, especially in Syria. Who would have imagined America invading Iraq and Islamists roaming on every corner as they please ... they [Islamists] have resources and money, and are very effective [communicators]. I imagine H felt he had no other choice, he's always been a proud kid, never wanted to ask us for anything. But it was obvious he needed money.

Although H's father kept blaming himself for his son having joined the militant Islamists, it was clear from his comments that economic marginalization and H's inability to provide for his family played a key role in his eventual decision to join the militant movement. The fact that groups help the youth out financially, by giving them monthly "salaries" and social aid, has surfaced a few times during my interviews with families of recruits. This is especially important given that 80 per cent of the unemployed in the country are under the age of 24 (2006 census).

B Prominent Islamist groups

In Syria, Islamists consist of: (1) former and dormant members of the Syrian Muslim Brotherhood residing outside Syria, many of whom once belonged to the militant wing of the Brethren; (2) Syrian Islamist groups such as Hizb al-Tahrir al-Islami (the Islamic Liberation Party), and Abu al-Qa'qa's group Ghuraba' al-Sham;[62] and (3) Syrian and non-Syrian Islamists who operate in the country and regionally as part of regional Islamist groups. This latter category includes Salafi-Jihadists from various nationalities and al-Qaeda-affiliated militant groups that are infiltrating Syria, mainly from Iraq, Jordan and

---

61 Private communication.
62 There are other smaller groups that are less active.

Lebanon.[63] The most prominent of the groups include: Jund al-Sham (allegedly under the leadership of Abu Mus'ab al-Suri) and al-Tali'a al-Islamiya al-Muqatila (the Islamic Fighting Vanguard) under the leadership of Abu Qutada al-Shami.

Hizb al-Tahrir al-Islami

The Islamic Liberation Party (Hizb al-Tahrir al-Islami) is the only known Islamist militant group believed to work from within Syria as well as across the region. It has ties with the Hizb al-Tahrir that is active in Jordan, although these are not clearly defined. It is also described by Syria experts as a shadowy offshoot of the Muslim Brotherhood's Fighting Vanguard, and as being strongly against reconciliation with the Syrian command. The group emerged from hibernation in the late 1990s, and announced their comeback by ambushing and killing several Syrian intelligence agents riding in a car on 30 December 1999, which resulted in a series of intense clashes with security forces that continued for four days. Some of the members caught were reportedly from Saudi Arabia and Jordan. The ambush prompted the state to launch a major crackdown in 2000.[64] In fact, representatives of the group have said that 1,200 of its members were arrested by the Syrian security forces in the December 1999–January 2000 operation against Islamists in Damascus, Homs and area villages. President Bashar al-Asad's release of Islamist prisoners soon after taking power included eight members of the party.[65]

Abu al-Qa'qa's group Ghuraba' al-Sham

It was argued in Chapter 6 that Syria's role as a transit corridor for militants heading to Iraq might have provided an outlet for Syria's jihadists to be active without risking a war with the Syrian state. This last purpose was to some degree the case of Mahmud Gul al-Aghasi, known internationally as "Abu al-Qa'qa'." Al-Qa'qa' has been known to mobilize and recruit jihadists in Syria, and help organize their infiltration into Iraq, which led many observers to think that he was operating with the support of the authorities.[66] Some claim that his radical profile was deliberately developed with the help of the Syrian state, particularly following the political command's 2003 decision to allow militant Islamists to enter Iraq from Syria.[67] Many radicals were drawn to his militantly aggressive

---

63 It is sometimes observed that a number of these Islamists have been funded and used by the Ba'thist regime to serve its own regional agenda and even to help it consolidate its power. But this is an unlikely scenario.
64 Moubayed, "Islamic Revival in Syria"; *APS*, 19 March 2001.
65 *APS*, 19 March 2001; *Al-Hayat*, 22 December 2000.
66 *Al-Ahram*, 8 June 2006; Al-Arabiya, 5 June 2006.
67 As mentioned earlier, Syrian officials insist that the decision was reversed in 2004, if it had ever been taken. It is argued that Syria's border with Iraq is so long that it is almost impossible to fully control. For available data on foreign jihadists in Iraq, see www.pjsage.com/products.htm and www.ctc.usma.edu.

Re-emergence of political Islam 195

sermons in the al-Shahrur mosque in Aleppo, in which he often declared his militant agenda against the American occupation of Syria's neighbour. It is not yet clear if the showdown that took place between Abu al-Qa'qa's groups and the Syrian security forces on 12 April 2006 was staged to end suspicions that the shaykh was collaborating with the state, or whether it simply reflected the fact that collaborators can turn against the regime whenever they wish to end their co-operation.

Abu al-Qa'qa' was killed on 28 September 2008, reportedly at the hands of an opposing *Takfiri* jihadist cell. But his militant vision is still promoted by the Syrian Association *Ghuraba' al-Sham*, and the group risks one day changing its focus to the domestic Syrian front.[68] It is important to note here that following al-Qa'qa's death, the Syrian state undertook to de-radicalize the Aleppo Islamic scene by assigning new shaykhs known for their moderate interpretations of Islam to the city's mosques, of whom the most prominent is Shaykh Mahmud 'Akkam who had studied under Arkoun at the Sorbonne in the early 1990s.[69]

Political aims and tactics

Despite their shared opposition to the regime, Syrian Islamists are distinct from Syria's Muslim Brothers and the Islamic Democratic Current partly because they prioritize being part of an international Islamist movement that deals with non-Muslims first, ahead of dealing with the "enemies within" (i.e. non-practising Muslims and Muslim secularists). This link to international Islamist cells gives the movement a degree of international extension or depth that the Syrian Brotherhood never really enjoyed, despite the fact that it had a number of foreign ties.

---

68 See Al-Arabiya TV, 2 July 2006; Al-Arabiya net, 4 July 2006; *Al-Hayat*, 30 September 2008. What is so interesting about Abu al-Qa'qa's case is that in the last year before his death, he became the head of Aleppo's Shari'a faculty. His appearance had changed drastically, but his message had remained quite jihadist in nature, although he encouraged jihad only with the external enemy in the occupied territories such as Iraq and Palestine, which is in agreement with the Syrian regime's message, despite the two parties' deeper ideological differences.

69 See 'Akkam's website: www.akkam.org. Regarding other groups, their leaders are Islamists who were initially members of the Fighting Vanguard and who fled overseas in the 1980s. Of those who fled, some continued their jihadi fight in Afghanistan by joining the International Jihadi Movement, which explains the prevalence of Syrians in the leadership and within the ranks of al-Qaeda. Following the American intervention in Iraq and the ensued chaos, the majority came back to Syria in order to operate across the Syrian–Iraqi border and in Iraq. These jihadists are today considered some of the leaders of Syria's Islamist movement. Among the most prominent names are: Mustafa Bin 'Abd al-Qader Sit Mariam Nassar (Abu Mus'ab al-Suri, a former Syrian Muslim Brotherhood member), Abu Basir al-Tartusi, 'Uthman Abu Umar (Abu Qutada al-Shami), 'Imad al-Din Bakarat Yarkas (Abu Dahdah, a former Syrian Muslim Brotherhood member), the Damascene Badran Turki Hisham al-Mazidi, also known as Abu Ghadiya, and Mahmud al-Aghassi (Abu Qa'qa'). Abu Ghadiya is charged by US officials with being an al-Qaeda militant and a key figure in smuggling fighters into Iraq and fuelling Sunni resistance. This claim justified, according to US officials, a raid on Sukkariya, a Syrian area on the border with Iraq. The raid supposedly targeted Abu Ghadiya, and ended in the death of eight Syrian citizens. For a profile on Abu Ghadiya, see BBC, 28 October 2008.

Syrian Islamists justify their focus on the "external front" by pointing to the need for being well-prepared first or in *Halat al-Jahiziya* (state of readiness), before heading into a fully fledged war with the Syrian regime. Indeed, in the current post-Saddam Iraq, they can conduct random terrorist attacks without being restricted by a fully functioning state apparatus. Thus their focus on the external foes first is partly a result of their judgement that they are not yet strong enough to take on the Syrian state and drive the whole country into a possible fully fledged civil war, though they hope to be in the future.[70] Syrian Islamists emphasize that the present state of mind and lack of the right Islamic teachings among Syrian Muslims necessitates caution, efficiency and great labours to avoid having the whole resistance collapse. They also argue that *al-Fiqh al-Jihadi* (jihadist jurisprudence) demands that the groups' members who are willing to sacrifice their lives engage in teaching Muslims the true meaning of jihad in Syria (the domestic front), so that soon enough Muslims can destroy the enemy within.

For the moment then, militant Islamists operating in Syria are still more interested in challenging external foes such as the United States in Iraq rather than directly challenging the Syrian regime. As a result, they warn on their websites against unleashing violence and individual jihad within Syria, since such actions could prompt a reaction from the Syrian security forces.[71] For example, the website *Minbar Suriya al-Islami* has routinely posted warnings to Islamists traversing Syria towards Iraq, cautioning against thinking that the Syrian environment is a friendly one just because of the regime's anti-American stance, and reminding hopeful fighters that many have fallen into the hands of the Syrian security forces before entering Iraq:[72]

> It is a great regret that many sad incidents have befallen enthusiastic brothers who have fallen into the hands of the Tyrants before entering Iraq, or have been killed in entire groups trying to make entry, without [having the chance of] presenting any danger to the American forces.[73]

To outside observers, Syria's Islamists might appear to be little more than isolated militant groups incapable of building a significant revolutionary momentum, despite a few armed clashes in Damascus, Hama and Hasaka. Yet this view should be tempered by the fact that they are operating in Syria on the tacit

---

70 See, for instance, "manhajoyat al-hazar wa al-bina' al-jahiziya fi al-fikr al-jihadi" [The doctrine of caution and building capabilities in the Jihadi activity], March 2006. Online: http://e-prism.org/images/mn-fekeh_al-Jihad_-_Mar06.pdf (accessed November 2008). See also Abu Basir al-Tartusi, "takafal allah lia bi al-sham" [God will take care of Greater Syria]. Online: www.tawhed.ws.
71 Translated by Stephen Ulph, see Stephen Ulph, "Syrian Website Calls for Experienced Mujahideen," *Terrorism Focus* 2(13), 13 July 2005. See also Minbar Suriya al-Islami, 3 July 2005 and 14 June 2005; *Al-Tajdeed* Forum, 25 July 2006.
72 See Minbar Suriya al-Islami: www.nnuu.com (10 January 2006 and 4 June 2005) (accessed 10 January 2006).
73 Ibid.

understanding that they do not target Syrians, and instead focus upon regional adversaries.[74] Effectively, therefore, one should not evaluate the groups and the success of their activities by only considering their fights with Syrian forces.[75]

One area in which the Syrian Islamists have recruited thousands is in the city periphery and rural areas.[76] These include those containing the Palestinian refugees, who are more vulnerable to the Islamist call due to their economic and social malaise, not to mention their fight against Israel and the United States which they see as an extension of the Israeli colonial project.[77] Accordingly, and based on the views expressed in the discussion forums of jihadist websites, it is only a matter of time before Islamists move from fighting the external enemy (such as the foreign troops in Iraq) to the "internal one," in this case, the Syrian state.

Certainly Syria is still perceived as being led by 'Alawi heretics. In fact, the relatively anti-Shi'i and anti-'Alawi point of view has spread across most of the Islamist forums and is featured in Islamist lectures, often under the title *al-Shi'a al-Rawafed* (The Shi'i Rejects).[78] Already, there have been postings in which Islamists have accused the Shi'as and the 'Alawis of acting like "pigs" and of worshiping *Allat* rather than *Allah*.[79] Another recurring theme is to attack Syrian 'Alawis for providing financial and ideological support to Lebanon's Hizbullah. Thus on 20 April 2002, one of the leading clerics of the Saudi Salafis, Sheikh 'Abdallah bin 'Abd al-Rahman al-Jabirin, issued a fatwa against Hizbullah because of its Shi'i discourse, saying:

---

74 See *Al-Hayat*, 5 January 2006. Ibrahim Hamidi calls it the "Gentleman" deal.
75 Abu 'Ubayd al-Qurashi, "madha ba'd ihtilal al-Iraq?" [What follows the invasion of Iraq?], *Majallat al-Ansar* website: www.tawhed.ws/c?i=91. Article summarized in William McCants and Jarret Brachman, eds, *Militant Ideology Atlas*, West Point, NY: Combating Terrorism Center, 2006, pp. 86–9.
76 *Al-Hayat*, 5 January 2006.
77 There are some 461,897 Palestinians in Syria today. Three-quarters of them live in Damascus, with the rest in the cities of Homs, Hama, Aleppo, Lattakia and Dara'a. Throughout the country there are ten refugee camps, with five around Damascus. See UNRWA: www.un.org/unrwa/refugees/syria.html; see also: www.un.org/unrwa/publications/index.html. The largest refugee camp in Syria is the Yarmuk Camp, an area in a Damascus suburb, housing around 137,000 refugees. Although a number of observers told me that the Palestinians are reluctant to join anti-regime Islamist groups because doing so could jeopardize their position in Syria. Indeed, they have no passports and nowhere else to go if ejected from Syria, which makes it especially risky for them to even consider joining – at least knowingly – an openly anti-regime group. Furthermore, Hamas's client relationship with Damascus certainly constrains the growth of anti-regime Islamists among the Palestinians who tend to be pro the resistance movement. If Palestinians do wish to become politically active, they would consequently tend to join the anti-Israeli and anti-American movements that are sponsored by the regime.
78 See "Muntadayat Mukafahat al-Shi'a al-Rawafed" at *Sahat Ahl al-Sunna* [the Sunni Space]. Online: www.antishe3a.com/vb/showthread.php?p=2779#post2779 (accessed 23 September 2009). Especially *Tahzir al-bariya min nashat al-Shi'a fi Suriya* [Cautioning the Righteous from the Shi'as' activity in Syria]. Online: www.ahlalhdeeth.com/vb/attach...6&d=1086382370.
79 See *Shabakat al-Difa' 'an al-Sunna* [the network for the defence of the Sunna]: www.d-sunna.net (accessed 13 August 2008).

198 Bashar al-Asad's era

It is prohibited to assist this rejectionist [*Rafidi*] party, nor to follow their command, or to pray for their success. We advise the Sunnis to wash their hands of them, and desert whoever joins them. They [the Sunnis] should elucidate their [the Shi'is] animosity to Islam and the Muslims, and their damages in the past and in modern times for the Sunnis. The Shi'is will always keep their hostility towards the Sunnis. They will always do their best to present the disadvantages of the Sunnis, to discredit them, and manipulate them. Therefore, whoever follows them enters their control, since Allah has said: whoever enters their command becomes one of them.[80]

On this point, Zarqawi's message to his fellow jihadists – which is reminiscent of Syria's Fighting Vanguard's statements in the 1970s – summarizes many of the messages posted regarding the Arab regimes and how they should be dealt with. In his message, Arab leaders are compared to the Ghassanids, who helped the Romans against the Muslim Arabs in ancient times. They are said to have surely rejected Islam and to have exited the Muslim Millat because they worshiped the God of the crusaders. In Zarqawi's portrayal, Arab leaders help fight the Muslims and steal their money and land. They are therefore a gang of heretics and criminals, and are to be fought.[81] As for the Ba'th regime in Syria, Abu Basir al-Tartusi asserts in his writings that jihad against the atheist 'Alawis is a *Fard 'Ayn* on all Muslims, and that it is indeed a fight that must precede the one against the rest of the other un-believers.[82] The following is a question asked about whether fighting within Syria has become a duty on every Muslim:

> Question: I had asked Shaykh Husseyn Bin Mahmood about the ruling on Jihad in Syria, if it is a *Fard 'Ayn* on all the country's youth ... but he gave me a general answer ... I hope you can tell us whether it is or not?
>
> Answer: Fighting this Nusayri ('Alawi) faction that is leading Syria in the name of the heretic Ba'th Party is a duty according to the Text, the Sunna ... and the majority of Islam's ulama' ... fighting against them is, to me, more important than fighting against all the rest ... and Syria will not regain its leading and awaited status ... its misery lifted ... until this heretical faction that embodies the sectarian Ba'thist political order ... [is removed] from the reins of power.

While these extremist statements would not have been taken seriously in the past, the Islamist militancy that has taken place in Syria starting in 2004 (see

---

80 Reuven Paz, "Hizballah or Hizb al-Shaytan? Recent Jihadi-Salafi Attacks against the Shiite Group," *Global Research in International Affairs (GLORIA) Center* 2(1), February 2004.
81 See http://e-prism.org/images/Zarqawi_-_Mujahidin_road_map_-_July_04.doc (accessed 21 November 2008).
82 Author's translation. See *Minbar Suriya al-Islami*, www.nnuu.com (accessed 10 January 2006).

Chapter 6) demonstrates that militants can back up their statements with actions, and increasingly so, Syrian observers argue, once foreign troops are out of Iraq. One high-ranking officer explained to me that:

> Extremists from all over the world and Afghanistan found an opportunity in a post-Saddam Iraq ... and the chaos that the Bush administration caused [in the country] will inevitably spill into Syria once foreign troops decide that their mission is over.

5 Conclusion

Syria's Islamic movement is far from homogeneous. Rather, the different groups that are emerging are distinct in terms of their opposition to, or endorsement of, the Syrian political order and command, but also in terms of their discourses and outreach methods. While the majority of the groups remain politically quietist and in alliance with the Syrian command, a number of them have developed overt political aims and do not see eye to eye with the Syrian state. Furthermore, some Islamists are growing militant in nature and believe that only a revolution from above can create a true Muslim society and the political order worthy of it. Although there is not yet a tangible insurgency, the Syrian Islamist movement is nonetheless re-emerging, and Islamist ideological and political outreach and framing are actively occurring within the largest Syrian cities. At the same time, the al-Qaeda-inspired Islamists operating in neighbouring Iraq claim to have developed an underground network within Syria. On their websites and in their statements they advise militants not to start a confrontation within Syria given the need to fight the foreign enemy first – that is, foreign troops in Iraq.

Overall, these groups' agendas and teachings are counter-hegemonic, they vie to topple the existing political orders, whether in Syria or in the region, and ultimately to take control of the state. At the heart of this "modernizing" search for political rupture and socio-political change from above lies the dream of re-establishing an idealized Islamic rule and way of life, as imagined by the movement's leaders.

9 Islamic activism and secularism in Syria

1 Introduction

This work has examined Islamic revivalism and its impact on Syrian secularism within the context of evolving state policy, and in often-dynamic interaction with a wide variety of other factors, both internal to the Islamic movement and external to it. The present chapter provides details from a number of interviews conducted during my research, thereby offering a glimpse into Syrians' attitudes and concerns regarding the Islamic question. In so doing, it also engages with some of the work's larger questions: What can an examination of the reasons behind the rise of Islamic religiosity and the concurrent decline of Ba'thist secularism tell us about the future of politics in the country? Has the Islamic movement achieved such a degree of momentum that the state can no longer contain it? How will economic liberalization continue to shape the relationship between the state and the Islamic forces, as well as state policy vis-à-vis the co-opted and growing sectors of society (i.e. the bourgeoisie and the Islamic civil society), in the process determining the nature of Syria's Islamic revivalism? Is the country's new civil society and opposition Islamically oriented? Do these newly forged state–Islam relations mark the beginning of *political* liberalization in Syria? And finally, will the secularization process that was originally initiated from above be resumed?

In examining these questions, it is important to reiterate the following intertwined factors that mark the current political reality in the country. First, the Islamic movement has once again become a powerful social phenomenon and a well established and organized civil society and social-welfare network capable of forging and sustaining close and personal relationships with the general public. Second, the Populist Authoritarian (PA) system that once put an end to the dominance of the liberal oligarchy has itself institutionalized a new oligarchy, with political power increasingly concentrated in the hands of a few families. These families have successfully combined private ownership with political power.[1] Finally, the political

---

1 To cite but a few of these new players: the Makhlufs, the As'ads, the Muhanas and the Da'buls. See Bassam Haddad, "Change and Stasis in Syria: One Step Forward," *Middle East Report* 213, Winter 1999: 23–7; Volker Perthes, "The Bourgeoisie and the Ba'th," *Middle East Report* 21(170), May–June 1991: 31–7.

elite have forged important alliances with Syria's religious figures,[2] and have in the process largely re-created the pre-Second World War socio-political order whose elite was indeed a mix of a business–religious coalition.[3]

In this chapter, I begin by examining the possibility of Syria's Islamic revival becoming a fully fledged Islamic opposition that is willing to openly challenge the secular political order. The first two sections of the chapter consider the possibility of an eventual overall Islamic takeover or Islamization of the state. I contend that even though the future is not easy to predict, the Syrian Islamic movement could easily repeat its historical pattern of shifting from being a social movement under a pro-elite Sufi leadership (in the 1920s) to a civil society activist movement (in the 1930s) before turning political (in the 1940s). This outcome would be a result of the current economic challenges that Syrians are facing – which was also the case during the previous cycle. In this sense, the facilitating condition of Islamic ideological framing and outreach would thus be structural inequality among Syrians. The last section of the chapter looks at the most recent containment measures taken by the current political command to try to stop the erosion of the country's secular culture, measures that represent a slight shift in the state's strategy. It also looks at today's Syrian secular groups, and offers a number of interviews with atheist and agnostic secularists, and pious Muslims who are also secularists in Syria. These interviews highlight some of the challenges that would face the Islamic movement if/when it gets more directly involved in politics.

2 The state's betrayal of the populist myth could come back to haunt it

A Islamic revivalism in light of economic recession

The ongoing development of Syrian society is occurring within a context of structural economic reforms and accelerated economic liberalization. Yet while this privatization and liberalization of the economy is aimed at sustaining the

---

2 Although these religious figures do not belong to the same traditional families that emerged in the early twentieth century and that defined Syria's Islamic environment at the time, these Sufi shaykhs still have had deep roots in Syria and within its Sufi orders, which since the late nineteenth century have helped to define the country's social and political scenes. See Philip S. Khoury, *Syria and the French Mandate: The Politics of Arab Nationalism 1920–1945*, Princeton, NJ: Princeton University Press, 1987, pp. 607–12.

3 In the early twentieth century, emerging Islamic movements – which later came together to create the Muslim Brotherhood – had close relations with, and roots within, Syria's Sufi orders. See Elizabeth Thompson, *Colonial Citizens: Republican Rights, Paternal Privilege, and Gender in French Syria and Lebanon*, New York: Columbia University Press, 2000, pp. 103–10. Concerning the Sufi–Salafi divide in Syria, see Itzchak Weismann, "The Politics of Popular Religion: Sufis, Salafis, and Muslim Brothers in 20th Century Hamah," *International Journal of Middle East Studies* 37, 2005: 37–59. Weismann explains that there is no necessary binary distinction, and that in fact Syrian Salafi thinkers had roots in the revivalist Sufi tradition, while the Muslim Brotherhood's leaders successfully combined both Sufi and Salafi elements and influences in order to mobilize the Syrian public.

202 Bashar al-Asad's era

current political system, it has simultaneously engendered a number of unintended challenges for that system. First, it has led to cuts in the number of jobs in the public sector, which has in the past generally absorbed surplus workers that the private sector could not absorb. These cuts, coupled with economic recession and rapid population growth (see Table 9.1), have resulted in a rise in the unemployment level in Syria that has left millions of citizens at risk of falling below the poverty line.[4] To illustrate these processes with some statistics, in 1994, 6.9 per cent of the active population was unemployed, while in 2004 that number had risen to 12.3 per cent, according to official government socioeconomic reports (see Tables 9.1 and 9.2 and Figure 9.1, which respectively show the population increase in Syria from 1990 to 2010, and the sharp increase in unemployment rates from 1994 to 2004).[5]

Second, the state-administered economic liberalization has prompted the gradual termination of the state's long-standing subsidization programmes and price intervention measures, which has hit the poor particularly hard.[6] Already in 2003–2004, 19 per cent of Syrians were at risk of falling below the poverty line, and as much as 11 per cent of the population could not afford basic necessities.[7] Indeed, as was alluded to in Chapter 6, the economic growth that paralleled Syria's *infitah* (opening) policies has largely bypassed the middle class and the poor, contributing to the development of an increasingly marginalized society. In fact, the Gini index's inequality measurement rose from 0.33 to 0.37, which shows that despite Syria's economic growth, inequality in the country rose by 11

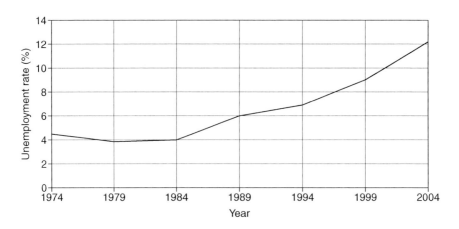

Figure 9.1 Unemployment rate from 1974 to 2004 (source: study published by the Syrian Bureau of Statistics, available at: www.cbssyr.org/studies/st7.pdf [Arabic]).

4 Al-Laithy, "Poverty in Syria: 1996–2004," UNDP Report, June 2005, p. 26.
5 Satoof al-Shaykh Husseyn, *Al-batala fi suriya 1994–2004*, Damascus: The Syrian Central Bureau of Statistics, July 2007, p. 32.
6 Ibid., pp. 32–5.
7 Al-Laithy, "Poverty in Syria," pp. 9 and 26.

per cent between 1997 and 2004,[8] and moreover is expected to have risen by 3 per cent more since 2004.[9] Thus while sales of such luxury cars as Maseratis, Porsches and BMWs were soaring in Syria in 2010 – with Syria being BMW's top-performing Middle Eastern market in 2009 – more modest cars could barely sell, which illustrates that wealth is no longer trickling down.[10]

Economic benefits have also been unevenly distributed, geographically speaking. That is, only certain cities – primarily Damascus and Lattakia – are reaping the benefits of the economic opening. Moreover, poverty rates in rural areas are significantly higher than the national average, and are sometimes more than triple those that prevail in urban areas. For example, in the rural north-eastern region, the percentage of people living on less than US$1 a day has increased at

Table 9.1 Human development 2009 data

Indicators year		Syrian Arab Republic
Total population (millions)	1990	12.7
	2007	20.5
	2020	26.5
Annual rate of natural increase of the population (%)	1990–1995	2.9
	2005–2010	2.5
Urban share of the population (%)	1990	48.9
	1995	54.9
Total fertility rate (births per woman)	1990–1995	4.9
	2005–2010	3.3

Source: UNDP, 2009 and 2007.

Table 9.2 Employment and unemployment numbers in 1994 and 2004

	1994	*2004*
Employed (thousand)	2,898.1	4,334.0
Unemployed (thousand)	216.4	607.5

Source: Study published by the Syrian Bureau of Statistics: www.cbssyr.org/studies/st7.pdf [Arabic].

8 Ibid., pp. 9 and 12. See also Eyal Zisser, *Commanding Syria: Bashar al-Asad and the First Years in Power*, New York: I.B. Tauris, 2007, pp. 111–18; the CIA World Factbook (accessed 16 September 2008); Syrian Central Bureau of Statistics Reports, online: www.cbssyr.org [Arabic]; UNICEF and the Syrian Central Bureau of Statistics, *al-Maseh al-'Unqudi Muta'aded al-Mu'ashirat*, 2006, online: www.cbssyr.org/people%20statistics/Final_Report_Syria_ARB.pdf. See also United Nations Development Programme Syria: www.undp.org.sy (accessed September 2008).
9 Reported by *The National* (UAE), 5 July 2010.
10 Ibid.

a rate that is ten times higher than the increase in urban areas.[11] The accompanying process of urbanization, which has proceeded apace since the early 1990s, prompted Leverett to note that: "the balance of urban versus rural Sunnis has shifted in favour of the former, creating a social climate potentially even more conducive than that of the early 1980s to Islamist resurgence." The rural exodus has indeed meant an increased number of poor Sunnis within the cities and thus adds to the number of potential recruits within these cities.[12] This even applies to the privileged cities, where only the upper classes can afford to partake in the emerging new consumption habits while the poor grow resentful of their inability to be part of the new consumerism (see Tables 9.3 and 9.4).[13]

Statistically speaking, Syrian GDP grew between 1996 and 2008. According to the World Bank, real economic growth averaged 3.4 per cent per annum between 1999 and 2003, around one percentage point above the country's population growth rate. And despite the decrease in oil production, real GDP growth averaged 5.1 per cent between 2004 and 2008. This growth was credited to the expansion in private investment, which itself was stimulated by the recent economic reforms and to cash inflows from oil-rich countries. Having said this,

Table 9.3 Poverty and inequality indicators in 2007

Human Poverty Index (HPI-1)	Probability of not surviving to age 40 (%)	Adult illiteracy rate (% ages 15 and above)	People not using an improved water source (%)	Children underweight for age (% aged under 5)
12.6	3.9	16.9	11	10

Source: UNDP Syria, 2007.

Table 9.4 Distribution of expenditures

Population deciles (poorest to richest)	Percentage of total expenditures
Poorest 20	7.24
Richest 20	45.25

Source: "Poverty in Syria," UNDP Syria, 2006.

11 Al-Laithy, "Poverty in Syria," pp. 16–17. See also UNDP Syria report, "The Impact of Subsidization of Agricultural Production on Development," October 2006, p. 6. Online: www.undp.org.sy/files/psia.pdf.
12 Flynt Leverett, *Inheriting Syria: Bashar's Trial by Fire*, Washington, DC: Brookings Institute Press, 2005, p. 36.
13 Leïla Vigual, "La 'nouvelle consommation' et les transformations des paysages urbains à la lumiere de l'ouverture économique: l'exemple de Damas," *Revue des mondes musulmans et de la Mediterrannée* 115–16, December 2006: 29–37.

other economists and UN studies report that when population growth and inflation are taken into account, the real growth rate for Syria is actually much less than calculated by the World Bank.[14] According to one reputable economist,

> data from national accounts ... suggest that per capita GDP growth between 1996 and 2002 was less than 1 per cent per annum. The increase in average salaries, after adjusting for inflation, was also a rather moderate 0.8 per cent per annum between 1997 and 2001. Moreover, a breakdown of GDP by expenditure reveals private (real) consumption grew at only 0.3 per cent per annum between 1996 and 2002. Hence, per capita real private expenditure should have declined by at least 2.0 per cent annually throughout that period.[15]

The net effect of Syria's economic liberalization (in concert with the recent global economic recession) has been the re-creation of a powerful economic elite that is growing at the expense of the regime's traditional socio-economic base of support. Moreover, political order and state control have proven to be much more difficult to maintain at this time of transitioning state–society relations. This is particularly the case because the regime is moving away from being a strongly interventionist welfare state, and is thus giving up the levers of control that it formerly wielded over society. And in the existing context of widening gaps between rich and poor, the increasingly autonomous and strong Islamic sector is not only able to attract more members, but can also pursue political change.[16] As will be shown hereinafter, a key factor in this process is the high number of young people in Syria.

B Economic liberalization, Islamic revivalism and the youth

Political and economic co-optation of the religious and bourgeois classes via economic liberalization, in concert with the weak economy, has produced new openings and spaces for Islamic outreach among Syria's youth. This is comparable to the 1970s and 1980s, when the generalized marginalization of the populace by the then-elites facilitated the leftist transformation of the political order. Effectively, the Syrian state is no longer a populist state, and thus is no longer seen as a unifying and supportive force by the country's middle and lower classes and the Syrian intelligentsia in general.[17] This shift in perceptions regarding the Syrian state is particularly marked among Syrian youth, a fact that is significant given that more than 50 per cent of the population in the country is

---

14 Zisser, *Commanding Syria*, pp. 113–14.
15 Al-Laithy, "Poverty in Syria," p. 9.
16 Because there are more marginalized people to draw upon as members. See introduction of Chapter 6 for more on the causal link.
17 A number of leftist groups have expressed their fears about the rising political role and influence Islamic elements have acquired in the last few years, since Bashar al-Asad's rise to the pinnacle of power.

under the age of 30. Syrian youth are likely further induced to adopt this viewpoint because they are disproportionately affected by unemployment (see Table 9.5 on youth unemployment rates in 1994 and 2004). Indeed, national surveys estimate that of the 16 per cent of Syrian citizens who are unemployed, more than half are between 15 and 30 years of age.[18]

At the same time that Syrian youth are feeling abandoned by the state, Islamic groups are using careful ideological framing and outreach programmes to appeal to them by addressing both their psychological and socio-economic burdens. Indeed, revivalist groups and charities often assert in their lessons and pamphlets and on their CDs that they alone are capable of meeting the youth's needs, be they psychological or material. The increasing visibility of their organizations and the efficacy of their charitable work give added force to these claims, and the fact that 80 per cent of the 100 charitable organizations in Damascus are Islamic testifies to their ability to provide for the needy.

In Egypt, economic liberalization – known as *infitah* – only added to the feelings of anomie and marginalization felt by the youth. Carrie Wickham writes about Egyptian youth in the aftermath of Sadat's *infitah* policies: "[T]here is considerable impressionistic evidence of two trends: first, that levels of political alienation are particularly high among urban educated youth and, second, that their alienation may have increased since the onset of political reform."[19] Although there are no nationwide opinion surveys on the subject of youth anomie in Syria, Wickham's observations about youth in Egypt seem to also accurately describe the situation of Syrian youth, many of whom are experiencing political and economic exclusion, are socially apathetic and face a strong likelihood of little to no social mobility in the future, short of "winning the Syrian *yanaseeb* [lottery]" (as one university student put it to me). This situation has prompted many of those with the means to leave the country and seek work in the Gulf region, with the hope of thereby gaining at least a comparable livelihood to that of their parents.

Table 9.5 Youth unemployment rates in 1994 and 2004

Age	1994	2004
15–19	13.8	11.6
20–24	16.8	21.4
25–29	16.5	18
30–34	13.8	14.7
35–39	10.6	11.5
40–44	8.2	7.5

Source: Study published by the Syrian Bureau of Statistics: www.cbssyr.org/studies/st7.pdf [Arabic].

18 Central Bureau of Statistics, *Syrian Statistical Abstract*, Damascus: Prime Ministry, 2006.
19 Carrie Rossefsky Wickham, *Mobilizing Islam: Religion, Activism, and Political Challenge in Egypt*, New York: Columbia University Press, 2002, p. 77.

Focusing then on only young, unemployed people, around 8 per cent of the Syrian population constitutes fertile recruiting ground for the Syrian Islamic movement, which is certainly a significant demographic for it to be able to tap into. The fears of secular observers are further amplified by the possibility of the Syrian Islamic movement following the Egyptian example and transforming into a Salafi movement. MP Shaykh Muhammad Habash referenced this concern about the possible radicalization of Syrians when he said that 80 per cent of Syrians are religiously conservative, yet "these do not have any political program, and when they think of politics, they look for a leader or a shaykh, one who could belong to either the reformers or the radicals."[20] Hence the need, at least according to the state, to present them with a tangible moderate programme.[21] Indeed, already, television programmes in Syria have remarked upon the problems facing Syrian youth and have noted the state's failure to address the situation.[22]

Impressionistic evidence from the 44 high school and university students that I interviewed in 2009 indicates that about half feel that Syria is heading down the same path as Egypt. Two of the students said that Syrians are always around "ten years late in messing it up," meaning ten years behind Egypt in this regard. Nineteen of the students were still optimistic and felt that Syria could never be like Egypt given its smaller size, its much higher literacy rate (around 85 per cent compared to 53 per cent in Egypt) and its higher per capita income.[23]

More broadly, a majority of the students that I interviewed felt that economic liberalization is more harmful than good for the middle class, and also felt that the gap between the lower and upper classes was growing wider. All believed that the 1980s were more egalitarian times in terms of money, and all were worried about the work prospects for youth, likely, they noted, to a greater degree than their parents and grandparents were when they were their age. They all agreed that the Syrian government was doing much better in terms of meeting the economic and social needs of youth than other governments in the Arab world, except for the oil-producing nations. Said one, "Syria has a lot of resources; we are the only country still self-sufficient and exporting wheat in the region."

Of course it is not certain whether these answers are representative of the views of the population at large.[24] It is also possible that I was given slightly

---

20 Muhammad Habash has stated this in a number of interviews on Syrian TV and in newspaper articles. See *Al-Hayat*, 18 June 2005.
21 See *Al-Hayat*, 5 April 2006; *al-Safir*, 6 April 2006.
22 Personal interviews; Syrian TV debates.
23 This is too small a number of people to constitute any sort of representative sampling. Yet while this informal sampling is not necessarily representative of the wider society, it does give a general sense of the thinking of urban youth.
24 I am aware of the limitations of these results; however, given the impossibility of carrying out more formal, larger-scale surveys in Syria's authoritarian political environment, such answers provide an important clue to opinions and views that would otherwise remain completely unelucidated.

more positive or negative answers because I am living abroad (since Syrians tend to be wary and even defensive in regards to such foreign attention). In general, however, the responses were in line with other informal conversations that I had with older Syrians regarding the country's young people. The responses uniformly expressed negative feelings about the economic liberalization process and Syria's apparent following of the path of *infitah* policies. And most of them agreed – even those who belonged to the upper-middle class – that only the rich youth are now getting a chance to prove themselves, with the rest having to take any available opportunities.

A majority of the youth seemed surprised by my question about whether religion would help them to cope with their socio-economic situation. Still, seven out of 44 (15 per cent of my sample) said that religion is very important, while 12 individuals (27 per cent of my sample) said that religion does not help at all. The rest said that religion helps on a spiritual level but is not an answer to their material problems, although they acknowledged that Islamic associations have helped a number of their friends and relatives when they were in dire economic circumstances. One student, 'Ammar, explained to me:

> We are held responsible for our future and for our destiny whether by our families or our society, and yet almost every part of our lives is beyond the scope of our control. In a world where agency is elusive, despite all claims that we are an empowered generation given the new technological advances and the Internet, only religion makes sense. Volunteering and working with Islamic associations and going to the mosque give us some control, if not over our lives, then at least over our afterlife.[25]

When I asked 'Ammar what he meant by "agency" and "control," he explained that

> the youth have no control over anything any more, not over their career, not over their marriage, and yet they are told that everything is possible. ... Our grievances are of an economic nature because money in this era opens all doors.

'Ammar's answer touches upon a number of issues: the question of marginalization and agency, the question of having control over one's destiny, and the feeling of disempowerment in a modernizing domestic and global environment. According to 'Ammar, Islamic groups have been more aware of these issues faced by today's youth, and are better suited to addressing them.

In the course of the same conversation, a friend of 'Ammar's asserted that "Islamic associations provide us with answers to our problems." When I said that Marxist groups also claim to provide their members with answers, and asked how Islamic groups are different, he answered,

---

25 Private communication, graduate student, University of Damascus.

they are more practical and pragmatic, I need a solution for now, I need a job, I need an apartment, I would like to get married one day, my aunt has cancer and the *shaykha* makes her feel better every time she visits. I don't believe that Marxists can solve these problems.

The answers of the two young men underline the gains that the groups in Syria's Islamic movement have made by transforming themselves into neo-fundamentalist organizations focused on moral change and charitable work rather than on politics. Indeed, beyond expressing solidarity with those experiencing difficult circumstances, Islamic groups help on two levels: they provide much-needed material support, and they reassure by combating the sense of failure and alienation that can be induced by modernity's often false claim that "all is possible," through an emphasis on the comfortable and familiar role of conformity with a clearly identified and identifiable spiritual group. In so doing, the socio-economic failures associated with the challenges of modernity are de-emphasized, and the successes associated with more easily fulfilled religious roles are emphasized.

Olivier Roy's conclusion that the entire Islamist movement is becoming neo-fundamentalist, with Islamism being "a moment, a fragile synthesis between Islam and political modernity, which ultimately never took place," reiterates that an increasing number of youth are attracted to the new Islamic groups precisely because of their move away from politics.[26] That is, it is their focus on the mundane and the everyday that has made the groups so pertinent to a generation facing the difficulties of transitioning towards a market economy.

3 Future trends in Syria: Islamizing or secularizing?

A Islam as modality for political change?

The Syrian state under Bashar al-Asad has moved to accommodate Islamic groups in order to ensure their support and allegedly to moderate them.[27] This strategy was pursued by President Bashar al-Asad and was strongly influenced by the fact that the different Islamic groups have achieved a stature that cannot be ignored. Indeed, despite their ostensibly pro-secular and pro-regime discourse, Islamic groups have shown that they are not just pawns of the state. Rather, they have successfully operated within the space available to them to advance a comprehensive cultural system, and thereby to expand their effective control over society in a way that has altered the governing political coalition and has challenged the secular heritage of the country, despite the regime's authoritarian nature.

Thus today, there are more Islamized spaces in Syria's public sphere – shops in neighbourhoods around larger mosques even avoid playing loud music (whether willingly or as a result of being asked), cafes have stopped serving alcohol and people do not eat outside during the fasting hours of Ramadan, all

26 Olivier Roy, *The Failure of Political Islam*, Cambridge, MA: Harvard University Press, 1996, p. 75.
27 See *Al-Hayat*, 5 April 2006; *as-Safir*, 6 April 2006.

things that would have been inconceivable ten years ago. This situation brings to mind Sa'id Hawwa, one of the main ideologues of the Syrian Muslim Brothers and of the Fighting Vanguard, who argued for the need to have Islamized spaces as pre-conditions for an Islamist renaissance that could ultimately spread to the political system.[28]

The increasing Islamization of the public sphere has been accompanied by an emboldening of politically quietist religious figures such as Salah Kuftaro and Sa'id al-Buti (as well as some of their followers), who have become more openly critical of the Syrian secular order over the last few years. Salah Kuftaro, who preaches to about 10,000 followers every Friday at the Abu al-Nur Mosque in Damascus and operates the largest Islamic charitable foundation in the country, has recently called for an "Islamic democracy" in Syria, and has pointed out the failings of secular Arab states in leading their countries.[29] Al-Buti has become more committed to orthodoxy as part of his call to hold on to the fundamental Islamic principles (*al-Tamasuk fi al-Thawabet*). He says that these fundamentals are timeless and universal; they cannot be altered or dismissed, hence one of his slogans, "renewal, not replacement" (*Tajdeed, wa laysa Tabdeel*).[30] Shaykh al-Buti has since the 1990s often discussed the misconceptions regarding the virtues of secularization, which many Syrians believe to be at the root of the West's intellectual and industrial revolutions. More recently, he has gone further by arguing that one can clearly recognize the "end of blindness and a demystification of European progress." He has also asserted that there is not a single Muslim left

> who would doubt whether Islam had political and social sufficiency, whether Islam was compatible with the sciences or not, because Muslims have put a stop to some of the traditional scholars' retrogressive perception of modern intellect and knowledge. Muslims are now ready to accept Islam as a comprehensive system of worship *and legislation.* [Italics added][31]

---

28 One of my interviewees explained to me that he was stopped by a policeman because he was eating while walking on the street during the fasting time of Ramadan.

> He asked me if I am Christian. I said: 'What is it to you?' And he said that it is not permitted to eat during Ramadan ... of course it is allowed, we are a secular state, but people are confused, they don't know their laws, the permeation of the religious message has made them think we have become a religious state ... their ignorance is a problem for all of us.
>
> Author interview, January 2010

29 Sami Moubayed, "Islamic Revival in Syria," *Mideast Monitor* 1(3), September–October 2006. Online. See also *Washington Post*, 23 January 2005; and *Daily Star*, 18 January 2005. Important to add here that Salah Kuftaro is serving a prison sentence for "embezzlement."
30 See Muhammad Sa'id Ramadan Buti, *al-Mazaheb al-Tawhidiya wa al-Falsafat al-Mu'asira*, Damascus: Dar al-Fikr, 2008.
31 Quoted by Andreas Christmann, "Islamic Scholar and Religious Leader: A Portrait of Shaykh Muhammad Sai'd Ramadan al-Buti," *Islam and Christian Muslim Relations* 9(2), 1998: 157.

Generally speaking, the Islamic discourse maintains that it is only after a majority of individuals in a society have chosen Islam and declared their obedience to its rules and principles that an Islamic society based on a contract of obedience to God can coherently emerge. One could interpret the notion of a contract of obedience to God as a form of socio-political contract, an interpretation to which Hawwa seems to be alluding. In his books, Hawwa proposes to counter the monopolizing, secularizing control of the state over education and information through a return to the mosque, the formation of local organizations around the mosque that are related in mission to the mosque, and the creation of a school or of study circles in every mosque. Taken together, these measures would constitute "the supportive environment for the emergence of new forces and [would] organize and guide the whole community back to Islam."[32] According to Hawwa, the mass return to Islam would lead to the state itself becoming "Islamic." Effectively, therefore, apolitical activities can lead to real political change, through Islamization of the state.

This suggestion that apolitical groups could transform into political activists is not perhaps so far-fetched as it might seem, particularly when one considers that the linkages between the state and the Islamic sector are not long-standing and inviolable. Thus if one party no longer deems the alliance to be in its best interests it will seek out other alliances, and will take with it the accrued benefits from the earlier relationships. This underlines that power is a capacity to dominate rather than simply the exercise of domination, and that that capacity presently rests both with the state and with the Islamic groups. Paulo Pinto alludes to this fact when he writes:

> Indeed, protests and public demonstrations done by the shaykhs and their followers against specific state policies do eventually happen. ... Despite their limited and pragmatic character, these protests remind the state that a general mobilization is always possible if its policies become perceived as a threat to society, or even better, to the religious community as such.[33]

Moreover, complete submission to the state harms the legitimacy of shaykhs; according to Pinto,

> the compromise between the shaykh and the state apparatus must allow both parties to be satisfied, yet the shaykh and his/her followers must remain distinct and above the logic of overt submission and control that organizes the webs of clientelism connecting different factions of Syrian society with the structures of the authoritarian state.[34]

---

32 Itzchak Weismann, "Sa'id Hawwa and Islamic Revivalism in Ba'thist Syria," *Studia Islamica* 85, 1997: 131–54.
33 Paulo Pinto, "Dangerous Liaisons: Sufism and the State in Syria," in S. Jakelic and J. Varsoke, eds, *Crossing Boundaries: From Syria to Slovakia*, Vienna: IWM Junior Visiting Fellows' Conferences, Vol. 14, 2003, p. 8.
34 Ibid., p. 8.

212 Bashar al-Asad's era

Indeed, the limited degree to which the shaykhs have subordinated themselves to the state also explains the latter's need to further accommodate these groups in order to maintain its ruling coalition, particularly since forcing them into submission is not an option. Yet this mechanism of control is self-defeating since more compromise invites the religious groups to appeal for still more manoeuvring space. And this effect is heightened if the religious sector has a wide social base of support. In other words, the balance between the political command's need to accommodate shaykhs contradicts its need to control a growing religious civil society in the long run, since "Their [the Islamic leaders'] collaboration can easily be transformed into open rebellion."[35]

Furthermore, although the Syrian Islamic agenda tends to follow a reformist, spiritual path and is thus very different from the militant, Islamist branch of the movement, there is still a pool of potential recruits that could switch from fundamentalism to Islamism and from pacifism to militantism. This might be due to the fact that militant Islamists and pacifist Islamic groups (whether Islamists or neo-fundamentalists) share many fundamental principles and beliefs; where they differ is in terms of their methods for actualizing those principles. As an example, Muslim Brothers such as 'Uqla did end up joining the *Takfiri* and militant Fighting Vanguard in order to pursue a political agenda that was initially set by the Muslim Brotherhood. It is in this vein that the following argument is made:

> just as Stalinism (and Pol Pot or Mao) was made possible by the mass of usually peaceful and naive believers in the Marxist Utopia, al-Qaeda and its nebula are permanently feeding up from the growing Islamic revivalist movement. To separate the two should be the goal of Muslims and non-Muslims alike, since they are all targets of jihadism. ... By making artificial distinctions between the two, one only postpones and avoids the real struggle.[36]

Notwithstanding the teleological inclination of the above argument, a related view has been widely argued and accepted, that political Islam is not disappearing from the political scene; rather, it is via neo-fundamentalism that Islamism "is spreading, becoming commonplace, being integrated into politics, leaving its mark on mores and conflicts."[37]

What emerges, therefore, is that what happens in the future will depend on the state's success at managing economic liberalization while still maintaining

---

35 Ibid., p. 9.
36 Michael Radu, "Al-Qaeda Confusion: How to Think about Jihad," *Foreign Policy Research Institute*, July 2007. Online: www.fpri.org/enotes/200707.radu.alqaedajihad.html.
37 Olivier Roy, *The Failure of Political Islam*, Cambridge, MA: Harvard University Press, 1996, p. ix.

authoritarian control over a mobilized and increasingly dissatisfied populace,[38] as well as on the success or failure of the Islamic outreach. The extreme delicacy of this balancing act makes it clear that the Islamic movement's formal entry into the political arena in the near future is possible, and perhaps even likely.

B The future of political Islamists

At the same time that the fundamentalists are making new attempts to impact upon the political realm, the political branch of the Islamic movement is also revitalizing itself and gaining ground with the re-emergence of the Muslim Brotherhood and the Islamic Current onto the Syrian domestic scene.[39] And in addition to the pacifist Islamist presence that is being increasingly felt, Syria has also witnessed the domestic re-emergence of militant Islamist activity (see Chapter 7). The radical Salafi character of this activity is especially striking given that the majority of Syrian Sunnis are orthodox Sufis, and signals the presence of an embryonic Salafi political movement in the country.[40] This Salafi movement might become more prominent and forceful once foreign troops exit

---

38 The present situation in Syria is reminiscent of the Egyptian example referred to by Wickham:

> [i]ndeed, an important finding is that even when opposition groups are denied access to the formal political order, ruling elites are unified, and the state's capacity for repression is high, an authoritarian regime may permit – or be unable to prevent – the emergence of "autonomous zones" in which mobilization is possible.
>
> Wickham, *Mobilizing Islam*, p. 94

See also Sylvia Chiffoleau, "La Syrie au quotidien: cultures et pratiques du changement Présentation," *Revue des mondes musulmans et de la Méditerranée* 115–16, December 2006: 1–21. For a critical analysis of the economic situation in Syria, see Thierry Boissiere, "Précarité économique, instabilité de l'emploi et pratiques sociales en Syrie," in É. Longuenesse *et al.*, eds, *Le travail et la question sociale au Maghreb et au Moyen-Orient*, *REMMM*, 105–6, Aix-en-Provence: Édisud, 2005; Marzuq, *Al-Faqr wa al-Batala fi Suriya* [Poverty and Unemployment in Syria], Damascus: Arab Centre for Strategic Studies, 2004.

39 In this regard it is important to note here that the Damascus Declaration signed in 2005, the Damascus–Beirut Declaration, the National Coordination Committee for the Defence of Basic Freedoms and Human Rights and the Committee for the Revival of Civil Society are all secular civil society movements that have acquired more attention after involving the Islamic opposition (the SIF). The Damascus Declaration and the Damascus–Beirut Declaration were signed by hundreds of Syrian dissidents in 2005 and 2006 respectively. Written by Michel Kilo, one of Syria's most prominent secular dissidents, the Damascus Declaration called for the abolition of martial law in the country and a return to democratic rule. The Damascus–Beirut declaration called for the normalization of relations between Lebanon and Syria following the Hariri assassination. The Syrian Political Command interpreted both documents as evidence that the country's opposition was conspiring against it. Walid Jumblatt, Lebanon's most vociferous anti-Syrian politician at the time of the assassination (although no longer is at the time of this writing), had called for an Iraq-like military intervention in Syria, and had met with members of the Syrian Muslim Brotherhood. Michel Kilo and ten other dissidents were arrested. Eight of them were later released, while Michel Kilo was released in 2009.

40 See Chapters 3 and 4 of this work.

214 *Bashar al-Asad's era*

Iraq, since its members will turn away from the *Mushrikun* (the non-believers), or in other words the external enemy – that is, Coalition troops – and focus their attention upon the *Murtaddun* (those who have abandoned Islam) or the domestic enemy.[41] As François Burgat writes:

> In order to be able to speak of an Islamist defeat as opposition, it would be necessary to prove that other political forces had replaced them – "secularist" forces which would thereby show themselves to have a superior capacity to mobilize support. We are far from such a situation ... in contesting national political orders..., the Islamists implacably continue to be both advance guard and main body of mobilised activity. In the Arab world, the conjectural success of state violence only now serves, in all probability, to reveal the society's general difficulty in making progress along the arduous road to democracy – a difficulty for Islamists, certainly, but also for the regimes and forces which claim to oppose them in the name of secularism. All this should not be taken as a denial of the fact that times change, for Islamists as much as for the regimes which they oppose.[42]

Ultimately, the future of Islamists in Syria is contingent on the state's next moves, both domestically and regionally.

C Isn't a religious political order inevitable?

The instability of the current Syrian secular order in light of the ongoing Islamic renewal underlines the degree to which the country's secular ideological groups have failed to effectively cope with the shifting political situation and the authoritarian setting, particularly in terms of maintaining a public profile. This is largely because the authoritarian setting means that their political activities must remain hidden from view; and given that political change is their primary focus, this means that they are relatively invisible and below the popular radar as compared to if they had an active programme of social activities aimed at engendering social change. Moreover, their failure to cope has been compounded by the fact that they can no longer depend on the Islamic movement having recruiting problems (which it used to have because its traditionalist and elitist discourse did not appeal to the Sunni rural populace and the subordinate classes). In fact, the current Islamic movement is banking on three new realities to help it recruit even more new members: first, the major rural exodus of Sunnis that took place in the 1980s and 1990s, which gives it a large new pool of potential recruits.[43] Second, the fact that the movement has now

---

41 See section on Hawwa, Chapter 4.
42 François Burgat, *Face to Face with Political Islam*, London and New York: I.B. Taurus, 2003, p. 182.
43 See Leverett, *Inheriting Syria*, p. 36.

enough funding and political acumen to engage rural inhabitants and the disenfranchised, particularly the economically alienated and politically excluded youth. And finally, the widespread dissatisfaction with the current regime due to its failure to provide for and satisfy the needs of the plebeian masses.[44] These factors, coupled with the manner in which the social setting has been transformed by increased levels of religiosity as well as the anaemic secular discourse within society, seem to indicate an almost inevitable move towards religious groups participating politically.

According to a number of Syrian observers, while the country's political system might seem stable from the outside, underneath it is a boiling mass of conflicting ambitions between avid pro-democracy secularists, old-guard interests and the rising religious elements. Part of the difficulty in sustaining a secular order is that the political system's relational borders with the Islamic sector have not been fully and formally delineated. At the same time, high-ranking officials and military officers agree that there is no longer a sure way to keep Islamic groups under the control of the state: "They are receiving financial aid from the Gulf region, essentially Saudi Arabia. Plus these are legitimate non-political institutions that are helping the impoverished and the needy." When asked about the Syrian secular system and what is left of it, one official stated that the regime is still secular but that society is making its own decisions. "Secularism cannot be imposed from above," he said, a statement that is reminiscent of Hafez al-Asad's 1983 speech about the impossibility of preventing the resurgence of overt Islamic religiosity in Syria.[45] Ultimately, the rising religiosity in Syrian society is increasing the number of potential members and the resources available for organized movements from below that are religious.

---

44 It is important to add here – since I have examined the question of fear in Chapter 7 – that the religious discourse is activating questions and fears about the after-life and an Almighty ('Ubudiyyat Allah). While the secularist ideology of the Ba'thist intelligentsia has hoped to separate citizens from congregational performances whose self-proclaimed links to the metaphysical was considered by Ba'thists a priori unscientific or irrational, the Islamic movement addressed the question of civic engagements from a different point of view. Its engagement with the political was done via recognition of an apparently much-needed metaphysical world. Indeed, Jürgen Habermas has more recently argued that European laïcism deprived their citizens of "semantic contexts that are indispensable to the moral health of their polities." This might be reflected in the words of one observer who, applying the same underlying logic to the Syrian context, noted to me: "how can leftist groups win if they would rather stay away from the metaphysical world?" See Eduardo Mendieta, "A Postsecular World Society? On the Philosophical Significance of Postsecular Consciousness and the Multicultural World Society: An Interview with Jurgen Habermas," *International Journal of Interdisciplinary Social Sciences*, 8 February 2010. Online: http://thesocialsciences.com/2010/02/08/rethinking-secularism-a-postsecular-world-society-an-interview-with-jurgen-habermas; Jurgen Habermas, *Between Naturalism and Religion*, Cambridge: Polity Press, 2006.
45 Personal interview, March 2008.

D Are religious groups pluralistic?

In light of the ascendancy of Syria's Islamic groups, it is worthwhile asking whether or not they are pluralistic in nature and thus whether they would tend to allow other viewpoints different from their own to exist should they gain political power. Jillian Schwedler tells us that only a group's "ideological commitments" can allow us to predict this, and that prior behaviour is a poor predictor.[46] This is an important insight, since it is steers us away from our intuitive inclination to emphasize the fact that all of Syria's official shaykhs have behaviourally accommodated the extant political system. In terms of ideological commitments, while shaykhs Ahmad Hassoun and Muhammad Habash have expressed pro-democratic and pro-secular stances, others have more recently voiced their disapproval of these systems that they say shunt religion into the private sphere. For instance, Salah Kuftaro's "Islamic Democracy" would promote a form of democratic rule that proclaims itself to be pluralist in nature, but that upon closer inspection turns out to not tolerate atheist discourses and parties, and to insist that God must always be part of the state's ideology and the citizen's life. For his part, al-Buti has been increasingly critical of Western systems for what he calls their secular thrust and Godless societies.

Whether the next generation of Syrian Muslims emerges into a socio-political system that seeks to radicalize them or not – or for that matter, which is pro-democratic or not, and accepting of non-believers or not – depends upon how successful moderate vs. radical Islamic groups are in their ideational framing and outreach methods, as well as on the evolution of the overall movement, which is difficult to predict given the *realpolitik* attitude of the overall movement and the fluid and complex environment in which the different groups operate.

4 Syrian secularism today: containment measures and current attitudes towards the Islamization of the state

A *The state's counter-measures*

In spite of the accommodation of the "moderate" and politically quietist Islamic groups and the resulting nominal shifts within Syrian secular culture, secularists in the country argue that it is important not to write off Syrian secularism just yet. One Syrian observer told me that

> a parallel [meaning entirely autonomous] Syrian Islamic sector has not *fully* developed just yet, and given Syria's very rich and diverse demographic environment, it is doubtful the Islamic revival will succeed in galvanizing enough of the populace to cause a bottom up change of this sort.

---

46 Jillian Schwedler, *Faith in Moderation: Parties in Jordan and Yemen*, University of Maryland, 2006, p. 18.

This view might prove to be correct in light of a number of "containment" tactics (examined hereinafter) deployed by the regime over the last few years. Indeed, the last five years have witnessed repeated waves of state intimidation being visited upon the Syrian Islamic opposition. Moreover, since 2008, the Syrian state has also started to nominally re-assert *secularism* and the importance of a secular political culture in Syria. These efforts have been in response to the increasing autonomy and popularity of both official and non-official Islamic groups, but also to a pragmatic rapprochement between the secular Syrian opposition and the Syrian Islamist opposition.[47]

The state's gradual targeting of the Islamic movement started with civil society. It has involved using emergency powers and restrictive legislation such as the Law on Associations and Private Societies (Law No. 93, which has been on the books since 1958) to control civil society groups' access and ties to the Syrian Islamists, and to prohibit Islamists from operating as legally recognized groups.[48] For instance, the Jamal al-Atassi civil society group was closed down in 2005 and its administration arrested for having read a statement to its attendees on behalf of the Muslim Brotherhood.[49] The Syrian state also arrested a number of Islamic groups' leaders, and waged a campaign against the dissidents in the media and through the most prominent *'ulama' al-sulta*.[50] The state justified this course of action by arguing that there was an "abuse" of the state's liberalizing political moves, confusion as to what civil society means, and that the oppositional activity on the part of civil society regarding political change was a recipe for chaos and instability.[51]

---

47 *Al-Hayat*, 27 July 2010; See also Zisser, *Commanding Syria*, pp. 86–91; and Joshua Landis and Joe Pace, "The Syrian Opposition," *Washington Quarterly* 30(1), Winter 2006–2007: 47–8. The action was directed at the entire civil society movement.

48 Under the provisions of Law No. 93, the Syrian Ministry of Social Affairs and Labor (MoSAL) controls the registration of all civil society associations and has wide jurisdiction to intervene in the internal governance and day-to-day operations of any association. Associations must notify MoSAL of their meetings, and representatives of the ministry have the right to attend. In addition, MoSAL has the authority to regulate the ties of any local group with the international community, ensuring that local associations are severely restricted in their ability to finance their operations or seek advice, expertise, support, and cooperation from abroad.
    http://makkah.wordpress.com/2007/10/31/strangling-human-rights-in-syria (accessed 10 June 2008)

49 In March 2005, the Ministry of Information rescinded the permits of two American-sponsored radio channels, al-Hurra and Radio Sawa. Syrian Ba'thist website All4Syria and Saudi website Elaph, both of which are known to be critical of the Syrian command (the former says that the regime is not secular enough, while the latter particularly focuses on its atheist elements), were also blocked. Reported by BBC Monitoring International Reports, 21 March 2005.

50 See the website of *Suria al-Hura* from March to July 2006, www.free-syria.com. The military pull-out from Lebanon in 2005 led to a cycle of containment, including interrogations and accusations, arrests, security summonses and harassment of civil society activists. See also Zisser, *Commanding Syria*, pp. 86–91.

51 Landis and Pace, "The Syrian Opposition," pp. 47–8.

218 Bashar al-Asad's era

In May 2005, the Kurdish Shaykh Muhammad al-Khaznawi was found dead, having died under apparently suspicious circumstances. His followers claim that he was assassinated following vociferous sermons at his mosque in which he denounced the Syrian regime. The shaykh had been described as a powerful enemy, particularly because his great charisma gave him a strong influence over attendees of his Qamishli-based Islamic institute,[52] where he taught the Quran and Islamic jurisprudence. While Syrian officials blamed his mysterious death on radical Islamists opposed to his reformist and inclusive interpretation of Islam, the shaykh's family and followers are convinced that the Syrian secret service assassinated him due to his recent ties with the SIF (the Syrian Muslim Brotherhood). After his death, tensions in the city of al-Qamishli were very high, resulting in instances of civil disobedience that caused the death of one police officer and the wounding of a dozen protesters.[53] Less than a year later, in March 2006, the state issued a bill that outlawed having political contact or forming alliances with any foreign element or government; this includes the Muslim Brothers, who are considered to be a "foreign group" by the Syrian state.[54]

Some observers have argued that the political command's moves against the opposition have been particularly prompted by its fear of an Islamist upsurge occurring due to an opportunistic use of the space created by the secular civil society during the Spring of Damascus. As explained by Eyal Zisser:

> This fear of a fundamentalist wave that threatened to sweep over the country had many partners, even outside the ranks of the regime, which could explain their support for it or more precisely their reservations about the activities of the reformist camp.[55]

In fact, the regime's fears materialized in February 2006, with the emergence of a new opposition coalition that united Ba'thist and former vice-president Khaddam with the Syrian Muslim Brotherhood in the National Salvation Front.[56]

The state for its part retaliated against the secular-Islamist alliance embodied by the formation of such groups as the SNF by sending a clear message. On 28 February 2006, the director of the Damascus *Waqf* (religious endowments), Muhammad Khaled al-Mu'tem, issued a decree re-banning theology lessons from Syria's mosques. The decree also reduced the frequency of lessons for the memorization of the Quran from daily to only once or twice a week. Mosques and *zawiyas* were told to shut between prayers, unless they received a special permit from the Ministry of *Awqaf*. Loudspeakers that broadcast the voices of the shaykhs to very large

---

52 One of the main Islamic institutes in Syria. Al-Qamishli is a northern city on the Syrian border with Turkey; the majority of its residents are of Kurdish origins.
53 See al-Khaznawi website: www.khaznawi.de/khaznawi/2005/3.htm. See also *New York Times*, 2 July 2005.
54 Landis and Pace, "The Syrian Opposition," p. 60.
55 Zisser, *Commanding Syria*, p. 93.
56 As noted earlier, this coalition ceased to exist in May 2009.

numbers of people assembled outside the mosques were banned during morning and evening prayers. Most importantly, the decree also banned mosques from receiving any donations (whether from Syrians living abroad or foreigners) without reporting them to the Ministry of *Awqaf*. It was only following a massive mobilization of the religious elite that parts of the ban were lifted, with the influential MP Shaykh Muhammad Habash intervening in parliament to resolve the situation. Beginning in 2007, the Syrian security court handed down prison sentences against dozens of individuals accused of belonging to the outlawed Islamist opposition.[57] On websites and in Arabic newspapers such as *Al-Hayat*, All4Syria and Cham Press, Syrians fought over whether Syria is/should remain a secular state or not, and engaged in many debates regarding what "secularism" actually means. The authorities refrained from getting involved in these debates.[58]

In mid-2007, the regime's relations with the Islamic movement seemed to have entered a new phase. That is, the state moved from accommodating moderate Islamic groups and containing Islamists to clearly and forcefully re-asserting Syrian secularism and insisting that it would be a mistake to forsake Syria's secular culture. This shift was deeper than simple declarations of intent from the president, since it involved a fundamental redeployment of high-ranking officers and civil servants to safeguard Syrian secularism and with it the regime itself.[59] Thus in May 2007, a two-day conference in the country entitled "Secularism in the Levant" featured Syria's most prominent secularists such as George Habash and Yasin al-Haj Saleh, and attracted much attention from the Syrian media.[60] In November 2007, the Grand Mufti of Syria, Ahmad Hassoun, re-asserted his commitment to secularism as a Muslim and declared that "secularism is not against religion" (*al-'Ilmaniya laysat did al-Din*).[61] This is different from his previous statements that Islam is compatible with secularism, since the emphasis was now on secularism as a fait accompli.

In 2008, a number of Islamic institutes that had previously been accommodated and tolerated by the state were shut down by a presidential decree, while a number of bureaucrats were dismissed due to their "religious backgrounds."[62] In 2008, legislative decree 35 included new regulations aimed at better controlling Syria's private schools, many of which are led by Islamic groups (see Chapter 6).[63] Thus

---

57 See reports by Syrian Human Rights Committee: www.shrc.org (for instance 28 August 2007 and 29 July 2010).
58 *Al-Hayat*, 29 March 2006; See also *As-safir*, 6 April 2006. For commentaries on the issue ranging from the secularists to the religious, see www.champress.com (30 March 2006). See also "Syria Rescinds Ban on Religious Lessons in Mosques": http://faculty-staff.ou.edu/L/Joshua.M.Landis-1/syriablog/index.html (30 March 2006).
59 *Al-Hayat*, 27 July 2010.
60 *Al-Hayat*, 22 June 2007.
61 See www.dw-world.de/dw/article/0,,2851007,00.html.
62 Reported by many Syrian and Lebanese websites and newspapers, including *Al-Hayat*, 27 July 2010.
63 *The National* (UAE), 14 July 2010; All4Syria: http://all4syria.info/content/view/2990/80 (19 July 2010); Elaph: www.elaph.com/Web/news/2010/6/5/574540.html.

220 *Bashar al-Asad's era*

the decree stipulated that a private institution can be closed by the authorities if it is proven that it encourages national division or factionalism or religious fanaticism, whether directly or indirectly.[64] In 2010, tight new regulations were imposed on private schools, and decree 35 stipulated that unlicensed schools will be pursued and fined.[65] These measures were introduced because a number of Islamist attacks within Syria, including the "Damascus Bombing" of 28 September 2008, were traced to domestic Islamic institutes. According to observers, the "Damascus Bombing" alerted the authorities to the *growth* of radical Islam within these "official" institutions. In early 2010, the state outlawed Hadi al-Bani's Islamic group, despite the fact that it had not been considered a negative influence on society one year earlier.[66] And in June 2010, the state banned the face-covering known as the *niqab* in the country's educational institutions. As a result, teachers wearing the *niqab* were removed from their posts and transferred into administrative positions. The minister of education has also hinted that more measures safeguarding Syrian secularism will follow. These moves were justified by claiming that Syria needs to retain and protect its secular heritage and secular methodology,[67] and that this sort of "radical," "non-Islamic" and "foreign" attire sends the wrong message to Syrian children regarding women, Islam and Syria.[68] The underlying idea is that the secular order is an organic vision of Syrian society, while the new religious manifestations are but a foreign invasion. More recent reports also claim that more closing down of Islamic schools and institutes is on its way in the country.

B A look at Syria's secular culture: final comments and interviews with pious and atheist Syrians

Syrian intelligentsia

This work has detailed the mass revival of an Islamic civil society in Syria, as well as its social, cultural and political achievements. But why have the Syrian Islamic groups managed to flourish under the repressive Ba'th authoritarian regime, while the secularists failed? The Islamic groups have gained greater autonomy and become more influential than their secular counterparts for a number of reasons: (1) the secularists were originally silenced by the Ba'thi state because they continued to act like a political opposition, unlike the majority of Islamic groups, who chose to survive the Ba'th era by focusing upon society's ethics rather upon than the political regime. (2) While Islamic groups enjoyed the psychological and monetary backing of the traditional capitalist elite, secular groups did not because they had leftist agendas, which made it easier for the

---

64 See SANA news: http://sana.sy/ara/2/2008/07/18/pr-184465.htm.
65 See SANA news: http://sana.sy/ara/2/2010/05/03/pr-285978.htm; *The National* (UAE), 15 July 2010.
66 *The National*, 14 July 2010.
67 Elaph: www.elaph.com/web/news/2010/6/574540.html (28 June 2010).
68 *Al-Watan* newspaper (Syria) (30 June 2010).

Ba'th to dismantle them. The Islamic groups were also not as easy to get rid of because of the ostensible sacredness of their religiously derived discourse.

Having said this, it bears emphasizing at this point that Syrian civil society is most certainly not entirely Islamic in nature, and indeed that notwithstanding the burgeoning Islamic revival and the power of the fundamentalists, the secularists are still a force in Syrian civil society, albeit one whose influence can only really make itself felt if democratization is instigated. Indeed, if one looks closely at recent events in Syria, it becomes clear that the secular civil society has had some noteworthy achievements under the presidency of Bashar al-Asad, which underlines that it is not yet a spent force. Examples include the establishment of the Forum of National Dialogue (*Muntada al-Hiwar al-Watani*) by Riyad Sayf in August 2000, the formation of the Cultural Forum for Human Rights (*al-Muntada al-Thaqafi li-Huquq al-Insan*) by Khalil Ma'tuq in 2001, the launch of the Suhayr al-Atasi's forum, the launch of the Petition of the 99 and the Petition of the 1,000.[69] Even after the supposed end of the Spring of Damascus and the state's decision to contain the rising opposition, the secular opposition continued to demonstrate more *political* stamina than the Islamists (though not as much militancy and social stamina) in asserting its opposition and demanding changes.

These various observations and insights regarding the situation in Syria are greatly informed by my interviews with a diverse group of Syrians. As a result, it makes sense to consider further pertinent excerpts from the interviews, as a basis for adding still more nuance to our understanding.

I asked one secular intellectual whether or not he believes that today's Islamic revival will mean the end of the secular system, and whether an Islamic state is the next step for Syria. He replied:

> No, not if it is a democratic decision made by the Syrian people. We are Sunni Muslims, 'Alawi Muslims, Kurdish Muslims, Druze Muslims, non-believer Muslims, agnostic Muslims, practising Muslims, non-practising Muslims, Muslims who converted to Christianity, Buddhist Muslims ... and all other non-Muslim minorities. So, no! However, if the region continues on its path, and the Ba'th regime with its Islamization tactic, it is possible that the state could be transformed into an Islamic vehicle. Then yes, an Islamic revolution from above, meaning Islamization of society from above, is possible.[70]

The question "is Islam the main identity of this nation?" prompted another observer to exclaim that this is like asking whether Christianity is the main identity of the French nation: "Of course Islam is the very identity of this nation, so is Christianity, so is secularism, so is paganism, so is our Roman heritage." He added:

---

69 Petitions drafted and signed by Syria's secular opposition requesting political change in Syria and forming the cornerstone of the Spring of Damascus.
70 Discussion with Syrian secularists, April 2009.

isn't it interesting that secular France does not need justification ... I mean they are all Catholics, and yet they're secular, their rivalries and internal struggles are political, ours are [seen as] factional ... when Syria is secular, it is not an ideological choice, but a pragmatic inclination that is made by minorities in order to disempower the majority Sunni.

Many secular observers argued to me that Syrians are intrinsically and historically more comfortable with a clear separation between religion and the state, notwithstanding that they are disillusioned with the Ba'thist state and its secular model. They claim that even if Islamists do ultimately gain access to the political arena, they do not have a solution for resolving the tensions within the system that arise from its accommodation of religiosity and its simultaneous claim to be Ba'thi secular. The concessions that the state made to accommodate the religious class have produced a system that perpetuates sectarianism, according to Syrian secularists, since it has created a religiously driven civil society that focuses on Good and Evil rather than justice. Some also note the lack of true free will and of a non-religious alternative in the basket of choices proffered by the Islamists:

> What the Islamists fail to see is that Syrians are no longer an Islamic nation. Islam is simply a sect, one faction among many others. The Islamic solution is a recipe for civil war because belief is not belief if it is forced upon us. People who are born into Muslim families have to be able to choose whether they want to be Muslims, Buddhists or simply undecided. This is what is missing from the *Shari'a* our Islamists want us so forcefully to abide by, we have no right to choose, we are destined to be Muslims. The right to faith has to include the right to no faith. No one religion has the right to force itself on people, not Islam, not Christianity, not Judaism. No power has the right to prevent choice in terms of belief.[71]

The same observer continued by drawing an interesting parallel: "The cancellation of freedom by the national party is very similar to [its cancellation by] the Islamic party. They think it is fine because they are Islamists, how different are they from the Ba'th?"

Both secularist and Islamic thinkers agree that Syria is a nation with a young population and thus tends to be more open to change. This means that doctrinal attitudes are far from set in stone and that they remain relatively dynamic, with a variety of different currents active in society at any one time. One result of this is that it is very difficult to accurately and definitively predict future trends. Yet it is possible to say with some certainty that an Islamist state in Syria could only arise in the absence of political alternatives, or in the unlikely event of a *coup d'état* by the Islamists. This is because the political Islamists are not universally popular among Syrians, a fact that can be lost amid the striking expansion in both popularity and funding of the Islamic civil society.

---

71 Personal interview with a Syrian secular intellectual, February 2008.

These misgivings regarding an Islamic state in Syria were confirmed during my informal discussions with Syrians. Indeed, a majority of those with whom I spoke – who included practising Muslims and pious Muslim women – do not wish to see such a state emerge. In the words of one school teacher:

> The West thinks we Muslims seek to be governed by Islamic states, this is evident in the ways the American leadership is organizing politics in Iraq, but this is not what Syrians want, despite the appearances. Of course, we all [Syrians] recognize the importance of Islam to guide our social and political interactions, even Christian Syrians seem to agree with us on this, nonetheless we are not interested in a reactive model [to the West], we would like to move forward, which means it is necessary to secularize in order to become part of the larger global system. This [secularization] does not contradict our religious beliefs, if anything it underscores the true democratic values [that are] deeply rooted in our Islamic faith.[72]

Another woman, who is a supporter of Dr Muhammad Habash's teachings, gave a similar response. She said that "If democracy necessitates secularization in Syria, then secularization it is." She added: "We have different religions, but we share the same faith and the same spirituality, we all believe in and love one God, and as long as our Constitution and governing bodies respect our Islamic heritage, secular configurations are welcome."[73]

A number of pious Muslims that I interviewed do not believe that an Islamic state can really solve their problems. One observer said that "an Islamic state would simply mean a state governed by Muslim leaders who would be governing according to their interpretations of the *Shari'a*." Another devout interviewee observed:

> Secularization does not equal Westernization, at least not within the Syrian context; we have contributed to it as much as the West has, was Ibn Rushd [Averroes] not an Arab and an Islamic thinker? Secularization is not necessarily corrosive to our culture and religion.

And according to still another interviewee: "Syrians of all ages still remember the fear and ignorance of life under the last Ottoman Caliphs."[74]

The same types of views came out during my open-ended interviews, particularly the judgement that an Islamic state is not the solution to Syria's political and economic difficulties. This latter viewpoint is clear in the work of Talhami, who says that

> [p]erhaps what the Islamist Movement symbolized for the Syrian people was not a political program but the civilizational heritage of Islam. It

---

72 Private communication, April 2009.
73 Private communication, March 2008.
74 Private communications, Damascus, April 2008.

appears that very few people took the Brotherhood's emphasis on the universal political bond of Islam and the inevitability of the universal Islamic state seriously.[75]

In other words, Syrians do not appear to want the Islamists to be a main political player, which underlines their failure to galvanize the Syrian masses, politically speaking. At the same time, however, this does not definitively mean that Islamization of the state is out of the question, especially given the country's Islamic revival and the dwindling vitality of its secular culture. Indeed, it might be this realization that prompted Syria's main Islamic opposition, the SIF (the Syrian Muslim Brotherhood), to emphasize its secular element over its religious one by associating itself with secular groups (see Chapter 8).

5 Conclusion

In addition to briefly reviewing the work's earlier arguments regarding the new Islamic reality in Syria, this chapter has examined the possibility of a rise in Islamist political activity within the context of the country's economic liberalization and its Islamic revivalism. The analysis drew upon a number of interviews that help to shed light on future trends in the country. It showed that while Syria's Islamic movement – which is apolitical – is growing and recruiting new members, the Islamist movement – which is politically oriented – has not yet achieved the same degree of success. This chapter has also emphasized the state's more recent deployment of a number of containment measures aimed at re-invigorating the weakening and shifting secular political culture.

The policies pursued under the presidency of Bashar al-Asad have proven to be a mixed blessing for both the state and for Syrian society. At the start of his presidency, authoritarianism was relatively de-emphasized such that the media and the emerging civil society became more daring in their critiques of the political order. This was clear in such TV programmes from the era as '*Asr al-Waldaneh* (The Era of Childishness), in which a Sunni intelligence officer and his ruthless 'Alawite right-hand man scheme to silence the freedom-loving, vital Syrian intellectual. At the same time, the elite seemed to be moving away from the economic illiberal stance of the old guard and towards an embracing of a de-centralized role for the state. This move was pragmatic, and showed the political command's readiness to adapt to new domestic, regional and international conditions. Yet the fact that it had to adapt simultaneously underlined the PA command's inability to keep its mobilization and co-optation measures in place without losing some of its grip on power to the business class and to an emerging Islamic civil society. More particularly, the adaptation seems to show the extant political command's recognition of the risks of having Islamic groups that it had for so long nurtured becoming vehicles of anti-étatist mobilization.

75 Ghada Hashem Talhami, "Syria: Islam, Arab Nationalism and the Military in Syria," *Middle East Policy* 8(4), December 2001,: 113.

Is this turn towards religiosity in civil society "a return to God" or what François Burgat called "the return of the forgotten sons of the south," that is, the return to prominence of the impoverished Syrian masses?[76] While it is impossible to discount the possibility that the turn towards religiosity is inspired by religious feeling, it seems more likely that it reflects the efforts by Syria's poor to cope with their often desperate circumstances. As we have seen, the structural reforms and the acceleration of economic liberalization over the last ten years have unquestionably impacted negatively upon poor Syrians, creating a class of people who find themselves increasingly marginalized in terms of economic and social well-being. And the marginalization of the "periphery" (poor) within the periphery (the impoverished nations) itself is certainly a recipe to re-Islamize this "south." Indeed, the state's emphasis in the 1990s and beyond on capitalist development and its concomitant retreat from its role as a provider of social benefits and an enforcer of basic civil rights has disproportionately affected disadvantaged groups. It has also made it possible for alternative providers of these benefits, in this case Islamic groups, to play a larger role in the lives of the urban lower and middle classes. In all likelihood, therefore, the turn towards religiosity in civil society is a result of the latter pragmatically espousing the religious rhetoric propagated by its new benefactors. Yet this pragmatic motivation does not make it any less significant, since it underlines the degree to which the Islamic movement is infiltrating society's *imaginaire* and in the process pushing the Baʿth and its secular ethos out of it. The seriousness of this situation for the Baʿth is of course further accentuated by the fact that its economic liberalization measures have re-created a bourgeois class of oppositional elites, one that is considerably more cohesive and conscious of its interests than the previous bourgeois class that was toppled in the 1940s and 1950s.

Yet while the bourgeoisie and pro-regime Islamic groups are willing to forgo access to political power in exchange for greater stability, prosperity and political access as well as more personal freedoms, anti-regime Islamists are not (let alone pro-democracy secularists). It is thus a problem from the command's point of view that the economic liberalization and the political upgrading that are giving some space to the politically ambitious within the bourgeois-religious class are doing the same to the Islamists. Indeed, the latter tend to see the extant political command's inclusive measures as a form of weakness, and furthermore believe that the increasing level of inequality in society will heighten popular discontent and thus weaken the command's base of support even more.

At the same time, it remains unclear exactly how numerous the victims of selective economic liberalization are and how efficiently they are being recruited. This lack of clarity tends to give Syrian secular groups hope, though this hope should perhaps be moderated by the overwhelming weakness of their outreach methods as a result of their obstinate focus on political participation and their

---

76 See Burgat, *Face to Face with Political Islam*, p. 70.

failure to present a compelling social vision. It seems safe to conclude that if the secular opposition remains focused only on political change, it has little chance of regaining a dominant position within civil society and the public sphere. But if secular groups deploy social outreach tactics similar to those used by the Islamic sector, a revitalization of Syria's secular sector can to one degree or another be anticipated.

10 Conclusion

1 Scope of study

This study explores Islamic revivalism in contemporary Syria. It uses a historical-institutional approach that traces the trajectory of the Syrian state's response to the Islamic movement, and analyses the shifts in this relationship over the course of two distinct political commands: the command of Hafez al-Asad and that of his son, Bashar al-Asad. In so doing, it elucidates how and why there has been a resurgence of Islamic activity in the country, and highlights the role of the secular Ba'thi state in facilitating it.

The topic is particularly important given that in 2004, 22 years of Islamist peace in the country ended with militant Islamist disturbances taking place in the heart of the capital city Damascus. From the point of view of political science more generally, it is also important because of the light it sheds on how system strains contribute to the creation of a collective movement, and on how regimes organize state–society relations to ensure their political survival. More particularly, it allows us to unpack the choices (and the limitations flowing from those choices) made by the Populist Authoritarian (PA) Syrian regime so as to contain the possibility of a viable Islamist alternative emerging, including its encouragement of an apolitical Islamic alternative.

There is also a clear lack of research on Islamic and Islamist activism in Syria other than a few works that narrowly focus upon certain prominent shaykhs and their teachings, despite the very palpable religious revivalism in the country. This absence, which is at least partly attributable to the difficulties in conducting research in the country, means that there has been very little attention given to the fact that Syria is a state in crisis because its PA regime model (with a focus on authoritarian) is increasingly unable to balance ideological commitments with concrete political actions. This crisis is being exacerbated by the effects of the war in neighbouring Iraq, as well as by economic recession and a widening gap between the rich and the poor. It is also being exacerbated by the country's Islamic sector, which is growing and deepening its control over society as a result of the new apolitical guise adopted by the state co-opted Islamic groups.

Ultimately, this study argues that the growing Islamic sector is changing Syria's secular culture and the social structures of society by taking advantage of the state's need to continue promoting economic liberalization while avoiding any political liberalization. Thus, while the traditional secular Ba'thist discourse, with its promotion of a clear distinction between religiosity and the public sphere, is being assailed from below, it is also being weakened from above as a result of the political command shifting its discourse about secularism from one that opposes overt piety in the public sphere to one that encourages a certain type of religiosity dubbed "moderate" and "fair." This underlines that Syria's secular system is moving away from *laïcité* and towards the Anglo-Saxon model of secularism.

2 Questions explored and findings

In its exploration of Islamic and Islamist revivalism in Syria, this study is animated by the following questions: Who are today's Syrian Islamic and Islamist groups? Why and how are they re-emerging as an important force in Syrian civil society and political circles after 22 years of relative silence? How has the state contributed to their re-emergence? Does Syria use Islamist groups as a mechanism for wielding influence in the region, particularly in Iraq and Lebanon? If yes, how is this affecting the Syrian domestic political scene? How successful are Syria's Islamic groups in recruiting followers within the authoritarian context of Syrian politics, and how is the Syrian state dealing with their re-emergence in light of Syria's multi-sectarian society and its secular model?

In answering these questions, the present study has re-examined the ways in which the secular Ba'th dealt with the Islamic militant opposition from its rise in 1963 to the seeming demise of the Islamist movement in Syria at the beginning of the 1980s. This re-examination is structured as a comparative analysis of the shifts in the state's responses to, and relationship with, the Islamic movement (independent variable), and its impact on Islamic revivalism (dependent variable) in the Syria of Hafez al-Asad and that of Bashar al-Asad. It illustrates how the Syrian political command is re-deploying in the face of recent challenges (i.e. the Syrian economic crisis and the new regional reality in light of the chaos in Iraq), and how it is using various domestic economic and socio-political survival strategies in order to keep religious discontent from boiling over into militancy, to eradicate the militant religious opposition and to limit popular unrest while still maintaining the unity of the regime coalition.

The study also offers an explanation for the Ba'th regime's shift from muting secularism and co-opting the religious class under Hafez al-Asad to promoting Islamic religiosity under the current command. In precipitating this shift, the state has employed an admixture of incentives and disincentives to consolidate its power and ensure its survival, in a manner typical of PA regimes. Thus it has concocted a new state–Islamic relationship and a new state–Islamic alliance, in an attempt to retain a considerable degree of control over society's resolute Islamic sector. In so doing, it has also produced significant changes in the nature of both the political system and society.

Despite the many similarities between the challenges facing Bashar al-Asad and those faced by his father, there are also some important differences, most significantly the former's need to address the inherent limits of the PA political model. These are producing a reconfiguration of state–society relations, and are causing Islamic groups to become a powerful and effective economic and social force.

My findings can be divided into two parts: the first analyses the changes at the state level. It shows how, in an attempt to consolidate power in a manner typical of PA regimes, the state apparatus helped to create a viable space for a new Syrian Islamic movement to grow and entrench itself in society. The other part considers the role of the Syrian Islamic groups in adapting to the new apolitical and controlled space provided by the state, and hence in advancing programmes of outreach that have been proven effective and efficient some 20 years later.

3 Theoretical analysis

This work's case study is part of an emerging analytical trend that bridges area studies, Islamic studies and broader political science theorizing, and contributes to the scholarship by extending the boundaries of research into Islamic groups. The study also provides new testing grounds for refining our understanding of the PA model, particularly of its limits.

Another major theme in the work is how economic decompression and selective liberalization have been closely linked to the political consolidation of the Syrian political order, but also to the seemingly paradoxical resurgence of Islamic discourse and activity within the public sphere. From a broader theoretical perspective, this work utilizes the socio-economic analytical paradigm to explicate the relationship between the Syrian state and the Islamic opposition. This paradigm's explanatory variables are best suited to illuminating not only the reasons behind the emergence of Islamism in the 1970s, but also the noticeable resurgence of Islamism in Syria today. The socio-economic school is effective because it takes into account the sectarian, regional and tribal aspects of the struggle, arguing that these are impossible to separate from the socio-economic cleavages when studying the relationship between urban Sunnis and rural compact religious minorities in Syria, though also insisting that the economic aspect ultimately trumps other cleavages when predicting choices and behaviours. This explains why the impoverished populace that supported the populist Ba'th in the 1970s and 1980s is today turning its eyes towards the populist Islamic movement. Importantly, the socio-economic paradigm can also explain the new attractiveness of Islam for Syria's urban masses, who once felt indifferent to the Islamic movement's position. It thus accounts for the variables addressed by social movement theory, namely the role of repression and of loss of socio-economic status in engendering militant opposition.

While this work employs theories and concepts from comparative politics and the socio-economy approach as a unifying framework of analysis, its interdisciplinary sensibilities and focus on intervening variables such as ideology, the role of women and the role of informal institutions allow it to also contribute to theory-building in the domain of Social Movement Theory. It does so by delineating new testing grounds for Social Movement Theory, through an empirical analysis of the factors that result in the re-emergence of religiosity within a supposedly secularizing authoritarian setting. These intervening variables shed light on: (1) the Syrian Islamic movement's successful use of available organizational space; (2) the movement's internal methods of outreach, more particularly its use of the intervening variables to expand membership and activities; and (3) the impact of the regional environment on domestic politics and vice versa.

4 Contribution

Despite the considerable attention devoted to the question of the Syrian Ba'thist struggle with the Muslim Brothers in the 1970s and the early 1980s, there is as of yet no other published work that deals with the impacts of that struggle on Syrian society today. Nor are there any other works that deal with the considerable social and political influence that the new Syrian Islamic movement has attained under Bashar al-Asad's command, a development that is especially important given the country's ethnic and religious heterogeneity and its widening class disparities. This work complements existing studies on Syria by examining the increasingly resurgent Syrian Islamic groups' roots, their social profiles and their ideologies. The findings elucidated suggest that Syria's new Islamic groups are proving more successful at permeating Syrian society than their earlier counterparts, and, moreover, than their secular counterparts as well.

In order to explain this development, the present study offers a typology of Syria's Islamic movement, dividing it into two streams: one encompasses neo-fundamentalist groups that are in alliance with the ruling elite, and the other those groups that are Islamist, anti-regime and driven by a clear anti-hegemonic thrust. Importantly, these two streams are not hermetically sealed off from one other – if anything, it was argued that each can empower the other, this in a context in which the socially liberal elements of the Syrian state and Syrian society continue to grow weaker. Indeed, the Islamic groups are today drawing support from the same circles that once propelled the statist Ba'th to power, by focusing on the marginalized elements in society that are now in particularly dire need because of the country's ongoing economic liberalization. In so doing, Syria's Islamic movement has taken control of the social milieu, and could potentially gain the political power that it has sought since the early 1930s. This underlines the degree to which the revivalist groups are no longer mere clients of the Syrian state. Rather, the limits of the PA model and the regime's survival strategies, coupled with the movement's efficient use of the organizational space that it has been given, have elevated the status of the Syrian Islamic movement to that of an ally of the state.

5 The work's main arguments

Part I

The first part of this work situates the study within its historical context, by examining secularism in Syria, the rise to power of a secular Baʻth Party, and the formation of the Syrian Muslim Brotherhood, first as an Islamic political democratic party and then in its shift towards militant Islamism. Part I provides an essential background to those who are less familiar with the Syrian case, and while some readers will already know much of the information that it contains, they will nonetheless gain from its re-examination of fundamental issues in that history.

Chapter 2 investigates Syria's secular political culture and surveys the Baʻthist secular doctrinal paradigm, tracing its different ideational sources and its most important theorists. The Baʻth Party's route to power and its implications are subsequently explored, before moving on to an examination of the Baʻth state's behaviour and its salient policies from 1963 to 1970, i.e. until the arrival of Hafez al-Asad to power.

Chapter 3 explores the formation and rise of Syria's Islamic movement by focusing upon the organization *al-Ikhwan al-Muslimin* (the Muslim Brotherhood) in Syria. The movement's base of social support is discussed, as is the socio-economic and political programme advanced by its creators. This background is necessary to understand the conflict that subsequently arose between the Baʻth regime and the Syrian Islamic movement in the 1970s and early 1980s, as well as the consequences of the conflict. It is also necessary in order to gain a full understanding of the reasons and complications underlying the relationship that exists today between Syria's various Islamic groups and the Syrian state.

Part II

The Islamic rebellion of the 1970s and early 1980s, as well as its consequences, are the main focus of Part II of this work. It lays the groundwork for understanding this rebellion by showing how in the 1960s and 1970s, the Islamic movement in Syria was supported by an alliance of traditional notables, merchants and religious 'ulama'. Its ideology advocated a status quo that was benefiting these groups, reflected their cultural values and was thought to provide a strong basis for drawing in a large segment of the urban masses in opposition to their Baʻthi antagonists. The project ultimately failed due to the alliance's elitist orientation, with Islam subsequently reclaimed by the Baʻth state apparatus and used as a tool for influencing the Syrian masses.

The main argument advanced in Part II is that the rise of Islamic political activism in Syria during the era of Hafez al-Asad was contingent on the Baʻth state's populist socio-economic and political policies, while its subsequent demise was due to the coercive and uncompromising strategy of the political command in dealing with the immediate and long-term threat to its rule. This is demonstrated through an examination of the Asad government's conflict with the Muslim Brotherhood from 1970 to 1982, which traces the socio-economic and political roots of the dispute and which delineates its bloody contours, paying special attention to the conflict's secular aspect (Chapter 4).

Chapter 5 focuses upon the decline in the 1980s of political Islam or Islamism as a model for change in Syria. It argues that although the Hama events described in Chapter 4 had a deterrent effect on the Islamist opposition, they also seemed to confirm the Muslim Brothers' accusations about the brutal nature of the Baʿth political command, and ignited a grassroots-driven revival of religious sensibilities. The state soon realized that, in spite of its various attempts to uproot the threat posed by Islamism, the traditional quarters' pervasive religious sensibilities were very resistant to state penetration, at least partly because of their autonomous economic base. This prompted the Asad regime to seek to quell the remnants of revolutionary Islam, co-opt the opposition and pre-empt future Islamic mobilization by creating a new legitimizing formula for itself that could replace the Baʿthist dogma while still avoiding political liberalization. The state thus undertook a two-part action plan, which ended up changing the Baʿth regime and its social policies as much as it affected Syria's Islamic movement. The first part saw the state move to destroy the institutional basis for ideological framing – and thus the opposition's capacity for such framing – while the second part sought to establish tighter state–society relations by co-opting the religious class, muting Baʿthist secularism and by instituting an official Islam from above (Chapter 5).

Ultimately, the state's new approach aimed to blur the borders between state and society so as to transform the conflict from one between an allegedly corrupt and authoritarian clique and Sunni Islam to one between moderate Islam and a de-stabilizing, reactionary and extremist Islam. More explicitly, the new strategy meant: (1) an increasing disregard for the secular principles of the traditional Baʿth ideology; (2) the creation of new alliances and institutions, so as to broaden the regime's social base of support beyond its traditional supporters and to control possible targets of Islamist outreach; (3) a relaxation of Syria's populist stance through a selective economic liberalization; (4) the creation by the state of an official Islam, dubbed moderate and correct, which was deployed to oppose and replace the one advanced by the Muslim Brotherhood and its allies; and (5) the use of regional Islamist groups in order to assert Syria's Arabist and nationalist stance while also influencing regional realities.

As a result of these moves, religious expression and practice were channelled through state-monitored institutions, and a *modus vivendi* with the mainly Sunni traditional bourgeoisie and the religious class was promoted. The selective economic liberalization that was deployed was meant to co-opt the business class, but also to mobilize certain "moderate" and "true" Sufi shaykhs and their communities on behalf of the regime, through the integration of the shaykhs into the state's clientelistic network. The government further constructed thousands of new mosques, established two dozen Islamic higher education institutes and developed a variety of other quasi-official religious institutions. All of these measures were intended to take over and replace channels that the Muslim Brotherhood had used for recruitment. Interestingly, the economic and political compromises deployed by the state, which were intended to sustain and upgrade the authoritarian system, had an unintended effect: they increased the resources and opportunities for organized challenges from below, especially Islamically based challenges, as a result of contributing to the omnipresence of religion in society.

Part II concludes that the regime's survival-oriented policies ended up establishing a new dynamic of state–society relations. Effectively, therefore, the control and co-optation measures of the Ba'th under Hafez al-Asad re-invigorated both Syria's Islamic movement and the Damascene bourgeois class. And while the state's balancing act between the different social forces was relatively successful in the 1980s, it became somewhat tenuous in the 1990s and even more tenuous under the presidency of Bashar al-Asad, to the point that today the country's Islamic movement and its bourgeois class are outgrowing the government's ability to control them. This highlights the degree to which the Syrian state's survival strategy has been fraught with paradoxes. Chief among them is the manner in which the co-optation of the country's Islamic groups has resulted in a shift within the secular discourse. That is, while secularism in the 1960s meant limiting religiosity to the private sphere, the definition changed in the 1970s and the 1980s as a result of the state becoming less strict in this regard. Thus its policies not only muted previous secularizing policies, but also sought to shape the Islamic message. This has resulted in the creation of a large Syrian Islamic sector that is growing powerful enough to encroach upon many aspects of Syrian life. In other words, far from being choked off, the Islamic movement in Syria was actually reinforced in the 1980s and 1990s, though its form changed from that of an illegal Islamist movement to a state-co-opted, neo-fundamentalist movement.

Part III

Part III shows that the old alliance between the elite and the religious class has re-emerged today, at the expense of socially and economically marginalized groups. This underlines the limitations of the PA political model, as well as its built-in contradictions. And faced with the fall-out from the chaotic situation in neighbouring Iraq and the impossibility of controlling the Syria–Iraq border, as well as an ongoing economic recession, the existing command has chosen to take previous measures even further. Thus the last decade has seen a clear shift in Syria's secular discourse, with civil servants and the whole state apparatus actively endorsing the revival of moderate Islam (and piety in general for that matter, both Christian and Muslim). At the same time, the economic liberalization initiated in the 1990s is being revitalized and broadened, while the Islamic sector is again being courted.

Part III demonstrates these points by focusing on the state's domestic and regional policies from Bashar al-Asad's rise to power in June 2000 up until the writing of this work. It argues that the manner in which the conflict between the Ba'th and the Islamic class was overcome has had a significant impact on today's Syria. In particular, this section notes that the current political command seems to be facing similar economic, social and geo-political challenges as those faced by the previous command, namely an economic crisis exacerbated by significant demographic growth, Islamist militant activity domestically and a new geo-political reality precipitated by a war in Iraq. But unlike his father, Bashar al-Asad's command is *also* facing a critical juncture in which reconfigured state–society relations have produced a situation that is no longer entirely under the state's control. This critical juncture is the natural outcome of the built-in limitations of the PA regime created by the Ba'th in 1963, as well as of Hafez al-Asad's mobilization and co-optation of Syria's Islamic sector.

Thus while Hafez al-Asad's regime was able to successfully co-opt Islamic groups, the current command's use of similar tactical manoeuvres strongly risks opening up an area for Islamic groups to re-transform from communal welfare groups back into active political actors. In other words, the increasing empowerment of neo-fundamentalist groups within Syria and of Islamists regionally, coupled with economic openings favourable to Syria's economic elite, may seem to be useful to the existing command – yet given the widening gap between the rich and the poor, as well as the inherent contradictions of the PA political model (particularly its aim of mobilizing social groups while also limiting their political participation), it is increasingly clear that today's Islamic sector has the capacity to challenge Syria's political order and to present a more broad-based challenge to the country's ideologically, religiously and ethnically diverse society in the longer run.

These points are elucidated in Part III. Chapter 6 shows that the new command of Bashar al-Asad felt it important to bolster its rule in the face of the growing popularity of the Islamic groups within Syria, as well as of various regional and international pressures, by increasing the profile of the religious element in society. This became even more urgent because the country's new bourgeoisie-elite was becoming a significant social force to contend with. But since the regime had less coercive capacity for repressing dissent, as well as because it needed to appear to still be moving forward with its announced agenda, economic co-optation through liberalization was pursued. As a result, the Syrian economic system is increasingly deserting its planned socialist structure: structural reforms and trade liberalization measures have been endorsed, private banks have been created, authorizations have been given to establish private insurance companies and a financial market has even recently been launched through the creation of the Syrian Stock Markets Authority. Yet while an increased liberalization of the economy would satisfy the powerful capitalist and *arriviste* elements linked to the state, it would also widen the gap between the impoverished masses and the elite. This would have the effect of further undermining the regime's populist and social-welfare orientation, since it would no longer be seen as in alliance with the lower and working classes.

In Chapter 7, the neo-fundamentalists, i.e. the apolitical, pro-regime Islamic groups, are examined. It is demonstrated that Syria's Islamic fundamentalist movement has broadened its base of support to the subordinate socio-economic classes, something that the Muslim Brothers never succeeded in doing. The overall discourse and the outreach methods of the groups are scrutinized, with particular attention given to their ideological framing and apolitical discourse, their network's dispersed, informal and personalized nature, and the psychological and financial support that they provide to their members. The success of these outreach tactics suggests that Syria's Islamic movement has largely usurped the state's populist role.

Chapter 8 finishes the task of mapping out Syria's Islamic groups, discussing the political Islamic opposition – the Islamists – in both its pacifist and militant guises. Chapter 9 concludes that the policy of economic liberalization and co-optation has been a double-edged sword for the current Syrian state, since it has led to the rise of an increasingly autonomous bourgeoisie that in the long term could present a united front against the state, and has also created a context in which the regime is no longer the most important supporter of the lower and middle classes. Under these circumstances, support for the regime strongly risks becoming increasingly conditional and critical. This is because the once-subsidized lower classes have been abandoned by the state, and will thus likely turn to the only other sector that has been allowed to prosper under the secular Ba'th, the Syrian Islamic movement. As was shown in Chapter 7, the latter has in fact begun acting as the new de facto backer of the unemployed and the poor in Syria.

I would like to conclude by emphasizing several points: first, the Ba'th secular state has empowered Syria's Islamic movement and its bourgeois allies in its attempt to control and contain them. Second, Islamic groups are not the simple product of Arab authoritarian co-optation measures, as many would likely argue. Rather, they have capitalized on the regime's structurally induced political weaknesses to achieve a commanding position within society, one that most secular social institutions have failed to achieve. Thus today, the Syrian Islamic movement is no longer a mere client of the state but has in fact become a powerful and increasingly independent ally of it. And finally, Syria is now at a crossroads. Though predicting the future is fraught with difficulty, it seems likely that the country faces two possibilities: the stability of a bourgeois–state alliance that excludes the plebeian masses, or the re-emergence of political instability due to the new Sunni capitalists feeling that they no longer need the minority-led state and as a result choosing to re-claim their past monopoly on political power. How these scenarios will impact upon Syria in light of its "fragile mosaic" of ethnic, religious and ideological cleavages, as well as its class stratifications, remains to be seen.

Bibliography

Primary and secondary sources

Ababsa, Myriam, "Contre-réforme agraire et conflits fonciers en Jazîra syrienne (2000–2005)," *Revue des mondes musulmans et de la Méditerranée* 115–16 – "La Syrie au quotidien: Cultures et pratiques du changement," December 2006: 211–30.

Abd-Allah, Umar F., *The Islamic Struggle in Syria*, Berkeley, CA: Mizan Press, 1983.

Abdelnour, Ziad K., "The Revival of Lebanon's Drug Trade," *Middle East Intelligence Bulletin* June 2001.

Abu Jaber, Kamel S., *The Arab Baʿth Socialist Party: History, Ideology, and Organization*, New York: Syracuse University Press, 1966.

Abu Khalil, As'ad, "Ideology and Practice of Hizballah in Lebanon: Islamization of Leninist Organizational Principles," *Middle Eastern Studies* 1, July 1991: 390–403.

'Aflaq, Michel, *Nuqtat al-Bidaya* [The Point of Commencement], Beirut: al-Mu'asasa al-'Arabiya, 1973.

'Aflaq, Michel, *Fi Sabil al-Baʿth*, Damascus: 1963.

'Aflaq, Michel, *Ma'rakat al-Masir al-Wahid* [The Battle of the Common Destiny], Beirut: Dar al-Adab, 1958.

Anderson, Lisa, "Democracy in the Arab World: A Critique of the Political Culture Approach," in Rex Brynen, Bahgat Korany and Paul Noble, eds, *Political Liberalization and Democratization in the Arab World: Theoretical Perspectives*, Boulder, CO and London: Lynne Rienner Publishers, 1995.

Apter, David, *The Politics of Modernization*, Chicago: University of Chicago Press, 1965.

(al)-Arsuzi, Zaki, *al-Mu'alafat al-Kamila* [The Complete writings], Damascus: Matabe'al-Idara al-Siyasiya lil Jaysh wal Quwat al-Musalaha, 1972.

Ayubi, Nazih, *Political Islam*, London: Routledge, 1994.

(al)-'Azm, Khalid, *Mudhakarat Khaled al-'Azm*, Beirut: al-Dar al-Muttahidah lil-Nashr, 1973.

Ba'd al-Muntalaqat a-Nadhariya li-Hizb al-Baʿth al-'Arabi al-Ishtiraki: Aqaraha al-Mu'tamar al-Qawmi al-Sades [Some of the Theoretical Starting Points of the Arab Baʿth Socialist Party: Adopted by the Sixth National Congress], Damascus: Maktab al-Thaqafa wa al-Dirasat wa al-I'dad al-Hizbi, n.d.

Babikian, Salem, "A Partial Reconstruction of Michel Aflaq's Thought: The Role of Islam in the Formulation of Arab Nationalism," *Muslim World* 67(4), October 1977: 280–94.

Badran, Tony, "Divided They Stand," *Mideast Monitor* 31 October 2006.

Barnamaj Itihad Shabab al-Thawra [Program of the Union of the Revolution's Youth], Damascus: al-Baʿth Printing Press, 1985.

Bar-Siman-Tov, Yaacov, *Linkage Politics in the Middle East*, Boulder, CO: Westview Press, 1983.

Batatu, Hanna, *Syria's Peasantry, the Descendants of Its Lesser Rural Notables, and Their Politics*, Princeton, NJ: Princeton University Press, 1999.

Batatu, Hanna, "Syria's Muslim Brethren," in F. Halliday and H. Alavi, eds., *State and Ideology in the Middle East and Pakistan*, Basingstoke: Macmillan, 1988.

Batatu, Hanna, "Syria's Muslim Brethren," *MERIP Reports* 110, November–December 1982: 12–20, 34, 36.

Ben-David, Alon, "Jordanian Indictment Reveals Operations of Jund al-Sham Terror Network," *Jane's Intelligence Review* 16 June 2003.

Blanford, Nicholas, "Hizballah and Syria's 'Lebanese Card'," *MERIP Reports* 14 September 2004. Online: www.merip.org/mero/mero091404.html.

Boissiere, Thierry, "Précarité économique, instabilité de l'emploi et pratiques sociales en Syrie," in É. Longuenesse, M. Catusse and B. Destremeau, eds, *Le travail et la question sociale au Maghreb et au Moyen-Orient*, REMMM 105–6, Aix-en-Provence: Édisud, 2005: 135–51.

Böttcher, Annabelle, "Islamic Teaching among Sunni Women in Syria," in Donna Lee Bowen and Evelyn A. Early, eds, *Everyday Life in the Muslim Middle East*, Bloomington and Indianapolis: Indiana University Press, 2002.

Böttcher, Annabelle, *Official Sunni and Shi'i Islam in Syria*, Florence: European University Institute, 2002.

Brockett, Charles D., "A Protest-Cycle Resolution of the Repression/Popular-Protest Paradox," in Mark Traugott, ed., *Repertoires and Cycles of Collective Action*, Durham, NC: Duke University Press, 1995.

Brynen, Rex, Bahgat Korany and Paul Noble, eds, *Political Liberalization and Democratization in the Arab World: Theoretical Perspectives*, Boulder, CO and London: Lynne Rienner Publishers, 1995.

Burgat, François, *Face to Face with Political Islam*, London and New York: I.B. Taurus, 2003.

Burgat, François and Dowell, William, *The Islamic Movement in North-Africa*, Austin, TX: University of Texas at Austin, 1993.

(al)-Buti, Muhammad Saʿid Ramadan, *al-Taʾaruf ʿala al-Dhat Huwa al-Tariq ila al-Islam*, Damascus: Dar al-Fikr, 2009.

(al)-Buti, Muhammad Saʿid Ramadan, *al-Mazaheb al-Tawhidiya wa al-Falsafat al-Muʾasira*, Damascus: Dar al-Fikr, 2008.

(al)-Buti, Muhammad Saʿid Ramadan, *wa Hazihi Mushkilatuna*, Damascus: Dar al-Fikr, 2008.

(al)-Buti, Muhammad Saʿid Ramadan, *al-Salafiya Marhala Zamaniya Mubaraka la Mazhab Islami*, Damascus: Dar al-Fikr, 2006.

(al)-Buti, Muhammad Saʿid Ramadan, *Kalimat fi Munasabat* [Words on Occasions], Damascus: Dar al-Fikr, 2002.

(al)-Buti, Muhammad Saʿid Ramadan, *al-Hiwar Sabil al-Taʾayush*, Damascus: Dar al-Fikr, 2002.

(al)-Buti, Muhammad Saʿid Ramadan, *al-La Madhhabiya: Akhtar Bidʾa Tuhadid al-Shariʾa al-Islamiya*, Damascus: Dar al-Farabi, n.d.

Byman, Daniel, *Deadly Connections: States that Sponsor Terrorism*, Cambridge: Cambridge University Press, 2005.

238 Bibliography

Central Bureau of Statistics, *Syrian Statistical Abstract*, Prime Ministry, Damascus: 2006.
Chiffoleau, Sylvia, "La Syrie au quotidien: cultures et pratiques du changement Présentation," *Revue des mondes musulmans et de la Méditerranée*, 115-16 – "La Syrie au quotidien: Cultures et pratiques du changement," December 2006: 1–21.
Christmann, Andreas, "73 Proofs of Dilettantism: The Construction of Norm and Deviancy in the Responses to 'al-Kitab wa'l-Qur'an: Qira'a Mu'asira' by Mohamad Shahrour," *Die Welt des Islam* 45, 2005: 20–73.
Christmann, Andreas, "Ascetic Passivity in Times of Extreme Activism: The Theme of Seclusion in a Biography by al-Buti," in Philip S. Alexander *et al*. eds, *Studia Semitica: The Journal of Semitic Studies, Jubilee Volume*, Oxford: Oxford University Press, 2005.
Christmann, Andreas, "'The Form is Permanent, but the Content Moves': The Qur'anic Text and its Interpretation(s) in Mohamad Shahrour's *Al-Kitab wa l-Quran*," *Die Welt des Islam* 43, 2003: 143–72.
Christmann, Andreas, "Islamic Scholar and Religious Leader: A Portrait of Shaykh Muhammad Sai'd Ramadan al-Buti," *Islam and Christian–Muslim Relations* 9(2), 1998: 149–71.
Cook, Steven A., "On the Road: In Asad's Damascus," *Middle East Quarterly* 3(2), December 1996: 39–43.
Cordesman, Anthony H., "The Department of Defense Quarterly Report on Stability and Security in Iraq: The Warning Indicators," Center for Strategic and International Studies, Washington, DC, 22 December 2006.
Daguerre, Violette, ed., *Huquq al-Insan wa al-dimuqratuya fi Suriya: 'Amal Jama'i li-'ishrin Baheth Suri* [Human Rights and Democracy in Syria: A Collective Work of Twenty Syrian Researchers], Paris: Commission Arabe des Droits Humains, 2001.
Daraj, Faysal and Jamal Barut, *The Islamic Parties, Movements and Groups*, Damascus: The Arab Center for Strategic Studies, 2006.
Dawn, Ernest, "The Rise of Arabism in Syria," *Middle East Journal* 16(2), 1962: 145–68.
De Jong, Fred, "Les confréries mystiques musulmanes au Machreq arabe," in Alexandre Popovic and Gilles Veinstein, eds, *Les Ordres mystiques dans l'Islam: Cheminements et situation actuelle*, Paris: Editions de l'EHESS, 1986.
Dessouki, Ali E. Hillal, ed., *Islamic Resurgence in the Arab World*, New York: Praeger, 1982.
Devlin, John F., *The Baʿth Party: A History from its Origins to 1966*, Stanford, CA: Hoover Institution Press, 1976.
Drysdale, Alasdair, "The Asad Regime and Its Troubles," *MERIP Reports*, November–December 1982.
Dunn, Michael Collins, "Islamist Parties in Democratizing States: A Look at Jordan and Yemen," *Middle East Policy* 2(2), 1993.
Eickelman, Dale F. and James P. Piscatori, *Muslim Politics*, Princeton, NJ: Princeton University Press, 1996.
Esposito, John, ed., *Political Islam: Revolution, Radicalism or Reform?* Boulder, CO: Lynne Rienner Publishers, 1997.
Esposito, John, "Islamic Movements, Democratization and US Foreign Policy," in Phoebe Marr and William Lewis, eds, *Riding the Tiger: The Middle East Challenge after the Cold War*, Boulder, CO: Westview Press, 1993.
Federal Research Division, *Syria: A Country Study*, Washington, DC: Library of Congress, 1988.

Felter, Joseph and Brian Fishman, *Al-Qaida's Foreign Fighters in Iraq: A First Look at the Sinjar Records*, West Point, NY: Combating Terrorism Center, 2007. Online: http://ctc.usma.edu/harmony/pdf/CTCForeignFighter.19.Dec07.pdf.

Gambill, Gary C., "Syria after Lebanon: Hooked on Lebanon," *Middle East Quarterly* Fall 2005: 35–42.

Gambill, Gary C., "Syria Rearms Iraq," *Middle East Intelligence Bulletin* 4(9), September 2002. Online: www.meforum.org/meib/articles/0209_s2.htm.

Gelvin, James, *Divided Loyalties: Nationalism and Mass Politics in Syria at the Close of Empire*, Berkeley, CA: University of California Press, 1998.

Gordon, Matthew S., *Hafez al-Assad*, New York and Philadelphia: Chelsea House Publishers, 1989.

Gorgas, Jordi Tejel, "Les Kurdes de Syrie, de la 'dissimulation' à la 'visibilité'?" *Revue des Mondes Musulmans et de la Méditerranée* 115–16, December 2006: 117–33.

Greimel, Hans, "Foreign Fighters Remain Threat in Iraq," *Associated Press*, 15 April 2003.

Guazzone, Laura, ed., *The Islamist Dilemma*, Reading: Ithaca Press, 1995.

Habash, Muhammad, "al-I'tiraf bi al-Akhar Mas'ala Siyasiya Aydan," in Adeeb Khoury ed. *Ishkaliyat al-I'tiraf bi al-Akhar*, Damascus, 2007.

Habash, Muhammad, *Al-Shaykh Muhammad Kuftaru*, Damascus: Dar al-Shaykh Amin Kuftaro, 1996.

Habermas, Jurgen, *Between Naturalism and Religion*, Cambridge: Polity Press, 2006.

Haddad, Bassam, "Change and Stasis in Syria: One Step Forward," *Middle East Report* 213, Winter 1999: 23–7.

(al)-Hafez, Muti' and Nizar Abaza, *Tarikh Ulama Dimashq*, 3 vols, Damascus: Dar al-Fikr, 1991.

Hajjar, Sami G., "Hizballah: Terrorism, National Liberation, or Menace?" Strategic Studies Institute, US Army War College (August 2002).

(al)-Haji, Muhammad 'Umar, *'Alamiyat al-Da'wa ila Allah Ta'ala* [The Global Call to Allah], Damascus: Dar al-Maktabi, 2007.

Haj Saleh, Yasseen, "Political Reform and the Reconfiguration of National Identity in Syria," *Arab Reform Brief* 14 June 2006. Online: www.arab-reform.net/IMG/pdf/ARB_14_Syrie_Yassin_Haj_Saleh_ENG.pdf.

Hamid, Hamida, "A Study on Conversion to Shiism in Syria," *Elaph* 7 January 2007.

Hatina, Meir, "Restoring a Lost Identity: Models of Education in Modern Islamic Thought," *British Journal of Middle Eastern Studies* 33(2), 2006: 179–97.

Hawwa, Sa'id, *Hadhihi Tajribati wa-Hadhihi Shahadati*, Cairo: 1987.

Hawwa, Sa'id, *Fi Afaq al-Ta'lim*, Cairo: Maktabat Wahaba, 1980.

Hawwa, Sa'id, *Tarbiyatuna al-Ruhiya*, Beirut/Damascus: Dar al-Kutub, 1979.

Hawwa, Sa'id, *Jund Allah Thaqafa zu Akhlaq*, 2nd edn, Beirut: n.d.

Heck, Paul L., "Muhammad al-Habash and Inter-Religious Dialogue" [Muhammad al-Habach et le dialogue interreligieux], in Baudouin Dupret, ed., *La Syrie au Présent*, Paris: Sinbad/Actes Sud, 2007.

Heck, Paul L., "Religious Renewal in Syria: The Case of Muhammad al-Habash," *Islam and Muslim–Christian Relations* 15(2), April 2004: 185–207.

Heydemann, Steven, *Authoritarianism in Syria: Institutions and Social Conflict*, Ithaca, NY: Cornell University Press, 1999.

Heydemann, Steven, "The Political Logic of Economic Rationality: Selective Stabilization in Syria," in Henri J. Barkey, ed., *The Politics of Economic Reform in the Middle East*, New York: St Martin's Press, 1992.

240 Bibliography

Hill, Fiona, "Syrian Women and the Feminist Agenda," in Paul J. White and William S. Logan, eds, *Remaking the Middle East*, New York and Oxford: Berg Publishers, 1997.

Hinnebusch, Raymond A., *Syria: Revolution from Above*, New York and London: Routledge, 2001.

Hinnebusch, Raymond A., "Calculated Decompression as a Substitute for Democratization: Syria," in Bahgat Korany, Rex Brynen and Paul Noble, eds, *Political Liberalization and Democratization in the Arab World: Comparative Experiences*, Boulder, CO: Lynne Rienner Publishers, 1998.

Hinnebusch, Raymond A., "Syria: the Politics of Economic Liberalization," *Third World Quarterly* 18(2), 1997: 249–65.

Hinnebusch, Raymond A., "State and Islamism in Syria," in Abdul Salam Sidahmed and A. Ehteshami, eds, *Islamic Fundamentalism*, Boulder, CO: Westview Press, 1996.

Hinnebusch, Raymond A., "The Political Economy of Economic Liberalization in Syria," *International Journal of Middle East Studies* 27(3), August 1995: 305–10.

Hinnebusch, Raymond A., "Class and State in Baʿthist Syria," in Richard T. Antun and Donald Quataert, eds, *Syria: Society, Culture, and Polity*, Albany, NY: State University of New York, 1991.

Hinnebusch, Raymond A., *Authoritarian Power and State Formation in Bathist Syria: Army, Party and Peasant*, Boulder, CO: Westview Press, 1989.

Hinnebusch, Raymond A., "The Islamic Movement in Syria: Sectarian Conflict and Urban Rebellion in an Authoritarian-Populist Regime," in Ali E. Hillal Dessouki, ed., *Islamic Resurgence in the Arab World*, New York: Praeger, 1982.

Hinnebusch, Raymond A., "Syria under the Baʿth: State Formation in a Fragmented Society," *Arab Studies Quarterly* 4(3), Summer 1982: 177–99.

Hinnebusch, Raymond A., "Political Recruitment and Socialization in Syria: The Case of the Revolutionary Youth Federation," *International Journal of Middle East Studies* 11(2), April 1980: 143–74.

Hizb al-Baʿth al-ʾArabi al-Ishtiraki, *Hawla Mafhum al-Hizb al-Thawri wa al-ʾIlaqa Bi-al Bunyatayn al-Fikriya wa al-Tanzimiya* [On the Concept of the Revolutionary Party and the Relation with the Ideological and Organizational Foundations], Damascus: Maktab al-Thaqafa wa al-Dirassat wa al-Iʾdad al-Hizbi, n.d.

Hourani, Albert, "Ottoman Reform and the Politics of the Notables," in Albert Hourani, *The Emergence of the Modern Middle East*, Berkeley, CA: University of California Press, 1981.

Hourani, Albert, *Syria and Lebanon*, London: Oxford University Press, 1946.

Husseyn, Satoof al-Shaykh, *Al-batala fi suriya 1994–2004*, Damascus: Syrian Central Bureau of Statistics, July 2007.

(al-)Iktissad Wal-Aamal "Special Issue about Investment in Syria," November 2000.

International Monetary Fund, "Staff Report for the 2006 Article IV Consultation," prepared by the Staff Representatives for the 2006 Consultation with the Syrian Arab Republic, 13 July 2006. Online: www.imf.org/external/pubs/ft/scr/2006/cr06294.pdf.

"Iran and Syria as Strategic Support for Palestinian Terrorism (Based on Interrogations of Arrested Palestinian Terrorists and Captured Palestinian Authority Documents)," Israel Defence Forces Military Intelligence, Document number TR6-548-02, September 2002. Online: www.mfa.gov.il/MFA.

ʿIssa, ʿAbd al-Qader, *Haqaʾiq ʾan al-Tassawuf*, Aleppo: Dar al-Irfan, 1993.

Jabbour, George, *Al-Fikr al-Siyasi al-Muʾaser fi Suriya* [Contemporary Political Thought in Syria], London: Riad al-Rayyes lil Kutub wa al-Nashr, 1987.

Joseph, Su'ad, "Gender and Citizenship in Muslim Communities: Introduction," *Citizenship Studies* 3(3), 1999: 293–4.
(al)-Jundi, Sami, *Al-Baʿth*, Beirut: Dar al-Nahar, 1969.
Kalmbach, Hilary, "Social and Religious Change in Damascus: One Case of Female Religious Authority," *British Journal of Middle Eastern Studies* 35, 2008: 37–57.
Kandiyoti, Deniz, "Women, Islam and the State," *Middle East Report* 173, "Gender and Politics," November–December 1991: 9–14.
Katzman, Kenneth, *Terrorism, Near Eastern Groups and State Sponsors*, Report for Congress, Washington, DC: Library of Congress, 2002.
Kaylani, Nabil M., "The Rise of the Syrian Baʿth, 1940–1958: Political Success, Party Failure," *International Journal of Middle East Studies* 3(1), January 1972: 3–23.
Kedourie, Elie, *Democracy and Arab Political Culture*, Washington, DC: Washington Institute for Near East Policy, 1992.
Kepel, Gilles, *Jihad: The Trail of Political Islam*, trans. Anthony F. Roberts, Cambridge, MA: Belknap Press, 2003.
Kepel, Gilles, *La revanche de Dieu: chrétiens, juifs et musulmans à la reconquête du monde*, Paris: Seuil, 1992.
Kepel, Gilles, *Muslim Extremism in Egypt: The Prophet and Pharaoh*, Berkeley and Los Angeles: University of California Press, 1986.
Khalidi, Ashraf, Sophia Hoffmann and Victor Tanner, *Project on Internal Displacement of Iraqi Refugees in the Syrian Arab Republic: A Field-Based Snapshot*, Bern: The Brookings Institution, University of Bern, June 2007.
Khalidi, Rashid, *Under Siege: PLO Decision-making during the 1982 War*, New York: Columbia University Press, 1986.
Khoury, Philip S., *Syria and the French Mandate: The Politics of Arab Nationalism 1920–1945*, Princeton, NJ: Princeton University Press, 1987.
Khoury, Philip S., *Urban Notables and Arab Nationalism: The Politics of Damascus, 1860–1920*, Cambridge: Cambridge University Press, 1983.
Kienle, Eberhard, ed., *Contemporary Syria: Liberalization between Cold War and Cold Peace*, London: British Academic Press, 1994.
Kienle, Eberhard, "Entre Jama'a et classe: le pouvoir politique en Syrie contemporaine," *Revue du Monde Musulman et de la Méditerranée* 59–60, 1991: 211–39.
Kriesi, Hanspeter, *New Social Movements in Western Europe*, Minneapolis: University of Minnesota Press, 1995.
Laithy, Heba, *Poverty in Syria*, UNDP Report (June 2005).
Landis, Joshua, "Islamic Education in Syria: Undoing Secularism?" in Eleanor Doumato and Gregory Starrett, eds, *Teaching Islam: Textbooks and Religion in the Middle East*, Boulder, CO: Lynne Rienner Publishers, 2007.
Landis, Joshua and Joe Pace, "The Syrian Opposition," *Washington Quarterly* 30(1), Winter 2006–2007: 45–68.
Lacey, Jim, ed., *The Canons of Jihad*, Annapolis, MD: Naval Institute Press, 2008.
Lawson, Fred, ed., *Demystifying Syria*, London: Saqi Books, 2009.
Lawson, Fred, *Why Syria Goes to War*, Ithaca, NY and London: Cornell University Press, 1996.
Lesch, David, *The New Lion of Damascus: Bashar al-Asad and Modern Syria*, New Haven, CT: Yale University Press, 2005.
Leverett, Flynt, *Inheriting Syria: Bashar's Trial by Fire*, Washington, DC: Brookings Institute Press, 2005.
Lewis, Bernard, "Islam and Liberal Democracy," *Atlantic Monthly*, February 1993.

McCants, William and Jarret Brachman, eds, *Militant Ideology Atlas*, West Point, NY: Combating Terrorism Center, 2006.
Mahmood, Saba, *Politics of Piety*, Princeton, NJ and Oxford: Princeton University Press, 2005.
Marzuq, Nabil, *al-Faqr wa al-Batala fi Suriya* [Poverty and Unemployment in Syria], Damascus: Arab Centre for Strategic Studies, 2004.
Mayer, Thomas, "The Islamic Opposition in Syria, 1961–1982," *Orient* 24, 1983: 589–609.
Ma'oz, Moshe, "Society and State in Modern Syria," in Menahem Milson, ed., *Society and Political Structure in the Arab World*, New York: Humanities Press, 1973.
Ma'oz, Moshe, "Attempts at Creating a Political Economy in Modern Syria," *Middle East Journal* 26(4), 1972: 389–404.
Mendieta, Eduardo, "A Postsecular World Society? On the Philosophical Significance of Postsecular Consciousness and the Multicultural World Society: An Interview with Jurgen Habermas," *International Journal of Interdisciplinary Social Sciences Journal* 8 February 2010. Online: http://thesocialsciences.com/2010/02/08/rethinking-secularism-a-postsecular-world-society-an-interview-with-jurgen-habermas.
al-Midani, Habanaka and 'Abd al-Rahman, *Sira' Ma' al-Malahida Hata al-'Azm*, Damascus, 1974.
Moghadam, Valentine M., *Modernizing Women: Gender and Social Change in the Middle East*, 2nd edn, London and Boulder, CO: Lynne Rienner Publishers, 2003.
Moghadam, Valentine M., "Gender, National Identity and Citizenship," *Comparative Studies of South Asia, Africa and the Middle East* 19(1), 1999: 137–57.
Mordechai, Kedar, *Asad in Search for Legitimacy*, Eastbourne: Sussex Academic Press, 2005.
Moubayed, Sami, "The Islamic Revival in Syria," *Mideast Monitor* 1(3), September–October 2006. Online: www.mideastmonitor.org/issues/0609/0609_4.htm.
Muslih, Muhammad, "The Rise of Local Nationalism in the Arab East," in Rashid Khalidi, ed., *The Origins of Arab Nationalism*, New York: Columbia University Press, 1991.
(al-)Nabusli, Ratib Muhammad, *Muqawimat al-Taklif*, Damascus: Dar al-Maktabi, 2005.
Nahj al-Islam, December 2007.
Nahj al-Islam, December 2008.
Nahyoum, Sadek, *Islam Didd al-Islam*, London and Beirut: Riyad al-Rayyes Books Ltd, 1994.
Nahyoum, Sadek, "Al-Muslima Laji'a Siyasiya," *Al-Naqed* 61, July 1993: 12–16.
Norton, Augustus R., *Hizbollah: A Short History*, Princeton, NJ: Princeton University Press, 2007.
Norton, Augustus R., ed. *Civil Society in the Middle East*, Boston, MA: Brill, 1994.
Norton, Augustus R., "Inclusion Can Deflate Islamic Populism?" *New Perspectives Quarterly* 10(3), Summer 1993.
Olson, Robert W., *The Ba'th and Syria, 1947 to 1982: The Evolution of Ideology, Party, and State*, Princeton, NJ: Kingston Press, 1982.
Oxhorn, Philip, "Conceptualizing Civil Society: A Political Economy Perspective," in Richard Feinberg, Carlos H. Waisman and Leon Zamosc, eds, *Civil Society and Democracy in Latin America*, New York: Palgrave Macmillan, 2006.
Paz, Reuven, "Hizballah or Hizb al-Shaytan? Recent Jihadi-Salafi Attacks against the Shiite Group," *Global Research in International Affairs (GLORIA) Center* 2(1), February 2004. Online: www.e-prism.org/images/PRISM_no_1_vol_2_-_Hizbullah_or_Hizb_al-Shaytan.pdf.

Bibliography 243

Perlmutter, Amos, "Islam and Democracy Simply Aren't Compatible," *International Herald Tribune*, 21 January 1992.

Petran, Tabitha, *Syria*, New York: Praeger, 1972.

Perthes, Volker, *Syria under Bashar al-Asad: Modernisation and the Limits of Change*, London and New York: Routledge, 2004.

Perthes, Volker, *Political Economy of Syria under Asad*, London: I.B. Tauris, 1995.

Perthes, Volker, "The Syrian Private Industrial and Commercial Sectors and the State," *International Journal of Middle East Studies* 24(2), May 1992: 207–30.

Perthes, Volker, "The Bourgeoisie and the Ba'th," *Middle East Report* 170(21), May–June 1991: 31–7.

Picard, Elizabeth, "Fin des partis en Syrie," *Revue du Monde Musulman et de la Méditerranée* 81–2, 1996: 207–29.

Pierret, Thomas and Kjetil Selvik, "Limits of Authoritarian Upgrading in Syria: Private Welfare, Islamic Charities, and the Rise of the Zayd Movement," *International Journal of Middle Eastern Studies* 41, 2009.

Pinto, Paulo, "Dangerous Liaisons: Sufism and the State in Syria," in S. Jakelic and J. Varsoke, eds, *Crossing Boundaries: From Syria to Slovakia*, Vienna: IWM Junior Visiting Fellows' Conferences, Vol. 14, 2003.

Pipes, Daniel, *Greater Syria: The History of an Ambition*, New York: Oxford University Press, 1992.

Pipes, Daniel, *In the Path of God: Islam and Political Power*, New York: Basic Books, 1983.

Pratt, Nicola, "Bringing Politics Back in: Examining the Link between Globalization and Democratization," *Review of International Political Economy* 11(2), 2004: 331–6. Online: www.jstor.org/pss/4177500.

Przewoski, Adam, "Some Problems in the Study of the Transition towards Democracy," in Guillermo O'Donnell, Philippe C. Schmitter and Laurence Whitehead, eds, *Transition from Authoritarian Rule: Comparative Perspectives*, Baltimore, MD: Johns Hopkins University Press, 1986.

Qurna, Ahmad, *Hafez al-Asad: Sane' Tarikh al-Umma wa Bani Majd al-Watan: 1970–198*, Aleppo: Dar al-Sharq al-'Arabi, 1986.

Qutb, Sayed, *Fi Ma'alem al-Tariq*, Cairo: Dar al-Shuquq, n.d.

Rabinovich, Itamar, *The War for Lebanon*, Ithaca, NY: Cornell University Press, 1985.

Rabinovich, Itamar, "The Islamic Wave," *Washington Quarterly* Autumn 1979: 139–43.

Rabo, Annika, "Gender, State and Civil Society," in Chris Hann and Elizabeth Dunn, eds, *Civil Society: Challenging Western Models*, London and New York: Routledge, 1996.

Radu, Michael, "Al-Qaeda Confusion: How to Think about Jihad," *Foreign Policy Research Institute* July 2007: 1–6. Online: www.fpri.org/enotes/200707.radu.alqaedajihad.html.

Razzaz, Munif, *al-tajriba al-murra* [The Bitter Experience], Beirut: Dar al-Nahar, 1969.

Roy, Olivier, *Secularism Confronts Islam*, trans. George Holoch, New York: Columbia University Press, 2007.

Roy, Olivier, *The Failure of Political Islam*, Cambridge, MA: Harvard University Press, 1996.

Roy, Olivier, *l'Echec de l'islam politique*, Paris: Le Seuil, 1992.

Sadeq, Mahmud, *Hiwar Hawla Suriya*, London: Dar 'Uqadh, 1993.

Sadowski, Yahya M., "Political Islam: Asking the Wrong Questions," *Annual Reviews in Political Science* 9, 2006: 215–40.
Sadowski, Yahya M., "The Evolution of Political Identity in Syria," in Shibley Telhami and Michael Barnett, eds, *Identity and Foreign Policy in the Middle East*, Ithaca, NY: Cornell University Press, 2002.
Sadowski, Yahya M., "Bathist Ethics and the Spirit of State Capitalism: Patronage in Contemporary Syria," in Peter J. Chelkowski and Robert Pranger, eds, *Ideology and Power in the Middle East*, Durham, NC: Duke University Press, 1988.
Sadowski, Yahya M., "Cadres, Guns, and Money: The Eight Regional Congress of the Syrian Baʿth," *MERIP Reports* 134, July–August 1985: 3–8.
Safadi, Mutaʾ, *Hizb al-Baʿth: Maʾsat al-Mawlid, Maʾsat al-Nihaya* [The Baʿth Party: The Tragedy of Birth, the Tragedy of the End], Beirut: Dar al-Adab, 1964.
Salkini, Ahmad, "Syrian Secularism: A Model for the Middle East," *Christian Science Monitor*, 13 July 2010.
Salloukh, Bassel, "Organizing Politics in the Arab World: State–Society Relations and Foreign Policy Choices in Jordan and Syria," McGill University: PhD thesis, 2000.
Schwedler, Jillian, *Faith in Moderation: Parties in Jordan and Yemen*, University of Maryland, 2006.
Seale, Patrick, *Asad of Syria: the Struggle for the Middle East*, London: I.B. Tauris, 1988.
Seale, Patrick, *The Struggle for Syria*, London: I.B. Tauris, 1986.
Seurat, Michel, *L'Etat de barbarie*, Paris: Collection Esprit/Seuil, 1989.
Seurat, Michel, "La Société syrienne contre son état," *Le Monde Diplomatique*, April 1980.
Seymour, Martin, "The Dynamics of Power in Syria since the Break with Egypt," *Middle Eastern Studies* 6(1), January 1970: 35–47.
Sfeir, George, "Islam as the State Religion: A Secularist Point of View in Syria," *Muslim World* 45(3), July 1955: 242–9.
Shahrur, Muhammad, *Tajfif Manabiʾal-Irhab* [Draining the Sources of Terrorism in the Islamic Culture], Damascus and Beirut: al-Ahali, 2008.
(al)-Sibaʿi, Mustafa, *Islamuna* [Our Islam], Damascus: Dar al-Waraq, 2001.
(al)-Sibaʿi, Mustafa, *Asdaq al-Itijahat al-Fikriya fi al-sharq al-Arabi* [The Sincerest Intellectual Directions in the Arab East], Damascus: Dar al-Waraq, 1998.
Sikkar, Nabil, "Hatmiyat al-Islah al-Iqtisadi fi Suriya" [The Inevitability of Economic Reform in Syria], *Al-Iktissad Wal-Aamal* 247, July 2000: 28–32.
Singerman, Diane, *Avenues of Participation: Family, Politics, and Networks in Urban Quarters of Cairo*, Princeton, NJ: Princeton University Press, 1996.
Smith, Christian, *The Emergence of Liberation Theology: Radical Religion and Social Movement Theory*, Chicago: University of Chicago Press, 1991.
Stenberg, Leif, "Young, Male and Sufi Muslim in the City of Damascus," in Jørgen Bæck Simonsen, ed., *Youth and Youth Culture in the Contemporary Middle East*, Aarhus: Aarhus University Press, 2005.
Stenberg, Leif, "Naqshbandiyya in Damascus: Strategies to Establish and Strengthen the Order in a Changing Society," in Elisabeth Özdalga, ed., *Naqshbandis in Western and Central Asia: Change and Continuity*, Istanbul: Swedish Research Institute in Istanbul, 1999.
Stepan, Alfred, "Multiple Secularisms of Modern Democratic and Non Democratic Regimes," in Craig Calhoun and Mark Juergensmeyer, eds, *Rethinking Secularism*, New York: SSRC Press, forthcoming 2010.

Stolleis, Friederike, "L'emprunt au féminine: réseaux de femmes et associations d'épargne a Damas," *Revue des Mondes Musulmans et de la Méditerranée*, 115–16 – "La Syrie au quotidien: Cultures et pratiques du changement," December 2006: 59–75.

(al)-Suri, Abu Mus'ab, "Mulahadhat Hawl al-Tajruba al-Jihadiya Fi Suriya" [Observations on the Jihadi Experience in Syria], in *Al-Thawra al-Islamiya al-Jihadiya Fi Suriya* [The Islamic Jihadi Revolution in Syria]. Extracts online: www.muslm.net/vb/archive/index.php/t-159953.html (accessed 11 November 2009).

"Syria, President Bush, and Drugs: the Administration's Next Iraqgate," *Subcommittee Staff Report, House Judiciary Committee's Subcommittee on Crime and Criminal Justice*, 28 October 1992.

Talhami, Ghada Hashem, "Syria: Islam, Arab Nationalism and the Military in Syria," *Middle East Policy* 8(4), December 2001: 110–28.

Talhamy, Yvette, "The Syrian Muslim Brothers and the Syrian–Iranian Relationship," *Middle East Journal* 63(4), 2009: 561–80.

Tauber, Eliezer, *The Formation of Modern Syria and Iraq*, London: Frank Cass, 1995.

Tessler, Mark, "Islam and Democracy in the Middle East: The Impact of Religious Orientations on Attitudes toward Democracy in Four Arab Countries," *Comparative Politics* 34(3), April 2002: 337–54.

Thompson, Elizabeth, *Colonial Citizens: Republican Rights, Paternal Privilege, and Gender in French Syria and Lebanon*, New York: Columbia University Press, 2000.

Tibawi, A.L., *A Modern History of Syria*, London: Macmillan, 1969.

Tilly, Charles, *From Mobilization to Revolution*, Reading, MA: Addison-Wesley, 1978.

UNDP, *Syria Report: The Impact of Subsidization of Agricultural Production on Development*, October 2006. Online: www.undp.org.sy/files/psia.pdf.

UNDP, *Poverty in Syria: 1996–2004*, New York: UNDP, 2005.

UNICEF and the Syrian Central Bureau of Statistics, *al-Maish al-'Unqudi Muta'aded al-Mu'ashirat*, Damascus 2006. Online: www.cbssyr.org/people%20statistics/Final_Report_Syria_ARB.pdf.

United Nations Economic and Social Commission for Western Asia, *Women and Men in the Syrian Arab Republic: A Statistical Portrait*, New York: United Nations, 2001.

US Department of State, *Patterns of Global Terrorism, 2003* (April 2004).

Van Dam, Nikolaos, *The Struggle for Power in Syria: Politics and Society under Asad and the Baʿth Party*, London and New York: I.B. Tauris, 1996.

Van Dusen, M.H., "Political Integration and Regionalism in Syria," *Middle East Journal* 26, Spring 1972: 123–36.

Vigual, Leïla, "La 'nouvelle consummation' et les transformations des paysages urbains à la lumiere de l'ouverture économique: l'exemple de Damas," *Revue des Mondes Musulmans et de la Mediterranée* 115–16, December 2006: 21–41.

Waldner, David, *State Building and Late Development: Turkey, Syria, Korea and Taiwan*, Ithaca, NY: Cornell University Press, 1999.

Webb, Edward W.F., "Turkey's France, Syria's France: La Laîcité in Two Ottoman Successor States," Conference on Migration, Religion and Secularism: A Comparative Approach (Europe and North America), Paris, 17–18 June 2005. Online: http://histoire-sociale.univ-paris1.fr/Collo/Migrations/Webb.pdf.

Wedeen, Lisa, *Ambiguities of Domination*, Chicago: University of Chicago Press, 1999.

Weisman, Itzchak, "The Politics of Popular Religion: Sufis, Salafis, and Muslim Brothers in 20th-Century Hamah," *International Journal of Middle East Studies* 37, 2005: 37–58.

Weisman, Itzchak, *Taste of Modernity: Sufism, Salafiyya, and Arabism in Late Ottoman Damascus*, Leiden: Brill, 2000.

Weisman, Itzchak, "Sa'id Hawwa and Islamic Revivalism in Baʻthist Syria," *Studia Islamica* 85, 1997: 131–54.
Weisman, Itzchak, "Sa'id Hawwa: The Making of a Radical Muslim Thinker in Modern Syria," *Middle Eastern Studies* 29, October 1993: 607–11.
Weuleresse, Jacques, *Paysans de Syrie et du Proche Orient*, Paris: Gallimard, 1946.
Wickham, Carrie Rossefsky, *Mobilizing Islam: Religion, Activism, and Political Challenge in Egypt*, New York: Columbia University Press, 2002.
Wiktorowicz, Quintan, ed., *Islamic Activism: A Social Movement Approach*, Bloomington and Indianapolis: Indiana University Press, 2004.
Winder, R. Bayly, "Islam as State Religion: A Muslim Brotherhood View in Syria," *Muslim World* 44(2–3), July–October 1954: 215–26.
Yacoubian, Mona and Scott Lazensky, *Dealing with Damascus: Seeking a Greater Return on U.S.–Syria Relations*, New York: Council on Foreign Relations, 2008.
Yakan, Fathi, *Al-Isti'ab fi Hayat al-Da'wa wa al-Da'iya* [Awarness in the life of the Da'wa and the Da'iya], Beirut: Mu'asasat al-Risala, 1997.
Yakan, Fathi, *Kayfa Nad'u ila al-Islam?* [The Way to Preach Islam], Beirut: Mu'assasat al-Risala, 1977.
Zakariya, Khodr, *Some Peculiarities of the Class Construction in the Syrian Society*, Tokyo: Institute of Developing Economics, 1984.
Zeine, Zeine N., *The Struggle for Arab Independence*, Beirut: Khayats, 1960.
Zisser, Eyal, *Commanding Syria: Bashar al-Asad and the First Years in Power*, New York: I.B. Tauris, 2007.
Zisser, Eyal, "Syria, the Baʻth Regime and the Islamic Movement: Stepping on a New Path?" *Muslim World* 95, January 2005: 43–65.
Zisser, Eyal, "Does Bashar al-Asad Rule Syria?" *Middle East Quarterly* Winter 2003: 15–23.
Zisser, Eyal, "Syria and the War in Iraq," *Meria* 7(2), June 2003. Online: http://meria.idc.ac.il/journal/2003/issue2/jv7n2a4.html (accessed 14 October 2008.

Newspapers

Al-Ahram
Al-Ahram Weekly
Al-Akhbar
Al-Baʻth
Al-Diyar
Al-Hayat
Al-Khaleej
Al-Liwa'
Al-Nahar
Al-Thawra
Al-Watan
Al-Watan al-Arabi
Asharq al-Awsat
As-Safir
Association France Presse
BBC Monitoring International Reports
Cairo News
Daily Star

Der Spiegel
Haaretz
Gulf News
Khaleej Times
Kuwait Times Daily
Middle East International
Le Monde
Le Monde Diplomatique
New York Times
Observer
Tishreen
Washington Post
Yediot Ahronot

Publications on the web

'Abd al-Karim al-Rifa'i group at: www.sadazaid.com
Abu Mus'ab al-Suri, *Da'wat al-Muqawama al-Islamiya* – extracts at: www.muslm.net/vb/archive/index.php/t-159953.html
Ahrar Suria (National Salvation Front) at: www.ahrarsyria.com; or Suriya al-Hurra at: http://Free-Syria.com
'Akkam's website at: www.akkam.org
Al-Marfa' at: www.almarfaa.net
Arab Gateway website at: www.al-bab.com/arab/countries/syria/bashar00a.htm
Arab Reform Initiative – Syria at: http://arab-reform.net/
Atassi Forum at: www.atassiforum.org
Ba'th Party at: www.baath-party.org/eng/constitution2.htm
Cham Press at: www.champress.net
Combating Terrorism Center at: www.ctc.usma.edu
Damascus Center for Human Rights Studies at: www.dchrs.com
Damascus Center for Theoretical and Civil Rights Studies at: www.dctcrs.org
Damascus Online at: www.damascus-online.com/history/documents/constitution.htm
Deutsche Welle at: www.dw-world.de/dw/article/0,,2851007,00.html
Egyptian Government at: www.egypt.gov.eg/english/laws/Constitution/index.asp
E-Prism at: http://e-prism.org/images/alkhatf.pdf
Federation of Syrian Chamber of Commerce at: www.fedcommsyr.org/economy.html
Joshua Landis at: www.syriacomment.com and http://faculty-staff.ou.edu/L/Joshua.M.Landis-1/syriablog/2005/06/capture-of-jund-al-islam-terrorist.htm
iBBC news at: www. news.bbc.co.uk/2/hi/business/7934644.stm
iCNN at: www.cnn.com/2008/WORLD/europe/07/21/spain.terror
iCNN Arabic at: www.arabic.cnn.com/2007/middle_east/4/2/shiite.syria/index.htm1.
Ikhwan website: www.ikhwanweb.com
International Constitutional Law Project Information at: www.servat.unibe.ch/icl/le00000_.html
International Labour Organization at: www.ilo.org/public/english/employment/gems/eeo/download/syria.pdf
Islamist website at: www.hurriyat.org [Down]
Islamist website at: www.ipv.org/wnm-e/classif.htm [Down]
Islamist website at: www.islam3.net [Down]

248 Bibliography

Islamist website at: http://almaqdese.com/c?i=98 [Down]
Islamist website at: www.taghreeb.org [Down]
Israel Ministry of Foreign Affairs at: www.mfa.gov.il/MFA/The+Iranian+Threat/Support+of+terror/Iran
(al)-Khaznawi website at: www.khaznawi.de
Knowledge at Wharton at: http://knowledge.wharton.upenn.edu/arabic
Kuluna Shuraka (All4Syria) at: www.All4Syria.info
Lajna Suriya li al-'Amal al-Dimuqrati at: http://sdwc.jeeran.com
Lajnat al-Tansik Min Ajel al-Taghyeer al-Dimocrati at: http://altansiksyr.free.fr
Minbar Suriya al-Suri at: www.nnuu.org [Down]
Muntadayat Mukafahat al-Shi'a al-Rawafed (Islamist) at www.antishe3a.com/vb/showthread.php?p=2779#post2779
Muqarabat Journal at: www.mokarabat.com
Nahda (Islamist) website at: www.alnahdaparty.com
National Salvation Front in Syria at: http://savesyria.org
Nida' (Damascus Declaration) at: http://annidaa.org/index.php
Nidaa' at: www.damdec.org
PJ Sage centre at: www.pjsage.com/products.htm
Press TV at: www.presstv.ir/detail.aspx?id=69800&sectionid=351020101
Pulpit of Monotheism and Jihad, Minbar of Tawhed and Jihad at: www.tawhed.net
Reform Party of Syria at: http://reformsyria.org
Reuters at: http://uk.reuters.com
Revue des mondes musulmans et de la Méditerranée at: http://remmm.revues.org/document3008.html
Risalat al-Tajdeed at: http://altajdeed.org
Sahat Ahl al-Sunna (the Sunni Space) at: www.antishe3a.com/vb/showthread.php?p=2779#post2779
Sa'id al-Buti website at: www.bouti.com
Shabakat al-Difa' 'an al-Sunna (the network for the defence of the Sunna) at: www.d-sunna.net [Down]
Shaykh Ahmad Kuftaro at: www.kuftaro.org
Shaykh Hassoun at: www.drhassoun.com
Shaykh Rajab at: www.sheikhrajab.org
Shaykh Wahba al-Zuhayli at: www.zuhayli.net
Sunnah, Salafi Islamist website at: www.alsunnah.net [Down]
Syria Report at: www.syria-report.com/article.asp?id=2897&rub=24
Syria Live at: www.syrialive.net/government/ministries/ministers.htm
Syria News at: http://syrianews.com
Syrian Human Rights Committee at: www.shrc.org/data/aspx/d4/3624.aspx
Syrian Human Rights Committee at: www.shro-syria.com
Syrian Ministry of *Awqaf* at: www.syrianawkkaf.com
Syrian Muslim Brothers at: www.ikhwansyria.com
Syrian Stock Exchange at: www.Syria-bourse.com.
Syrian Vision (al-Markaz al-Suri li al-Dirasat wa al-Tanmiya al-Dimucratiya) at: www.syrian-vision.com
Syria's Labour Force Survey, 2006 at: www.ilo.org/public/english/employment/gems/eeo/download/syria.pdf
Tajdeed Movement (Shaykh Muhammad Habash) at: www.tajdeed.org
Tayar al-Suri al-Dimuqrati at: www.tsdp.org

Thawra Community at: www.tharwacommunity.org
Thawra Project at: http://arabic.tharwaproject.com
This is Syria at: www.thisissyria.com
UNIFEM at: www.unifem.org.jo/attachment/743.doc
US Treasury at: www.treas.gov/press/releases/hp834.htm and www.ustreas.gov/press/releases/js1538.htm

Index

Note: Page numbers in *italics* denote tables.

Ababsa, Myriam 123
`Abidin, Abu al-Yusr 45
al-'Absi, Shukri 134, 135
Abu al-Nur foundation 90, 159, 164–5
Abu Ghudda, `Abdul Fatah 38, 44, 49, 71, 79, 93
Afghanistan 127, 130
`Aflaq, Michel 18, 21, 22, 24, 26, 29, 31, 32
agency 208
al-Aghasi, Mahmud Gul *see* al-Qa'qa, Abu
agricultural policy 27, 33, 43, 63, 95, 122–3
Ahl al-Bayt society 132, 133
Ahmad, Kamal 187
al-Ajuri, Akran 128
Akkam, Mahmood 139, 195
al-Mustaqbal newspaper 135
al Nadhir newspaper 91
al-Qaeda 127, 130, 134, 135, 136, 140, 191–2, 193
al-Tayar al-Islami al-Dimuqrati see Islamic Democratic Current
`Alawis 61, 69, 70, 74, 88, 93–4, 133, 197
alcohol 41
Aleppo 43, 44, 47, 49, 63, 72, 76, 77, 79; Artillery School attack (1979) 74, 75; riots (1973) 70–1
Algeria 53, 114
alienation, youth 206, 209
AMAL movement 104
al-Amiri, `Umar Baha' 38
Anglo-Saxon secular model 16, 18, 21, 115, 143, 228
apoliticalism 106, 146–50, 175, 211, 227
Arab Ba'th Socialist Party *see* Ba'ath Party
Arab-Israeli War (1967) 34, 41, 47
Arab League 122

Arab nationalism 23, 24, 26, 28
Arab Revival Movement 21
Arab Socialist Party (ASP) 22, 34
Arab Socialist Union 76
Arafat, Yasir 49, 134
armed forces *see* military
Armenians 7n23, 22n26, 24
al-Arsuzi, Zaki 18, 23, 24, 70, 89
`*As al-Waldaneh* (The Era of Childishness) TV programme 224
Asad Institute for Memorizing the Quran 90–1
al-Asad, Bashar 5, 6, 105, 107, 114, 115, 143, 228, 229, 230, 234; foreign policy 125–9, 131–2; inaugural speech 115n10, 120–1; and secularism 1–2, 114, 115
al-Asad, Hafez 5, 6, 30, 34, 63, 70, 71, 77, 89, 104, 107, 112, 228, 234; on Aleppo massacre 75–6; assassination attempt 77; death of 1; and regional politics 73, 102; rise to power 54–6, 58; and secularism 72, 100–1, 143
al-Asad, Rif'at 84
Atasi, Nur al-Din 33
al-Atasi, Jamal 76
al-Atasi, Suhayr 221
atheism 33–4, 46, 67, 70, 89, 143, 144
al-`Attar, `Isam 38, 44, 48, 49, 71, 76, 181
authoritarianism 8; *see also* Populist Authoritarian (PA) system
`Awwad, Shaykh Muhammad 49
`Ayyash, `Abdul Ghani 30
Al-`Azm, Khalid 44

Badran, Tony 183
Baha'is 69
Bakdunes, Su'ad 171
Balila, `Aref 135

al-Bani, Hadi 118, 163, 168–9, 220
banks 32, 104, 121–2, 128, 132, 234
al-Banna, Hasan 38
Baqdash, Khaled 29
Bar-Siman-Tov, Yaacov 46–7
al-Baroudi, Bilal 135
Batatu, Hanna 38, 60, 61, 62
Ba'th Party 3–4, 5, 10, 15, 19–20, 31–4, 37, 43, 44, 147, 231; ascent to power 27–31; co-optation strategy 5, 82, 85–106, 98, 106, 112, 118–19, 142, 172, 228, 232, 233, 234, 235; Conference (2005) 2; constitution 25; containment tactics 217–20, 224; formation 21–2; monopolization of power 70, 82; *Muntalaqat* text 45, 47; and Muslim Brotherhood 53–81; National Command 31, 32; power struggles within 58; Regional Command 31, 32, 58; secular doctrine 20–1, 23–6, 45–7, 67, 70, 82, 83, 116, 228, 231 (muting of 5, 88–94, 98–9, 100–1, 106, 114, 115, 116, 143, 228, 232, 233; reactions to 45–7); social base 54, 55, 60; support base 82; unity, freedom and socialism principles 26–7, 75
Ba'th (Resurrection) Arab Party 21
Ba'thist Revolution (1963) 19
Batikha, Isidor 116
Bayanuni, Abu al-Nasr 76, 79
al-Bayanuni, Abu Fateh 93, 115
al-Bayanuni, 'Ali Sadr al-Din 78, 115, 132–3, 181
belonging, sense of 157
Benford, Robert D. 64
Berbers 24
al-Bitar, Salah 18, 21, 22, 31, 32
Blanford, Nicholas 129
bookstores 155
Böttcher, Annabelle 45–6
bourgeois class 36, 58, 86, 94–8, 106, 112, 142, 225, 233, 234
Britain 29
Brysk, Alison 64
bureaucracy 32, 45, 55, 83, 96
Burgat, François 214, 225
business elite 95, 124, 137, 159, 224, 232
al-Buti, Muhammad Sa'id Ramadan 90, 91, 148, 152, 155, 163, 167–8, 180, 187, 210, 216

Camp David peace agreements (1978) 73, 103
capitalism 43, 46

Center of Islamic Studies 164, 166n63
charitable organizations 137, 158–9, 172, 173, 206
Christians/Christianity 1n1, 2, 7n23, 17, 22n26, 24, 39, 47, 58, 71, 72, 233
Circassians 22n26
civil rights 225
class 36, 41, 42, 60–3, 86, 124; *see also* bourgeois class; middle class; working class
clientelism 95, 232
co-optation strategy, Ba'athist regime 82, 85–106, 98, 106, 112, 118–19, 142, 172, 228, 232, 233, 234, 235
colonialism 46
Committee for Human Rights 73
Communists 24, 28, 29, 30, 36, 49, 69, 76, 181
comparative politics 7, 229
conformity 157, 209
Constitution: (1920) 16; (1950) 19, 39; (1953) 19; (1973) 20, 55, 70, 71
containment tactics, state 217–20, 244
corporatism 83, 86–8
Corrective Movement (1970) 34, 54–5, 75
corruption 62, 75, 83, 95, 96
Cultural Forum for Human Rights 221

Dabbagh, 'Adnan 74
Dahdah, Abu 195n69
Damascene National Bloc 28
Damascus 28, 42, 43, 44, 47, 49, 62, 72, 76, 84, 138, 140
Damascus-Beirut Declaration 213n39
Damascus Declaration for Democratic and National Change 178, 182, 213n39
Damascus International Book Fair 156
Damascus Securities Exchange 122
Damsacus bombing (2008) 3n12, 134, 142, 220
Dar al-Arqam 38
Darwish, Haj 187
Da'wa wa al-Tabligh groups 176
Democratic National Bloc 76, 77
al-Din, Adnan Sa'ed 49, 71, 78, 79, 181
al-Din, Badr 148
disbelief (*Jahiliyya*) 69
divorce 139
dress 2, 3, 6, 11, 101, 115, 157, 165n60, 220; *see also* veiling
Druze 22n26, 58
Drysdale, Alasdair 59, 62–3

economic crisis 4, 83, 144, 228, 234

economic growth 121, 123–4, 202, 204–5
economic liberalization 8, 9, 54, 83, 95–7, 106, 112–13, 119–25, 201–9, 212–13, 225, 228, 229, 232, 233, 234, 235; and private sector 75, 96, 119, 120, 121, 123–4, 142–3; and social welfare 113; and youth 205–9
Economic Security Court 96
economy 37, 41, 43, 60–1, 62–3, 94–8, 178–9, 184–5; Muslim Brotherhood agenda 36, 37, 40–2
education/educational system 27, 37, 106, 138–9; religious 138–9, 151–2; secularization of 2, 16, 20–1, 45, 115
Egypt 35, 47, 59, 64, 73, 74, 117, 131, 154, 207; and Israel peace accords (1978) 73, 103; Muslim Brothers in 41, 43, 44, 53; and Suez War 29; union with 29–30, 31; youth alienation 206
Eickelman, Dale F. 86
Ekko, Fu'ad 187
elections 43, 44; participation of independents in 93, 117–18
emergency powers 217
employment 203; women in 99–100; see also unemployment
ethical renewal 148–50, 153, 163–6, 172, 174n2
exiles 2, 93, 115

Faculty of Islamic Mission 91
al-Fadel, Muhammad 73
family 20, 99, 101, 139
al-Farhan, Ishaq 49
Fatah al-Islam (FAI) 72, 76, 134–6, 142
Faysal, King 73, 74
fear 157–8
feudalism 36, 43
Fighting Vanguard 48, 49, 53, 55, 72, 74, 76, 77, 78, 191, 194; attacks on regime 71, 73; ideology 67–8
financial aid 158–9, 193, 235
Financial Intelligence Unit 2
financial market 122, 234
fiscal policy 61, 121
Foley, Lawrence 134
foreign policy 102–6, 107, 118, 125–37
foreign trade 60, 61
Forum of National Dialogue 221
France 28, 29, 36, 39
free trade agreements 122
freedom 26, 27
freedom of expression 41
fundamentalists/fundamentalism 6, 148, 162–71, 175; see also neo-fundamentalism
funding 159, 215
Future Movement 134–5

gambling 41
gender relations 98–102, 106
geo-political approach 8, 9, 184
Ghabbaz, Fatima 171
Ghadiya, Abu 195n69
Ghadry, Farid 182
al-Gharbi, George Ibrahim 142
Ghassanids 198
Ghaza, Muhammad 71
Ghuraba' al-Sham 193, 194–5
Global Jihadist group 192
Greater Arab Free Trade Agreement (GAFTA) 122

Habanaka, Shaykh Hasan 45–6, 47, 70
Habash, Ahmad 116
Habash, George 219
Habash, Huda 163, 170
Habash, Muhammad 118, 132, 139, 152–3, 155, 163, 164, 165–6, 180, 190, 207, 216, 219
Habermas, Jurgen 215n44
al-Hadibi, Hasan 68
Hadid, Marwan 48–9, 68, 69, 70, 71
al-Hafez, Amin 31, 33
al-Halabi, Abu Rashid 192
Hama 63, 74, 76, 79, 232; battle (1982) 79, 80–1, 82, 181; riots (1973) 70–1; uprising (1964) 49, 69–70; Uprising of March (1980) 77
Hamas 103–4, 127, 128
al-Hamed, Muhammad 38
Hamshu, Muhammad 118
Harika, Ignatius 39
al-Hariri, Rafiq 118, 128
al-Hariri, Sa'ed 134–5
al-Hariri, Ziyad 31
Hassoun, Ahmad Badr al-Din 116, 118, 122, 148, 149, 153, 155, 169–70, 180, 190, 216, 219
Hatina, Meir 68
al-Hawrani, Akram 22, 28, 30, 70, 76
Hawwa, Sa'id 49, 68–9, 70, 71, 78, 79, 81, 175, 210, 211
headscarves see veiling
Heck, Paul L. 166
hijab see veiling
Hinnebusch, Raymond A. 36, 40, 46, 60, 61, 62, 80, 89, 93, 94, 97, 119, 184

Hizb al-Tahrir al-Islami (Islamic Liberation Army) 193, 194
Hizbullah 103, 104–5, 127, 128, 129, 130, 133, 197
Homs 28, 47, 72, 74, 76
human rights 73
Hunaydi, Mazyad 30
al-Husayni, Kamil 118

Ibn Taymiya 48
ideological framing 9, 66, 154–8, 172, 192, 206, 232, 235
Import Substitution Industrialization (ISI) 97n53
imports 60, 61
industry 61, 63
inequality 124, 143, 202–3, *204*
inflation 62, 205
informal networks/institutions 160–2, 172, 230, 235
inheritance 101, 139
intelligence services (*mukhabarat*) 76, 84, 88, 135, 142
interest rates 121
internal group structures 65
international dimension 9
International Jihadi Movement 195n69
International Monetary Fund (IMF) 121
International Muslim Brotherhood 49, 71
investment: domestic 123; foreign 121
Iran/Iranians 93–4, 103, 104, 105, 106, 131–3, 177, 187, 188
Iraq 29, 30, 78, 79, 103, 113n5, 130–1, 136, 193, 194, 227, 228, 233; US-led invasion and war 3, 118, 125, 126, 127, 144, 186, 189, 234
Iriksusa, Na'im 166
Islam 24, 36, 39, 65, 69, 72, 223–4; as modality for political change 209–13
Islamic Activism 6
Islamic Democratic Current 177–80, 181, 189, 213
Islamic Liberation Army (*Hizb al-Tahrir al-Islami*) 193, 194
Islamic Nation (*Umma*) 41
Islamic Renewal 6
Islamic Revivalism 6
Islamic Salvation Front (FIS) 53, 141
Islamic as a term 5
Islamic University of Pakistan 91
Islamist groups 174–99, 213–14, 222, 230, 231; militant 174, 189–99, 212, 234, 235; pacifist 8, 174, 176–89, 212, 235; *see also* Fighting Vanguard; Muslim Brotherhood; Syrian Islamic Front
Islamist as a term 5–6
Isma'ilis 61, 69
Israel 73, 102, 103, 104, 105, 132, 178, 197; and Egypt peace accords (1978) 73, 103; formation of 18; and Lebanon 79–80, 82, 105, 127–9; (1967) war with 34, 41, 47; and Palestine 127–8, 132, 136; and Suez War 29
al-'Iti, Yasser 178

al-Jabi, Sa'id 175
al-Jabirin, `Abd al-Rahman 197
al-Jadid, Salah 30, 33, 34, 54n1, 58
Jama'a concept 56
Jamal al-Attasi group 217
Jam'at 160, 161–2
Jam'iyat Hifz al-Ni`ma al-Khayriya 166
al-Jerudi, Munir 30
Jews 7n23, 22n26
jihad 68, 69, 152–3, 165, 191, 196
Jordan 35, 49, 78, 79, 103, 117, 193
judiciary 16
Juha, Khayr 171
Junblatt, Walid 183, 213n39
Jund al-Sham 130, 135, 136, 140, 194
al-Jundi, `Abdul Karim 30
al-Jundi, Khalid 47
al-Jundi, Sami 31
justice system 83–4
justifiable action, boundaries of 65

Kan'an, `Uthman 30
Kandiyoti, Deniz 98, 100
Khaddam, `Abd al-Halim 181, 182, 183, 184, 218
Khalas, Ibrahim 46
Khayrallah, Zein al-Din 49, 76, 84
al-Khaznawi, Muhammad 163, 187, 218
Kienle, Eberhard 56
Kilo, Michel 135, 213n39
kinship culture 56, 57
al-Kizbari, Ma'mun 44
Kuftariya Naqshbandiya 154, 162, 163–4
Kuftaro, Ahmad 45, 90, 148, 150, 155, 164, 170, 187, 190
Kuftaro, Amin 150, 163
Kuftaro, Salah 210, 216
Kuftaro, Wafa' 164, 170
Kurdish Coordination Committee 141
Kurdish Democratic Party 187
Kurds 7n23, 22n26, 24, 91, 185–7
Kuwait 131

254 *Index*

al-Kuzbari, Nabilah 171

laïcité 15, 18, 21, 115, 215n44, 228
land reform 27, 61, 95
Landis, Joshua 182
Law on Association and Private Societies 217
League of National Action 23
Lebanese National Movement 71
Lebanese Open Faculty of Islamic Studies 91
Lebanon 72, 80, 82, 106, 129, 132, 133, 134, 135, 136, 183, 194, 213n39; Hizbullah and 103, 105, 127–8, 129, 133; independence from French 104; as market for goods 95n44; Syrian withdrawal from 118, 125
Leverett, Flynt 120, 204
liberalization 146; political 75, 112, 200, 228, 232; trade 121, 122, 234; *see also* economic liberalization

Mahmood, Husseyn Bin 198
Makhlouf, Rami 130
Maktabi, Nadhir 166
al-Malki, Adnan 29
marginalization 208, 225
Maronite Christians 71, 72
marriage 20, 139
Ma'tuq, Khalil 221
al-Mazidi, Badran Turki Hisham 195n69
media 91, 106, 154
merchant class 54, 61–2, 63, 124, 159, 231
Merhi, Ahmad 135
Mezza political prison 115
Mezzeh Attack 3n12, 140
middle class 22, 42, 43, 60, 62, 63, 86, 124, 202
Middle Path movement 163, 167–8
militants/militancy 1, 3, 8, 47–50, 55, 68, 69, 140–2, 146n2, 174, 189–99, 212, 228, 231, 234, 235
military 2, 27, 29, 30, 31–2; Ba'ath purge of 45, 58; Muslim Brotherhood and 43; religious practice in 116; Sunni representation in 57–8
Military Committee 30, 31, 32, 33
Minbar Suriya al-Islami website 196
minority rights 41
al-Mir, Ahmad 30
modernization 17, 40
modernizers 8
money laundering 2
morality 2, 19

mosques 85, 92, 117, 137, *138*, 151, 211, 218–19, 232
Mossad 104
Moubayed, Sami 182–3
Mount Qasyun 140
Mughniya, 'Imad 133
Muhammad, Prophet 117; Danish cartoons 116–17
Muhammad's Battalions 48
Mukhabarat (intelligence services) 76, 84, 88, 135, 142
Muntalaqat text 45, 47
Murtaddun 69
Mushrikun 69
Muslim Brotherhood 2, 3, 6, 32, 34, 35–44, 53, 55, 57, 58, 63, 76, 77–8, 84, 85, 96, 177, 178, 183, 193, 213, 218, 231, 232; and Damascus Declaration 182; as a democratic party 43–4; dogma 38–9; execution of members 74–5, 77; formation 37–8; militantism 47–50, 69–71, 146n2, 189, 231; national political participation 43, 44, 47; as pacifist group 180, 190; political agenda 39–41; release of imprisoned members 92–3, 115; social base 36, 37–8, 43, 60, 65–6, 66; socio-economic agenda 36, 37, 40–2; support base 41–3, 62; *see also* Fighting Vanguard; Syrian Islamic Front (SIF)
Muslim Brothers of Hama 38
Muslim World League 90n30
Mu'tazila doctrine 166
al-Mu'tem, Muhammad Khaled 218

Na'ama, Ibrahim 73
al-Nabusli, Ratib Muhammad 155, 190
Nadwat study groups 160, 161–2
Nahj al-Islam 91, 156–7
al-Najar, Ghassan 178
Naqshbandi Kuftariya Sufi order 90, 163
Nasrallah, Hasan 129
Nasser, Jamal 29–30, 44, 47, 55
Nasserites 34, 49, 69, 70, 181
National Alliance for the Liberation of Syria 78, 80
National Bloc coalition 44
National Democratic Grouping 181
national identity 37
National Progressive Front (NPF) 3, 54, 66, 77, 83, 84, 87, 114, 117, 118
National Salvation Front (NSF) 133, 181n26, 182, 183, 218
National Union 30

national unity 18, 26, 54
nationalism 86, 105, 106; Arab 23, 24, 26, 28
Nationalist Party 36
nationalization 32–3, 41, 61
Necessary State Violence strategy 77
neo-Ba'ath Party 33–4
neo-fundamentalism 82–107, 209, 212, 230, 234, 235
networks, informal and associational 160–2, 172, 235
New Vanguard 155
al-Nihlawi, Lieutenant Colonel 44
9/11 attacks 127, 130
niqab 220

'Odat, Hussein 156
oil 120, 124
Olson, Robert W. 69n54, 73–4
Ottoman Empire 16, 28, 36
outreach methods: Islamic movement 153–62, 172–3, 206, 230, 235; Islamist militant groups 192–3

Pace, Joe 182
pacificism/pacifists 8, 174, 176–89, 212, 235
Palestine/Palestinians 43, 103–4, 105, 126, 127–8, 132, 136
Palestinian Authority 49
Palestinian Front for the Liberation of Palestine-General Command (PFLP-GC) 103
Palestinian Islamic Jihad (PIJ) 103, 104, 128
patriarchy 99
patron-client relationships 103–6, 113, 126
patronage networks 95–6
peace accords (1978), Egypt-Israel 73, 103
peasantry 60, 86, 87
People's Council 54
People's Party 28, 36
personal relationships 160–1
Personal Status Law 45, 98, 99, 139
Perthes, Volker 97n53, 127
Petition of the (99) 221
Petition of the (1000) 221
Pinto, Paulo 211
Piscatori, James P. 86
pluralism: political 93, 117–18; of religious groups 216
political culture approach 8, 55, 56–9
political economy approach 8, 9, 57, 66
political Islam *see* Islamist groups

political liberalization 75, 112, 200, 228, 232
political opportunity structures 65
political pluralism 93, 117–18
political prisoners 140–1; release of 2, 115
politics of the notables era 22
polygamy 99, 101, 139
popular democracy 45
population growth 120, 125, 202, *203*, 205
Populist Authoritarian (PA) system 5, 97, 111, 112, 119, 143, 183, 200, 227, 230, 233, 234
poverty 202, 203–4
prayer 2, 92
presidency, eligibility for 71
presidential monarchical system 55
price controls 95
private sector 86, 96, 113, 146; economic liberalization and 75, 96, 119, 120, 121, 123–4, 142–3; re-invigoration of 75, 94–8; women in 99, 100
private sphere 20, 233
privatization 41, 120, 123, 124, 125, 201
professional syndicates/associations 72, 73, 76–7, 84–5, 87
Progressive Democratic Kurdish Party 187
public sector 94, 202; women in 99, 100
public sphere: Islamization of 3, 209–10; secularization of 20
publishing houses 155–6

Qadiyanis 69
al-Qa'qa, Abu 193, 194–5
Qubaysi sisters 163, 170–1
Qutada, Abu 192n58
Qutb, Sayed 68, 69, 191
Quweidar, Haifa' 171
Quweyder, Muna 171

radicalization 114, 117, 152, 167, 180, 207
radio 91, 106, 154
Radu, Michael 134
Rajih, 'Abd al-Salam 118
Ramadan, Shaykh Sa'id 49
Reform Party of Syria 182
regional dimension 4, 7, 9, 57, 83, 102–6, 107, 113, 125–37, 144, 230, 232, 233–4
religion 3, 15, 16, 18–19, 20–1, 24, 42, 45, 46, 47, 66, 72, 75, 76, 101, 116, 118, 143, 150, 164, 208, 222
religious banners 117
religious class, state co-optation of 86, 88–94, 101, 106, 228, 232
religious diversity 37, 116

religious institutions: purging of 85; state re-appropriation of 88, 89, 90–1, 232; *see also* mosques; schools
religious teachers and leaders (ulama) 19, 20, 42, 45–6, 47, 49–50, 61, 62, 89, 175, 231; women as 169–71
Renewal of the Religious Discourse conference (2004) 2, 116
repression 65, 66, 229
research methodology 9–10
Revolutionary Youth Federation 86–7
ridda (conversion) 69
al-Rifa'i, Sariya and Usama 166
al-Rifa'a, `Abd al-Karim 150, 163, 166
Roy, Olivier 209
rural exodus 62, 125, 214
rural sector 57, 58, 61, 95, 203, 215, 229

Sa'adeh, Antoon 18
Sadat, Anwar 73, 74
Sadeq, Bashir 30
Sadeq, Mahmud 88
Sadowski, Yahya M. 95–6, 175
al-Sadr, Musa 104n84
Sahwa (awakening) 68
Salafis/Salafism 38, 48, 68, 76, 92, 135, 136, 150, 168, 176, 190, 191, 193, 213–14
Saleh, Yasin al-Haj 182, 219
Salem, `Adan 156
Salkini, Ahmad 116
Salloukh, Bassel 87
al-Satar, Muhammad `Abd 148, 155
Saudi Arabia 29, 73, 74, 105, 131, 135, 177, 215
Sayf, Riyad 221
schools 137, 138–9, 219–20; purging of 83, 85
Schwedler, Jillian 64–5, 216
scientific socialism 34
Seale, Patrick 7, 74
sectarianism 55, 56–7, 58, 59, 67, 143, 222
secularism 1–2, 36, 179, 214, 215, 216–24, 225–6; Anglo-Saxon model 16, 18, 21, 115, 143, 228; Ba'th doctrine 20–1, 23–6, 45–7, 67, 70, 82, 83, 116, 228, 231 (muting of 5, 88–94, 98–9, 100–1, 106, 114, 115, 116, 143, 228, 232, 233; reactions to 45–7); in education 2, 16, 20–1, 45, 115;
Syrian model 15–21, 57, 231 (overview and historical roots 15–17; underlying reasons behind agenda for 17–19)

security forces see intelligence services (*mukhabarat*)
Sednaya political prison 140–1, 142
services sector 99
Seurat, Michel 40, 56
Shahrur, Muhammad 152, 180, 190
al-Shami, Khalid 115
Shaqfa, Muhammad Riyad 180n21
Shi'ism 104–5, 106, 132–3, 136, 137, 187–8, 197–8
al-Shishakl, Dalal 171
al-Shishakli, Adib 43, 44
al-Siba'i, Mustafa 17, 19, 36, 38, 39, 40, 43, 47, 68, 155
Snow, David A. 64
Social Movement Theory 7, 8, 9, 55, 64–6
Social National Party 24
Social Unionists' Movement 31
social welfare 6, 37, 113, 125, 158–9, 179, 225
socialism 23, 26, 27, 34, 45, 57, 62
socio-economic factors/school 36, 55, 57, 59–64, 229, 231, 232
Soviet Union 34, 46, 97n43, 103
speech, styles of 3, 6
Start Your Project programme 122
state-society relations 5, 8, 59, 82, 83, 83–5, 86–8, 112, 205, 227, 229, 232, 233, 234
Stenberg, Leif 159, 164
strikes, March 1980 76–7
students 42, 62, 87, 95
subsidization 123, 202
Sudanese Faculty of the Pillars of Faith 91
Suez War (1956) 29
Sufan, Sami 31
Sufis/Sufism 38, 48, 68, 76, 90, 92, 95, 149–50, 166, 176, 213
Sunnis 35, 61, 63, 66, 75, 93–4, 105, 106, 132, 136, 137, 139, 177, 232, 235; bourgeoisie 95; Kurdish 187; in military 57–8; numbers 7n23, 22n26
al-Suri, Abu Mus'ab 140, 191–2, 192, 194, 195n69
Suwaydani, Ahmad 33, 34
Syria Today 156
Syrian Islamic Front (SIF) 78, 79, 80, 82, 92, 141, 177, 180–9, 218, 224
Syrian Social National Party (SSNP) 28, 29, 36
Syrian Stock Markets Authority 234
Syrio-Soviet Friendship Association 73

al-Tabba', Fa'izah 171

Index 257

al-Tabsha, Hatem 180
Tajdeed movement 154, 163, 164–6
Takfiri groups 176
Talas, Firas 130
Talhami, Ghada Hashem 39, 93, 223–4
Taraqji, Nahidah 171
al-Tartusi, Abu Basir 195, 198
taxation 96, 121
television 91, 106, 132, 154
terrorism 2
textualists 8
Third Crusader Campaign 191
Tlas, Mustafa 34
tolerance 2
trade: foreign 60, 61; liberalization 121, 122, 234
Tsabihjii, Raja 171
Tu'ma, Ahmad 178
al-Turk, Riyad 93
Turkey 122
Turkomans 22n26

'Ubayd, Hamad 30
'Umran, Muhammad 30, 33
unemployment 120, 125, 202, *203*, 206
United Arab Republic 29–30, 44
United States 79, 102, 103, 126–7, 130, 131, 133, 135, 197; and Iraq 3, 118, 125, 126, 127, 144, 186, 189
unity, national 18, 26, 54
universities 42, 90, 117
Uprising of March (1980) 76–7
'Uqla, 'Adnan 76, 78, 79, 80, 81, 191, 212
urbanites 54, 57, 58, 61, 63, 229
urbanization 204

Van Dam, Nikolaos 56–9, 75
veiling (hijab) 2, 6, 15, 92, 101, 102, 157, 165n60, 167n70
violence 65–6

Wahhabi 105, 191
war on terror 127
websites, Islamic 155, 196
Wedeen, Lisa 89
Wickham, Carrie Rossefsky 64, 154, 206, 213n38
Wiktotowicz, Quintan 64
women 9, 20, 87, 98–102, 106, 139, 157–8, 159–60, 165, 192; dress code 2, 6, 92, 101, 102, 115, 157, 165n60, 167n70; employment status 99–100; as religious leaders 169–71
Worker's Party 76
working class 42, 234
World Communist Revolution 33

Yarkas, 'Imad al-Din Bakarat *see* Dahdah, Abu
Yarmuk Palestinian camp 142
youth 205–9, 215
youth brigades 86–7
Youth of Muhammad 37
al-Yusuf, Ibrahim 74

al-Za'im, 'Abd al-Satar 71
Zamar, Muhammad Haydar 192
al-Zarqawi, Abu Mus'ab 130, 134, 198
Zayd movement 151, 154, 163, 166–7
Zionism 18, 34
Zisser, Eyal 218

Taylor & Francis
eBooks
FOR LIBRARIES

Over 23,000 eBook titles in the Humanities, Social Sciences, STM and Law from some of the world's leading imprints.

Choose from a range of subject packages or create your own!

ORDER YOUR FREE 30 DAY INSTITUTIONAL TRIAL TODAY!

- ▶ Free MARC records
- ▶ COUNTER-compliant usage statistics
- ▶ Flexible purchase and pricing options

- ▶ Off-site, anytime access via Athens or referring URL
- ▶ Print or copy pages or chapters
- ▶ Full content search
- ▶ Bookmark, highlight and annotate text
- ▶ Access to thousands of pages of quality research at the click of a button

For more information, pricing enquiries or to order a free trial, contact your local online sales team.

UK and Rest of World: **online.sales@tandf.co.uk**
US, Canada and Latin America:
e-reference@taylorandfrancis.com

www.ebooksubscriptions.com

A flexible and dynamic resource for teaching, learning and research.